Unlikely Partners

Unlikely Partners

CHINESE REFORMERS, WESTERN ECONOMISTS,
AND THE MAKING OF GLOBAL CHINA

Julian Gewirtz

 Harvard University Press

CAMBRIDGE, MASSACHUSETTS   LONDON, ENGLAND   2017

Second printing

Library of Congress Cataloging-in-Publication Data

Names: Gewirtz, Julian B., 1989– author.
Title: Unlikely partners : Chinese reformers, Western economists,
   and the making of global China / Julian B. Gewirtz.
Description: Cambridge, Massachusetts : Harvard University Press,
   2017. | Includes bibliographical references and index.
Identifiers: LCCN 2016011267 | ISBN 9780674971134 (hard cover :
   alk. paper)
Subjects: LCSH: Economic development—China. | China—Economic
   policy—1976–2000. | China—Economic policy—2000– | China—
   Foreign relations—1976– | East and West.
Classification: LCC HC427.92 .G478 2017 | DDC 338.951—dc23
   LC record available at http://lccn.loc.gov/2016011267

Contents

Abbreviations

CASS	Chinese Academy of Social Sciences
CCP	Chinese Communist Party
CCTV	China Central Television
DRC	Development Research Center
FDI	foreign direct investment
GATT	General Agreement on Tariffs and Trade
GDP	gross domestic product
GNP	gross national product
NAS	National Academy of Sciences
NGO	nongovernmental organization
NPC	National People's Congress
PBOC	People's Bank of China
PLA	People's Liberation Army
PRC	People's Republic of China
RMB	renminbi
SEZ	special economic zone
SPC	State Planning Commission
WTO	World Trade Organization

Unlikely Partners

Introduction: River Crossings

In THE ERA of Deng Xiaoping, who led China during its transformation from a poor country to a global economic power, China's reformers often used a pithy expression to describe their method: "crossing the river by feeling for the stones." The phrase is usually interpreted to mean that China would move forward through trial and error, with the precise endpoint not apparent and the pathway not known clearly in advance. But the river itself was an apt metaphor. Chinese civilization grew up along two rivers, the loess-rich Yellow River and the fast-winding Yangtze River, but it was not those rivers China's reformers had in mind. They meant the river as a metaphor for movement, flux, constant transformation. The "crossing" would itself be through currents and over flowing waters, with the markers only unseen stones. The river is a symbol of change, and crossing it would be an uncertain journey toward a changed future.

The scope of China's transformation over the past forty years staggers the mind. China is now the world's largest economy by purchasing power parity and is expected to overtake the United States as the largest economy by gross domestic product (GDP) by 2025. This enormous transformation of China's economy and in the lives of its people since Mao's death in 1976 has been shaped by a vast and important change in the way the Chinese leadership thinks about

the organization of the economy. Mao's communist ideology regarding the economy has been replaced. Since the early 1990s, China's ruling Communist Party has defined its economic system as a
"socialist market economy." That self-understanding is enshrined in
all the Party's major ideological documents as well as in the Chinese
constitution. The "river" China crossed to reach the socialist market
economy—and the "stones" it groped for along the way to arrive at
a changed China—is the story of this book.

A "socialist market economy": Is it "socialist"? Is it "market"? How
did people come to promote and accept this seeming oxymoron?
How did this union of opposites actually become the official designation of the Chinese economy?

The socialist market economy is the result of Deng Xiaoping's
promises to make China modern, wealthy, and powerful. When
Mao died, socialist China was mired in poverty and isolated from
the outside world. Within two years, the feisty Deng, who stood at
four feet, eleven inches and made frequent use of his personal spit-
toon, had replaced Mao's designated successor, Hua Guofeng. After
the disastrous years of the Great Leap Forward (1958–1961) and the
Cultural Revolution, China was an economically ravaged nation of
nearly one billion people, with a per capita GDP of only US$175 in
1978.[1] Deng and his supporters attributed this situation to problems
in the socialist command economy that had guided the People's Republic of China (PRC) since its founding in 1949. With "reform and
opening," Deng declared a momentous break with the inefficient traditional socialist economy and stated his intention to find a form of
socialism that did not "boil down to shared poverty."[2] His top officials articulated the mantra of "crossing the river by feeling for the
stones" as the pragmatic, experimental guide to reform.[3]

In this quest to modernize and grow the economy, Deng attached
unprecedented importance to the work of China's economists and
allowed his main economic official—Premier Zhao Ziyang, with his
oversized black-rimmed glasses and graying crown of swept-back
hair—to encourage economic policy makers to think boldly. But as
Zhao acknowledged in his posthumous memoir, "My earliest understanding of how to proceed with reform was shallow and vague. . . .
I did not have any preconceived model or a systematic idea in mind."[4]

Because China's leaders realized that they understood the path ahead only in a "shallow and vague" way, they embarked on a process of learning from abroad on a scale that has few parallels in human history. As this country of one billion people grew economically and deepened its ties with the outside world through trade and investment, its leaders also sought an extraordinary array of foreign economic ideas to help the country become a global economic powerhouse. Many participants have called this era a "golden age" of reform and intellectual openness.[5] This "golden age" saw the end of decades of inefficient and unproductive central planning and launched China on a path to become a global power.

Under Mao, intellectual exchanges had all but ceased. Especially during the Cultural Revolution (1966–1976), thinkers and writers—whether economists or novelists—were often viewed as threats to the state who needed to be "reeducated." Yet almost from the moment Mao died in 1976, all this changed. Economic expertise became critical to the goals of China's leaders—and economic policy makers began what Deng called "taking a look around," a casual-sounding phrase that belies the intensity of their efforts.[6]

The experiences of countries that had experimented with transition from a socialist economy were clearly relevant, but Zhao, Deng, and other leaders urged an even wider-ranging effort. In 1978, Deng told a vice premier before a trip to Western Europe: "We ought to study the successful experiences of capitalist countries and bring them back to China."[7] General Secretary Hu Yaobang declared, "We must learn to do economic work from all who know how, no matter who they are."[8] This official position produced tremendous—though never unconditional—receptivity to incorporating market elements into China's socialist system, drawing on what Deng called "useful capitalist methods."[9]

These views were highly controversial within China. Less than a decade earlier, the ultra-leftist leadership of Mao's wife had insisted that economic exchanges with the West were a "betrayal to the nation" and she had furiously denounced "worshippers of foreign things and bootlickers for foreigners."[10] Mao himself frequently stated that making China "self-reliant"—independent of what he saw as the subjugations of foreign trade, capital, intellectual exchange, and policy influence—was one of his key goals, although of course he diligently studied the foreign Marxist classics and, during the early period of his rule, he had loyally carried out the orders of his Soviet "elder brother."[11] Denunciations of "betrayal" and "bootlicking" were part of a broader Mao-era program of thought-policing and maintenance of the Party line that sometimes could be a matter of life and death: tens of thousands of intellectuals and officials were purged as "rightists" and died during Mao's rule. This discourse criticizing those who embraced foreign ideas remained a powerful line of attack even during the Deng era—and it hindered but did not stop China's reformers.

With unequaled granularity, significance, and scale, Chinese economists scoured the globe for the economic ideas that could help China "cross the river by feeling for the stones." Invitations and delegations went out to Hungary, the United States, Japan, the United Kingdom, Yugoslavia, West Germany, and Argentina. Journeys to and from China became an integral part of "crossing the river"—and they, too, were "river crossings" of their own, voyages to lands that were sometimes strange and sometimes unexpectedly familiar.

The sheer quantity and variety of Chinese economists' engagement with ideas from abroad is one of the most remarkable aspects of China's economic transformation. The result—that China would be a socialist state propelled by market forces to wealth and power on the global stage—was codified into the Chinese constitution in 1993, when China was renamed a "socialist market economy."[12] That conception endures to this day as the ideological and policy engine of China's global economic power.

This book brings to light the story of how between 1976 and 1993 Chinese intellectuals and decision makers sought to remake the state-market relationship in their country with the help of foreign economists. These stories allow us to see anew how China emerged from the isolation and poverty of traditional socialism to become a global economic behemoth. China's opening up triggered an enormous transmission of knowledge and expertise to Chinese economists and policy makers—new ideas that permeated the entire intellectual environment and played a major role in the evolution of Chinese Communist Party (CCP) ideology and policy.[13]

When we examine the ideas of the Chinese policy makers and economists who guided this transformation, we discover that Western economists were crucial if unlikely partners in the reform process. More than is widely known or acknowledged, China's economic interconnections with the West are not only in the realm of economic transactions of trade and investment, but in the realm of economic ideas as well.[14]

This claim constitutes an attempt to see the reform period anew, through basic characteristics of that period that have often been ignored. Indeed, for all the academic and popular attention that China's astonishing economic transformation has received, interactions with foreign economists are almost unknown outside China. Nearly every major book on the period only briefly mentions that international economists visited China, that Chinese economists had read works by European and North American economists, or that international institutions, especially the World Bank, provided valuable policy guidance.[15] In recent years, leading Chinese economists have acknowledged the importance of these exchanges to the development of both their own thinking and their country's reform ideology and policy, creating new sources, largely in Chinese, for historians to draw on.[16] But no account has presented the full stories of these visits or analyzed these interactions as central to China's dramatic debates over ideology and policy after Mao's death.

Interactions with foreign ideas form an enduring theme in China's history, particularly during the "century of humiliation" at the hands of foreign imperial powers beginning with the First Opium War in 1839. China's conflicted relationship to modernization often played out through negotiations with Western ideas. At the end of the nineteenth century, the Qing official Zhang Zhidong championed reforming the Qing dynasty (1644–1911) through a system of "Chinese learning for fundamental principles and Western learning for practical application" (*Zhongxue wei ti, xixue wei yong*). The late Qing writer Zheng Guanying's *Words of Warning to an Affluent Age* (1893) called for emulating Great Britain to bring industrialization and constitutional monarchy to China. The eminent scholar Yan Fu used the activity of translating Adam Smith, Herbert Spencer, and

John Stuart Mill to discover how the Chinese state could regain "wealth and power."[17] Perhaps most significantly, even the founding of the CCP in 1921 was itself the result of an intervention by the Communist International (Comintern), established in Moscow in 1919. The Comintern sent emissaries, including Grigori Voitinsky and Henk Sneevliet, translated key texts into Chinese, established a military academy, and trained individuals in the Soviet Union.[18] Mao's intellectual contributions later often sought to rebut the direct importation of Soviet ideas and to emphasize the Chinese identity of China's socialist revolution and the "Sinification of Marxism."[19] In the minds of its Communist rulers, China's ability to "stand up"— as Mao described the founding of the PRC in 1949—was in many ways closely connected to its ability to find a ruling ideology that was not a wholesale foreign importation, but rather could be portrayed as a Chinese product of China's leaders examining the country's characteristics.

Despite this dynamic, the predominant narratives about Western influence on China before the PRC have often been told as one-sided stories of Western advisers—missionaries, scientists, and military experts—who came "to change China."[20] This book, however, replaces the abstract idea of "changing China" that existed in the fantasies of often uninvited foreign advisers with a firm foregrounding of the partnership between Chinese reformers and Western economists. These twentieth-century partners in reform worked collaboratively to transform China's economy according to the needs of China and the demands of the CCP leadership. To be sure, in some cases, the lure for Western advisers in the reform era was Chinese reformers who were so clearly open to outside influences in the decades after Mao's death. That pedagogical structure was typically the superficial *form* of these exchanges, which makes it tempting to try to understand them in line with the older model of advisers whose success was judged on whether or not, or to what extent, the foreigners indeed "changed China." But that model is insufficient when we try to understand the actual processes at work in the years after 1976, with advisers who were actively sought out by the Chinese leadership, and whose advice led Chinese audiences to interpret and to select among competing or contradictory foreign viewpoints. The processes were varieties of partnership in which the agency of the Chinese reformers was paramount.

One reason for this complex and plural dynamic is that there was no single audience in China for the ideas and proposals of foreign economists. Zhao Ziyang often acted as the arbiter and decider in debates over economic policy. At times he met personally with foreign economists, a sign of the importance attached to their visits to China. But he rarely engaged at length with these visiting experts. Instead, he drew on a flexible network of Chinese economists and policy makers to interpret the advice from abroad. Some of these economic experts reported directly to the State Council, which Zhao led as premier, or were affiliated with central policy-making organs like the System Reform Commission (Guojia jingji tizhi gaige weiyuanhui, abbreviated as Tigaiwei) and the Research Office of the State Planning Commission (SPC). Others staffed government-run research institutions, most notably the Chinese Academy of Social Sciences (CASS), while universities like the prestigious Peking and Tsinghua universities employed others. Some economists even served in multiple capacities simultaneously, creating an institutional environment that blurred the distinction between policy making and research, and in which internal and external debates were fluid and often difficult to distinguish. For example, bold maneuvers to influence senior leaders frequently appeared in the pages of the official newspaper, *People's Daily*, or the CASS journal *Economic Research*—and whether an idea got past a publication's censors was often a key test of its political viability. Many other senior CCP leaders sought foreign ideas to bolster their own positions, and still others repudiated the notion that "Western doctors" might travel across the seas to prescribe "Western medicine" for China's woes.

To fully understand these exchanges, we must inhabit the positions of both the host and the visitor and strive to see through both pairs of eyes at once. Instead of a cause-and-effect schematic or a teleological pull toward "conversion" or "progress," we find a constantly negotiated receptivity. This pragmatic and eclectic approach granted coherence to the idea that a Chinese leader might, all in the span of a single year, meet with and praise the ideas of a socialist economist, a free market fundamentalist, and a neo-Keynesian. There was extraordinary variance in the economists the Chinese leadership invited—and an even more extraordinary variance in what the Chinese leadership wanted from these interactions.

These Chinese and foreign partners changed China together, but there was no checklist of proposals that were either accepted or rejected. There do exist examples of direct influence, but the more revealing account focuses less on categorizing which foreign ideas did and did not "change China" and more on recreating and examining the dynamics these foreign interventions produced—processes, forms, and rhythms of interaction that push us to broaden our theories of influence in transnational exchanges of economic development strategies. These dynamics were variable and textured, like a range of different chromatics scattered across a wide spectrum. As we shall see, there were cases of direct or short-term influence. Chinese policy makers' travel abroad brought back ideas to China that became inspiration for policy, like Vice Premier Gu Mu's sojourn in Western Europe, which introduced the idea of special export-processing zones that would eventually germinate into the special economic zones (SEZs) in Shenzhen, Zhuhai, and elsewhere. At other times, foreign economists' travel to China brought ideas that immediately became central to Chinese policy debates, such as János Kornai's 1985 visit to China and his analysis of socialist enterprises' "soft-budget constraints" and "investment hunger." There were also cases of indirect or long-term influence. Chinese leaders traveled abroad to developed countries where the sight of prosperity was startling and inspiring, like Deng Xiaoping's trips to Japan and the United States. At other times, foreign economists brought ideas to China that laid the foundation for long-term reforms of the economic system, like James Tobin's proposals for establishing modern institutions of monetary policy in 1985. Some visits led to a fundamental reshaping of the way the discipline of economics was taught in China, such as the econometrics courses that Lawrence Klein and Gregory Chow organized. Other cases fell elsewhere on the spectrum. Some visits were simply window-dressing to bolster the leaders' credibility with the aura of a distinguished Nobel laureate or an Ivy League professor. Other visits helped Chinese reformers make more effective critiques of the planned economy, like the lectures by Polish exile Włodzimierz Brus in 1980, but sometimes the visits also provided new targets for conservative attacks, as occurred in 1981 with the Czech reformer Ota Šik, whose speeches were denounced in a special directive by the Secretariat as "anti-Marxist" and "wrong."[21] As Šik's case illustrates, the activity of influence could at times be counterproductive by galvanizing the opposition and providing targets for the critics of reform.

Such examples indicate the variety and texture of the interactions. They are events that encapsulate a crucial if often forgotten characteristic of China's reform process: Chinese economic policy makers invited and learned from economists from countries that had experimented with socialist transition and from countries with conventional liberal market systems. The "socialist market economy" system that China gradually adopted reflects these multiple influences.

These stories of the multifaceted transnational partnering in China's economic reforms suggest a new way of thinking about how economic ideas spread from the West to the "developing world." The earlier way of understanding these processes has been variously termed the "Washington consensus" and "modernization theory." Broadly speaking, these arguments contend that modernization, globalization, and economic and political liberalization are the key sources of economic progress necessary to improve the lives of people in developing countries. In this didactic model, which emerged during the Cold War, the sources of progress come from Western advisers and international organizations like the World Bank.[22] This book argues that even though these actors played a critical role, they were not merely bringing global norms to China; instead, the "local context" of China is what drove the "transnational flows" of ideas as China became a global powerhouse.[23]

In other words, this is not properly understood as a story of modernization theorists transplanting their norms on a developing country, but rather as a story of the developing country's outreach and interpretation of those ideas and norms. Foreign influence was a contested process that gave agency to Chinese reformers, rather than the inevitable trajectory toward modernization-as-Westernization in many conventional models of influence in economic development and economic policy making.[24] I have used the word "partners" to capture these interactions' complexity, with the deliberate purpose of suggesting both the importance of the local-foreign interactions and also the *variety* of these interactions—by no means all long-term collaborative partnerships, but including brief interactions and also including the complexities of attraction and resistance that can constitute short-term or long-term partnering relationships.

At the same time, this book also shows distortions in the way that official Chinese narratives characterize the reform process and gives us new insights into the actual workings of Chinese economic policy debates. First, it restores the purged Zhao Ziyang to his rightful place at the center of what is too often shorthanded as "Deng Xiaoping's economic miracle," a heroic narrative of China's transformation in the years following Mao's death with Deng Xiaoping as its sole architect. Because of Zhao Ziyang's ouster during the Tiananmen crackdown in 1989, he has been written out of the history of the period, taking with him the fuller and more accurate account of many of the policies he oversaw, including accounts of exchanges with Western economists.[25] Zhao's name almost never appears in print in China, making it exceptionally difficult for PRC scholars to write openly on these activities.[26] (Some examples are particularly egregious: *Breaking Through: The Birth of China's Opening-up Policy* by former vice premier Li Lanqing, which was promoted by its publisher as "a particularly detailed history" of "China's economic reform and opening to the outside world," does not mention Zhao Ziyang's name.) But using a wide range of sources that can now be obtained in China, combined with materials available outside China including a new compilation of leaked documents published in the summer of 2016, it is possible to reconstruct a more complete picture of the reform era that also—as any such account must—returns Zhao Ziyang to the center of the action.

Second, the stories here undermine the CCP's portrayal of the reforms as a largely internal process, proof of the CCP's ingenuity and wisdom. The foreign involvement is typically unmentioned when Chinese leaders describe the development of China's economic thinking. For example, Foreign Minister Wang Yi recently claimed that "socialism with Chinese characteristics" was "grown out of the soil of China," and former vice premier Zeng Peiyan has written that since 1978 the CCP has demonstrated "great daring and resolve" in creating the socialist market economy, the development of which he fully credits to "Chinese Communists."[27] True in part, these statements omit important dimensions of the full story in order to boost the CCP's legitimacy in the present. China and Chinese officials of course deserve great credit for China's economic growth, but there is insufficient acknowledgment of the role of economists from outside of China who also significantly impacted the making of China's socialist market economy.[28]

The book proceeds chronologically from Mao's death in 1976 to 1993, when the "socialist market economy" was formally accepted by the CCP. Focusing on a set of key characters, it follows the tumult and drama of the CCP's transformation of its ideas and policies about the economy, and the crucial role of partnerships with foreign economists.

I begin by charting the return of economic experts to the top echelons of the CCP policy-making apparatus after Mao's death, the promotion of reformist leaders like Premier Zhao Ziyang, and their newfound intellectual embrace of the possibilities of markets. Initially, in the early 1980s, Chinese reformers like the newly restored senior economists Xue Muqiao and Ma Hong engaged with Eastern European thinkers to explore how to reconcile socialism and markets—and find justifications for Deng's claims that markets do not mean capitalism. Conservatives at the highest levels of Party power, led by CCP elder Chen Yun and ideologue Deng Liqun, consistently fought back, temporarily stymieing reforms and international exchanges. But in 1984, reformers successfully redefined the Chinese economy as a "planned commodity economy"—with "commodity" a byword for tolerating some measure of market forces—and established a dual-track price system that allowed goods to be bought and sold outside the state plan. After these victories, however, rapid growth created new worries that the Chinese economy was overheating, a fear that strengthened the hand of the conservatives and caused disagreements among the reformers about how to respond, with the leading factions headed, respectively, by the economists Wu Jinglian and Li Yining. During this crucial period of debate, at Zhao Ziyang's orders, the reformers staged their most ambitious international exchange yet: a 1985 conference onboard a cruise ship, the S.S. *Bashan*, sailing down the Yangtze River. This conference provides a case study in the varieties of transnational exchange of economic ideas, with particular attention to the differing impacts of two foreign attendees, János Kornai and James Tobin. In the wake of this conference, Chinese economists and officials increased their economic sophistication and widened the scope of their policy goals, even as they openly disagreed about the next steps. In 1987, reformers made a series of major ideological breakthroughs at the Thirteenth Party Congress that enshrined the central role of the market and charted a path forward under Zhao Ziyang, newly promoted to CCP general secretary. Zhao continued striving to find the best ideas from around the world and to put them into practice, only in the end to fail as inflation soared and student protests in the spring of 1989 allowed the conservatives to purge Zhao and brutally crack down on dissent. In 1992, however, Deng Xiaoping used his paramount authority to restart reform, as a new generation of leaders took the reins of power and set out a reform agenda drawn substantially from Zhao's agenda of the late 1980s. Under the mantle of the "socialist market economy," which was included in an amendment to the Chinese constitution in 1993, China was on its way to becoming a global economic superpower.

The meeting of ideas between China and the West must be understood as a central element of the period 1976–1993. With partnering dynamics of picking and choosing, reformulating, occluding, and disguising influence, one crucial but underappreciated reason that China made such enormous progress during this period was its remarkable openness to finding the best ideas from around the world and applying them to China's circumstances.

This book is a work of history, but the implications of this history are deeply relevant to the current moment. Many of the issues I chronicle concerning the relationship between the state and the economy remain the pivot points of today's fervent debates in China—both as echoes of and direct linkages to this history. Many of today's key actors participated as young officials in this history, including Zhou Xiaochuan, now governor of the People's Bank of

China (China's central bank), and Lou Jiwei, now the Minister of Finance. Indeed, it should come as no surprise that these officials have continued to engage international expertise or that institutions like the World Bank and a new generation of Western economists continue to be connected to China's top officials and reformers. These officials acknowledge that China can "learn from beneficial experiences" abroad, but maintain a tough stance that China should "never indiscriminately copy" foreign "concepts and models."[29]

Thus the argument that foreign economists were the active partners of CCP reformers during the "golden age" of reform has significant implications for the present time because, alongside these measured endorsements of learning from abroad in some quarters, a pervasive theme of top Chinese leaders has been to decry with newfound intensity "hostile foreign influences" that are "exporting ideology" to the professions and even the bureaucracy in China.[30] A leaked internal Party communiqué from April 2013, a few months after Xi Jinping became general secretary of the CCP, revealed that central leaders believed that the "ideological situation" was in a state of "complicated, intense struggle"—and that struggle was largely between "Western anti-China forces" and a self-reliant China under the system of "socialism with Chinese characteristics." The communiqué declared, "Western anti-China forces and internal 'dissidents' are still actively trying to infiltrate China's ideological sphere" and "carry out Westernization."[31] Reports claim that Xi himself used the phrase "hostile foreign forces" repeatedly in internal speeches since he came to power.[32]

Rhetoric about a Manichean "intense struggle" against Western influences persists in China today, even as the CCP leadership's version of the history behind China's socialist market economy—"grown out of the soil of China"—remains a point of pride. In the face of these aggressive attacks on Western influence and self-serving claims about the history of a prior era, the stories this book tells are living, sometimes dangerous narratives, and they offer us a way to view today's gilded age from the vantage point of a true golden age. The fierce, freewheeling debate that flourished under Zhao Ziyang—about what socialism truly meant, whether markets and wealth could be allowed, and what sort of society China should become—may be the stuff of history. But China's future will depend on continuing and deepening the debates and the benefits that accrued from these exchanges of ideas to strengthen China. It may even depend on acknowledging the fact of partnership between Chinese reformers and Western visitors—and carrying it forward into the twenty-first century.

1

The Great Helmsman Departs

T HE CLOCKS IN Beijing struck midnight. Chairman Mao Zedong was dying.

Ten minutes later, on September 9, 1976, the man who had founded the "New China"—the Great Helmsman who had presided over his nation with a fiery utopian vision and murderous rage, attaining the godlike status of a potentate who was everywhere greeted with wishes to live for 10,000 years—had died. At age eighty-two, he had been in failing health for years and, after suffering a severe heart attack on May 11, had declined rapidly.

Propaganda posters were prepared, with black-lettered exhortations to "turn grief into strength" below an image of crowds of workers and soldiers, clenched fists upraised and eyes fixed on the sky. There a dazzling, serene apparition of Mao's face floated, surrounded by the red sunbeams described in songs such as the Cultural Revolution anthem "The East Is Red."[1]

The funeral was set for September 18, 1976. Mao's designated successor, Hua Guofeng, would deliver the main eulogy, the valediction of the Chinese Communist Party (CCP) to the man who had led it to victory in the Civil War and whose grand ambitions and delusions had made the history of the New China a story of bloody tumult and revolutionary change.[2]

Millions of people massed in the streets of the city around Tiananmen Square, where the red and yellow flag of the People's Republic of China (PRC) flew at half-staff. Wearing funerary white, the crowd bowed and, for three minutes of silence, mourned. Paying respects where Mao lay in state, draped in the flag of the CCP, textile workers and People's Liberation Army (PLA) soldiers wept and wailed over the body of the leader whose image had hung in every home throughout the country he had ruled.[3]

Speaking to the crowd, Hua voiced "most profound sorrow" over the death of "our esteemed and beloved great leader and the great teacher of the international proletariat and the oppressed nations and oppressed people." The death of Mao, leader and teacher, was a loss for the world, but nowhere would that loss be felt more keenly than in China. Ordinarily, Hua rarely looked somber, with his rosy, round cheeks and toothy grin, but on this day he spoke with great gravity. "It was under Chairman Mao's leadership that the disaster-plagued Chinese nation stood up," Hua declared. But even though Mao was gone, his ideas would keep China safe: "Against [our] forces armed with Mao Zedong Thought, any enemy that dares to intrude will certainly be drowned in the vast ocean of people's war." Hua cited a lengthy list of Mao's key ideas and "admonishments": "Never forget class struggle," fight against capitalism and imperialism, follow the authority of the CCP, and build China into a "powerful socialist state." Hua thundered, "The correctness or incorrectness of the ideological and political line decides everything."[4]

"Everything" depended on the correctness of "the ideological and political line," but with Mao's death China had lost the longtime supreme arbiter of what was "correct" in China's ideology and politics. Although Hua's eulogy made Mao's legacy sound secure, it was in fact highly contested. Over the next two years, well before the "reform and opening up" under Deng Xiaoping, the ideological contest was fierce. This competition would open up a new focus on developing China's economy and a new way of thinking about economics, thus triggering new thinking about looking outside China for economic ideas.

A team of four radical ideologues known as the "Gang of Four," including Mao's wife, Jiang Qing, was pushing to play a dominant role in the CCP policy-making process. Along with Jiang, the Gang consisted of Zhang Chunqiao, Wang Hongwen, and Yao Wenyuan, who had amassed power during the chaotic and destructive Cultural Revolution and fanned the flames of criticism of Deng and others who threatened their power. Jiang continued to speak in a Cultural Revolution–inflected language of existential class struggle, telling students at Tsinghua University that their fight was not yet over.[5] Yet Jiang's stature, tied to the Gang of Four as well as to Mao himself, was nonetheless limited. Observers inside the Kremlin wrote, "After Mao's death, there is no single exceptional personality on the Chinese scene. . . . [T]he efforts of the new Chinese leadership will be focused on bringing back internal order in the country as well as battling the economic difficulties."[6] Jiang's presence undermined Hua's ability to be an "exceptional personality," but, in the eyes of both external observers and many Chinese leaders, she was certainly not a viable replacement.

Thus, within several weeks of Mao's funeral, Hua and his allies among the CCP elders—especially Ye Jianying, often called Marshal Ye, a distinguished former military leader with sterling CCP credentials, including participation in the Long March of 1934–1935—decided that the Gang of Four's actions were endangering their leadership and had to be stopped. During a secret overnight Politburo meeting, Hua, Ye, and their allies planned to arrest the Gang and their close associates. The Gang would be charged with the crime of instigating a "counterrevolutionary" plot to "overthrow the dictatorship of the proletariat" and to take control of the country.[7] On October 6, Hua and Ye put their plan into action: summoning the members of the Gang of Four to a purported Politburo meeting, they placed all four under arrest. Shortly thereafter, they arrested thirty of the Gang's closest allies in Beijing, quelled pro-Gang dissent in Shanghai, and placed under surveillance others who were deemed suspicious.[8]

It was a rapid and dramatic show of strength. Announced on October 18, the news was met with public jubilation, with drunken students and teachers all emptying store shelves of liquor in Beijing's university district.[9] When photographs of Mao's memorial a month earlier were subsequently published, the Gang of Four had vanished, airbrushed out of memory and replaced by the Beijing horizon.[10] Shortly thereafter, Hua helped to cement his own legitimacy by revealing a short message Mao had allegedly scratched out shortly before his death. "With you in charge, I am at ease," Mao had written.[11] And Hua was now, for the first time, firmly "in charge."

With the Gang of Four toppled and his own legitimacy strengthened, Hua could assert his authority over the all-important "ideological and political line." He took on the project of editing volume 5 of Mao's *Selected Works*, an opportunity to interpret Mao's legacy and highlight elements that would be important to China's present and future—an illustration of the importance of "documentary politics" in asserting authority within the CCP.[12] The key essay by Mao that Hua highlighted was his 1956 speech, "On the Ten Major Relationships." This document contained one of Mao's strongest endorsements of balanced economic development among heavy industry, light industry, and agriculture and of giving some autonomy to factories and enterprises; Mao also criticized the Soviet Union for suffering from "a shortage of goods on the market and an unstable currency," in contrast to a more plentiful and stable Chinese economy. Mao presented "faster growth in economic construction" as the "only" way China could strengthen its national defense and he firmly stated that it was wrong to "prohibit erring comrades inside the Party from making amends." Finally, Mao called on China to "learn from the strong points of all nations and all countries" and to learn "with an analytical and critical eye, not blindly, and we mustn't copy everything indiscriminately and transplant mechanically." China needed to do this because it was both "poor" and "blank," like "a blank sheet of paper, which is good for writing on."[13] In contrast to Mao's speeches during the Cultural Revolution decade, the "Ten Major Relationships" emphasized economic growth, reconciliation with "erring comrades," and learning from abroad—key priorities in the aftermath of the arrest of the Gang of Four.[14] That October, propaganda posters were pasted up with images of ferocious revolutionaries, fists raised and teeth bared, clutching Mao's *Selected Works* above the message, "Angrily denounce the monstrous crime of usurping the power of the Party by the 'Gang of Four' anti-Party clique!"[15]

Hua and his leadership team immediately began to sketch out a policy agenda, often as a process of criticizing "ultraleftist" ideas, which were ascribed to the purged Gang of Four. One of Hua's immediate priorities was to develop China's disordered and backward economy. Structurally, China operated under a chaotic and weak system of central planning, in which the central authority issued commands to state-owned enterprises that then obtained inputs and sold outputs at rigid state-set prices. However, economists have demonstrated that Chinese central plans frequently had "shortfalls of up to 25 percent of the commodities being allocated built into them." In 1975, for example, actual steel output had fallen fully 36 percent short of the plan target, and grain was 9 percent below the plan target.[16] Similarly, enterprises were essentially under no central pressure to fulfill their plan objectives.[17]

The Chinese economy had endured years of stagnation, and Hua wanted to change that. The Gang of Four had opposed "promoting production" on the grounds that it was an ideologically impure activity, and Hua openly repudiated that view. Instead, at a State Council work conference on November 5, he foregrounded the need to raise living standards. Shortly thereafter, as Frederick C. Teiwes and Warren Sun have shown, Hua supported national conferences on economic issues, including industry, finance, agriculture, technology, and capital construction. In an important December 1976 speech, Hua boldly suggested that "revolution"—a key term for the leadership of the revolutionary CCP—could be defined as "liberation of the productive forces."[18] Only a few months after Mao's death, change was underway.

Although Hua's eulogy for Mao had explicitly called for "deepen[ing] the struggle to criticize Deng Xiaoping and repel[ling] the rightist deviationist attempt to reverse correct verdicts," by the end of 1976, it was clear that many Party leaders wanted to give Deng another chance. That year had been a tumultuous one for Deng, a wily revolutionary who had been labeled China's "number two capitalist roader" early during the Cultural Revolution but had reemerged in

1974 as first vice premier under Premier Zhou Enlai. Zhou, Deng's revolutionary comrade from their days as young communist converts in Paris, had been Deng's indispensable mentor. Zhou's key agenda, the "Four Modernizations," sought to modernize China's agriculture, industry, national defense, and science and technology, in opposition to Mao's utopian radicalism. Although the Four Modernizations were released under Zhou's name, by 1976 they were closely associated with Deng.[19] Indeed, during the preceding decades, Deng had become linked with a practical, development-oriented socialist agenda, sometimes openly disagreeing with Mao, whom he had once truly idolized, according to Alexander Pantsov and Steven Levine. By 1962, Deng praised policies that created economic incentives for peasant households to produce more crops, anathema to Mao, and first used an aphorism with which he would become closely identified. "It doesn't matter if the cat is black or yellow, as long as it can catch mice, it is a good cat," Deng had said. (Over time, this metaphorical cat would change from "yellow" to "white.") These views, alongside Deng's decades-long association with Zhou and his deep ties to the military, help to explain his rehabilitation in 1976.[20]

After Zhou died on January 8 of that year following a long period of illness, Deng delivered the eulogy, a sign that he was well positioned to succeed Zhou as premier.[21] But the Gang of Four, incensed by the Four Modernizations, revived the Cultural Revolution criticisms of Deng, branding the documents that articulated the Four Modernizations as "poisonous weeds" and decrying Deng as a "rightist deviationist." With Zhou dead, Deng had lost a powerful protector—and, on January 26, Hua Guofeng was named acting premier, seemingly ending any hopes Deng might have harbored. In early April 1976, when crowds gathered at the Monument to the People's Heroes to mourn Zhou as part of the traditional commemorative activities of the Qingming Festival, they also criticized Jiang Qing and the Gang of Four and wrote messages in praise of Deng. On April 5, the crowds were encircled by a Politburo-ordered militia and driven away, in what became known as the Tiananmen Incident. On April 7, Hua was made premier and vice chairman of the CCP, a clear signal that the verdict on Deng would not yet change and that Hua was to be Mao's designated successor.[22]

But, by January 1977, with the Gang of Four purged and a renewed focus on garnering support for Hua's regime and on helping China modernize, Deng no longer seemed so toxic to China's elder leaders. They, like Deng, were largely of the same generation as Mao or slightly younger (Deng, born in 1904, was ten years younger than Mao). On January 6, 1977, the Politburo met and, according to Ezra Vogel, privately determined that Deng would soon be allowed to return to work in some capacity. Although no decision had been made that suggested Deng would have responsibility for economic policy, the growing sense that his reinstatement "was simply a matter of time," in Vogel's words, sent a clear, positive message to Chinese economists and economic policy makers[23]—legions of whom similarly had been labeled "rightists" and attacked for committing ideological crimes ranging from "bourgeois liberalism" to "economism" during the Cultural Revolution.[24] One of those economists, Xue Muqiao, at the age of seventy-two wrote, "I am ready to contribute my last bit of strength to work with my comrades and to do whatever work is within my power."[25]

In many ways, Xue Muqiao was the leading figure of his genera-tion of intellectuals and economic policy makers.[26] With his tightly buttoned Mao jacket, graying crew cut, and square-rimmed glasses, Xue may have looked like a typical apparatchik, but his background exemplified the variety and vagaries of the career paths of his gen-eration. He helped author the first five-year plan and led several government economic, industrial, and statistical organs before being attacked during the Cultural Revolution, but he returned to a posi-tion of great influence after Mao's death. Xue's intention "to con-tribute my last bit of strength" was also shared by the experienced economic planner Ma Hong, a man of the same generation who like-wise had been influential at the highest levels of power and had fallen to the depths of powerlessness. Born in 1920, Ma had joined the CCP at seventeen and by 1952 he had become a senior staffer at the State Planning Commission (SPC), helping to draft the first five-year plan. But when the SPC leader allegedly attempted to chal-lenge Zhou Enlai's leadership, Ma was purged along with much of the SPC staff. After the disastrous Great Leap Forward, Ma returned to work on China's economic recovery, but he was again purged during the Cultural Revolution.[27] Another prominent member of this generation, Deng Liqun, who was an expert on Party ideology, had similarly survived the maelstroms of the Mao era. Born in 1914, he had become influential by helping to purge the writer Wang Shiwei, who was expelled from the CCP after criticizing Mao in 1942 and was secretly executed in 1947.[28] Deng Liqun also served as secretary to Liu Shaoqi, China's head of state. When Mao turned against Liu—branding him China's "number-one capitalist roader" during the Cultural Revolution and condemning him to torture and prison, where Liu died in 1969—Deng Liqun was also purged.[29] Like Ma Hong and Xue Muqiao, Deng Liqun was allowed to return to work only at the end of Mao's life.[30] In the initial years after Mao's death, these figures were united in their basic goal of righting the tilted ship of China's economy, though their views would evolve and eventually diverge substantially in the 1980s.

Alongside these elder officials who were eager to draw on their "last bit of strength" to oversee China's economy after Mao's death, at least two other distinct younger generations were returning to work from the Cultural Revolution's "decade of chaos." One generation had finished its academic studies before the Cultural Revolution, when training in political economy made these individuals suspect as "rightists." By 1976, this middle-aged generation had accumulated some expertise but was eager to discover new ideas that would avoid the disasters that had kept China poor and had prevented them from participating in policy making. For example, Liu Guoguang had studied political economy in the Soviet Union and worked at the Chinese Academy of Sciences in the 1950s (before the creation of the Chinese Academy of Social Sciences in 1977) as an economics researcher. He had translated Soviet statistical texts into Chinese and had a strong interest in Eastern European economies, but, during the preceding decade, he and his ideologically suspect colleagues had been cut off from developments in Soviet economics and had also been unable to affect Chinese policy.[31]

A third, even younger generation had its education disrupted by the Cultural Revolution. Forced to go to the countryside for "rustication" and "reeducation through labor," members of this generation encountered the bare facts of China's indigence: "The poverty was real," one researcher recalled. "I remember going to a village where they had only one blanket for the whole family, and only one bowl." Amid the ferment and tumult of the years following Mao's death, these young people began to return to the cities and their studies with this painful awareness in mind—an awareness that fit well with an environment in which change was afoot and foundational ideas seemed up for debate as never before.[32]

Returning to work after the precarious, traumatic existence as "rightists" during the Cultural Revolution, the generations of economic experts who offered themselves to "do whatever work is within my power" found shifting winds blowing across the landscape of Beijing's elite politics. On February 7, 1977, the *People's Daily*, *Red Flag*, and the *Liberation Army Daily* published an editorial that directly addressed the question of Mao's legacy. The editorial, supported by Hua Guofeng, announced that the CCP would "resolutely uphold whatever policy decisions Chairman Mao made, and unswervingly follow whatever decisions Chairman Mao made." This idea quickly became known as the "two whatevers" (*liangge fanshi*), after its blanket endorsement of Mao's decisions—as contradictory and destructive as those decisions may have been.[33]

In contrast to his endorsement of the doctrine of the "two whatevers," Hua continued to advance economic policies that bore little resemblance to the agenda that Mao had pursued for much of his rule. A Party work conference convened on March 10, 1977, issued major decisions about the importance of the Four Modernizations, opening China's economy to the outside world, and strengthening Party rule. At the work conference, spurning Hua's line, Chen Yun spoke out in favor of allowing Deng Xiaoping to return to work.[34] Chen was a Party elder who had played a critical role in overseeing periods of economic success during the Mao era and was regarded as a powerful independent voice in the senior leadership. Ye Jianying, whose status was similarly above questioning, also advocated reversing the verdict on the Tiananmen Incident and returning Deng to the leadership.[35] The "two whatevers" policy raised doubts about the viability of rehabilitating Deng and the many other leaders and experts who had been attacked during the Mao period, but Chen Yun and Ye Jianying's vocal support for Deng suggested that these powerful senior elders had no intention of upholding "whatever" decisions Mao had made.

Despite this uncertainty, China's economists pushed ahead with their efforts to organize and influence policy debates. On April 13–14, the Economic Research Office of the SPC invited more than one hundred "theoretical workers" in Beijing to attend the first national discussion forum on the principle of distribution according to labor, an idea that Karl Marx discussed in his *Critique of the Gotha Programme* (written in 1875 and published by Engels in 1891). Both Marx and V. I. Lenin believed this principle was necessary during the early stages of socialism; as discussed in Beijing in April 1977, to encourage workers to produce, both "spiritual" and "material" incentives were allowed (permitting "material" incentives had earlier made a principal target of vociferous criticism by the Gang of Four).[36] Xue Muqiao attended the forum and several days later he submitted a letter to Deng Xiaoping and Li Xiannian, another of the CCP's "Eight Immortals," as the group of eight elderly Party leaders who wielded substantial power during this period would become known because of their long history as revolutionary leaders. Xue, noting that his Party membership had been reinstated only in September 1975, wrote, "Over two decades, we have learned from experience that too much control leads to rigidity, while too little control causes disorder. This remains an unsolved quandary in China, as well as in other socialist countries." To deal with this "quandary," Xue advocated bold research and aggressive policy decisions that would promote "balanced and rational growth" under the leadership of the senior Party elders. "It seems that discussion of the 'forbidden territory' cannot be entered into without the express support of leaders in the [CCP] Central Committee," he wrote. "I fear it is hard to break through into forbidden territory without Central Party leadership taking responsibility."[37]

What "forbidden territory" might Xue have meant? In a society in which Hua Guofeng's interpretation of "revolution" as "the liberation of the productive forces" was a bold claim, "forbidden territory" could include much of what a senior economist in Xue's position might think and do. Mao, in the words of Roderick MacFarquhar, wanted "a China that was pure though poor."[38] Any attempt to make China rich thus might have been an attempt to make Chinese socialism less "pure," and, indeed, such an agenda might also suggest overruling Mao's vision for China, which the new doctrine of the "two whatevers" forbade. Liberating the "productive forces" and reappraising Mao's legacy both seemed to be prohibited, stymieing the ability of Xue and his colleagues to return to work without fuller support from the "central Party leadership."

At the same time, however, Hua's regime moved quickly to grow China's underdeveloped economy. Between 1975 and 1977, power and transportation shortages had led to underutilization of as much as 30 percent of industrial capacity, permitting enormous room for improvement.[39] On April 19, the *People's Daily* published an editorial trumpeting the need for a "new leap forward," a period of intensive growth and economic ambition.[40] At a conference that began later that month and continued until May 13, Hua delivered a speech on prioritizing economic work and introduced but did not develop an important idea: he cited the existence of "objective economic laws" that China needed to obey.[41] This concept showed the extent to which, in practice, Hua's embrace of the "two whatevers" was only partial. Although Mao had sometimes made statements suggesting an independent economic sphere (e.g., in his speech on "The Ten Major Relationships" in 1956), other statements left little doubt about his position: In January 1967, Mao said, "Political work is the lifeline of all economic work."[42] In socialist society, a *Red Flag* editorial declared, "There is no 'pure learning,' and all kinds of learning are . . . subordinate to politics."[43] The Maoist vision left no room for "objective economic laws" that might be separate and not "subordinate" to political laws—and yet, to Hua and his lieutenants in the spring of 1977, the goal of economic growth evidently outweighed such ideological scruples.

To demonstrate support for economic research and provide an institutional base for economists to work, in May 1977 Hua Guofeng approved the creation of the Chinese Academy of Social Sciences (CASS) as an institution independent of the Chinese Academy of Sciences.[44] The purpose of the organization was, in the words of one senior official, to act "as an assistant to the Party and to the government."[45] Three officials who were closely associated with Deng Xiaoping and the State Council Political Research Office during this period—Hu Qiaomu, Deng Liqun, and Yu Guangyuan—assumed top posts at CASS and began to recruit economists to return to Beijing.[46] Sun Yefang, a leading economist during the early PRC period who had been demonized as "a figure assuming command of [the] black line in economic circles" during the Cultural Revolution, was rehabilitated and became a senior adviser to CASS.[47] During the same period, numerous government organs established or reestablished their own "economic research institutes," including the State Statistical Bureau (since renamed the National Bureau of Statistics), the Ministry of Finance, and the People's Bank of China, the country's central bank. Xue Muqiao was appointed to lead an important research institute under the SPC.[48] This core set of economists, who quickly developed dense networks and numerous institutional affiliations, would drive economic analysis and policy formulation for the Party's reform-oriented faction.[49]

With their many official stamps of approval, these economists began issuing criticisms of the Gang of Four's economic policies. Because the Gang of Four was now universally disparaged, the criticisms helped to define the value of the discipline of economics in terms that were ideologically palatable across the spectrum of official opinion. Yu Guangyuan, a Party member since the 1930s who had been a senior researcher at the State Council and the first director of the Economic Research Institute of the SPC, led the charge. He was viewed by his colleagues as "an extraordinarily well-read scholar" who, like members of the "Miscellaneous School" that existed in the pre-Qin dynasty Hundred Schools of Thought period, had a mind that sought to integrate diverse ideas by finding their merits and avoiding their pitfalls.[50] Yu Guangyuan's credibility and his "miscellaneous" style of mind made him well suited to criticize the Gang of Four's economic theories and organize a series of seminars that helped to unify political economists of different backgrounds.[51] CASS economists also readied to reestablish the journal *Economic Research*, which had been published by the Chinese Academy of Sciences before the Cultural Revolution and would now become

China's leading journal for theoretical and applied economic research.[52] In public statements during the several months after the establishment of CASS, the elder generation of China's economists struck a pragmatic tone, emphasizing the value of experience. "If you do not proceed from reality, and summarize experiences, it will very difficult to engage in socialist economics," Xue Muqiao argued in a speech at the Central Party School. Ideologically driven policies had produced contradictory and often negative results, Xue observed: when grain was taken as the "key link" by ideologues, Chinese agriculture boomed and grain prices remained low, but when steel became the "key link," production fell and the economy foundered.[53]

Implicit in Xue's statements was an important idea: economic knowledge and the tests of experience, rather than political imperatives, should be the means for diagnosing China's economic problems and determining economic policies. This key step to restore the status of professional economists—the experts within the Chinese policy-making apparatus who were committed to this approach—is easy to take for granted, but it would prove critical to the success of China's reform policy development.[54]

This energy emerged at a critical moment in Chinese elite politics more broadly. A re-empowered Deng Xiaoping began to criticize openly the "two whatevers" policy and, in doing so, undercut Hua Guofeng, with whom the "two whatevers" was becoming almost synonymous. On May 24, 1977, Deng said bluntly in a conversation with several allies, "For us to apply what Comrade Mao Zedong said on one particular question to another" or "to apply what he said under one particular condition to another—all this certainly will not work!" Of course, Deng realized that his status was on the line because Mao had authorized his dismissal—but his claims were far larger. Deng suggested Mao had believed that if he were posthumously given "an assessment of 70 percent for achievements and 30 percent for mistakes, that will be quite all right."[55] In distancing himself from the "two whatevers" doctrine, Deng created a new but still ideologically viable alternative to the reviled Gang of Four. In July, the third plenum of the Tenth Central Committee of the CCP voted to formally restore Deng's positions and on July 21 Deng delivered a speech on improving the treatment of intellectuals, striking a tone very much in line with the new flourishing of activity at institutions like CASS. Shortly thereafter, Deng supported the Party's decision to resume China's national college entrance examinations, which had been eliminated during the Cultural Revolution, providing a new generation of intellectuals and students (beginning with the "third generation") with the opportunity to resume or begin their education.[56] He had leveraged his initial portfolio in education, science, and technology to great effect. Deng was back, and he made the restoration of status and opportunity for China's intellectuals one of his first priorities.

Yet Hua was still China's paramount leader and he continued to wear the legitimating mantle as Mao's designated successor. In line with his May 1977 speech and his emphasis on liberating "the productive forces," Hua encouraged his advisers and officials to begin drawing up plans for China's economy to grow—and to grow rapidly.

With these goals in mind, China's leadership began to adopt a remarkable new policy: to travel far and wide, across national borders and ideological boundaries, to seek new ideas. On July 26, 1977, the SPC issued a report to the Politburo recommending that senior officials organize study tours to foreign countries to conduct "investigatory work" on other countries' economies and practices.[57] One senior delegation had already visited the United Kingdom and France to study enterprise management, producing few concrete results but awakening the curiosity of the delegation members, many of whom had never before traveled to a capitalist country.[58] Early the following year, Hua would highlight this element of his agenda to the Politburo and, by the best scholarly count, during 1978 twenty-one delegations with participants at the vice premier or vice chairman level traveled to fifty-one countries.[59] The recommendation of the July 1977 report was the first clear articulation that senior Chinese officials intended to learn from systems vastly different from their own. The SPC report sidestepped the question of what this learning would be used for, beyond technical know-how; to say more at this stage might have raised exceedingly difficult ideological questions.[60]

As Hua was encouraging his officials to look abroad, he faced a potent challenge back home. From August 12 to 18, he convened the

Eleventh Congress of the CCP, a national meeting of the top CCP leadership and over 1,500 delegates, held in the Great Hall of the People in Beijing. The reinstated Deng Xiaoping used the opportunity to deliver a powerful alternative to the "two whatevers" doctrine that he had criticized in conversations the previous spring. What Deng proposed was a cleverly re-appropriated phrase from Mao's writings: "seeking truth from facts." Rather than clinging to ossified doctrines or repeating "empty phrases," Deng suggested that all matters of ideology would need to be accountable to—and, potentially, adjusted in response to—hard "facts."[61] Less than one year after Mao's death, Deng was using Mao's own words to provide a path to "truth" that was distinct from the Maoist views Hua had endorsed. In a world where economists worried about treading on "forbidden territory" and claims that "there is no 'pure learning'" remained fresh in the memories of survivors of the Cultural Revolution, the prospect of a different official source of "truth" was, by implication, a direct challenge to Hua's leadership.

At the same time, it was clear that Hua was not entirely holding himself to the strict standard required by "upholding whatever policy decisions Chairman Mao made," and nowhere was this clearer than in foreign affairs. From August 30 to September 8, Hua hosted the eighty-year-old leader of Yugoslavia, Josip Broz Tito, in Beijing, following a series of diplomatic overtures. Tito had become an international symbol of "revisionist" socialism after he broke with the Soviet Union's economic model after World War II, defying Josef Stalin and developing a system based on independent worker-run enterprises (instead of state-run enterprises) that allowed for management decisions and profits to be shared among workers. Mao had repeatedly called Tito a "revisionist," part of a "clique of renegades and scabs," and had said that his regime's economic success was not socialist but came simply from "copying the bourgeoisie."[62]

Tito's visit to China made it clear that Hua was both prepared to engage with foreign countries that Mao had deemed abhorrent and ready to recognize that multiple varieties of socialism existed in the world—and this visit could even be called, as one Chinese scholar has written, the "starting point" of the CCP's "willingness to resort to reforming" Chinese socialism.[63] Regardless, it is unquestionable that Hua's meeting with Tito—and the return of a visit by Hua that the two leaders planned for later in 1977—showed the extent to which criticisms of "revisionism" and "copying the bourgeoisie" in a changing China were no longer ultimate transgressions. "Comrade Tito was the first to recognize that socialism should not be confined to one model," praised the leading Party theoretician Hu Qiaomu.[64] China, by implication, had also come to "recognize" this fact.

Yet divisions ran deep about how to understand China's system and define China's goals, as revealed by a series of editorials and essays published that autumn. On September 12, an essay written by the SPC and published in the *People's Daily* laid out a traditionally Maoist understanding of the "great guiding principles for socialist construction," emphasizing class contradiction and struggle, though it did not entirely omit "promoting production."[65] However, later that month in the same newspaper Chen Yun and another senior theoretician each published essays raising previously verboten questions that did not accord with the "two whatevers," such as whether distribution according to labor was "a socialist or a capitalist principle" and, in Chen Yun's case, calling for the Chinese leadership to "firmly uphold the revolutionary style of seeking truth from facts," a clear indication of support for Deng.[66] Both documents showed that important senior figures within the CCP had decided that the Maoist embrace of class struggle was no longer the critical "guiding principle" of China's future.

Even if Deng Xiaoping, Chen Yun, and others had decided by autumn 1977 that the "whateverist" agenda was not best for China, they did not yet offer a systematic answer to the question of what, exactly, had gone wrong. When Yu Qiuli, a survivor of the Long March who was chairman of the SPC, spoke to the Politburo Standing Committee about this question, he focused his attention on the flaws in the creation and implementation of state plans, asserting that "the roots of planning problems" did not stem from "the central planning system itself but rather [lay] in the failure to implement correctly its premises and requirements."[67]

This was a powerful idea with pleasing ramifications for those who did not want to have to change China's governing ideology: the problems of China's economy, in other words, were not caused by the "premises" of the traditional socialist planning system, but rather by specific flaws in Chinese implementation of that system. The solution, under this framework, would be for China to eliminate the flaws and make better plans. Larger ideological questions could be put off for the time being.

However, other Chinese economists seemed less immediately satisfied with this simple and conservative solution. The dissatisfaction grew from their interest in what other economic systems could teach China in its pursuit of the Four Modernizations. On November 23, the newly established CASS Institute of World Economics, the Economic Research Office of the SPC, the Research Office of the Ministry of Trade, and the Foreign Affairs Bureau of the Ministry of Finance—among other government research agencies—held a joint seminar in Beijing to discuss economic growth and development issues in the United States, Japan, the Soviet Union, West Germany, and elsewhere, with the goal, as one participant observed, of "realizing the Four Modernizations and catching up with the rest of the world."[68] Discussing in early December how China could research capitalist economics, Xue Muqiao quoted Lenin: "We are convinced that [Marx's] theory has only laid the foundation stones of that science on which the socialists must continue to build in every direction, unless they wish to be left behind by life."[69] Like Hua's invitation to Tito, these discussions indicated an increasing willingness among Chinese officials and economists to engage with alternative models, whether "revisionist" Yugoslav socialism or the capitalist practices of Western countries such as the United States and West Germany. These ideas extended all the way to the most senior level of the Chinese leadership, with Deng Xiaoping commenting, in a discussion on the sixth five-year plan then being drafted, that Romania had recently achieved a growth rate of 14 percent. This, Deng said, was the kind of goal that China should also pursue, even if it required China "to learn how to use . . . foreign things."[70]

As China's new leaders discussed people and places once considered anathema, some theoreticians began to explicitly challenge the notion that Mao's ideas could provide a consistent and comprehensive guide to policy and ideology. Hu Yaobang, a free-thinking revolutionary who had been one of the youngest participants in the Long March and had become a top administrator at the Central Party School in March 1977, rose to be one of the loudest voices encouraging his colleagues not to rely solely on Mao Zedong Thought to determine what was correct. In December 1977, in a speech at the Central Party School, Hu suggested that, in addition to studying Mao's ideas and writings, "practice" should be a second "criterion in judging the truth." Echoing Deng, who was himself also selectively echoing Mao, Hu cited the principle of "seeking truth from facts" and insisted, "If you polemicize about whether a line is correct or not without regard for practice or with your eyes closed to the facts of history . . . you will only be taken in and deceived."[71] Hu, an important protégé of Deng, made clear that the Chinese leadership's increasing willingness to consider new economic ideas and partners had vast ideological implications—and powerful forces desiring to advocate for these changes, especially within a bastion like the Central Party School, were stirring.

Such debates over ideology became critical matters in economic policy early the following year, when Hua Guofeng presented his vision for China's economy at the February 1978 National People's Congress (NPC). Boosted by the rapidity of the economic rebound over the previous year—when production in industry and agriculture had risen 10.7 percent, with steel production, for example, rising 16 percent—Hua had been pushing for ever-higher growth rates, even stating at one point that 10 percent was too low.[72] His economic vision sought to fuel rapid growth with imports of foreign technology and foreign capital.[73] In this, Hua relied on Yu Qiuli and his "Petroleum Group," a moniker earned because they had built their careers in the petroleum industry (Yu had formerly headed the Daqing Oil Field).[74] Hua's ten-year development plan introduced at the NPC sought to boost investment in heavy industry (steel production targets were set at 60 million tons annually by 1985 and 180 million tons annually by 1999), to mechanize agriculture, and to use imported foreign technology to create new manufacturing plants.[75] In 1978, as a result of this policy China signed contracts to import US$7.8 billion in equipment—a stunning amount for a single year—and the total volume of imports and exports was 39 percent higher than that in 1977.[76]

This vision quickly earned the unfortunate moniker of the "foreign leap forward" (*yang yuejin*, sometimes translated as the "Western leap forward" or the "great leap outward"), a reference both to the rapid-growth policies of the Great Leap Forward and the rapid embrace of "Western" or "foreign" (*yang*) technology and capital to produce that growth. The "foreign leap forward" was a symbol of two dynamics that coexisted uneasily: on the one hand, China's readiness under Hua to introduce foreign capital and technology and to learn from abroad; on the other hand, an impatience for fast results that reminded Chinese observers of Mao's disastrous policies during the Great Leap Forward.[77]

Hua's agenda, unsurprisingly, was in keeping with Yu Qiuli's comments that the "premises" of Chinese socialism were correct but that problems had arisen because of errors in implementation. In addition to these contentious economic policies that sought faster economic growth, Hua's regime continued to oversee an increased emphasis on research in economics and social sciences, with a mid-March article in the *People's Daily* declaring, "It is imperative to allow research in the social sciences to prosper as never before."[78] Later that month, in a discussion with Hu Qili and Deng Liqun on division according to labor, Deng Xiaoping praised the research that had been undertaken and encouraged further work.[79]

But many senior economists felt great frustration with an economic situation that, as a result of Hua's policies, was teetering on the brink of disaster. Despite striking a positive tone at the official meetings, Xue Muqiao returned home, slumped in his chair, and began to cry. "The national economy has come to the brink of collapse," he choked out to his daughter. She recalled that she could hear the frustration in his voice. "I still feel that now is better than before, with the Gang of Four—so how is it that we are so close to collapse?"[80]

The perception that China's economic policy was still not producing optimal results fueled a new wave of delegations sent abroad to study foreign economies. Yu Guangyuan was the senior economist on an official delegation to Yugoslavia and Romania, dispatched on direct orders from Hua, between March 9 and April 6, 1978.[81]

China's leaders had "long misunderstood" Yugoslavia, Yu wrote, praising the "beautiful" and "expanding" cities they visited, and admitting, "Our general impression is that they had developed faster than us these years."[82] The key message of the trip accorded with Yu's "miscellaneous" mind: the delegation "concluded that multiple forms of socialism were legitimate," driving home a point that had been symbolically represented by Tito's visit to Beijing the previous year.[83]

A second delegation of senior economists, including Sun Yefang, would spend five weeks in Yugoslavia that winter; it returned praising Yugoslav "enterprise autonomy" and believing, as Sun wrote, "The Yugoslav example provided valuable experience for other countries to choose their own road of socialist construction according to their specific conditions"—a point made clearly with China in mind.[84] The breathless praise of the Yugoslav economy was not universally shared; many Chinese economists were critical of that system, which they thought encouraged enterprises to ask for too much from the central government and thus should not serve as a model for China. But even critics of Yugoslavia's economic policies had generally stopped arguing that its socialism was illegitimate.[85] With a new-found sense of permission, Sun Yefang also wrote to Hungarian colleagues about arranging a visit to study Hungarian socialism during the following year.[86]

During the busy spring of 1978, Deng Xiaoping's allies also spear-headed two decisions that would have vast ramifications for the future of China's reforms. First, Deng sent to Guangdong an important revolutionary elder, Xi Zhongxun, who was tasked with solving the problem of residents fleeing the poor provinces for the rich British colony of Hong Kong. Xi, like Deng, had only recently been rehabilitated, after suffering several purges and periods of imprisonment during a tumultuous career. But Xi (the father of China's current president, Xi Jinping) had been close to Zhou Enlai and voiced his strong commitment to bringing the Four Modernizations to Guangdong.[87]

Second, Deng's August 1977 article on "seeking truth from facts" and Hu's December 1977 comments on "practice" and "truth" provided the basis for a searing editorial, published in May 1978, titled "Practice Is the Sole Criterion for Testing Truth." Written by a group of thinkers and writers associated with Hu Yaobang at the Central Party School, this essay argued that, as Michael Schoenhals has summarized, "A theory in itself can never be the criterion of truth, although it can be the truth. All theories are dependent on, and will always have to be judged against, practice," as well as being "constantly 'supplemented, enriched and corrected.'" After input from and approval by Hu Yaobang, the essay appeared in *Guangming Daily* on May 11 and was reprinted in the *People's Daily* and by Xinhua News Agency the following day. Suddenly the arguments made in the article were catapulted up the ranks and came to the attention of the CCP leadership. Conservatives were incensed, claiming the essay was theoretically "erroneous" and politically "an even greater problem . . . very bad, very bad," even accusing its authors of being "out to cut down the Red Banner of Mao Zedong Thought," according to a former editor of the *People's Daily*, whose rage was shared by many of Hua Guofeng's supporters.[88]

Of course, far more than ideological abstractions were at stake: the quarrels over what the CCP would embrace as the "truth criterion" represented a fundamental choice about how China would develop. Would "facts" and "practice" allow for policy experiments, or would the traditional strictures of Maoist ideology and socialist planning prevail? The writers of the "practice" essay soon acknowledged the obvious: the claim that "practice is the sole criterion of truth" was closely connected to the Dengist agenda of "seeking truth from facts."[89] Early that summer, Deng himself spoke out in favor of the correctness of the "practice" doctrine, comments that Li Xiannian echoed shortly thereafter.[90] Deng, with his power on the rise, pushed ahead with "seeking truth from facts" even as senior ideologues debated the merits of this view.

One important manifestation of this agenda borrowed from Hua's playbook: sending a delegation, led by Vice Premier Gu Mu, to Western Europe, in order to conduct research on how to realize the Four Modernizations through practice. Before the group left, Deng told Gu, "We ought to study the successful experiences of capitalist countries and bring them back to China."[91]

From May 2 to June 6, 1978, Gu Mu and his delegation of central and provincial officials traveled through France, Germany,

Switzerland, Denmark, and Belgium. Their goals, Gu recalled, were to investigate the level of modernization in industry, agriculture, science, and technology; economic development in the 1950s and 1960s; and the experience of organizing and managing socialized production in capitalist countries.[92] This was the first time Gu had been out of the country, and he did not know, he wrote, what the "capitalist world" would look like. He and his delegation experienced three "breakthroughs." First, there had been dramatic postwar economic development in Western Europe, so the way in which countries there regulated their economies no longer resembled the capitalism the Chinese had learned about from the Soviet Union. Second, the leaders of the capitalist countries were very interested in China's economic development. Third, there were many "internationally accepted practices" that China could also use. Returning to China, Gu wrote a long report on what he and his colleagues had learned, which he submitted to the Central Committee and the State Council and presented in a report to the Politburo at a session chaired by Hua Guofeng on June 30, 1978.[93]

The discussion proceeded for three and a half hours. The top leaders present—including Hua Guofeng, Ye Jianying, Li Xiannian, Wang Zhen, and other Politburo members—praised Gu's research and spoke out in support of the ideas he had brought back from Western Europe. "This allows us to see our own situation more clearly. It will not do to go without comparisons," they agreed.[94] At this Politburo session, as well as at private conversations he held with Deng Xiaoping, Gu advocated one idea in particular: "adopting the practice used in some Western countries of establishing industrial processing zones closed off from surrounding areas, where foreign businesses could invest and establish factories under a tax-free regime, and directly exporting production." This idea was further expounded by a SPC official, who suggested that Guangdong could be a site for some of these policies. These early proposals aligned with experiments already underway at the local levels that were percolating upward, such as the experimental industrial zone in Shekou, Guangdong, of the China Merchants Group of Hong Kong, which would be formally ratified in January 1979. At this point in 1978, Gu and the central leadership did not fully articulate a vision for what would become known as the special economic zones (SEZs), but these discussions helped lay important conceptual groundwork. Gu would also become an advocate for bolder policies in international economic relations.[95]

In a sign of how partisan China's ideological debates had become by the summer of 1978, the Dengist group that had rallied around "seeking truth from facts" and "practice as the sole criterion of truth" received a substantial boost from a speech delivered by the senior theoretician and CASS president Hu Qiaomu on July 28, 1978, on observing "objective economic laws." Hu was perhaps the Party's leading writer of important official documents.[96] He had coauthored the April 1977 speech in which Hua used this term, but he now applied it to undermine Hua, knowing full well that "objective economic laws" would be seen as a ringing endorsement of Deng's agenda.[97]

In the speech, Hu Qiaomu presented "objective economic laws" as a central priority for the Party. "Many cadres leading our industrial, agricultural, and other economic work do not recognize or do not want to recognize economic laws and their objectiveness," Hu bemoaned. "They consider that economic laws can change according to political needs." These were serious errors; instead, the task of those leading comrades should be "to skillfully apply the objective economic laws in order to correctly formulate and implement plans." Furthermore, in order to learn how to do this, China must both "strengthen the study of economics" and "make learning advanced foreign things a requirement." Hu elaborated, "Only in this way can we quickly increase our ability to do things according to objective economic laws and to accelerate the pace of the Four Modernizations."[98]

The powerful connection Hu's speech drew between the goal of realizing the Four Modernizations and the work of China's economists and economic policy makers was an important step. The "study of economics" had not previously received as lucid, official, or forceful an endorsement. In February, Hu had spoken with Xue Muqiao about Xue's observation that China's "economic theory workers" were not skilled at "combining theory with practice." Further, Xue had said, "Economic theory research institutes very seldom interact with economic work departments, they don't even look at statistical materials, and they must search in foreign books for Chinese statistical information; this situation cannot continue."[99] By asserting the need to "observe objective economic laws," Hu gave tremendous importance to the work of scholars and officials, separating their policy work from their previously ruinous ideological crimes like "deviation to the right." And it was clear this would require learning from both socialist and capitalist countries. At the same economic theory forum, the conservative chairman of the SPC, Yao Yilin, reportedly quoted Lenin's foreboding line about dealing with capitalists: "When you live among wolves, you must howl like a wolf."[100]

Yet Deng and others around him were aware that learning to "howl like a wolf" would take time and careful training. That same July, Deng met with an American education delegation led by geophysicist Frank Press, the primary science adviser to President Jimmy Carter. During these meetings, Deng sought and received approval to send thousands of Chinese exchange students to the United States in the immediate future.[101] After all, if "practice" were to be "the sole criterion of truth," then future Chinese leaders would need to see what an advanced economy looked like in practice before they could begin to build one in China.

Thus, by mid-1978, an astonishing intellectual opening was underway—with economic ideas at its center. As Chinese leaders investigated the alternative forms of socialism being practiced in Eastern European countries that were formerly branded as "revisionist," they also rehabilitated economists whom Mao and his supporters had persecuted during the Cultural Revolution and put new emphasis on "objective economic laws." Those empowered economists (as well as scientists and others) helped lay the groundwork for a much broader engagement with the nonsocialist economies, especially the capitalist countries in Western Europe and North America. In addition to the foreign technology and cooperation that Hua had welcomed to China, foreign economic ideas were also entering elite conversations.

Yet the broader context of the theoretical war against the "two whatevers" meant that far more was at stake in learning from abroad than simply academic curiosity. As Deng and Hua jostled for position at the top of the CCP apparatus, ideology became a battleground for raw power—turning the investigations abroad into a dangerous game in the blood sport of Chinese politics.

2

Pushing Off from the Shore

⌘ DENG XIAOPING's vision for China's future may have
been on the rise by the summer of 1978, but Hua Guofeng continued
to behave like China's leader and to develop his agenda. In July, he
and Hu Yaobang—the important Deng protégé who had spearheaded
the "truth criterion" debate—met to discuss Hua's ambitious goals
to modernize China. Hu, a supporter of rapid economic growth,
would later recall that the long conversation had made him tremendously excited about Hua's vision, despite their other disagreements.[1]
A meeting of the State Council early that month supported this vision and determined that China could intensify its rapid industrial
boom. Participants blamed the Gang of Four for China's economic
backwardness and loyally asserted that China's recovery since Hua
came to power boded well for future growth.[2] Other socialist countries, aligned against China, were quick to criticize Hua—in a private
conversation, Soviet foreign minister Andrei Gromyko praised the
Polish government for its "strong stance in condemning the Chinese
leadership's policies"[3]—but Hua had made his decision: economic
growth was now firmly the top priority of the Chinese Communist
Party (CCP).

To achieve that goal, Hua and other senior leaders set out to
find new ideas, establishing a pattern of examining foreign ideas and
models. Hua traveled abroad in August, on an itinerary that included

Yugoslavia and Romania, where Yu Guangyuan had conducted research earlier in the year. Hua's delegation included the Party secretary of Sichuan province, Zhao Ziyang. Several years later, Zhao—who had spent four years working in a factory in Hunan province during the Cultural Revolution—would become premier of China and its chief economic reformer, but during the trip he was simply a promising provincial leader. Like the previous Chinese delegations, Hua was most interested in Yugoslav enterprise management, which stressed self-management and enterprise autonomy. Upon returning to China, Hua instructed Zhao to experiment with these policies in Sichuan.[4] Zhao's industrial enterprise reforms in Sichuan, which focused on restructuring and consolidating management, evidenced "significant borrowing from the Yugoslav experience."[5]

Separately, by October 6, when the *People's Daily* published Hu Qiaomu's speech on observing economic laws, Deng had already taken aggressive steps to advance his own agenda.[6] On October 19, Deng Xiaoping arrived in Japan, which offered him and other senior leaders a close look at a capitalist economy. Deng Liqun recalled, "In my lifetime, the 1978 study tour to Japan was my first immersed look at capitalism. Prior to this, I had never been to a capitalist country"— much the same sentiment that other Chinese leaders had voiced on their inaugural trips to the West.[7] Deng's trip to Japan, where he and his delegation toured factories and markets, showed what prosperity could look like if a country followed "objective economic laws."[8]

Japan would be an important source of financing and technical expertise for China in the subsequent decades. As the Japanese economy boomed—leading some analysts to foresee a future with "Japan as number one"—Japanese investment poured into China, reaching US$532.5 million by 1991, 12.2 percent of the total foreign direct investment in China, behind only that of Hong Kong.[9] In science and education, Japan also provided technical training to Chinese counterparts—and Japan inspired Deng Xiaoping, Deng Liqun, and others with a vision of modernization just across the East China Sea. But in the arena of economic ideas, Japan's role was many orders of magnitude smaller than its value to China as a source of investment, trade, and training.[10] Some Japanese economists would come to China to offer advice, and senior leaders, especially Hu Yaobang, continued to develop ties with Japanese counterparts throughout the 1980s. But intellectual interactions with Japanese economists were far less systematic than engagement with Eastern European countries that had experimented with reforms to socialism or with Western capitalist countries that were regarded as the originators and developers of liberal market ideas.

In the weeks after Deng returned from Japan, the central Party work conference convened, providing him and his allies with a major opportunity to solidify their power. At the work conference, which opened on November 10, fierce criticism of the "two whatevers" doctrine was expressed and intense speeches were made that called for the overturning of Mao-era verdicts. Hua, sensing that Deng's supporters had won over much of the Party leadership, accepted many of the demands, including a reversal of the verdict on the 1976 Tiananmen Incident. This had the effect of partly undermining Hua's legitimacy, which was founded on decisions made in the wake of the Tiananmen Incident and the anti-Deng atmosphere that had prevailed in the months before Mao's death. On December 13, Deng delivered a speech—drafted by Yu Guangyuan and Hu Yaobang—in which he articulated his goals for China's leadership in powerful, inclusive terms and suggested a new era was dawning in China.[11] The CCP had to "emancipate the mind" from the strictures of outdated ideology and misguided notions. "Revolution takes place on the basis of the need for material benefit," not just "the spirit of sacrifice," Deng declared. "Emancipating the mind" would involve learning advanced science, technology, management, and economics. "We must learn to manage the economy by economic means. If we ourselves don't know about advanced methods of management, we should learn from those who do, either at home or abroad," Deng added.[12] Most of all, the call for "emancipating the mind" showed the immense power of Deng's commitment to "seek truth from facts" and ended weeks of contentious meetings on a resounding note of inclusive optimism. By the time the work conference concluded on December 15, it was clear to the participants that Deng, not Hua, would be China's paramount leader in the years to come.

These internal decisions were unveiled at the third plenum of the Eleventh Party Congress, which met from December 18 to 22. The decisions made at the work conference were announced and ratified; although Hua remained the titular leader of the government and Deng received no new title, both domestic and foreign observers realized that Deng was now in charge. Chen Yun, now a formal member of the Politburo Standing Committee, spoke of the leadership's newfound ability to realize the Four Modernizations. He and Deng sat together—two old revolutionaries, still clad in their dark Mao jackets, preparing to lead their country into what they proclaimed was a new era.[13] The meeting, one of the most famous events in China's modern history, announced that the chaos and waste of the Mao period were finally over. A new era of "reform and opening up" was beginning, with the promise of wealth, power, and participation in the global community. And Deng Xiaoping was the man who would lead China forward.

However, it is important to recognize that, at the famous third plenum, no clear endpoint of the process was established. China's economic policy makers did not believe that the time of the planned economy had ended or that a market economy was their clear goal.[14] Yu Guangyuan recalled that "reform ideas were generally embryonic" at the third plenum.[15] Zhao Ziyang, one of Deng's favorites and the future premier, agreed, writing in his memoirs: "My earliest understanding of how to proceed with reform was shallow and vague. . . . I did not have any preconceived model or a systematic idea in mind."[16] Instead, China's leaders prioritized determining the problems of the old system and taking incremental, experimental steps to improve economic management—that is, what they famously called "crossing the river by feeling for the stones."[17] This pragmatic mantra broadcast that they were committed to trial and error, an unequivocal turn away from the massive disasters of the Mao era's utopian visions and steely plans.

Immense shifts occurred in 1978—from the "foreign leap forward" to "reform and opening," from Mao-era isolation to dozens of study trips abroad, and from Hua Guofeng to Deng Xiaoping. In December, at a meeting in Havana of the Soviet-bloc organization tasked with coordinating policy toward China, an East German report decried "China's policy of allowing more Western influence to shape its domestic policies and economic strategies," an assessment the Soviet leadership would also voice repeatedly in internal reports.[18] Both inside and outside the country, China was clearly on the move. But even its leaders did not know where it was headed.

The Soviet bloc's criticism of China received what seemed to be astonishing confirmation when, on December 15, 1978, the United States and China announced normalization of diplomatic relations effective January 1, 1979, following intensive negotiations during 1978.[19] This breakthrough, crucial in its own right, also gave a significant boost to Deng's campaign for "reform and opening"—it was, in a sense, a swift victory for Deng's broader agenda. Only several days later, on January 6, the Party center granted Xi Zhongxun approval to begin seeking foreign investment in Guangdong. This would allow Guangdong to build factories that could manufacture industrial products for export and eventually led to Gu Mu's appointment to a new position as head of the Special Economic Zones Office, coordinating Guangdong's activities. By the end of January, the Shekou industrial zone at the tip of Shenzhen, just across Deep Bay from Hong Kong, had been established, and a first project— involving scrap metal exports to Hong Kong—had received formal approval.[20]

Coming in swift succession, these developments emphatically demonstrated the diplomatic and economic transformations that "reform and opening" would entail in practice. Deng set out on a visit to the United States from January 28 to February 5—the historic introduction to the American people of a world leader whom the U.S. Secretary of State Cyrus Vance called "impatient, feisty, self-confidently outspoken, direct, forceful, and clever." Deng, named *Time*'s "Man of the Year" in 1978 under the title "Visions of a New China," toured American factories (including those at Boeing and Ford Motor Company), beamed for the cameras wearing a 10-gallon hat in Texas, and met with leading political figures across the country. Deng, who was thrilled and astonished by what he saw, tossed and turned at night, going several days without sleep. Ezra Vogel has argued that the images of Deng in the United States "introduced the Chinese public to a modern way of life. . . . A whole new way of living was presented to them, and they embraced it."[21] In this sense, the

Time cover had at least two meanings: the Deng administration's ambitious plans as well as the new lifestyles and ideas that Chinese people were able to see for the first time.

Yet the debates that would expand and justify these "visions of a new China" were intensifying. Beginning in mid-January, as controversy over taking "practice as the sole criterion of truth" continued to swirl, Hu Yaobang convened a conference in Beijing on theoretical principles, suggested by Ye Jianying after the December plenum. Leading Chinese intellectuals spoke out about the changes to China's governing ideology that they thought would be necessary to legitimate and guide the policies of "reform and opening." A variety of groups met under the umbrella of the conference, including a session led by Yu Guangyuan to discuss and praise the Yugoslav economic reforms.[22] The attendees presented bold ideas, including a proposal by two theoreticians that China was in what they called the "early stage of socialism" or "undeveloped socialism," an argument they claimed could legitimate a wide variety of enterprise management and organization, whether state owned, private, or foreign owned.[23] Mao had used the term "initial stage of socialism" in passing in November 1958, but he had not fully explained what he meant by it and he never subsequently returned to it; it would be revived in 1986–1987 and eventually would become a signature component of Zhao Ziyang's work report at the 1987 Party congress.[24] But in 1979, such ideas were clearly too freewheeling for some: Deng Liqun, who remained committed to conservative reform and whom Deng Xiaoping had once mocked as stubborn as "a Hunan mule," attended very few of the conference sessions.[25] Yet, perhaps most importantly, scholars have observed that the necessity of a "theory conference" at this pivotal turning point in the CCP's history—despite the emphasis on "facts" and "practice"—revealed the "belief that the rectification of ideas [was] a prerequisite for the rectification of policy."[26] Deng's call for "emancipating the mind" and policies intended to "liberate the productive forces" were, it seemed, two kinds of inextricably connected freedoms.

How far would these freedoms extend? Beginning in late 1978, as educated young people sent to the countryside during the Cultural Revolution returned to the cities, in Beijing several "big-character posters" were mounted on a wall on Xidan Street that became known as "Democracy Wall." These posters, written by intellectuals of several generations, called for increased rights and freedoms for the Chinese people. Their criticisms were wide ranging, including direct attacks on Mao, Marxism-Leninism, and the CCP. In December, twenty-eight-year-old Wei Jingsheng posted an essay on the wall announcing a concept he called the Fifth Modernization—namely, democracy. "We do not want to serve as mere tools of dictators with personal ambitions for carrying out modernization," Wei wrote, mocking the Four Modernizations. Many of China's leaders, including Hua Guofeng, had sent their own children to the countryside, but they had not foreseen that "reeducation" might push these young people toward demands for democracy. Deng soon clamped down on freedom of expression at Democracy Wall, destroying the wall and imprisoning activists such as Wei.[27] The mind, Deng's actions showed, could be "emancipated" only within the bounds of the CCP's authority.

With Deng's work on the political front and Hu Yaobang's work on ideology, Chen Yun moved to take greater control over the economic portfolio from Hua. On March 8, Chen wrote an outline of his views on "the plan and market question," which revived his ideas from the 1950s and 1960s and called for a dominant planned economy, with a small, ancillary role for "market adjustment."[28] Further, on March 14, Chen presented his "readjustment" (tiaozheng) plan.[29] His signature initiative sought to cool growth and balance the expansion of heavy industry, light industry, and agriculture. It was clearly opposed to the rapid-growth policies of Hua Guofeng and Yu Qiuli's "Petroleum Group," but it also included an attack on "those like Gu Mu 'who came back from overseas inspection trips blowing the wind of more foreign loans and higher speed.'"[30] In addition to the new policy of "readjustment," Chen also established a Finance and Economics Commission at the State Council, which he and Li Xiannian would lead, providing them with an institutional base from which to oversee future economic policy making. The commission also included Yao Yilin, Gu Mu, Bo Yibo, Yu Qiuli, and Wang Zhen.[31] Frederick C. Teiwes and Warren Sun, drawing on the work of the Chinese scholar Xiao Donglian, have written that this group was "a happy reunion of leading economic officials, two-thirds of whom had been ousted during the Cultural Revolution."[32] With an experienced coalition empowered at the State Council, Chen set out to implement the goals he had articulated in mid-March.

Chen has often been caricatured as an exclusively conservative force in China's reform—sometimes in tension with Deng and often in contrast to the more liberal Zhao Ziyang. Chen's views in fact were substantially more complex.[33] A consistent advocate of incorporating market mechanisms into the socialist planned economy, Chen believed China should continue to rely on the plan as "fundamental and predominant" but should allow markets to emerge as "supplementary and secondary." Throughout the reform era, he would support reforms in line with this vision, but he would push back sharply against ideas that were more expansively pro-market or that he feared would undercut socialism or CCP authority.[34] While Deng's personal legitimacy "rested squarely on his ability to 'deliver the goods'" (as Joseph Fewsmith has explained Deng's tendency to prioritize "breaking precedent and producing high growth rates"), Chen had earned his stripes through precise managing of the planned economy. Chen was thus highly sensitive to the problems that emerged when bold policy changes of any sort were made, the sort of details Deng might have regarded as minutiae. Chen's priority throughout his career was *balance:* a combination of a balanced budget, balanced allocation of inputs and investment, and balanced output throughout the economic sectors.[35] To achieve balance, Chen believed in hard work, not bold thinking. Fewsmith writes, "[A]s he summarized his approach, it was necessary to spend 90 percent of one's time on study and investigation and only 10 percent on making decisions."[36]

During the Mao era, Chen had been an economic specialist, but it might be more precise to call him an economic repairman. After the CCP won the Chinese Civil War and inherited an economy riddled with inflation, Chen tamed it; after the reckless and disastrous Great Leap Forward, Chen (along with Zhou Enlai and Deng Xiaoping) helped to mend the damage. The market sometimes proved to be a useful auxiliary tool in these repairs. After the Great Leap Forward, for example, the introduction of some agricultural market incentives in the rural areas helped the country recover from the massive famine.[37] Yet those incentives constituted simply one of several tools in the repairman's toolbox, and his consistent goal was a well-functioning planned economy. Thus Chen was a conservative, but a complex conservative: he wanted to maintain the socialist economy above all else, but also to make it work better.

At a minimum, Chen seemed to envision himself as playing a similar role now that Deng had become paramount leader. Particularly in the first years of Deng's tenure, however, he sought to set the entire economic agenda. His priorities remained balanced planning and cautious, slow growth—which, during the Deng era, often placed him in opposition to younger, more ambitious reformers who aimed to fundamentally transform China's system of economic organization. Specifically, Chen opposed deficit financing and sought to avoid inflation at all costs. In 1979, he spoke of the "bitter lessons" he had learned from China's experiences with inflation earlier in the twentieth century and he made it clear that under his watch he would not allow China to repeat those "bitter" experiences.[38] Chen believed that the history of capitalism was a "history of inflation," and, according to Deng Liqun's recollections, he had said at the start of the reform era: "When it comes to allowing inflation to develop the economy—I fear it, I fear it, I fear it."[39]

In the elite politics of reform-era China, Chen was a major power broker. In addition to Deng Liqun, Chen's high-level allies included his protégé Yao Yilin, the vice premier and financial official who had supported Chen's economic work throughout the history of the People's Republic of China (PRC), and Bo Yibo, a revolutionary elder who had worked with Chen during the period of economic reconstruction after the Great Leap Forward, had served as chairman of the State Economic Commission, and had been attacked as a "rightist" fixated on "economism" during the Cultural Revolution.[40] Chen Yun and Deng Xiaoping, famously photographed triumphant together at the third plenum in December 1978, gradually grew less close, as they disagreed about the value of new ideas that promised faster growth in China. By 1984, the redefinition of the Chinese economy as a "planned commodity economy" revealed that Chen's approach was no longer the order of the day; his views would

therefore place him in stark contrast to the ambitions of the reformers as the decade progressed. Deng, Zhao Ziyang, and their
economic lieutenants no longer wanted to improve the traditional
socialist economy or to repair it when things went wrong. They
wanted to create a new system. But during this period, Chen and
Deng acted as allies.[41]

In March 1979, China's senior economist Xue Muqiao delivered a
speech at the State Enterprise Management Research Office that
sought to unite the agendas of Deng and Chen. Xue explicitly connected the errors of Mao's economic policies to the errors of Hua's
economic policies, which he said were both marked by impatience for
rapid results, or "blind pursuit of an impractically high pace of development."[42] During the Great Leap Forward, data on iron production
had been blatantly "fabricated," Xue wrote, and some village leaders
had allowed many people to starve to death, both manifestations of
errors in economic policy. But after giving voice to these Chen-style
criticisms of impatience and excess, Xue switched to using Deng's
favored language. "How can we observe objective economic laws?"
Xue wondered aloud. "This is a new question that has emerged over
the past year." Xue stated firmly that Chinese economic policy makers
would need to use their "nearly thirty years of experience" and to
"borrow from the experiences of other countries"—and it was not
necessary to completely eradicate anything that might look or sound
like "capitalism" from the economy.[43] Echoing Deng, Xue concluded
bluntly, "Why should a socialist society exalt poverty?"[44] The days of
Mao's vision of a China "pure though poor" were over.

However, Deng Xiaoping was absolutely unwilling to let this ferment of new ideas and policies undercut the authority of the CCP.
In a speech to a reconvened second session of the conference on
theoretical principles that Hu Yaobang had initiated in January,
Deng provided a four-part program that asserted the continued primacy of the CCP, in what might be considered an authoritarian
political counterpart to the liberalizing economic Four Modernizations. Deng introduced these "Four Cardinal Principles" in a speech
on March 30, 1979. The four principles were keeping to "the socialist road" and upholding the "the dictatorship of the proletariat,"

the leadership of the CCP, and Marxism-Leninism and Mao Zedong Thought.

At the same time that Deng put forth these strict limits on expression, he maintained the importance of acting "in accordance with objective economic laws," a direct reference to Hu Qiaomu's speech. In a major step, he declared that the CCP would support those "theoretical workers" (meaning, in this case, economists) who supported this mission. Echoing Lenin, Deng called for "more talk about economics and less about politics," reiterating the necessity of "catching up" in the social sciences and learning "whatever is progressive and useful in the capitalist countries." However, Deng maintained that intellectuals must also "criticize whatever is reactionary and decadent" in those societies.[45] In a speech designed to affirm, simultaneously, Deng's insistence on maintaining the power of the CCP and his commitment to economic reform, these comments about "the capitalist countries" showed an attitude in flux: Deng wanted to extract what was "useful" and shun what was "reactionary and decadent," but he did not offer a clear formulation about how precisely to recognize and separate those contradictory elements.

Although shows of Party strength in these speeches and in the clampdown on the Democracy Wall movement made clear the limits on expression and disagreement that Party leaders were willing to tolerate, they did not silence China's reform-oriented economists. More than 300 scholars from the Chinese Academy of Social Sciences (CASS), the Economic Research Office of the State Planning Commission (SPC), and the State Statistical Bureau gathered at Wuxi, in Jiangsu province, in April 1979 to debate China's reform policy priorities.[46] The conference allowed China's re-empowered "economic workers" to offer competing policy ideas for China in the period ahead. One bold proposal came from the improbable team of the gregarious Liu Guoguang and the mild-mannered Zhao Renwei, two economists affiliated with CASS's Institute of Economics, who called for an end to a "lopsided emphasis on planning to the neglect of the market," and proposed immediate reform to state-owned enterprises, particularly an expansion of the freedom to set prices, which provoked heated discussion.[47] A Party central work conference, also held in April, also focused on problems in enterprise management and, most importantly, set out a guiding economic agenda of "readjustment, reform, consolidation, and improvement" (*tiaozheng, gaige, zhengdun, tigao*), thereby expanding Chen Yun's "readjustment" agenda to include a broader set of objectives.[48] Zhao Ziyang, Gu Mu, and others supported this "Eight-Character Policy."[49] These reformist leaders also supported the April 1979 announcement approving the establishment of special economic zones (SEZs) in Guangdong and Fujian provinces. Hua Guofeng presided over the meeting, with both Hu Yaobang and Guangdong Party secretary Xi Zhongxun praising Hua's support for these reforms.[50]

Gatherings of economic experts, such as the Wuxi conference, and institutionalizing measures like the establishment of the State Council's Finance and Economics Commission were both part of a larger process during the post-Mao period of solidifying the role of economic expertise in crafting Chinese policies. In late June and early July, the State Council extended the formal role of economic expertise and policy input by establishing four Small Groups on reform, organized to conduct "large-scale investigations" and to "mobilize research." Yao Yilin delivered an address to senior economists and officials, alongside speeches by Sun Yefang, Yu Guangyuan, Deng Liqun, and others.[51] Yao called for the research groups to be willing to study present-day and historical problems, both in China and in foreign countries—including reforming socialist countries such as Yugoslavia, Romania, and Hungary ("Where had they hit snags? How did they resolve them?")[52] and "capitalist countries, in order to understand the lessons of their experience and what merit they have."[53] Zhang Jingfu led the group researching reform of the economic management system, known as the System Reform Group, with Xue Muqiao as one of the deputy heads.[54] Ma Hong led the Structural Reform Group, Wang Daohan led the Institutional Reform Group, and Yu Guangyuan led the Theory and Method Group. On July 19, members of the Politburo Standing Committee issued orders to the groups, stressing the importance they attached to their research because "after ten years of turmoil, the problems have really piled up." Each relevant ministry would send some of its most talented researchers, the senior leaders promised.[55]

For the moment, this talent would be drawn largely from members of the generation that had graduated from college around the time of the PRC's founding and had begun their careers before the disruptions of the Cultural Revolution. A prototypical member of this middle-aged generation was Wu Jinglian, who found his skills in high demand in 1979.[56] Wu Jinglian had studied Marxist political economy during the 1950s. When the Cultural Revolution broke out, Wu was a target of persecution for his ties to the senior economist and "black hand" Sun Yefang. Wu's mother, a teacher, had been attacked during the Cultural Revolution for contact with foreigners, and Wu had been punished as a "revisionist seedling."[57] Along with many other economists, Wu was sent to rural Henan province for "reeducation through labor" and subjected to beatings and criticism. Forced to criticize his mentor Sun, Wu returned to Beijing after his persecution ended with the advice of his friend Gu Zhun, a prominent intellectual whom he had met during their "re-education," echoing in his head: Gu had encouraged the charismatic and outspoken Wu to learn English, search for new ideas, and criticize central planning.[58]

Wu was assigned to work with Ma Hong at the Structural Reform Group and Yu Guangyuan at the Theory and Method Group, while also occasionally helping at the Institutional Reform Group. As the groups conducted their research, they would settle on an overall approach, "Have big changes in mind but start out with small changes." They would submit their reports to the SPC and other government agencies.[59]

During the same period, Chinese officials took the important step of establishing international partnerships with nongovernmental organizations (NGOs), which the changed diplomatic environment—especially the normalization of U.S.-China relations—newly permitted. That spring, senior officials quietly approached the Ford Foundation, an American NGO focusing on promoting international cooperation, for what internal Ford Foundation papers called "help in their efforts to catch up with developments in this country and elsewhere during China's long period of isolation." The Ford Foundation agreed and quickly began to design ambitious plans for collaborative economic activities in both the United States and China.[60]

As the Chinese leaders began to organize a formal role for economic expertise in the government and to reach out to international
partners to bring new knowledge to China, they also took action.
On July 13, 1979, the State Council issued an important decision that
some enterprises would be selected to have greater autonomy, including retaining a portion of profits.[61] Although it seemed this
policy might introduce significant changes to enterprise incentives
and the Chinese economy as a whole—after all, industrial profit for
the previous year had comprised 17 percent of the estimated gross
national product (GNP), and 6,600 enterprises had begun to implement this reform by the end of 1979—in fact it had little effect.
Chinese economists soon discovered that the low marginal retention
rate built into the equation used to calculate profit retention meant
that the system created extremely weak incentives for enterprises.[62]
More ambitious reforms were necessary to create stronger incentives. These fumbling early attempts at enterprise reform demonstrated that Chinese officials were indeed moving toward combining
plan and market, but they still had only a rudimentary understanding
of how to deploy market mechanisms most effectively.

Even outside the formal bureaucracy, Chinese economists were
organizing and conducting research intended to have a direct impact on government policy. Ma Hong announced, "We plan to summarize our experiences over the past three decades . . . [and] to
study the history, experience, and current conditions of the economic
structures of certain key foreign countries. Our goal is to explore
the laws governing the development of economic structures, and find
an economic structure that conforms to our own unique conditions."[63] For example, on July 27, the Chinese Society of Quantitative Economics was founded.[64] Another related case was the serial
Economic Reference Material, which began publication in early 1979,
soliciting contributions from numerous economists to provide policy
makers with regular updates on economic theory and research, focusing on foreign economics. Over one hundred issues in 1979 featured foreign economies and trends, more than half the total number
of issues published that year, including the developed capitalist countries in Europe and Asia, as well as the socialist countries in Eastern

Europe and the Soviet Union.[65] These efforts evidenced a clear interest in the utility of market mechanisms, although how to apply these ideas to Chinese socialism remained highly controversial even to storied reformers like Sun Yefang.[66]

Part of this controversy, of course, related to Mao Zedong's explicit condemnations of markets, capitalism, "rightism," and "bourgeois liberalization." What were China's new rulers to make of the man who had been their leader, prophet, scourge, and comrade? Although Deng and his allies had outmaneuvered the "two whatevers" faction and upheld "practice as the sole criterion of truth," thus overturning many Cultural Revolution–era verdicts, they had not directly and comprehensively addressed the issue of Mao's legacy and Party history. By autumn 1979, Deng Xiaoping decided that it was time. On October 1, 1979, after drafting by Hu Yaobang, Deng Liqun, and Hu Qiaomu, Ye Jianying delivered a speech on China's National Day, commemorating the founding of the PRC thirty years earlier. Ye's lengthy speech—of which the octogenarian official was too weak to read more than the opening and the closing at the National Day ceremony—presented a reworked narrative of the CCP's pursuit of building a "modern powerful socialist country" since the Party's founding in 1921. The speech admitted that the Party had made mistakes during Mao's rule, caused by the "impatience" of its leadership. Ye's statements were an unprecedented admission of errors made by both the Party and Mao himself.[67] The formality of this assessment, under the name of one of China's most senior revolutionary elders, marked a major historical reevaluation that clearly undercut the legitimacy of the "two whatevers." On an even more abstract level, this reworking and reevaluating of history provided yet another sign that Deng and his allies were consciously working to frame their own initiatives in epoch-making historical terms.

The historical reevaluation would also clearly mark a formal end to the period of "placing politics in command" over economic policy and would further legitimate Hu Qiaomu's analysis of the necessity of "upholding objective economic laws." Later in October, economists in Beijing issued public statements criticizing "political sermons and philosophical jargon" in economics—comments reported approvingly in the *Guangming Daily*.[68] In this changing political and intellectual context, Chinese economists made a new series of bold claims in their articles, many of which were published in the CASS journal *Economic Research*. One declared that economic planning was "a subjective process of economic activity in which man learns to know the objective laws and acts accordingly." China, the author wrote, had failed on this score: "Our plans, dictated by the higher authorities who paid little attention to objective realities, courted disaster." Now that this situation had changed, the author demanded that enterprises be given numerous "rights," including "the right to take independent action" and "the right to make a profit."[69] Writers in this vein did not intend to throw out economic planning. Instead, they proposed that these rights, in line with the "objective laws" of economic development, were the only way to correct the profound failures of planning in China and to make an economic plan that was "based on reality, reflects reality, and bears on reality," an emphasis that shows how necessary the Dengist language of "facts" and "practice" had become in justifying arguments about economic policy.[70] Other articles called for fixing China's broken statistical collection system, asserting it was not "a rightist ideological deviation if one conducts statistical analysis of the national economy on the basis of statistical data."[71] Although applying such charged language on seemingly banal matters such as statistical data may seem excessive, in context this was the normal vocabulary of "theoretical workers" in a socialist state, and China's economists were pushing to legitimate the ideas and tools they would need to craft better economic policies in the years to come.

As Deng Xiaoping prepared to advance his agenda, he assembled a core team of advisers that included Hu Yaobang, Yao Yilin, and Deng Liqun. Deng Xiaoping also planned to elevate to the central leadership Zhao Ziyang, who had become famous throughout China for his policy successes in Sichuan.[72] A new generation of reform-minded provincial Party officials had attracted to the attention of central leaders through rapid economic successes in the years immediately after Mao's death, with Zhao and Wan Li, Party secretary of Anhui province, as the most prominent examples. Zhao's and Wan's successes were associated with breaking away from Maoist economic models and remaking the rural economy in their provinces. Beginning in 1977, Wan was a vocal advocate of the "household responsibility system" in agriculture, which allowed individual households to make decisions about their own farms, a stark contrast to the Maoist policy of collectivization, and analogous policies in rural industry.[73] In turning to the household responsibility system, Wan was reviving a policy that had been promoted in 1956–1957, producing intense ideological opposition, and was introduced once again after the catastrophe of the Great Leap Forward—before once more being curtailed by 1963. This controversial history did not deter Wan, who led the formulation of the province's "Regulations on Several Questions of Current Rural Economic Policy," which fleshed out these policies, even encouraging farming on private plots and directly engaging in rural industry, calling for independent production teams and small-scale production outside the plan.[74] When a brutal drought ravaged Anhui in 1978, Wan used the catastrophe to promote use of the household responsibility system in farming, which incentivized workers by promising that if they worked harder during the drought they would be allowed to keep more food, and other responsibility systems in small-scale rural industry.[75] Meanwhile, the success of Zhao's similar agricultural policies in Sichuan—the "Sichuan Experience" David Shambaugh has argued was a "blueprint" for many subsequent agricultural reforms around the country—earned him the praise of farmers and peasants throughout the province.[76] Zhao's experiments in Sichuan, some of which were initiated at Hua's orders after their joint trip to Eastern Europe, had boosted agricultural output by 25 percent and industrial production by 81 percent during his first three years on the job.[77] Rural reform would transform the lives of hundreds of millions of Chinese and become one of the success stories of the reform era. It occurred largely at the provincial and local level, but came with its own battles and complexities. As scholars expand the reappraisal of the period 1976–1993, they will continue to deepen our understanding of these important dynamics.[78]

After Deng's ascendance in December 1978, rural reform in Anhui spread, and sped ahead. "Now the question is one of getting the masses to raise productivity," Wan said. "As long as production is increased, any method is fine." In a comment that the opening of relations between Tito and Hua had made permissible, he noted, "There is individual farming in Yugoslavia, but it is still recognized as a socialist country."[79] In 1979, signs of support for these policies came from Beijing, where Hu Yaobang had invited the reformist intellectuals Du Runsheng, Chen Yizi, and others to plan the establishment of a central group dedicated to rural development.[80] In April 1980, in recognition of their success, both Wan and Zhao became vice premiers of the State Council, and in May the policies they had championed received high-level endorsement from Deng.[81]

Several months later, Zhao would again be promoted, replacing Hua as premier. Within a few years, Zhao had gone from being a successful provincial administrator to one of China's top leaders and the Party's chief economic reformer. His easy smile, square-rimmed glasses, and graying crown of swept-back hair would make him a recognizable figure throughout the world, including in the United States, where in 1984 he jubilantly locked arms with President Ronald Reagan as they walked together at the White House.[82] In 1980, when he was named China's new premier, Zhao seemed to be a uniquely skilled official with proven ability in managing the economy during the period of "reform and opening"—making him an important addition to the team Deng was assembling to govern China.

Tremendous changes had taken place in 1978 and 1979: a wave of senior-level trips to study foreign countries, the normalization of relations with the United States, and the beginning of foreign investment in Guangdong and other coastal areas. Taken together, this new model of collaboration with foreigners marked the end of an era. During the Mao period, foreigners were allowed almost no access to the Chinese economy, meaning that the primary type of interaction with Western thinkers was inviting fellow travelers who were encouraged to act as propagandists for the regime at home. One prominent example of this type of visitor was Cambridge University economist Joan Robinson, who had been swept up in admiration for Mao in the 1950s and 1960s. Attending the National Day celebration in Beijing in 1957, she had shaken hands with Mao but was "too shy to make a remark."[83] A renowned economist who had often been mentioned as a contender for the Nobel Prize, Robinson's main academic career involved contributions that extended Keynesian ideas of growth to the long run; a major interpreter of Marx and John Maynard Keynes, she had dedicated her career to fighting what she denounced as "the sophistries of classical economics," and she had written with delight that, under Mao's leadership, China offered the "final proof" that communism was a viable "substitute" for capitalism.[84]

Robinson had not gone to China to offer her expertise, to participate in the economic policy-making process, or to interact meaningfully with her Chinese peers. Instead, she went to pay homage and to report back to global leftist audiences. In this way, she represents one end of the spectrum of the CCP's interest in Western economists: an extreme case of an intellectual who went to China to observe a highly distorted vision of what was occurring and to report that information back at home.

The examples of how far Robinson was willing to go to support Mao's policies are remarkable and numerous. After her first trip to China, she returned to the United Kingdom praising the murderous "Three Antis" and "Five Antis" campaigns as "pretty fair."[85] She lent her approval to the Great Leap Forward, the utopian campaign to create self-sufficient local communities that could feed their people and produce surplus but that failed spectacularly, exacerbating a massive famine and leading to the deaths of tens of millions of people.[86] Robinson chastised rumor-mongering "critics" who were "shedding crocodile tears over the 'famine.' "[87] Her most notorious boosterism came during the Cultural Revolution, which sought to purge Chinese civilization of traditions that might prevent China from achieving the goal of full communism and caused the persecution of at least 36 million people as class enemies and the deaths of between 750,000 and 1.5 million people, according to an estimate in one prominent study.[88] Robinson, however, deemed the Cultural Revolution, with its chanting, wrathful Red Guards, "picturesque and startling," noted its "historical necessity," and praised how China was advancing toward its goal of "self-reliance."[89] Many believe that this writing was the major reason she failed to be awarded the Nobel Prize that so many of her colleagues believed she deserved.[90]

Even when Robinson returned to China in 1978, with Mao dead and his policies being changed, her views did not change substantially.[91] Leading voices in China were openly admitting at internal meetings that the production statistics issued during the Great Leap Forward were "false" and that, in some areas, "not a small number of people had starved to death," as Xue Muqiao put it[92]—but Robinson continued to praise the "open-mindedness" of Mao and the "striking achievements of the authorities in China" who were able to "come through the years of harvest failure—1959, 1960 and 1961—without either famine or inflation."[93] On this visit, the magazine *World Economy* summarized the arguments she had made in her speeches and interviews in China. "Robinson believes that Western countries are now in the midst of a serious crisis. . . . The outlook is very bleak." Robinson allegedly claimed that the era of postwar prosperity in the Western countries was permanently over and asserted, "China's socialist system is superior, because it provides for the needs and interests of the people, allocates resources in a reasonable way, and plans economic development, which the Western capitalist system cannot match."[94]

Yet Robinson's one-way street of paying homage and bolstering the regime abroad was no longer the order of the day. "It was deflating to be told that the Cultural Revolution is over and that the new aim of policy is modernization," she reflected in 1979. "We know only too well what it is like to be modern."[95] That same year, Deng Xiaoping said plainly that his goal was to "turn China into a great modern and powerful country within this century."[96]

During the final months of 1979, the new model of collaborative international engagement, intellectual ferment, and political transition that grew out of Deng's goals expanded and deepened. In October 1979, a major American economics delegation visited China, and two important Chinese delegations traveled to Western capitalist countries. From October 8 to 27, the American delegation—chaired by the econometrician Lawrence Klein (who would win the Nobel Prize the following year) and including the Harvard expert on the Chinese economy Dwight Perkins, the Stanford economist Lawrence Lau, the agricultural economist Irma Adelman, and the Nobel

Prize–winning neoclassical economist Kenneth Arrow—traveled around the country giving lectures, meeting with senior officials and scholars, and initiating partnerships.[97] The Americans met with Vice Premier Gu Mu to inaugurate relations between China and both the American Economic Association and the Committee on Scholarly Communication with the PRC, which funded the trip.[98] They also met with Xu Dixin, a vice president of CASS, and Chen Daisun, a professor at Peking University who had received his PhD from Harvard in 1926, overlapping with many giants of the field, including Bertil Ohlin and Edward Chamberlain.[99] The delegation praised "the eclectic nature of China's search for new methods" of running the economy, though they were stunned at the low level of economic knowledge they encountered in nearly all their meetings.[100] At a seminar with students and officials, Arrow discovered that many people knew about the debates between Keynesians and monetarists, but only one person had heard of "rational expectations." Arrow reflected in his diary, "The joining of theory and empirical work is just beginning."[101] Recognizing this situation, Klein left the trip with an idea: he would organize a seminar on econometrics in Beijing the following year with funding from the Ford Foundation.[102]

During the same period, Hua Guofeng journeyed to France, West Germany, Great Britain, and Italy. In West Germany, his hosts noticed, "Hua had not mentioned Mao's name once in his speeches in the Federal Republic."[103] Hua's decision to omit explicit references to Mao likely reflected the reevaluation of Mao's historical position underway in China in the wake of Ye Jianying's National Day address. Meanwhile, his hosts in Great Britain saw the trip as a valuable opportunity to give Hua and his delegation "the best possible impression of British interest in China."[104] It would allow British officials and businesspeople "to influence and impress Chinese political, economic, and commercial thinking at the highest level."[105] The timing was off, however, given Hua's declining status in China, but the exposure and positive interactions with Western leaders—including even the free-market standard-bearer Margaret Thatcher—were received favorably by the Chinese delegation. Zhao Ziyang, who traveled to Great Britain, France, Greece, and Switzerland that same year, reacted positively to what he saw and noted the high degree of specialization and trade among the various regions of Western Europe.[106] When Zhao passed along his report to senior leaders, Bo Yibo wrote that the document was "inspirational and tremendously educational."[107]

Another major delegation to the West, led by Ma Hong, was composed of senior economists, including Xue Muqiao, Liao Jili, and several researchers from the SPC Economic Research Office and CASS.[108] From the trip's first moments, the members of the delegation became keenly aware of China's poverty. Flying to Paris on October 3, Xue recalled, "The meal on the plane was richer than a state banquet." On October 4, Xue went to a shopping mall and was stunned: "The goods were in much greater supply than those in Beijing."[109]

The entire delegation traveled around the United States from October 7 to November 3. The trip was structured around visits to universities, including Harvard, the Massachusetts Institute of Technology, the University of Pennsylvania, Indiana State University, and Stanford, and included trips to seventeen U.S. companies. The delegation's original intention was to study business management, the uses of foreign investment, and how the government intervenes in the U.S. economy. However, Xue wrote in his diary that their access was much more limited than they had hoped, so they were not able to conduct significant research on the latter two subjects. The delegation's meeting at Stanford with Arrow, who had recently returned from China, particularly impressed his Chinese interlocutors.[110] "China is a large, populous country, rich in natural resources, and with a certain amount of technological equipment," Arrow reportedly said, "but it is most backward in its management." Ma Hong, in particular, reflected that the trip had allowed him to see vividly how undeveloped Chinese management levels were by comparison to those in the United States.[111] For men who had survived invasion, revolution, famine, and ostracism in China, a warm welcome from American colleagues was an unlikely and moving milestone. The group spent its last day in California at the beach, writing poems to commemorate the occasion.[112]

Back in Beijing, many of these economists and their peers began to organize a professional economics network, with the goal of disseminating useful information to their colleagues. On November 10, 1979, they published the first *Communication of the All-China Federation of Economics Societies*, which included a speech by Yu Guangyuan and numerous essays, including material on "Western economics."[113] The All-China Federation of Economics Societies existed in name only and would not actually take form until May 1981, but the journal helped to advance the development of a community of economic experts throughout the country. By December, CASS was issuing several bulletins of job openings and new opportunities for social scientists and economists.[114]

The environment seemed to be warming for China's economists. On November 26, 1979, Deng lent further personal support by declaring, in no uncertain terms, that it was time for China to get rich—and to pursue policies that would allow wealth and power to flow into China. "The Gang of Four said it was better to be poor under socialism than to be rich under capitalism. This is absurd," Deng said plainly, in a conversation with the American scholar Frank B. Gibney. "Of course, we do not want capitalism, but neither do we want to be poor under socialism. What we want is socialism in which the productive forces are developed and the country is prosperous and powerful."[115] Deng continued:

> It is wrong to maintain that a market economy exists only in capitalist society and that there is only "capitalist" market economy. Why can't we develop a market economy under socialism? Developing a market economy does not mean practicing capitalism.[116]

Economic expertise would be critical in creating a socialist system that could successfully incorporate market mechanisms and renounce a state of perpetual poverty.

To that end, from late November to late December, a delegation of economists and theorists (including Yu Guangyuan and Liu Guoguang) traveled to Hungary, an Eastern European country with decades of experience in implementing market reforms to central planning. Sun Yefang had requested the trip in 1978, and the Hungarian side arranged for them to visit dozens of projects.[117] In the

course of twenty-one meetings, they spoke with Hungarian economists and economic officials, learning about Hungary's experiments
with "socialist markets" and other reforms. After they returned to
China, the cerebral Yu Guangyuan in particular frequently discussed what they had learned and wrote the *Report on an Investigation into Hungary's Economic System*, which was widely circulated.[118]
Deng Liqun gave voice to the general sentiment when he recalled
that the trip to Hungary had suggested to Chinese leaders of all
stripes that China's problems "were not only China's but were
common to all socialist countries."[119]

Chinese economists and policy makers demonstrated that they
were aware of the changes that had occurred in socialist economies
and they were actively making distinctions among them. "In our internal discussion, we held the view that among the Eastern European
countries, only Yugoslavia and Hungary were undertaking genuine
reforms and that the other countries' steps were too small," recalled
one ambassador and official during this period. "We wanted to make
big strides."[120] Interest in countries such as Hungary and Yugoslavia
revealed the intensity and variety with which Chinese economists
responded to Deng's rhetorical question, "Why can't we develop a
market economy under socialism?" Although the trips to the United
States and the study of "Western economics" were, in 1976–1979,
largely instrumental, focusing on management and technical questions, trips to the socialist countries in Eastern Europe were explicitly intended to compare their systems to China's, with the goal of
bringing new ideas back to Beijing.

Two significant dynamics were thus at play by the end of 1979. The
first was the newfound prominence of economic experts in China's
policy making, the result of a process that had taken off after Mao's
death in 1976 and had intensified under Deng. These economists,
stationed at government institutions and universities, actively ex-
changed ideas and opinions, helping to shape the ideological and
political debates of the moment. They traveled abroad together to
study foreign economies, and they regularly reported on their latest
findings to top Party leaders, who were hungry for expertise and
ideas within the boundaries of politically acceptable discourse. The
second was the continued commitment to socialism in the minds of

many reformers. "Reform and opening" was not an agenda to dismantle socialism in China but, rather, was intended to strengthen and enliven it. Deng's decision to "seek truth from facts" led to the firm conclusion that China urgently needed to make up for lost time.

Distancing the CCP from Mao's often misguided policies, Deng Xiaoping, Chen Yun, and their allies knew they wanted the Chinese economy to become more successful—but, as they surveyed countries ranging from Yugoslavia to the United States, they did not yet know what sort of system was needed to reach these goals. Finding answers to this profound challenge would result in nearly fifteen years of contestation, tragedy, and transformation.

3

A Swifter Vessel

⟨⟩ IN THE EARLY years after the beginning of "reform and opening up," the first important visit to China by a foreign economist began on a cold New Year's Eve. The venue was a nondescript gray building in Beijing's old center, to the west of Tiananmen Square. Instead of the sloping tiled roofs and leafy courtyards of the imperial city, this structure could have been built in any socialist capital from Budapest to Hanoi. Dozens of China's leading economists climbed up four flights of stairs to gather inside the meeting hall of the Institute of Economics of the Chinese Academy of Social Sciences (CASS). They had braved the last frigid December day of 1979 to hear the first of a series of lectures from the Polish-born Oxford economist Włodzimierz Brus.[1] His visit exemplified the search for models of reformed socialism in communist Eastern Europe—countries that, like China, had implemented central planning and found it wanting.

CASS provided a base for many top Chinese economists to advise Party officials. As the cases of Sun Yefang, Ma Hong, Yu Guangyuan, and others demonstrate, the institutional support for social science research and the newfound prestige top Party leaders attached to economics allowed these individuals an opportunity that had long been denied during the fearful "lost decade" of the Cultural Revolution: They could read more widely, write more freely, and demonstrate interest in outspoken critics of socialism. These activities, just a few years earlier, would have destroyed their careers and their lives, causing them to be branded "capitalist roaders," "rightists," or worse.

One of the most eager readers of foreign thinkers was Liu Guoguang, a CASS economist and coauthor of a bold paper on the relationship between the plan and the market presented at the Wuxi Conference in April 1979. In July 1979, Liu, who had studied political economy in Moscow shortly after the founding of the People's Republic of China (PRC), came across Włodzimierz Brus's work while reading about international reforms to socialism.

Brus was a famed advocate of what was often called "market socialism," a system based on the idea that market mechanisms were ideologically and practically compatible with socialism.[2] As early as 1960, he began to develop the concept of a "planned economy with a built-in market mechanism," explaining that enterprises would use the "profitability principle" to make autonomous decisions.[3] However, at the same time, "The principle of central plan primacy, and hence the primacy of national economic interests as a whole, is preserved. . . . Application of the market mechanism is not intended to supplant the plan, but to create an instrument for implementing it."[4] To Brus, market mechanisms were tools to make planned economies work better.[5]

Brus's life story embodied the conflicting values his scholarship hoped to reconcile. Born to a Jewish family on the banks of the Vistula River in central Poland, he had married young and seen his life torn apart in 1939, when Poland was invaded from both sides. The young Brus lost track of his family, continuing his economic studies at the University of Leningrad amid the churning chaos of World War II. Upon returning to Poland, he discovered that the Nazis had transported his parents, sister, and his wife's family to the Treblinka concentration camp, where all of them had died.[6]

After this tragedy, Brus's life continued to take dramatic turns. He discovered that the beautiful Jewish girl he had married before the war, whom he assumed had died in Treblinka along with her family, was still alive, living under a new name. But this joyful luck did not lead to an easy reunion. Helena Wolinska, as she was then known, had become the mistress of a leading officer of the secret police in the new Stalinist regime in Poland. It took over a decade for her to extricate herself from the relationship and return to Brus in 1956.[7] In communist Poland, Brus, too, rose to prominence. Earlier in his career, he had praised Stalinist economics, but now he became notable for his forceful advocacy of a more efficient and growth-producing form of "market socialism" and his claim that greater political democracy was necessary for a socialist state to thrive. After a period of worker strikes that seemingly supported his criticisms, Brus's influence gradually waned within the Polish United Workers' Party as the political and economic situation stabilized. Facing a rising tide of anti-Semitism in Polish politics, he resigned from the Party in 1968 and soon thereafter sought refuge in Great Britain.[8]

At Oxford, Brus continued to advance the ideas of market socialism that had made him famous. He taught economics at Wolfson College and published several books. Intellectually, he remained a man with one foot in his socialist homeland and one foot in his new capitalist home. He adopted the style of an Oxford don, dressing in suits and silk ties, though he never lost his Polish accent.[9] He remained both within and without socialism, striving to create a synthesis of the socialist ideals to which he remained committed and what he perceived as the need for a more participatory and competitive economy, which would help guard against the kinds of abuses that had shaped his difficult life.

It is easy to understand, then, why Brus's ideas excited a Chinese intellectual like Liu Guoguang, who had survived the disasters of Mao's China: Brus offered a new theory about the central problem of how to reconcile socialism and markets, hammered out of the furnace of tragedy in a history not unlike China's. Liu persuaded his superiors at CASS to invite Brus to deliver several lectures in China.[10] The opportunity to do so came in September 1979, when another economist in Liu's generation, Dong Fureng, traveled to England to attend an International Economic Association conference at Cambridge and visited Oxford, where he personally extended an invitation to the Polish exile.[11] Dong also shared with Brus the experience of studying Marxist economics in the Soviet Union.[12] Brus accepted the invitation, and the visit was scheduled for late December 1979 and early January 1980.[13]

The final days of 1979, shortly before Brus arrived, were a heady time for Chinese economists, as a landmark work of Chinese economic thinking was published: Xue Muqiao's *Research on Questions about China's Socialist Economy*.[14] The book offered a sweeping, detailed survey of China's economy and the problems of its socialist system. It was particularly noteworthy because Xue had incorporated input and drafting suggestions from hundreds of colleagues, giving the book authority.[15] Xue's allegiance to Deng Xiaoping's new administration was clear: Xue had criticized Hua Guofeng's "foreign leap forward" during the previous two years, contending—as many other Chinese economists also believed—that the positive results had been largely the consequence of recovery after the chaos of the Cultural Revolution and did not prove Hua's policies were correct.[16] Stressing "objective economic laws," Xue wrote, "It is these laws that decide the line, framework, and policies, and not the line, framework, and policies that decide the laws." Firmly criticizing "leftist mistakes," Xue's book provided a broad theoretical survey of the new economic agenda Deng had come to represent. Xue maintained that socialism remained the right path for China; the challenge the leadership faced was to determine how to move from "underdeveloped socialism" toward a more prosperous society.[17] The book was an enormous hit: its initial printing sold out, and by 1984 it had an astonishing total print run of 9.92 million copies.[18] At no time since the founding of the PRC had it seemed so clear that economics was at the center of the country's concerns. In this environment, Brus came to offer ideas about what might happen next.

Shortly after Christmas, when Brus arrived in China, several economists with a strong interest in Western economics received him, including Dong Fureng and Zhao Renwei, a mild-mannered CASS scholar with excellent command of English. Zhao was assigned to accompany Brus for his entire visit.[19] On December 30, the night before Brus's first lecture, Zhao handed Brus a list of ten questions that he and his colleagues hoped the visiting scholar would address. The questions asked about "the differences between market mechanisms in a socialist economy and in a capitalist economy" and the "meaning" of "market socialism," as well as about the Eastern European experiences.[20]

Zhao's questions exemplified two important dynamics. First, he and his colleagues felt an urgent need for both conceptual analysis (questions about "market mechanisms" and "enterprise autonomy") and experiential or historical analysis (questions about the Soviet, Yugoslav, and Hungarian reforms). Second, by asking Brus what "market socialism" and a "mixed economy" meant, Zhao indicated that he and his colleagues believed that they had large gaps in their knowledge even on international socialist economic theory.

Encouraged to give a wide-ranging presentation, Brus began his lectures with a broad overview of the socialist economic system. He distinguished three levels of the economy: macroeconomic decision-making, enterprise decision-making, and individual and household decision-making.[21] From this schema, he presented four models of the socialist economy: "war communism," in which all three levels were centralized; the "centralized model," in which household decision-making was decontrolled; "the planned economic model with market mechanisms," in which enterprises were also decontrolled; and "market socialism," in which all three tiers of decision-making were decontrolled.[22] ("Decontrolled," in this context, meant delegating decision-making power from the central plan to the relevant level of the economy.) Before CASS scholars and officials from the State Council agencies, Brus argued strongly for the superiority of the third model, stressing above all that China's enterprises needed greater autonomy, with latitude to be more responsive to market dynamics.[23] These reforms, he asserted, would increase efficiency and actually maximize realization of the government's socialist objectives, without the innate problems of the command economy.[24]

In addition to his lectures at the Institute of Economics, Brus met with prominent economists and officials, including Vice Premier Bo Yibo, one of the "Eight Immortals" of the Chinese Communist Party (CCP).[25] On the one hand, these high-level meetings helped build support for the report Zhao Renwei was already preparing on Brus's recommendations for China. On the other hand, at a more general level, the sessions were important because they involved senior Party officials meeting with an economist who had been rejected by the

Communist Party in his own country and who espoused views that were more pro-market than the official CCP line. After the meeting with Vice Premier Bo, Zhao Renwei, with input from Wu Jinglian and a multilingual Party translator named Rong Jingben, composed a summary of Brus's speeches and submitted it to a variety of government and Party agencies, including the Central Committee, the State Council, and the National People's Congress (NPC).[26]

Yet perhaps the most symbolically meaningful encounter of Brus's visit to China was his meeting with the seventy-two-year-old economist Sun Yefang. In 1961, in the brief economic policy reappraisal that took place in the wake of the Great Leap Forward, Sun had argued for reform of the planned economy, criticizing what he called economic "overcentralization" and excessive emphasis on gross output under the plan.[27] But Sun was soon attacked as a secret agent of capitalism who had infiltrated the Party and was denounced and imprisoned.[28] His next public appearance, in 1977, marked his rehabilitation after great suffering and solitary confinement during the Cultural Revolution.[29]

Brus's and Sun's proposals shared striking similarities, but the two men had never before crossed paths. Brus went to visit Sun at the hospital where he lived, his health failing after the many years of imprisonment. Wu Jinglian, a student of Sun, excitedly observed the harmony between the ideas of his teacher and the foreign guest about the need to "decontrol" enterprises while retaining strong central authority over the economy.[30] Speaking in Polish and Russian, the pair spent forty minutes together; Sun, writing in his diary, regretted that their time together had not been longer.[31] According to their former students, the two men ended the encounter deeply impressed with each other.[32] To Wu, Zhao, and other students of both Chinese and Western economics, Brus's meeting with Sun symbolized the end of a decades-long separation between critics of the command economy in China and in the West.[33]

Brus's visit remained vivid in the minds of his Chinese interlocutors, including Vice Premier Bo. At a January 15, 1980, speech to Party officials, Bo said he had gleaned that, in contemporary socialism, three basic models existed: the centrally controlled Soviet model, the Yugoslav model that emphasized regional decentralization and enterprise autonomy, and the Hungarian model, which was somewhere between the two. Bo then moved to reminisce. "Not long ago, the Oxford professor Brus visited China, and we had a conversation. . . . He advocated distinguishing these three models and found the Hungarian model to be relatively praiseworthy. But he also stressed that nowhere in the world was there an absolutely ideal socialist model with no flaws." The utopian revolution for which Bo had fought as a Party guerrilla—and which Bo had discussed between laps in a pool with his longtime swimming partner, Mao Zedong—must have seemed a world away. Reflecting on Brus's visit, Bo left no doubt that China had entered a new era: "I am inclined to agree with his view," he concluded.[34]

On January 16, the day after Bo's address, Deng delivered a speech to cadres in the Great Hall of the People, articulating his vision for the years ahead, which his biographer has called "the first major address after Mao's death to define the overall goals for the coming decade."[35] In this speech, titled "The Present Situation and the Tasks Before Us," Deng placed renewed emphasis on the idea that economic development and modernization were the "core" of China's future and "the essential condition for solving both our domestic and our external problems" (a "bitter lesson" Party leaders had learned since 1957). Citing the "fundamental change" in ideology since Mao's death, Deng praised "the thesis that practice is the sole criterion for testing truth." He laid out one of the central challenges facing China: "In economic development, we are searching for a road that both conforms to China's actual conditions and enables us to proceed more quickly and economically" and to "combine planned regulation with market regulation."[36] The need for this "road"—a path that traced the unique and uneven landscape of China in the 1980s but that also used the most effective teachings and techniques from around the world to move ahead "quickly and economically"—was, in Deng's telling, the top priority for the decade ahead.

Before China could blaze this trail, several problems, in Deng's estimation, had to be confronted. First, although "the leading comrades of our economic departments" had done good work since being restored to their positions, they were still behind from having been "shunted aside for many years" during the Cultural Revolution and they "don't have a very good understanding of either domestic or international developments," leading to serious "shortcomings in their work." To remedy these deficiencies, Deng urged economists and economic officials to "study the new situation and new problems with an open mind."[37] Deng made clear to the gathering of "leading comrades" that he viewed intensive study of both "domestic" and "international developments" as a necessity.

Second, and more troublingly, Deng warned that "some people, especially young people, are skeptical about the socialist system, alleging that socialism is not as good as capitalism," a clear reference to the Democracy Wall activities that he had suppressed the previous winter. But Deng did not only denounce the "young people" who had criticized socialism and the regime; he made an important distinction that would undergird the Party's ideology in the coming years. "The socialist system is one thing, and the specific way of building socialism another," he argued. Criticizing the "specific way of building socialism" that had failed China was permissible, Deng suggested, but "the socialist system" itself, understood broadly and pragmatically, was above criticism. "In the future, we must—and certainly will—have abundant facts with which to demonstrate that the socialist system is superior to the capitalist system. This superiority should manifest itself in many ways, but first and foremost it must be revealed in the rate of economic growth and in economic efficiency."[38]

One final note concluded Deng's speech: a discussion of the ideal of cadres who were both "red" (that is, loyal CCP members) and "expert," a distinction that Mao had initially presented as mutually reinforcing but later came to believe were in opposition (some analysts have even interpreted the Cultural Revolution as a "'class struggle' of red versus expert").[39] But Deng unmistakably argued for a synthesis: "Being 'expert' does not necessarily mean one is 'red,'" he declared, "But being 'red' means one must strive to be 'expert.' . . . We cannot reconcile ourselves to lagging behind others; if we do, we will not survive. But how many of our Party members, and particularly our leading cadres, have mastered professional knowledge? Can we go on in this way?" Good cadres, in other words, would be *both* "red" and "expert." As previously noted, one component of this expertise would come from studying "international developments." But for "red" and "expert" cadres, Deng added an additional warning: "When we study . . . capitalist society, we must never allow ourselves to worship capitalist countries, to succumb to corrosive capitalist influences or to lose the national pride and self-confidence of socialist China."[40] Deng, it seemed, believed expertise gleaned from "capitalist countries" was both necessary and risky.

In the month after his address, Deng chose the lineup of new leaders he would appoint to spearhead China's reforms—leaders who exemplified the Dengist emphasis on economic development and would replace the defeated Hua Guofeng and his allies. Zhao Ziyang, who had been Party secretary of Sichuan province, was made nominal vice premier but de facto premier; Zhao would be formally named premier the following September.[41] Politburo member Hu Yaobang became chairman of the CCP (he would become Party general secretary in 1981). At this point, Hua's career, in decline since 1978, was essentially ended; he retained only ceremonial titles. Power had passed to a new generation of reformers backed by Deng—and Zhao Ziyang would be in charge of the economic arena.

In March, Hu took advantage of his new position as Party chairman to elaborate on Deng's comments in his January address. Quoting Mao, Hu intoned, "We must learn to do economic work from all who know how, no matter who they are. . . . We must not pretend to know when we do not know." He added, "History will once again prove that the vast number of our cadres are able to master things which they do not now understand!"[42] The message was clear: under the leadership of Deng, Hu, and Zhao, those who could "learn to do economic work from all who know how" would shape China's future.

In keeping with Hu's call, study exchanges with Europe and North America continued throughout 1980. The State Planning Commission (SPC) sent a delegation to Switzerland, West Germany, and France in early 1980, and several top officials from the State Economic Commission—including Ma Hong and senior cadre Yuan Baohua—conducted a tour of West Germany, Switzerland, and Austria from April to June of that year, studying enterprise management and vocational training.[43] West Germany, where Hua Guofeng had also traveled, sent experts to China. Most notably, Armin Gutowski, president of the Hamburg Institute for Economic Research, visited China to discuss the country's business practices and economic policies. Gutowski's "vivid descriptions of West Germany's market economy made a deep impression on his audience," one former Chinese official recalled.[44] In 1979, Ma Hong had bemoaned the shock of discovering China's low level of enterprise management and management education after his trip to the United States; now, in 1980, these new exchanges focused on tackling those problems.[45]

Enterprise reform had the potential to penetrate the heart of China's socialist system, presenting what Joseph Fewsmith has called "critical and sensitive ideological questions at the same time that it inevitably caused economic problems and threatened the fiscal interests of the state."[46] Diverse and contentious proposals appeared during this period, including Liu Guoguang's moderate plan to gradually increase enterprise responsiveness to market demand, Dong Fureng's bold proposals to separate economic and political ownership, and CASS scholar Jiang Yiwei's radical suggestion (based on Yugoslavia) to shift to an "enterprise-based economy," in which enterprises were run under a system of worker management.[47] Xue Muqiao's reform group at the State Council also produced proposals in December 1979 and again in August 1980 that emphasized the need for greater enterprise autonomy, but they only hinted at concrete measures relating to enterprise reform. The proposals stated that "comprehensive reform" was the main goal for the latter part of the 1980s, but "comprehensive reform" remained an amorphous term, completely undefined.[48] Deng Xiaoping himself proposed a system of "factory manager responsibility under the leadership of a factory management committee or a board of directors," with the radical suggestion that Party committees might be eliminated in enterprises, as his preferred means for boosting enterprise autonomy.[49] This range of proposals emphasized critiques of the existing system over nuanced policy formulation, producing no clear changes to enterprises beyond the weak profit retention system implemented in July 1979.

As China's leaders grappled with these controversial policy questions, they began to formalize new institutional frameworks for seeking expertise and input from Chinese economists. In April 1980, the Central Finance and Economic Leading Small Group, which Zhao had taken over from Chen Yun in March, invited a group of senior economists, including Xue Muqiao, Sun Yefang, and Ma Hong, to consult on the sixth five-year plan.[50] In early July 1980, Xue received direct orders from Zhao and the Central Finance and Economic Leading Small Group to establish a State Council Economic Research Center, to attend biweekly Secretariat seminars on economics, and to consult with the new Office on System Reform (Tigaiban).[51] The increased involvement of Xue—who had been attacked along with Sun Yefang during the Cultural Revolution as an advocate of "revisionist fallacies"[52]—brought the many younger economists who worked under him closer to the center of the reform debates, while also acting as a potent symbol of the priority given to economic development by Deng's new administration.

With Hu Yaobang's calls for "learn[ing] from all who know," Chinese officials also turned to one international institution that had been unwelcome in Mao's China: the World Bank. China had been a founding member of the bank in 1944 at the Bretton Woods Conference. However, since the end of the Chinese Civil War in 1949, Taiwan had effectively represented China at the bank.[53] During the Cultural Revolution, the World Bank was rarely mentioned—but, when it was, it was depicted as an agent of American "imperialism," giving loans that upheld "the aggressive interests of the United States," as one propagandist wrote in 1962.[54] But Deng Xiaoping—who had first seen New York City through the glass windows of the United Nations as an emissary of Mao—seemed to believe that this global financial institution could give China its much-needed financial and technical support and perhaps even provide economic analysis and policy input.

In the summer of 1979, Chinese officials began laying the groundwork. A small group of Chinese officials extended a confidential invitation to Edwin Lim, a top Asia official at the World Bank who spoke Chinese. Lim, a cosmopolitan career bank officer, was born in the Philippines and attended Princeton and Harvard, where he received his PhD in economics.[55] Based in Washington, DC, Lim often passed through Beijing on his way to bank meetings in Southeast Asia, and on one of these trips he gathered with officials from the Bank of China, the Ministry of Foreign Affairs, and the Ministry of Finance, who revealed that Party leaders were considering applying for World Bank membership.[56]

In mid-April 1980, following further overtures from the Chinese embassy in Washington, DC, World Bank president Robert McNamara visited China, meeting with Deng and other top CCP officials.[57] At this meeting, Deng said to McNamara, "We are very poor. We have lost touch with the world. We need the World Bank to catch up."[58]

Given this sense of urgency, negotiations moved forward swiftly, and on May 15, 1980, China formally rejoined the World Bank.[59] The first delegation, which included Lim and Shahid Husain, the bank's vice president for East Asia and the Pacific, visited China in the summer of 1980; they met with a variety of officials, including Zhao Ziyang, who told them that the bank could play an important role in helping China "cross the river by feeling for the stones." Husain committed that the bank would be "a partner" in China's reforms.[60] World Bank lending began the next year, but, before lending could commence, the bank required that China permit it to complete a comprehensive country report, which would determine borrowing eligibility and lending targets.[61] Lim explained to his Chinese counterparts that a World Bank report involved extensive fieldwork and data collection in order to analyze and model the Chinese economy according to bank standards. Although Lim's counterparts initially expressed concern about allowing foreigners such substantial access to closely held information, government officials and economists soon communicated a different message to Lim: They realized the World Bank could provide them with the kind of advanced analysis of the Chinese economy that they did not have the training to perform themselves.[62] In July 1980, Lim and several teams of World Bank economists would set to work on this first report, which, when it was eventually released in 1983, exceeded 1,000 pages and received the endorsement of Premier Zhao Ziyang, who would circulate it widely to Party cadres and shortly thereafter would request a second survey.[63]

Although the range of new perspectives that individuals such as Brus and institutions such as the World Bank introduced to China had delighted reformist leaders, some conservative officials were displeased by this intellectual direction. These conservatives found a domestic beacon in Chen Yun, who believed that Chinese socialism could involve a small measure of decentralized market activities that would enrich the socialist state, but he remained committed to a strongly centralized socialist plan and believed change needed to be gradual. Conservatives in particular praised the first five-year plan (1953–1957), on which Chen had worked under Zhou Enlai. Chen's signature policy achievement was a planning-focused technocratic agenda that drew on Soviet planning and technology to promote socialist industrialization and modernization of the Chinese economy. Chen Yun was an ardent supporter of China's relations with the Soviet Union and, according to Zhao Ziyang, deeply mistrusted the United States and other capitalist countries—attitudes shared by many of the conservatives who admired Chen.[64]

One of Chen Yun's closest allies was Hu Qiaomu, the Marxist theoretician and former CASS president who had spoken in 1979 of the need for China's economic policy to obey "objective economic laws." Hu took a hardline conservative position about what such "objective economic laws" actually were. Along with his frequent collaborator and ally, the ideologue Deng Liqun, Hu believed that if central government policy incorporated a "commodity economy"—a Soviet byword for an economy that incorporated competition and market forces—Chinese socialism would be ruined. It is worth pausing to note that a "commodity economy," contrasted with a "product economy" in Marxian economics (most famously, in Stalin's 1951 *Economic Problems of Socialism in the USSR*), would become a pivotal term in Chinese reform debates. In a product economy, the sale of a product from one state-owned enterprise to another does not involve a change of ownership because both enterprises are owned "by the whole people"—but, in a commodity economy, ownership changes with a sale. The ideological implications were enormous, but so were the real economic implications; the issue of a "commodity economy" was one major case in which seemingly arcane Marxist vocabulary had major and direct implications for economic activity and advancing on-the-ground economic reform.[65] People such as Hu Qiaomu and Deng Liqun, both politicians and theoreticians, understood this intersection well.

Like his more market-oriented peers, however, Hu Qiaomu took advantage of the hundreds of translations of foreign works produced in the late 1970s to read widely and to look for ideas that would bolster his agenda. He discovered that Marxist theoreticians had produced valuable work during China's decades of isolation. Among the many treatises translated and published after Mao's death, Hu was particularly drawn to Belgian theorist Ernest Mandel's two-volume *On Marxist Political Economy*, which was published in French in 1962 and appeared in China in 1979. Mandel criticized Stalin but attacked advocates of the introduction of "commodity-money relationships" (i.e., market exchanges and prices as the result of supply and demand) to the socialist economy, regarding economic incentives and distribution according to work as tantamount to capitalism. Denied permission to travel from Belgium to many other Western countries (including the United States, France, and West Germany), Mandel served as an adviser to Che Guevara, who allegedly praised *On Marxist Political Economy* as offering a possible model for Cuba.[66] In Mandel, Hu Qiaomu had found a kindred spirit.[67]

In May 1980, at a CASS meeting, Hu argued that Chinese economists should be reading Mandel and suggested paying less attention to thinkers such as Brus, who operated outside a strictly Marxist framework. Mandel "relies on his own independent observations and the collection of large quantities of data, which is seldom utilized in Marxian economics," Hu stated. At the same time, Hu praised Mandel because "he still perseveres with the basic viewpoints of Marxism . . . and definitely accepts what Marx said." Mandel's work obeyed "objective economic laws," but did not use those laws to contradict the all-important Marxist orthodoxy.[68]

The tireless Hu Qiaomu went even further in trying to whip up what later writers would refer to as "the Mandel Tornado." He was especially taken with Mandel's chapters on the Soviet economy, excessive production, and socialist economics, and he circulated excerpts widely. He even wrote a letter to General Secretary Hu Yaobang and Premier Zhao recommending the book to the Central Committee and suggesting it might be a useful way of thinking about China's reforms. As Hu Qiaomu used his influence to push Mandel's ideas, Wu Jinglian and Zhao Renwei—two younger economists familiar

with the wider range of international ideas available to China—
believed strongly that, although the Mandel book was a socialist
classic, it was not appropriate as a basis for China's reforms. They
decided to fight back.[69]

Their stature was too low to confront Hu Qiaomu right away, so
they first turned to one of their mentors, Ma Hong. Ma agreed with
their views and organized a session to discuss the book at the CASS
Institute of Economics. There, Zhao Renwei, Wu Jinglian, and their
frequent collaborator Rong Jingben acknowledged the value of Mandel's critique of Stalin but argued that Mandel was, in many ways,
"even more leftist" than Stalin, so many of his proposals were simply
not relevant to China's main goals under Deng.[70] Ma also invited
Bao Tong, Zhao's secretary (chief of staff), who quietly took detailed
notes on the critique.[71] Shortly thereafter, the "Mandel Tornado"
dissipated.[72]

Although the different ideological camps disagreed about which foreign thinkers were most important for Chinese economists and
policy makers to study, they agreed it was necessary to increase the
level of technical sophistication of Chinese economists. Frustrated
by the limited set of analytic tools with which they were familiar in
1980, Chinese economists intensified their efforts to receive technical training from European and American counterparts.

One area in which they requested training was econometrics. An
American delegation headed by Lawrence Klein of the University of
Pennsylvania was invited to give an intensive seminar on mathematical economics for officials and academics in the summer of 1980.[73]
The delegation included Lawrence Lau and Theodore W. Anderson
of Stanford and Gregory Chow of Princeton.[74] The seminar was
funded by the Ford Foundation, which provided several hundred
thousand dollars to support exchange activities with China that year.
"We see China as seriously trying to move toward incentives, markets, [and a] freer econ[omic] system," said the Foundation's executive
vice president, David Bell, in a speech. "There is a historically important opening here [and] we would like to help Chinese—and the rest
of us—benefit from it."[75]

For seven weeks in the summer of 1980, Klein, Chow, Lau, and
the other distinguished American econometricians held court in the

gorgeous confines of an island at the center of the Summer Palace, surrounded by crystalline waters. "It can be said that the econometric approach gave empirical content to economic theory. At the same time it can be used to test theory or validate theory," Klein explained in an introductory lecture on his life's work. "Econometrics is a decision-making tool" that can help policy makers examine alternatives and predict outcomes.[76] They lectured on mathematical and statistical methods for modeling economic behavior and were received by Vice Premier Yao Yilin. Yet it was not all pleasure and glamour, the sharp-eyed Liu Guoguang recalled. "The professors were tired out in the hot summer days with only fans turned on."[77]

Despite the heat, Klein, found his Chinese students "hungry for education" and "enthusiastic" participants. After the seminar, CASS established an Institute of Quantitative and Technical Economics, staffed by many students who had first been introduced to econometrics within the walls of the Summer Palace.[78] Other workshops and academic exchanges on econometrics and economic modeling involving notable American scholars of the Chinese economy, especially Gregory Chow and the Harvard economist Dwight Perkins, would follow: that November, a group gathered at the Frank Lloyd Wright–designed Wingspread House in Wisconsin (also funded by the Ford Foundation), and many other such seminars occurred thereafter.[79]

Foreign teachers were not the only experts running seminars on foreign economics. To deepen and broaden these skills, the State Council Theory and Method Research Group, which Yu Guangyuan directed, also launched a Foreign Economics Lecture Series. A total of sixty lectures, which attracted leading economists from the State Council, other government agencies, research institutes, and universities, were held once a week beginning in 1979.[80]

The economists in charge of the lecture series were affiliated with the China Foreign Economics Research Association, an informal group founded in 1979 that included the Harvard-educated Peking University professor Chen Daisun.[81] But the guiding spirit of the lecture series was Li Yining, another professor at Peking University. Li outlined the impetus behind the initiative in his first lecture, delivered in intense, ambitious tones. "We not only do not really understand the recent ten or twenty years of economists' research in

Western bourgeois countries, but also are relatively unfamiliar with recent developments in economic circles in the Soviet Union and Eastern Europe," he said.[82] Although he urged his peers to be wary of capitalist influences, Li stressed, "contemporary bourgeois economic theory also has some elements that are available for us to refer to and draw on," citing a diverse toolkit that ranged from "the investment multiplier" to "econometric methods."[83] Li Yining also organized a flurry of translations in 1979 and 1980, emphasizing developments in the West in both macroeconomics and microeconomics.[84] Portions of the tenth edition of Paul Samuelson's classic textbook *Economics* were published, but, unlike the English-language version, this first Chinese version was pitched to economists and policy makers rather than university students, with an introduction that stressed the textbook's ability to help readers address economic policy problems.[85]

For Li Yining, who had been attacked during the anti-rightist movement and again in the Cultural Revolution, when his hair had been forcibly shaved off and he was condemned to six years of manual labor, Chinese economists could not truly advance reform until they made up for lost time and mastered these international ideas.[86] Li's efforts epitomized the sense among so many Chinese economists who had suffered during the Cultural Revolution that the period had not only been a "lost decade" in terms of economic development; it had also been a "lost decade" for Chinese economics. Translations and lecture series were envisioned as part of a broad strategy of catching up—a strategy that required Chinese economists to master economic ideas from both the relatively familiar territory of the "Soviet Union and Eastern Europe" and the stranger and more troubling terrain of the "Western bourgeois countries."

Despite these efforts, by August 1980 China's efforts to "catch up" seemed profoundly imperiled. Investment exceeded planned levels, skyrocketing to RMB 75.8 billion, and state revenue had fallen. Inflation began to climb, reaching 8.4 percent in urban areas by the autumn of 1980, and advocates of readjustment, such as Chen Yun, were poised to set a new policy agenda.[87] At a meeting in November of top leaders, including Deng Xiaoping and Chen Yun, Yao Yilin presented a report outlining the troubling economic situation. Zhao

Ziyang, his thick Henan accent overlaid with urgency, responded, "Right now the most dangerous problem is the inflation that will emerge next year if we don't manage things well. It's a hidden crisis, and it will explode."[88] Deng deferred to Chen in responding to Zhao and Yao. Although Chen echoed Deng's line that "leftist" ideas were "a fundamental error" in the making of economic policy, he characterized excessive investment and poor budgeting as manifestations of such errors; in other words, he used the opportunity to reiterate the need for further retrenchment and readjustment policies along the lines that he had been advocating all year.[89]

Furthermore, some Party leaders demonstrated an increasing international awareness by linking this brewing crisis to the strikes that had followed an inflationary spike in Poland, leading to the birth of Solidarity, the independent trade union that unsettled the communist world.[90] That autumn, both Hu Qiaomu and Chen Yun explicitly warned that if inflation produced an economic crisis in China, a Polish-style movement could emerge in China, with Hu Yaobang responding that he was "full of alarm" about the prospect. Conservatives effectively used this fear of Polish-style chaos to argue for braking hard on the reform policies, producing a substantial impact on the thinking of top leaders all the way up to Deng.[91] Poland had become a symbol of emerging dissent within the communist world—a specter that haunted even the reformist leaders of the CCP.

4

Navigating the Crosscurrents

◁◁◁◁ GIVEN THE ESCALATING crisis in the economy, reform-oriented economists pushed forward with their efforts to learn "from all who know how." In September 1980, the vice president of the Chinese Academy of Social Sciences (CASS), Yu Guangyuan, met with a Swedish reporter to discuss China's development. Yu projected confidence about the teetering economy. Echoing a speech that Hu Yaobang had delivered in March 1980, Yu told the reporter he hoped China would continue to engage broadly with Western economists in the coming years. "It's very helpful to have discussions with people from far away," he said. For example, Yu continued, "From an egotistical point of view, [foreigners] raising many questions was also very helpful to me, because it shows how others raise questions and what things concern them."[1]

Yu's seemingly offhand comments went further than any prior utterance by a prominent Chinese official about engagement with international ideas. Yu's statement that it was helpful to hear "how others raise questions" and "what things concern them" suggested that Chinese economists sought to understand not only the content of Western economists' proposals and ideas but also their way of thinking. This goal makes clear why it was especially important to host meetings, lectures, and visits, rather than simply to rely on transmission through texts, because less articulable qualities of the mind would be most accessible through in-person encounters.

Shortly after Yu's September interview, CASS hosted a series of lectures by a visitor whose worldview and experiences differed dramatically from those of Brus: the American economist Milton Friedman.[2] When Friedman celebrated his sixty-eighth birthday in 1980, he was perhaps the most famous economist in the world. The University of Chicago professor had appeared on the cover of *Time* in 1969, in an issue that trumpeted the "new values" that would define the coming decade.[3] Academically, Friedman established himself as a brilliant scholar of consumption policy, monetary history, and monetary and fiscal policy; in American public life, he was a polemical advocate for a particular brand of free-market fundamentalism, supporting the presidential campaigns of Republican candidates Barry Goldwater and Ronald Reagan.

One of Friedman's best-known works, *Capitalism and Freedom*, theorized the intersection of these two roles: "What the market does is . . . to minimize the extent to which government need participate directly in the game"—which, in turn, he believed would end "inflation and high taxes."[4] He had won the Nobel Prize in 1976, with a citation that praised both his contributions to "the renaissance of the role of money in inflation and the consequent renewed understanding of the instrument of monetary policy" and "his liberal belief in the positive, built-in properties of a functioning market economy," out of which "derives his negative view of the ability of governmental authorities to intervene in market mechanisms."[5] The Nobel Committee recognized Friedman's dual identity, which had made him an indispensable figure in professional economics and a divisive figure in international public debates.

Indeed, earlier in 1980 before he and his wife, Rose, visited China, the couple released a popular overview of their ideas, *Free to Choose*, a full-throated defense of free-market principles. *Free to Choose* made Friedman's name virtually synonymous with a totalizing faith in free-market ideology—a faith that China's leadership refused to accept alongside "market mechanisms." In a television interview with Phil Donahue in 1979, Friedman maintained, "The world runs on individuals pursuing their separate interests." He then moved to attack socialism. "You think China doesn't run on greed?" he asked. "If you want to know where the masses are worst off, it's exactly in the kinds of societies that divert from [free-market principles]."[6] By

1980, Friedman's stature as a recognizable face in American civic life rested on this brand of free-market fundamentalism.

Thus it came as a surprise when, on October 15, 1979, Friedman received an invitation from the Committee on Scholarly Communication with the People's Republic of China, which had ramped up exchanges after U.S.-China relations were normalized on January 1, 1979. Friedman was invited to participate in the "first lecture exchange program" between the United States and China, following "nomination" by the Chinese side.[7] Friedman soon also received a letter from a research fellow at CASS who had written his master's thesis under Friedman's supervision at the University of Chicago from 1948 to 1950. After receiving a follow-up invitation from CASS, Friedman accepted quickly, but he noted in a letter to a friend that the invitation was "a phenomenon that I find almost literally incredible."[8] The world's leading advocate of free-market fundamentalism was to be the first official representative of a new academic exchange with the People's Republic of China (PRC).

How "incredible" was Friedman's invitation? In other words, how much did China's economists know about him, monetarism, and Keynesianism by the time Friedman received his invitation in late 1979? It is clear the younger generation of economists had come across his name in their wide reading about "world economics" that commenced after 1978. Li Yining, the Peking University professor who had led the Foreign Economics Lecture Series, was knowledgeable about Friedman's criticisms of Keynesian ideas about consumer spending and income.[9] Yang Peixin, a rapidly rising official at the People's Bank of China (PBOC, China's central bank), had met Friedman while traveling in the United States. Speaking to an audience of banking officials after his trip, Yang explained the primary difference between the "two factions" in American economics in broad generalizations: "Keynesians advocate inflation, and Friedman is opposed to inflation."[10] Ironically, Friedman thus seemed to share the priorities and concerns of China's younger, internationally minded economists, fearful that the "capitalist" scourge of inflation would derail their country's economic reforms.[11]

The senior generation of Chinese economists, however, had not yet encountered Friedman's work when their younger colleagues arranged for him to visit China. The historical record demonstrates this fact in somewhat circuitous ways. During Xue Muqiao's 1979 tour of the United States, the Chinese officials attended a formal dinner at the University of Pennsylvania. Only one American could speak Chinese, a graduate student named Martha Avery who considered herself a disciple of the Chicago and Austrian schools of economics. As she relayed subsequently in a letter to Friedman, "I was amazed to learn that he [Xue Muqiao] had never read the works of either [the leading proponent of the Austrian school, Friedrich Hayek, or Friedman]. Declaring that a serious gap in his economic training, I promised to send him some books," and followed up with *Capitalism and Freedom*. Xue acknowledged the gift and said that he had commissioned a translation "so that I and my friends may read these works."[12] Members of the younger generations of Chinese economists saw Friedman as an inflation-fighting genius; the older generation of Xue and his "friends" had simply never heard of him.

It seems that China's economists contacted to Friedman because of his international fame and his expertise on money and inflation; his controversial persona was evidently all but unknown to them. Upon Friedman's acceptance of the invitation to visit in 1980, a CASS official wrote to Friedman, stressing that Chinese economists above all else were interested in learning about the "cause and solution" of "inflation." He added, "Our colleagues in the Institute are familiar with your superior achievement in the academic world."[13] These CASS experts did not expect that this "superior achievement" undergirded a commitment to spread free-market ideology.

Milton and Rose Friedman arrived in Beijing on September 22, 1980. The trip was a struggle from the moment the couple got into the car sent to pick them up at the airport, when Friedman complained about the "terrible body odor" of a man in the passenger seat who was "dressed as a worker," who turned out to be a deputy director of CASS. Friedman proceeded to deliver four lectures to audiences from both CASS and the PBOC, on topics from "the mystery of money" to "the Western world in the 1980s."[14] Leading figures of the two senior generations of Chinese economists, including the middle-aged Wu Jinglian, the seventy-nine-year-old Tsinghua academician Chen

Daisun, and CASS vice president Xu Dixin, attended, as did many graduate students and young officials. At these sessions, Friedman opened by directly confronting the idea that inflation was only an "incurable disease in capitalist society," stating that inflation "is not a capitalist phenomenon," nor is it "a communist phenomenon." Instead, he announced, "Government is the fundamental source of inflation."[15] He concluded, "[T]he most important implication of the analysis is to use free private markets over as wide an area as is politically and economically possible."[16] It is clear that Friedman wanted to persuade his listeners of the necessity of free private markets, not just to teach them about the mechanisms of counter-inflationary policy making. Friedman claimed his ideas were "non-ideological," but, in the context of China in 1980, his fundamental premise that governments caused inflation and his principled advocacy of "free private markets" were both radical convictions that went far beyond the sanctioned views that usually echoed from the corridors of CASS to the halls of the Chinese leadership compound at Zhongnanhai.[17]

Friedman's frustrations boiled over at a lunch one afternoon, when a Chinese researcher mentioned "the internal contradictions of capitalism," a standard Marxist phrase. Friedman responded by "stating firmly" that there were no such contradictions and he proceeded to launch an attack that included sharp observations on Marx's incorrect predictions about the future of capitalist development and aggressive assertions that ordinary people lived better in capitalist countries than communist countries. One can imagine the horrified reaction of his listeners, who were quite prepared to listen to a Western economist discuss "the mystery of money" but had not expected to face an ideological philippic at lunch. The next day, several CASS economists went to Friedman's hotel room and delivered a long lecture on the triumphs of the Chinese Communist Party (CCP)—an education as well as a warning.[18]

The Friedmans departed China on October 12, with Milton angrily exclaiming that the Chinese officials whom they had met were "unbelievably ignorant about how a market or capitalist system works" and that the professional economists "had only the vaguest and most ill-informed understandings of 'bourgeois' or 'capitalist' economics."[19] The Chinese side, meanwhile, had learned the hard way about Friedman's dual persona and that his expertise on inflation could not be separated from his ideological intensity. The economists he met, despite their eagerness to engage with a foreign expert, resisted his heated criticism of socialism. Yang Peixin remembered Friedman as "extraordinarily stubborn," someone who "thinks the world socialist experiment has failed," and "would not speak politely no matter how high your position." Yang added that it had become clear that it was "impossible" to reconcile Friedman's views with an acceptance of socialism, so the Chinese economists' arguments with him were "a complete mess, until we were flushed with anger."[20] Friedman's 1980 visit to China was met with exasperation on both sides.

Friedman's final comments also provided insights into a critically important question: By autumn 1980, how advanced was the understanding of Chinese officials and economists about the "market mechanisms" they hoped to implement as part of China's "reform and opening"? In Friedman's judgment, these economists were clearly totally "ill informed." Indeed, interactions with Brus, Friedman, and others seem to have heightened awareness by Chinese leaders of the limitations of their understanding of how markets operated and what it might mean, in both theory and practice, to implement market reforms under socialism.[21]

These limitations were particularly frustrating to Chinese reformers in late 1980 because the conservatives were on the march, and China's market-oriented economists were ill-equipped to fight back. Facing a widespread fear of inflation—the "capitalist" scourge that, before the Deng era, propagandists had claimed did not exist in China—the new leadership team of Deng, Hu Yaobang, and Zhao Ziyang backed off from ambitious reform plans, instead deferring to Chen Yun's emphasis on "readjustment," a resurgence in administrative interventions and planned regulation of the economy with the aim of rapidly bringing down deficits and stabilizing the economy. Because Chen was in poor health, Li Xiannian, Yao Yilin, and Zhao Ziyang, submitting to the fears of what might happen if China did not head off inflation and avert an economic crisis, took over crafting the actual readjustment policy. Zhao continued to celebrate the fact that China "has escaped from the chains of 'left' thinking," but the readjustment policy was endorsed at the Party's central work conference in December. The reformers' more ambitious policy proposals—such as increasing enterprise autonomy and creating special economic zones—would be put on hold during this period of readjustment.[22]

At that conference, Chen Yun used his time on the stage to go on the attack. "Foreign capitalists are still capitalists," he warned the audience of officials. "Some of our cadres are still very naive about this." He further urged that these "naive" cadres lessen their emphasis on "theoretical studies, economic statistics, and economic forecasting" and instead prioritize "conducting experiments, and constantly summing up our experiences."[23] Chen thus made it clear that he believed this policy readjustment should also be an intellectual readjustment, shifting away from interest in international "theory" and modern economic "statistics" and "forecasting," and toward a more traditional, pragmatic, and inward-looking focus on cooling down China's economy.

In his December speech, Chen Yun first urged cadres to "cross the river by feeling for the stones," a pragmatic doctrine that in the public imagination would come to be more closely associated with Deng.[24] Chen's pragmatism was narrow and focused on policy, not ideology. In his speech at the central work conference, he clearly envisioned this metaphorical river as flowing within China's borders, with stones made from indigenous materials. Even more importantly, the pragmatism this slogan described was not intended to encourage ideological eclecticism or intellectual engagement with "foreign capitalists"—at least in its initial presentation. An irony of this famous slogan is that it would come to be deployed to ends that clearly contradicted Chen Yun's vision.

Despite Chen's warnings, international exchanges continued even during this period of readjustment. In late 1980, the reformist CASS economist Xu Dixin led a delegation to the United States, dispatched to learn about the latest developments in practical management of the U.S. economy, focusing on issues ranging from industrial balance to taxation.[25] Furthermore, the lecture series by the Foreign Economics Research Group that Li Yining had inaugurated continued its popular lectures, which were subsequently published in book form.

The series occasionally devoted entire session to individual economists. Toward the end of the series, the mild-mannered Zhao Renwei delivered a talk reflecting on Brus's visit, followed by a lecture on another Eastern European socialist reformer, Ota Šik. A prominent Czechoslovak economist, Šik was best known for his reformist socialism as well as his role as vice premier and economics minister during the country's brief 1968 Prague Spring. His circuitous career had begun in the art academies of Prague, where he studied painting before joining the resistance to the Nazi invaders. Sent to Mauthausen, a concentration camp in Austria, Šik survived World War II and threw himself into the study of economics, eventually rising to become the top economist at the Czechoslovak Academy of Sciences. In 1965, the country's communist government adopted some of his policies—which called for a smaller role for central planning and increased reliance on the market—before Prime Minister Alexander Dubček appointed him vice premier. Šik avoided the violent crackdown during the Prague Spring only because he was on a trip to Yugoslavia in August 1968, when Warsaw Pact troops invaded the country and put an end to its reforms.[26] Šik, like Brus, ended up an exile, teaching at the University of St. Galen in Switzerland.[27]

The roots of Šik's ideas stretched back decades. In the 1920s and 1930s, several prominent economists associated with the Austrian School of economics, especially Ludwig von Mises and Friedrich Hayek, criticized socialism on the grounds that economic planning would never be feasible because planners would be unable to successfully calculate prices, output, and other key variables. Socialist economists, most famously Oskar Lange and Abba Lerner, responded by arguing that such a calculation was in fact feasible and would allow socialism to be superior to capitalism. But how would the central government plan the economy with the same knowledge as what Hayek called the "man on the spot" and the same efficiency as the market? How would central planners accurately forecast trends and respond swiftly as changes occurred in the economy?[28]

When computers offered a dramatic leap in processing speeds and previously impossible calculation potential, advocates of a more efficient and responsive form of socialist planning saw a vast new opportunity. In 1963, Lange wrote that the task of proving Hayek wrong would be "much simpler" now. "Let us put the simultaneous equations on an electronic computer and we shall obtain the solution in less than a second. The market process with its cumbersome *tâtonnements* [the market's trial-and-error 'groping' toward equilibrium] appears old-fashioned."[29] Šik shared this enthusiasm for computers, as did reformers in Hungary and Yugoslavia who initiated programs to reform or "develop" socialism in the late 1960s and early 1970s. But, right or wrong, an overwhelming sense soon emerged that these reforms—and not just the popular movements of 1968—had failed.[30] By the time that Šik went to China, he was not only an exile from his homeland; he was, in most of Europe, associated with an intellectual movement that had foundered. Chinese reforms, it seemed, might offer him another chance.

In China, Šik became a figure of fascination for reform-minded economists. Delivering a lecture on Šik in 1980, Rong Jingben, an official at the CCP Central Compilation and Translation Bureau who frequently collaborated with Wu Jinglian and Zhao Renwei, held up the Czech economist as an example for all those who studied socialism: "He deeply feels the need to conduct incisive research on the theory of plan and market under socialism." Rong focused on both Šik's criticism of the planned economy and ideas about combining plan and market to achieve socialist ends, especially his view that a primary goal of the reform should be to liberalize price signals.[31] In an interview, Rong, who had translated Marx's *Das Kapital* into Chinese, indicated that Šik's brilliance had been clear to him from afar: "He translated *Das Kapital* [into Czech] and it took him only one year, while it took me more than ten years!"[32]

The main text on which Rong drew for his lecture was Šik's *Plan and Market under Socialism*. This book fiercely criticized the "directive system of planning," which Šik saw as inefficient and irrational.[33] Šik understood the command economy, in which centralized authorities determined the quantities and prices of goods that national enterprises should produce, as having its basis in "super-structural, political, or moral incentives" (rather than "material incentives"), which he deemed unable to generate "really optimum development."[34] In addition, Šik wrote, "erroneous decisions in planning" had proven numerous, the result of imperfect market information and faulty predictions about consumer demand. As a result, he concluded, "It is therefore essential for a real market to function as a continual criterion and corrector" of the inefficiencies and errors of planning.[35]

Šik considered many ways to develop a corrective "real market," but prices occupied the most prominent place in *Plan and Market under Socialism*. He advocated "socialist commodity-money relationships," involving "a constant confrontation and direct mutual balancing of people's interests as producers and as consumers"—an apt description, albeit in socialist terms, of market prices as the equilibrium result of supply and demand.[36] In other words, Šik argued that letting the market forces of supply and demand determine prices—as opposed to the command economy's state-set prices—was the only way of creating incentives and transmitting information that would achieve "really optimum development." Still, Šik operated within a socialist framework; his advocacy of market solutions was cautious, lest reforms toss the baby out with the bathwater. "Relatively free price formation" was permissible "under socialism" only because "government price bodies cannot predict in detail the demand trends, nor even assure that production may react immediately to every detailed change in demand," he wrote, recalling the Hayek-Lange debates over socialist calculation.[37] Social welfare and economic development of the society as a whole remained Šik's paramount goals; like Brus, he argued that market mechanisms would serve as a highly useful tool to aid the government in advancing its overall socialist mission.

In another well-known work, *The Third Way* (between capitalism and communism), Šik stressed that this theory was especially valid for developing countries. "The type of economic, political, and cultural set-up peculiar to the developing countries bears no relation to the socialist measures appropriate to the needs of industrially and culturally advanced countries," he wrote. "It may well be that a developing country can follow its own specific road to socialism, but it cannot skip the industrialization phase, nor can it fail to evolve, as far as possible, a high degree of division of labor with accompanying development of the market mechanism."[38] Thus Šik positioned his model as necessary—even unavoidable—for developing countries such as China that hoped to progress along the "road to socialism." In addition to these theoretical writings, Šik's practical (albeit brief) experience implementing Czech reforms in 1968 appealed to Chinese economists and led them to give particular credence to his proposals.

Šik's diagnosis of the problems of the price system in planned economies resonated strongly with China's situation. Prices had been essentially frozen for over a decade; from 1965 to 1979, general retail prices had increased by an annual rate of only 0.2 percent, and similar rates had applied to industrial prices. Under this system, both incentives and information were profoundly distorted.[39] Party leaders had determined that reform should begin with an economic reorientation, away from investment (total state fixed investment declined from 18.6 percent of gross national product [GNP] in 1978 to 14 percent in 1981, most of which came from heavy industry, the traditional focus of central planning) and toward production of consumer goods in light industry, which increased output by 36 percent during 1980 and 1981.[40] But they knew that these quick supply-side successes would have limited long-run effects as long as the price system remained unchanged. In such an environment, strong interest in Šik's work led Liu Guoguang to recommend that CASS invite the Czech economist to visit China in the spring of 1981. Wu Jinglian was selected to accompany Šik on his month-long stay, during which Šik would travel to Shanghai and Suzhou, in addition to delivering five lectures in Beijing.[41]

Šik arrived in Beijing on March 19, 1981, looking every bit the Communist apparatchik, with a dramatic gray bouffant hairdo and black thick-rimmed glasses. But the first words he spoke at his opening lecture revealed what his appearance belied. "This is the first time in twelve years that I have come to a socialist country," Šik said. "I feel happy to be here." In an emotional register, he described his personal story and exhorted the audience of economists and officials to think boldly and speak frankly about the long-term problems of the socialist system—to "have the courage to change our theories."[42]

Referencing the experiences of Czechoslovakia, Šik outlined the broad argument of his subsequent lectures: "The socialist economy cannot be without a market mechanism. Directive planning cannot substitute for the market. The market I am referring to is a socialist market. I believe that to automatically equate the market with capitalist relations is an error." Markets, Šik said in a comment that recalled Deng Xiaoping's exhortations, did not mean capitalism. Launching into a comprehensive critique of the command economy, whose problems he believed to be innate, Šik proposed a reformed socialist system in which a "macro-distribution plan" governed reformed enterprises that responded to consumer demand.[43] In subsequent lectures, Šik fleshed out the idea of the "macro-distribution plan," discussed proposed changes in the ownership structure of enterprises, and elaborated on the role of the market mechanism in socialist economic management.[44] These lectures also gave Šik an opportunity to introduce his audience to applications of advanced quantitative tools to socialist economic problems.[45]

In his concluding lecture, Šik crystallized his arguments and presented a forceful case for the direction of reform in China. He asserted that "price reform" should be "the primary step of reform of the economic system."[46] "I believe that the goal of price reform is a complete transition to free-market prices, but [on the way] it is necessary to move incrementally," he said, noting that this "incremental" adjustment was particularly important when demand exceeded supply, as it currently did in China.[47] He described a transitional two-track price system in which the state continued to set a guidance price but allowed enterprises freedom to sell goods within certain limits of the state-set price, increasing enterprise competitiveness and efficiency.[48] These changes would increase the state's ability to focus on managing aggregate demand, as opposed to the planned-economy's focus on aggregate supply.[49] In the meantime, to minimize the distortion of the state-set prices, Šik suggested that the Chinese government make use of advanced computer price calculations to conduct large-scale input-output analyses under a two-channel price system based on both labor and capital.[50] In this way, potential economic chaos from excess demand pushing up prices too quickly would be kept under control, while the transition would still move ahead.

After each of Šik's lectures, Wu Jinglian wrote lengthy summaries and sent them to CASS president Ma Hong and vice president

Yu Guangyuan. Wu attempted to connect Šik's ideas to the work of China's leading economists—noting, for instance, that Xue Muqiao's emphasis on "reform of the system of price administration" in 1980 was consistent with Šik's much more detailed and sophisticated argument to the same end.[51] Ma Hong then immediately sent the reports to Premier Zhao Ziyang.

The response from above came swiftly and was enormously positive. Zhao proposed that Šik be hired as a consultant to CASS, visit China once a year, and hold an additional seminar with the highest-level economists in order to further discuss his recommendations for China. CASS officials, wary that the unprecedented idea of hiring a foreign economist might open them to criticism from conservative forces in the Party, ignored Zhao's first proposal, but quickly moved to arrange the seminar the premier had suggested.[52] With the direct encouragement of China's top policy maker and the presence of many of the guiding minds behind China's reforms, the stage was set for an influential encounter.

On Šik's last day in China in early April, he met with Xue Muqiao, Liao Jili, Ma Hong, and others, as well as one of Zhao Ziyang's secretaries, Bai Meiqing. Xue and Šik entered into a long dialogue about price reform that took up almost the entire time allotted for the meeting, with Šik illustrating how he believed China could use input-output tables and two-stream capital-labor pricing to improve socialist efficiency, encouraging Xue to use such techniques to "adjust" prices before embarking on total liberalization.[53] Xue, recalling the lectures by Armin Gutowski in 1979, felt more strongly than ever that price reform would be the "key link" to the overall success of the reforms.[54] After Šik left China and Bai Meiqing gave an account of the meeting to Zhao Ziyang, the premier responded with a forceful decision: The State Council would create a Price Research Center under the leadership of Xue Muqiao and Ma Hong.[55]

Within weeks of the Czech economist's visit, the highest levels of the CCP leadership had responded to his proposals with clear intellectual and institutional support. The newborn Price Research Center began to implement Šik's transitional pricing strategy. It hired several Czech price-calculation consultants who had been recommended by Šik, including Jiři Skolka, who also ran instructional workshops in the technical training of officials who could oversee the price reforms.[56] The center began a massive effort to calculate prices that better reflected what in 1981 Šik called "socialist commodity-money relations." Selecting 1,200 categories of products, the center surveyed 7,000 enterprises, 10,000 farms, and 5,000 shopping centers.[57] With this extraordinary quantity of data, the center used Šik's two-channel price system to calculate prices derived from both labor and capital inputs.[58] Price experts praised the results of this equation as significantly "more rational" than earlier pricing schemes.[59] Under Xue's direction, the Price Research Center continued its work over the next several years. In 1982, the prices of one hundred minor commodities were entirely set by the enterprises. By 1983, the number of commodities had grown to 350.[60] The Price Research Center conducted another comprehensive price calculation in 1983, hoping to improve on the 1981 results.[61] In both analytic and institutional terms, Šik's ideas had become part of the Chinese system. Later, Šik's longer-term goals for the price system would also become part of the Chinese leadership's reform agenda.

Beyond prices, the lectures by Brus and Šik fundamentally changed the way in which Chinese reformers conceived of their own endeavor. By the time Šik departed China, "Chinese economists felt that we had fallen behind," Wu Jinglian said. "In the past, we thought that reform would only be some policy measures to bring out the (economic) initiative, but, hearing the two of them lecture, we realized that it would entail a transformation of the system."[62]

While these visits and changes were underway, in the first half of 1981 the Party leadership was largely preoccupied with settling old scores. As early as August 1980, Deng had begun to publicly discuss the need to assess Mao's legacy, telling the journalist Oriana Fallaci, "[I]n the evening of his life, particularly during the Cultural Revolution, he [Mao] made mistakes—and they were not minor ones—which brought many misfortunes upon our Party, our state and our people," although Mao's errors were "secondary" to what Deng described as his "great contributions." Deng added, "[W]e will forever keep Chairman Mao's portrait on Tiananmen Gate as a symbol of our country, and we will always remember him as a founder of our

Party and state. . . . We will not do to Chairman Mao what Khrushchev did to Stalin."[63]

Deng's goal was to render a formal judgment on Mao's leadership and Party history that would, as Ezra Vogel argues, simultaneously preserve the Party's legitimacy and "show why those officials criticized by Mao now deserved to return to work, and to legitimatize the undoing of the high levels of collectivization and class struggle of the Mao era."[64] Deng appointed an ideologically diverse group, chaired by Hu Yaobang, with the wordsmith Hu Qiaomu and the dogma-defending Deng Liqun as primary drafters. Their task was to write what would become known as the Resolution on Party History.[65] Hu Qiaomu had participated in the drafting, thirty-five years earlier, of the 1945 Resolution on Party History, which recast the period 1921–1945 as a historical process supporting Mao's consolidation of power—and Hu Qiaomu believed that the new document still needed to present strong arguments for preserving socialism, even if it was going to change attitudes toward Mao.[66] But as Hu Qiaomu and Deng Liqun worked on the new resolution in late 1980 and early 1981, Mao's rule was no longer the endpoint of historical progress. They regularly met with Deng Xiaoping to discuss their drafts and they also incorporated the views of Chen Yun, who pushed for primary emphasis on both Marxist-Leninist theory and Mao Zedong Thought.[67] Over 5,000 officials and Party members were shown drafts and given the opportunity to comment, with the majority of the document written by late November 1980—though it would take another half-year to finalize the most sensitive parts of the text and, in particular, to deal with Hua Guofeng.[68]

The final result, approved on June 27, 1981, and publicized on July 1 (the sixtieth anniversary of the founding of the CCP), attempted to bring decisive ideological closure to the Maoist period. It solidified the downfall of Hua Guofeng in the political arena and represented a victory for Chen Yun's historical contribution to economic policy.[69] The Resolution on Party History praised Mao's theoretical contributions and the period 1949–1956 as a time when the Party "scored major successes" in economic development and "the people's livelihood improved perceptibly," attributing these policies to Chen Yun and Deng Xiaoping. Yet, the document's tone became more critical beginning with the Great Leap Forward in the late 1950s: "Comrade Mao Zedong and many leading comrades . . . had become smug about their successes, were impatient for quick results, and over-estimated the role of man's subjective will and efforts." The document then moved to the Cultural Revolution, specifically blaming Mao and calling it "the most severe setback . . . since the founding of the People's Republic," which "led to domestic turmoil and brought catastrophe to the Party, the state, and the whole people."[70] It would later be said, as a kind of shorthand, that Mao was 70 percent right and 30 percent wrong.[71] Mao's portrait would still look out over Tiananmen Square, but his vision for China's future was buried.

Deng and his new administration did not stop with Mao's death in 1976. China had suffered between 1976 and 1978 because of "the 'Left' errors in the guiding ideology that Comrade Hua Guofeng continued to commit." The document presented the moment of Deng's solidification of power at the third plenum in December 1978 as "a crucial turning point of far-reaching significance in the history of our Party since the birth of the People's Republic," when Deng "made the strategic decision to shift the focus of work to socialist modernization." Deng had won out in the struggle for control of the CCP, and Hua Guofeng was reduced to a parenthetical aside between two long sentences, the eras of Mao and of Deng. Hua was the un-fortunate whipping boy at Deng's court, blamed for nearly all the problematic policies put in place between the downfall of the Gang of Four and the 1978 third plenum, even those Deng himself had supported at the time.[72]

Sixty years after the CCP had been founded in Shanghai, Deng claimed credit for the decision to launch the "reform and opening" and called that decision a "turning point" of world-historic stature. "Socialism and socialism alone" remained China's goal, but "economic construction" was the Party's central task. Crucially for the period ahead, the document gave equal place to the study of "economic theory and economic practice" in order to determine how to achieve the goals of this new era—wealth and power.[73] This "Resolution" made it clear that there would be no turning back. What remained unresolved, however, was how to forge a way forward.

*   *   *

Searching for answers about what might come next, many prominent Chinese economists proceeded to travel abroad. The spirit of "reform and opening" and the search for ideas with relevance to China's situation and goals justified such trips, which included Dong Fureng's 1979 visit to Oxford, Ma Hong's 1979 and 1980 tours of universities and factories on both sides of the Atlantic, and Yu Guangyuan's travels to Europe in 1980.[74] At the same time, these economists developed personal relationships with key international peers and a critical distance from China's heated debates over reform policy.

The trips were not simply ceremonial junkets, and their significance becomes clearer on closer inspection. In August 1981, for example, Yu Guangyuan selected Wu Jinglian to attend a small International Economic Association conference in Athens on the topic of "The Economics of Relative Prices." That year, at the age of fifty-two, Wu, together with Dong Fureng and Rong Jingben, had begun taking intensive English classes at Beijing's No. 2 Foreign Language School in an attempt to improve their language skills, which until then had been largely limited to reading.[75] After all, activities such as international economics conferences, with participants from around the world speaking in accented English and through interpreters, were linguistically demanding for the Chinese economists. Middle-aged Wu's determination to improve his English revealed his intense desire both to understand Western ideas more fully and to represent China and Chinese economists on an international stage.

At the Athens conference, economists from socialist and capitalist countries presented papers on price-related issues. The distinguished group included the seventy-seven-year-old Sir John Hicks, as well as the Soviet economists V. R. Khachaturov and Leonid Kantorovich (the Soviet Union's only Nobel laureate in economic sciences). But the economist whose presentation attracted the most attention was János Kornai, a professor at the Hungarian Academy of Sciences who would take up an appointment at Harvard in 1984.[76] Once an enthusiastic communist, he had become disillusioned as he witnessed Hungary's political repression, economic inefficiency, and failed revolution in 1956.[77] Kornai, who remained a Hungarian citizen even as he built his career internationally, had just published *Economics of*

Shortage (1980), an incisive analysis of the socialist system focusing on the problem of "shortage," which he believed to be "chronic" and characteristic of the planned economy.[78] For the firm or enterprise under socialism, Kornai described a permanent state of "investment hunger," defined as an "almost-insatiable demand" at the firm level for inputs and factors of production, as a result of persistent system-wide shortage.[79] Kornai was a committed intellectual, once caricatured in the pages of the *New York Review of Books* as sharing a bed with a disembodied brain, and he had dedicated his career to "knock[ing] away the intellectual foundations of the publicly owned, bureaucratically planned economy."[80]

Kornai's major idea presented at the Athens conference was his analysis of the "soft budget constraint." This crucial concept showed that, under a planned economy, the firm "is not limited by fear or loss of failure"—in more practical terms, loss-making in the firm's finances does not bring negative consequences to the firm. The vicious cycle of chronic shortage in a socialist economy ensures that excess demand for a firm's outputs always exists; at the same time, the state perpetually compensates the firm for any losses, which Kornai called the state's "paternalism" toward the enterprise.[81] In his speech at the 1981 conference in Athens, Kornai surveyed these ideas, dwelling in particular on the firm's weak price responsiveness in the case of the soft budget constraint and using the occasion to call for further reform in Hungary.[82] Most of all, he stressed that shortages and soft budget constraints were "system-specific trouble[s] of the socialist planned economy"—the most original claim of *Economics of Shortage* and, by implication, its most damning criticism of economic planning, although at this point in his career Kornai did not explicitly oppose socialism.[83]

Kornai's presentation drew a sharp rebuke from Khachaturov, president of the Soviet Economic Association and a vehement supporter of the socialist planned economy. "One gained an impression from this paper that socialist economies invariably had deficits, that the socialist economy was typified by shortages, scarcities, and so on. This was a rather distorted picture," Khachaturov protested.[84] He admitted that shortage could occur in a socialist system, but he blamed bad or "imbalanced" planning for the problem. Better planning, he claimed, could fix these problems: "Such imbalances could be, and should be, eliminated."[85] Kantorovich remained silent.[86]

But an unlikely voice, not heard previously in the conference discussions, spoke up in Kornai's favor: Wu Jinglian. "In his paper, Professor Kornai had analyzed the functioning of a specific model of a socialist economy. Chinese experience made it easy to understand his analysis," Wu said.[87] Chinese economists had observed these issues, especially "the paternalistic relationship" of the government and enterprises, "serious waste" in enterprise management, and "the disappearance of the function of prices as carriers of information about supply and demand." Wu praised Kornai for providing a rigorous conceptual apparatus, "putting forward the questions in a fundamental manner and in more concrete form" than Chinese economists had been able to do.[88] Providing examples from China's experience to support Kornai's critique, Wu concluded his lengthy comment by speaking directly to Kornai, saying he was "sorry not yet to have read" *Economics of Shortage*.[89] The other economists—including Kornai, who had never before met a Chinese economist—were astonished at this unexpected intervention.[90]

After the session, Wu approached Kornai to reiterate his support for the Hungarian's ideas. Kornai's reaction, however, was mixed. Although he was grateful to find an ally, he knew little about China or Wu's position there and he mistrusted Wu's intentions.[91] Wu said he hoped they would stay in touch, and Kornai responded only vaguely.[92] Even so, no doubt because of the surprise of Wu's impassioned comments, China was frequently referenced during the remaining days of meetings. Hicks, in his closing remarks on "profit," finished with a veiled reference to the debate about Kornai's presentation. He "did not think it impossible that a socialist system might find ways of making use of [profit], in appropriate forms." Indeed, he added, "Perhaps we could more easily see it fitting into Chinese communism than into Russian."[93]

In Wu's developing awareness of China's place in the context of international economic ideas, this 1981 conference and his excitement at encountering Kornai's work marked an important turning point.[94] The value of Western economics to China had crystallized in Wu's mind: It could help China's economists solve the problems they faced "in a fundamental manner and in more concrete form," with profound implications for both theory and policy. Wu returned to China buoyed by what China might be able to achieve and energized to make a name for himself in China and, perhaps, around the world.

In September 1981, shortly after Wu returned to China, he attended a meeting of the Federation of Chinese Economists, a new organization created as an academic nexus for China's economists. Despite the lingering chill of the "readjustment, reform, rectification, and improvement" policy, China's reform-oriented economists had reason to be optimistic. The Price Research Center was carrying out its efforts to rationalize China's price system, and plans were being made to spread experiments with profit retention to all state-owned enterprises. Barry Naughton has noted that a multiplicity of new outside-the-plan retail and distribution channels developing at this time meant that enterprises were increasingly handling procurement (perhaps even as high as 40 percent of consumer manufactures) through voluntary contracts rather than planned allocations.[95] Thus some market-oriented incentives had begun to appear even in areas of the economy ostensibly still under the state plan; in this sense, reformist economists began to realize that the readjustment policies had laid the groundwork for a new wave of reforms.

On September 3, 1981, CASS vice president Yu Guangyuan delivered a speech to the Federation of Chinese Economists, which sought to encourage other Chinese economists to pursue international intellectual engagements. What they had already learned clearly excited them: Šik's lectures had been released as a special issue of a CASS economic journal, which sold out rapidly over the summer, and further plans were underway to translate and publish his books *Plan and Market under Socialism* and *For a Humane Economic Democracy*. Šik wrote a letter to Wu Jinglian and Rong Jingben, delighted and surprised at this wave of interest. "Even if in my homeland today I am ignored and ostracized," he wrote, "at least I have the satisfaction that the economists of as great and culturally rich a country as China view my ideas as current and practical."[96]

In his September speech, Yu Guangyuan showed he did indeed view ideas from abroad as "current and practical." He declared, "Researching international economics is indispensable." However, he more narrowly than in his 1980 interview defined how China should process these ideas: China should "critically absorb the useful content, based on national conditions."[97] Yu stressed that, in learning how foreigners thought about problems, the most important goal of engagement with Western economics was to discover and "critically" isolate "useful content" that related to China's situation. Wide-ranging research was less important than an approach that identified the most relevant ideas, like iron filings in sawdust, using the magnet of China's "national conditions" and needs.

By late 1981, China's economists had asserted the importance of their discipline and were poised to innovate a path forward for their country. They had heard from an eclectic chorus of foreign voices, ranging from Joan Robinson to Włodzimierz Brus, and from Milton Friedman to Ota Šik. China had taken important steps toward participating in the world economy, including rejoining the World Bank, and Chinese economists had begun to receive training in advanced economics and econometrics. They were hungry to learn more about how markets functioned and, like the political leaders to whom they reported, they had become even more ambitious about the prospects for transforming China into a wealthy, powerful, and modern country.

But their successes thus far were exceedingly fragile. Self-assertive reformers like Wu Jinglian, Dong Fureng, and Li Yining had outmaneuvered the older conservatives when it came to which international economists were in vogue, but the conservatives still held many of the most important cards. Chen Yun's success in implementing readjustment policies and shaping the 1981 Resolution on Party History demonstrated that the power he and his advisers held seemed to be waxing, not waning. The gathering of reformist energy and optimism at the Federation of Chinese Economists was hard won but precarious. Listening to Yu Guangyuan urge his audience to push onward, no one in the assembled crowd knew for certain whether they were making progress or merely spinning their wheels.

"Hopefully nothing unexpected intervenes and we can be together again in the coming year," Šik wrote in a late December greeting to his Chinese friends.[98] Only the most paranoid among them could have guessed that the situation for China's reformers was about to take a precipitous turn for the worse.

5

Through Treacherous Waters

◈◈◈ Chinese New Year, the Spring Festival, is a time of new beginnings. In 1982, China Central Television (CCTV) hosted its first-ever Spring Festival gala in Beijing, featuring four hours of performances and celebrations. One People's Liberation Army (PLA) soldier, a beautiful young soprano from Shandong province named Peng Liyuan, thrilled the audience with her rendition of "On the Fields of Hope," catapulting her to celebrity. Thirty years later, Peng—having married the future Chinese president Xi Jinping and given up professional singing—would become first lady of China.[1]

Although much of Beijing's population was watching Peng's breakout performance, three senior officials at the State Planning Commission (SPC) had received an urgent summons from Chen Yun, the man who had set China's economic agenda for the previous year.[2]

Despite Chen's success in pushing through his readjustment policy, the Spring Festival found the man who had briefly set the agenda for the Chinese economy frustrated. In debates over formulating China's seventh five-year plan, Chen sensed that reformist officials might be planning to push more market reforms and not adhere to the principle of "the planned economy as primary and market regulation as supplementary." To reassert this principle, Chen called together a group that included his protégé Yao Yilin, director of the

SPC, and Song Ping, the deputy director. Chen reminded them about the successes of the period 1949–1956, when national plans made under his guidance kept the economy unified and prices fixed, preserved the state's monopoly on the purchasing and marketing of goods, and advanced the cause of Chinese socialism. Song Ping concurred. "It's well and good to bring out [enterprises'] initiative, but the national plan should still be binding over everything," he said. "Now planning is not welcome!"

"Planning is not welcome!" Chen repeated angrily. He had gathered his planners together "on the first day of the new lunar year," he explained, to instruct them to fight back. Yao Yilin defended the reform policies, but Chen was emphatic. Concluding the meeting, he forcefully instructed his planners to remember past experience and to "keep your feet firmly on the ground!"[3]

The dogma-defending Deng Liqun, closely associated with Chen as head of the Policy Research Office of the Secretariat of the Chinese Communist Party (CCP), echoed Chen's claims in speeches and articles. "We must be careful not to 'enliven' the planned economy out of existence," he said, pointedly referring to the plan as China's "lifeblood."[4] (The term "enliven" generally meant to increase responsiveness to market forces, although here Deng Liqun's usage is obviously sarcastic.) Conservatives were on the attack. The impact on both policy and personnel was immediate. Plans made in 1981 to spread experimental profit retention schemes to all state-run enterprises were cancelled.[5] Deng Liqun also led the preparation of materials that directly attacked the reform-oriented views of Xue Muqiao, Liu Guoguang, and several other economists at the Chinese Academy of Social Sciences (CASS), who were consequently pressured to offer self-criticisms for having advocated a "commodity economy," the Soviet euphemism for an economy governed by market forces ("commodity relationships"), which Ota Šik, among others, had used.[6] The meaning of the term "commodity economy" was clear to Zhao Ziyang. Ma Hong had once asked him, "What is the difference between a socialist commodity economy and a socialist market economy?" Zhao replied that there was "no difference," explaining, "Using 'commodity economy' is simply a matter of decreasing commotion, since many people find it easier to accept."[7]

Zhao was willing to soften the blow for the conservatives, but he knew where he wanted to strike. Yet in early 1982, the conservatives seemed to have figured out reformers' stratagems and were trying to head them off.

At the same time, Chen decided to target the influence of "foreign capitalists" that he had decried the previous year. In coastal cities, where joint ventures and foreign trade were flourishing, Chen perceived the insidious presence of smuggling and graft.[8] In January, the Central Committee sent out a message warning about these problems, with a handwritten note from Chen Yun that demanded "a hard and resolute strike, like a thunderbolt." This was the start of what, in March and April, became a "Strike Hard Campaign" against economic crimes. One propaganda poster, showing a virtuous man in a white shirt refusing a bribe of liquor and cigarettes, called for businessmen to "resist noxious influences."[9] As part of the campaign, Chen Yun and his conservative ally Hu Qiaomu targeted "sabotage and erosion of our system by class enemies using decayed capitalist thought" and insisted on "preserving the purity of communism." As their statements make clear, the campaign, nominally targeting smuggling and corruption, had larger implications. As a national campaign, it included an ideological component so powerful that Premier Zhao found himself unable to move forward with his reform agenda.[10]

A high-stakes battle had begun over the extent to which China's reforms would be allowed to reshape the fundamental relationship between the state and the economy. Conservatives wanted to "strike hard" against more than only "economic crimes"—they wanted to take down the thinkers whose ideas they believed undermined the "purity of communism." In April 1982, they found their target.

That month, the CCP Secretariat, under Deng Liqun, published a stunning attack titled "Ota Šik's Anti-Marxist Economic Reform Theory." Based on a collage of quotations, the Secretariat accused Šik of seeking to undermine the CCP and being an "antisocialist element." The information Šik had presented while in China was "wrong and should be revoked," the directive declared. Galleys of the book that Wu Jinglian and Rong Jingben had been preparing on

Šik's and Włodzimierz Brus's visits were branded "invalid" (*zuofei*) before the book could be published.[11] Šik's proposals for introducing market prices and enterprise reforms, as well as his consistent emphasis on the vices of planning and the virtues of market correction, had clearly infuriated Chen's faction. The reformers' enthusiasm for Šik's ideas had made him into an easy mark. Deng Liqun and his conservative allies, sensing an opportunity in early 1982, fired away with their most powerful ideological weapons.

Yu Guangyuan anxiously attempted to fight back, stating in a May speech, "Some problems have not yet been studied thoroughly and the viewpoints on others are in confusion. . . . We ought to maintain a cautious attitude in branding viewpoints as Marxist and anti-Marxist."[12] But Yu's defensive maneuvering was unsuccessful. Within a year of his 1981 visit, Chen Yun's faction had vilified Šik as an unwelcome and subversive intruder. He did not return to China as scheduled—and even as the Price Research Center busily continued its work, all direct acknowledgment of his influence was eradicated.

Šik, in Switzerland, wrote worriedly to the Chinese counterparts who had suddenly fallen silent. "A variety of rumors about the political changes in China are currently swirling," Šik wrote to Yu Guangyuan, pleading for information. After another Chinese correspondent stopped responding to his letters, the Czech exile feared something terrible had befallen him, writing that he was "very worried" and "really scared that something is going on with you." Although he did not receive a formal explanation from his Chinese correspondents, Šik, who had been thrilled the previous year that the Chinese found his ideas "current and practical" while he was "ignored and ostracized" at home, understood the vagaries of life in a communist state. When he received a note from a Chinese colleague after months of frantic letters that had gone unanswered, Šik quietly accepted the excuse of "excessive work" his correspondent gave. He seemed, tacitly, to understand that there had been "difficulties," as he wrote to Yu Guangyuan the following year.[13]

These "difficulties" were indeed substantial in early 1982, and reformers in the Party looking to escape the growing influence of conservative forces determined that a new high-level institution would be necessary to serve as a gathering point for their efforts. That spring, Zhao Ziyang, An Zhiwen, and others established the System Reform Commission (often abbreviated as Tigaiwei). On March 30, 1982, with Bo Yibo, Xue Muqiao, Ma Hong, and An present, Zhao described his ambitions for the new organization. It would "unify theory and practice" and examine different economic models from around the world, while pulling together the efforts of the government's many different research units and experts to propel the reforms forward.[14] An Zhiwen made his vision clear : "I have done two things in my life. The first was to sincerely study the planned economy, and the second is to sincerely study how to transform the planned economy."[15]

Aiming to unify more fully research and policy making, the System Reform Commission replaced the prior State Council research groups under Xue Muqiao and Ma Hong.[16] Some scholarship suggests that the creation of this crucial commission may have been prompted by Chinese economists' study of Hungarian reforms; Hungary had created a Committee on Reform of the Economic System, which included both theoretical economists and economic policy makers and served many of the same functions in Hungary's reform as the System Reform Commission did in China's.[17] In China, the System Reform Commission drew on a core group of experts and maintained strong networks throughout the central and regional governments to disseminate the ideas and policies it would develop.[18] On May 4, the System Reform Commission partnered with other State Council reform researchers to release a draft document calling for "further developing discussion of theoretical questions in economic system reform," especially "the relationship between the commodity economy and the planned economy." They explicitly pushed back against the view of "some comrades" who believed that these two systems were "diametrically opposed" and that socialism could not encompass a commodity economy.[19] The new System Reform Commission had set itself a formidable task.

The establishment of the System Reform Commission indicated a shift in the thinking of the reformist faction of the Party, as well as a defensive reaction to conservative pressures. With its unifying institutional arrangement and ambitious agenda, it indicated a growing belief among Chinese reformers that the problems in traditional socialist planning were innate to the system itself. Under Zhao Ziyang's leadership, it had become clear that a more aggressive and comprehensive reform agenda would need to be developed— if the reform-oriented economists and policy makers could first overcome the thwarting forces of conservative retrenchment.

In these treacherous waters, the State Council's Price Research Center also had to deal with an awkward holdover from the visits of Brus and Šik: a conference scheduled for the late spring, planned with the World Bank, to bring Brus and other Eastern European economists to China to discuss further applications of the Eastern European reform experience. When Liu Guoguang, who had been responsible for the invitations extended to Brus in 1979 and to Šik in 1981, conceived of the idea, he had clearly hoped to follow up with an even more substantial success. He and Wu Jinglian decided shortly after Šik left China to approach the World Bank's Edwin Lim and request a larger-scale conference for 1982.[20]

However, the vicious attacks on Šik in the intervening months made the Chinese side extremely nervous. Although Xue Muqiao, senior pricing official Liu Zhoufu, and Liao Jili of the System Reform Commission all still planned to attend, they determined beforehand that the conference should not be publicized and that the report written at its end would likely not be widely circulated, even internally.[21] The briefing on the conference submitted to Zhao Ziyang, Bo Yibo, Yao Yilin, and other top officials noted explicitly, "Both sides have agreed that the information and content of this exchange will, without exception, not be reported on or shared openly through publication." Of course, Zhao remained highly interested in the Eastern European reforms: In a mid-June meeting on the subject with Liu and others, Zhao asked numerous questions on the variety of reform paths and observed, "No country has yet solved it." He encouraged his economists to forge ahead—"no idea can be dismissed without first being studied," he said—but also advised them to be discreet, even remarking that they should not publicize any internal lectures they might hold on the Eastern European reforms.[22]

On July 8, 1982, the delegation of Eastern European economists arrived in China and traveled to Moganshan, a spectacular mountain resort in Zhejiang province.[23] The group included Brus, the former Polish price commissioner Julius Struminsky, the former Czech deputy prime minister Jiří Kosta, and the Hungarian official Peter Kende. Liu Zhoufu, Xue Muqiao, and Liao Jili delivered stiff orations to open the conference.[24] Liao framed the invitation of foreign experts as making good on Deng's calls to "seek truth from facts" and "emancipate the mind," emphasizing both the leadership's focus on "readjustment" and the progress made so far. Looking ahead, Liao identified several major challenges China faced, which hewed closely to Chen Yun's priorities, including correcting imbalances in production and upholding the planned economy as primary and market regulation as supplementary.[25]

Over five days, the foreign experts presented on a variety of topics: Brus summarized recent economic and institutional developments in the Soviet Union and Eastern Europe,[26] Struminsky discussed the divergent decision-making experience of the Soviet Union and Hungary with regard to pricing policy, and Kosta surveyed Eastern European experiments with a range of economic incentives. In addition to prices, the discussion focused on whether the reforms should be implemented all at once or piecemeal and gradually. The Eastern European experts unanimously supported a sweeping, immediate reform of the entire system, claiming their experiences proved incontrovertibly that this would be the only way for China to implement an effective reform policy without becoming trapped by vested economic interests and political opposition.[27] This "all or nothing" approach to the problems of socialist transition—a "big bang" that would terminate command economy structures and relationships overnight—would be theorized as "shock therapy," a painful but necessary stroke to cut the bonds of socialist planning.[28]

Edwin Lim also spoke at the 1982 conference, discussing reform and development in a comparative perspective. He stressed to both sides that policy options for China, a large, poor country, should be assessed using standards different from those used for industrialized Eastern European countries.[29] In directing these comments to both sides, Lim perhaps hoped to make two points. First, he signaled to the foreign experts—likely with the discussion of the speed and sequencing of reform in mind—that they should present their analysis of Eastern Europe as descriptive of Europe and not prescriptive for China.[30] Second, aware of the chilling political climate, he may have been signaling to the Chinese that he agreed with the Party reformers' statements about the proper approach to foreign economic ideas. Lim, as a middleman in these intellectual transactions, was demonstrating that he understood how to placate his audience, knowingly minimizing the ostensible importance of the ideas shared at the conference to maximize his longer-term ability to operate in China.

The visiting experts made speeches on a staggering range of topics, including ownership and modes of operation, the planned and market prices of labor, and wages and bonuses, which evidently frustrated the already distracted Chinese participants. To cope with these conditions, Xue Muqiao took long morning walks in the bamboo-wooded hills of Moganshan.[31] He composed two classical-style quatrains, venting his exasperation:

> In a deep valley, the cascade washes off the dust of the
>   secular world;
> The depths of a forest spring console the strained spirit.
> Amid endless protocol, a mountain of paperwork and a
>   sea of meetings,
> It would be better to snatch a brief rest and tend to real
>   affairs of state.

The second quatrain read:

> The "reform and opening" is tremendously complicated;
> Chinese and foreign thinkers are pondering it together.
> Do not obsess over having a complete vision in mind;
> These are times when even an old horse does not know
>   the way.[32]

In the ancient Chinese tradition of the scholar-official who expresses his deepest feelings about public affairs through poetry, Xue gave voice to a profound ambivalence about his duties as a leading architect of the reform policy. The "sea of meetings" at Moganshan would not help China find its way forward; Xue suggested that the challenges China faced were so new that they were beyond the former experiences of anyone, Chinese or Western. A pun in the last line added an additional dimension to these lines: "Old horse" (*lao ma*) contains the same character used in Marx's name (*ma*), perhaps suggesting that Xue was referring both generally to old experiences and specifically, at an ulterior level, to the tenets of Marxist political economy that no longer sufficed for China.

The visiting economists toured China after the conclusion of the conference. At the end of their trip, they sent word to Beijing that, after seeing China's poverty, they now believed that a single-stroke approach to reform would not work. A gradual approach to reform would be necessary after all. "Before their observation and study (of China), the scholars advocated the adoption of a 'package' approach, in line with the successful experience of the Hungarian reform. After their observation and study of China, they had changed their views, saying that regional economic disparities are too large, and the situation is very complicated."[33]

This was the final knell of the conference's lack of success: political circumstances had undermined its potential for substantial relevance to China, and the European experts had almost immediately and totally reversed their policy recommendations. Xue, Liu, and Liao wrote a short summary and submitted it to a circle of leaders affiliated with the System Reform Commission; as promised, no public commentary or announcement was made.[34] Reform-minded policy makers and economists perceived a need for better ideas from the outside world, but the 1982 Moganshan Conference had not delivered.

The conference participants hurried back to Beijing to prepare for the Twelfth Party Congress scheduled for September. Scholars have generally viewed this congress as a success for the conservatives under Chen Yun, who played an outsize role in the drafting of its major documents.[35] Its report, penned in the name of CCP general secretary Hu Yaobang, echoed Chen's public statements, asserting the primacy of the planned economy and the "supplementary," "subordinate and secondary," role of market mechanisms "within the scope determined by the state's unified plan."[36] At a meeting on December 2 on the sidelines of the fifth session of the Fifth National People's Congress (NPC), Chen delivered the most vivid articulation to date of his views. Comparing the relationship between the market and the plan to a bird and a cage, he said:

> You mustn't hold the bird in your hands too tightly, or it would be strangled. You have to turn it loose, but only within the confines of the cage; otherwise it would fly away. The size of the cage should be appropriate. . . . In short, enlivening the economy and regulation through the market can only operate within the framework of state plans, and must not depart from the guidance of planning.[37]

For the moment, reform seemed truly stalled, locked up in Chen's birdcage. China's reform-oriented economists seemed temporarily stuck, too, unsure about how to tackle this fresh challenge.

Desperate for new ideas, China's reform-oriented and increasingly cosmopolitan economists did not stop looking beyond the thin bars of the gilded birdcage. One of the boldest among them was Peking University professor Li Yining, who, in addition to helping lead the Beijing lecture series of the Foreign Economics Research Group, had published on debates in Western economics and, in particular, on the challenges to Keynesianism. "These trends are worthy of our attention," Li argued. Although Li Yining had never traveled to Great Britain, he became fascinated by what he read about the debates on the relationship between the state and the economy then raging under the new prime minister, Margaret Thatcher.[38]

In 1982, despite the conservative environment, Li Yining and his colleague Luo Zhiru published the most comprehensive study of the British economy produced during this period, titled *The English Disease*, referring to the economy's stagnation. Calling England the "first country to have a capitalist system of industry" and "the world's factory," Li and Luo framed their study as an attempt to explain how British industrialization had functioned, why it had run into problems with inflation and unemployment, and what its prospects were for revival.[39] Writing in the familiar language of Marxist political economy—discussing the "contradictions" of English society and the interests of the "ruling bourgeois class"—they offered withering criticisms of the nationalization of industry and the government's promulgation of price controls and labor management schemes. "The British government playing a growing role in the economy" has a relationship with "the deepening and complications of 'the English disease,'" they wrote.[40] English socialists, they noted, were the first advocates of policies like nationalization—although they argued persuasively that these "socialist" policies quickly "converged" with the Keynesian ascendency in postwar Britain. The result was a system of "capitalist planning" and the eventual creation of a "welfare state."[41]

On nearly every page of *The English Disease*, Li and Luo described phenomena in England that could apply equally to China in the early 1980s. Indeed, Li would admit in a subsequent interview that the book was intended to be "a diagnosis of China's economic ailments" and a way of writing "about the stagnation of Chinese industry," which Li worried was "too sensitive" in 1982 to tackle directly.[42]

With "changes in objective political and economic realities, economic policy must also undergo major changes," they stated, emphasizing that British economists and government officials found consensus around the need to shift from planning to "long-term demand management."[43] Finally, they praised the "opposition to state intervention" of Thatcher and concluded, "A model that does not have to change has never existed and will never exist."[44] The book's criticisms of the effects of nationalization on British industry and of planning and labor market controls on the economy's robustness applied directly to China, and its positive summary of Thatcher's "plans for invigorating the economy through privatization" offered the beginning of arguments for ownership reform of Chinese state-owned enterprises, for which Li would become famous later in the 1980s. In a sense, then, the titular "English disease" was a Chinese disease as well—and Li and Luo's book was a gauntlet thrown down for Chinese reformers, challenging them to shake off the stifling influence of the conservatives and work harder to cure the disease.

Wu Jinglian, meanwhile, prepared for a very different sort of challenge. He was to spend three semesters, January 1983 to July 1984, at Yale University in New Haven, Connecticut, as a visiting scholar funded by the Ford Foundation.[45] While there, Wu conducted some research on enterprise management but he spent most of his time attending introductory macroeconomics and microeconomics lectures, finally receiving the systematic education in modern economics that he had struggled to find in China. He subsisted mostly on steamed cabbage until his wife arrived in the latter part of his stay, but the opportunities that studying in the United States presented kept his spirits high.[46] He traveled throughout the East Coast, meeting Edwin Lim in Washington, DC. In addition to his academic work, Wu had his first in-depth experience seeing how a market economy functioned in practice.[47]

Given the important debates playing out in China at the time, Wu's decision to spend time outside China must be viewed in light of not only the general political and intellectual retrenchment but also, specifically, the virulent attacks on Šik, whom Wu had accompanied, translated, and written about. It was a bad time to have partnered intellectually with someone who was officially accused of spreading "anti-Marxist economic theory."

Yet, as Chinese reformers reviewed the events in 1982, they discovered something remarkable: China's economy had largely avoided the horrors about which the conservatives had warned. Industrial production had risen by 7.7 percent, and the budget deficit had fallen to 2.6 percent of revenue (from 11.7 percent in 1981).[48] Would Chen Yun's "birdcage" thesis suffice, or was a new way of understanding the relationship between the plan and the market necessary if the administration of Deng Xiaoping wanted to make good on its promises?

In early 1983, reformist leaders began to answer this question by making clear that they were finished waiting. In mid-January, General Secretary Hu Yaobang delivered a speech to the Secretariat in which he said, emphatically, "We must appropriately speed up reform. Many comrades are crying out for this." Anticipating disagreement, he encouraged those cadres with differing opinions to air their views but he stressed they "should not obstruct" progress. Zhao Ziyang reiterated these comments in February.[49] Shortly thereafter, Zhao gave his blessing to experimental "comprehensive urban reform" in the southern metropolis of Chongqing.[50] His decision appeared to test the waters for a future expansion of urban reform, with the need to lay the groundwork for the seventh five-year plan in mind. In a deliberate rebuke to conservatives who had opposed international exchanges of economic ideas, Zhao emphasized, "The aim of our foreign economic and technical exchanges is of course to raise our capacity for self-reliance."[51] Harking back to the Mao-era emphasis on "self-reliance," Zhao asserted the renewed centrality of "foreign economic and technical exchange" as he and his allies revived their dormant reform agenda.

Despite these positive signs, a sad passing occurred in early 1983: after a long and painful battle with liver cancer, Sun Yefang, the hero of many of China's reformist economists, died in a Beijing hospital at the age of seventy-five. Xue Muqiao, his close friend and ally during the darkest days of the Cultural Revolution, visited him there on the afternoon of February 12. His voice weak but persistent, Sun urged Xue to continue fighting for the cause of reform. It was the last time the two friends would meet.[52]

Sun's death fired up the reformers who had viewed him as their godfather. In the heat of the summer, tensions between reformers and conservatives escalated rapidly. In early June, Zhao Ziyang emphasized the need to change direction from the readjustment agenda presented at the Twelfth Party Congress. "It is imperative to speed up structural reform of the economy," he contended. Pushing for a higher growth rate while nodding to readjustment, Zhao emphasized that China should "fulfill or overfulfill" plan targets and he noted that investment and construction in the fields of energy and transportation—necessary to lay "a solid foundation" for growth—"had failed to reach the amount planned" during the time of readjustment. "For a considerably long time to come, we will strive to expand socialist production and commodity exchange," he declared. The invocation of "commodity exchange" prompted Zhao to deal with the sensitive subjects of ideology and economic thought. The goals for China were "essentially different from the profit-grabbing and anarchic commodity production characteristic of the capitalist system of private ownership," he argued, decrying "the decadent ideology of 'putting money above everything else.'" In line with this distinction, Zhao praised the fact that "the persistent, erroneous tendency to belittle knowledge and discriminate against intellectuals has gradually been corrected," but he made it clear that his embrace of intellectuals like the System Reform Commission economists did not relieve Chinese thinkers of continuing ideological obligations to socialism.[53]

Some conservative leaders were incensed over Hu Yaobang and Zhao Ziyang's movement from readjustment to faster reform. Chen Yun sent a letter along these lines to Zhao, suggesting that he felt a much stronger message about the continuing centrality of socialism was necessary.[54] That same month, Deng Liqun and his allies launched a campaign against "spiritual pollution," which not only re-ferred to Western influences but also, in the words of one Chinese theoretician, "was a shorthand for the dangerous ideas being pro-pounded by these thinkers that, as Party propagandists argued, could in the long run threaten the Communist Party's ideological su-premacy and its monopoly on power."[55]

The Campaign to Combat Spiritual Pollution officially started when Deng Xiaoping used the term in a speech at the autumn 1983 second plenum, and it reached a ferocious peak in the following months. Articles and meetings decrying the "sugarcoated bullets" of "bourgeois ideology," like detective novels and pornography, prolif-erated rapidly. Despite his earlier statements about the risks of "leftist" tendencies, Deng's endorsement of the campaign allowed conservatives to explicitly target "right" tendencies "spreading the feeling of lacking confidence in socialism, communism, and the lead-ership of the Party," including "academic research" laden with "cap-italist germs."[56] Scholars have observed that conservative clout was so powerful in this period that Deng even permitted himself to be "censored": In a new volume of his *Selected Works* published that year, his controversial proposal for enterprise reform by creating a factory manager responsibility system vanished without explanation.[57]

It was, in other words, a brief reversion to a Cultural Revolution–style ideological campaign. The combined intensity of the campaigns to Strike Hard against Economic Crimes and Combat Spiritual Pol-lution led to a dramatic spike in executions; the *Economist* reported that sentences of death by firing squad were meted out to 24,000 people in 1983 alone.[58] At one execution in the southern city of Fuzhou, a reporter noted that twenty-seven of the twenty-eight people executed had fallen "into the abyss of perdition after having watched pornographic video tapes."[59]

However, the ferocity of the campaign roused Zhao Ziyang, Hu Yaobang, and other top reform-oriented policy makers to push back strongly, and the tide once again turned. Joseph Fewsmith has argued that "overwhelmingly positive economic news," especially a 10.2 percent increase in the output value of industry and agriculture due to the reforms, "undercut the credibility of conservatives." Enterprise losses, for example, fell from RMB 5.6 billion in 1982 to RMB 3.7 billion in 1983. That November, Zhao counterattacked: "Reform and opening, and invigorating the domestic economy, are the unswerving policy of the central government. Now we are talking about spiritual pollution . . . but this mainly refers to the ideological front. The central government does not use these formulations on the economic front." He further argued to Deng Xiaoping that the conservatives' campaign would cause serious damage to China's development, condemning China to further "backwardness," and that it must be stopped. Deng, thus persuaded, decided to intervene, using his paramount authority to halt the campaign.[60]

Reformist economists immediately called for renewed engagement with Western economics. Chen Daisun, the distinguished Harvard-educated scholar, published a major article in the Peking University newsletter, which was reprinted in the *People's Daily* on November 16, 1983, as a sign of official endorsement. Chen prescribed further intensive study of Western economists' ideas as a means of solving specific economic problems. He asserted that the shift in attitude toward Western economists at the end of the 1970s had helped to propel the early-stage reforms to success and he argued that Chinese economists could not turn their backs on the "speculative analysis, quantitative techniques, and management methods" about which they had been learning. "To call international economics useless, or reactionary, or to shun it out of fear, is one-sided ridiculousness," he wrote. "We can learn to take advantage of some aspects," especially in seeking to improve the operation and management of enterprises.[61] As 1983 came to a close, reformers began to regain the ground they had lost over the previous two years.

Urban and industrial reform returned to the top of the agenda. First, Deng Xiaoping reaffirmed his support for the special economic zones (SEZs) by visiting Shenzhen, Zhuhai, and Xiamen in late January and early February 1984 and opening up more coastal cities. "In establishing special economic zones and implementing an open policy, our guiding ideology is clear: not to restrain, but to free," Deng said.[62] On March 27, at a speech to the State Council, Zhao Ziyang praised the results of the Chongqing experiment in "comprehensive urban reform" (including the reform of commercial distribution channels by creating China's first "trading center")[63] and urged the expansion of reforms to state-owned enterprises and the labor system.[64] A few days later, the *People's Daily* published a letter from fifty-five factory managers pleading, "Please Untie Us!"[65] Under Zhao's leadership, ten Provisional Regulations on Further Expanding the Decision-Making Powers of State-Owned Enterprises were drafted and approved by the State Council on May 10, 1984. These regulations substantially increased enterprise autonomy: State-owned enterprises could now freely produce above state quotas, sell such goods at prices within 20 percent of the state-set price, and retain 70 percent of the funds allocated to buy new fixed assets.[66] Within the following month, the State Council also approved a report, written by the Ministry of Commerce, on advancing urban reform.[67]

In negotiating the terms of these regulations at a State Council meeting on May 4, Zhao had promised, "We will necessarily remain committed to planning, so what could be wrong with freeing up the enterprises a bit on this basis?"[68] Even the SPC, long a holdout against reforms, finally agreed to a further reduction of its control over enterprises and pricing.[69] (Fewsmith persuasively argues that the SPC "felt that it had no other choice given the political atmosphere [in favor of reform] prevailing at the time," though he notes officials there would subsequently stall and undermine implementation.)[70] These changes marked a shift toward realizing Deng's vision of greater managerial responsibility, so controversial only a year earlier, and codified ideas for which Xue Muqiao, Liu Guoguang, Wu Jinglian, and others had argued. The May regulations were what three participants subsequently called "a step of historic significance" in the direction of increasing the marketization of state-run enterprises.[71]

Enterprise reform received a further boost that summer when Gregory Chow, the Princeton econometrician, visited Beijing to conduct a seminar on "microeconomic theory" at Peking University. Chow was becoming a principal academic liaison between the United States and the People's Republic of China (PRC), meeting regularly with university and research institute leaders, including partnerships with CASS and exchange activities funded by the Ford Foundation. Along with the Harvard economist Dwight Perkins, the Chinese-speaking Chow chaired the American Economic Association's U.S.-China Economic Liaison Committee, using his connections and his credibility in econometrics and applied economics to draw in other American economists. In 1982, Nobel laureate Theodore Schultz had written to Chow, "I continue to be uneasy about some of the soft economics that some US economists promote in their China ventures"—a worry that, evidently, he had no fear would be realized in Chow's "China ventures."[72] During Chow's summer 1984 trip, he, his wife, and his young daughter met with Zhao Ziyang, an event televised and described on the front page of the *People's Daily* on July 6, including a photograph of the urbane Chow in a dark suit and striped tie, with his legs crossed and hands folded, speaking as Zhao looked on, smiling.[73] At the meeting, Chow frankly said China's knowledge of economics was "not ideal" and "definitely below" international standards, stressing the importance of economics education for both students and officials.[74] Chow also met with Xue Muqiao, Ma Hong, and Xu Dixin at CASS. Writing to his colleagues after he returned home, Chow hypothesized, "The meeting and the publicity might partly signify the importance which the Chinese government places on modern economics."[75] The particular focus on microeconomics further suggested that his Chinese partners wanted both to glean knowledge about reforming enterprises and to display, with unusual fanfare, China's premier interacting with an American expert.

It is worth pausing to ask why the Chinese side so fully endorsed Chow as a middleman and interlocutor. Of course, his Chinese ancestry and ability to speak Mandarin were an enormous help—but it was just as likely that his Taiwanese background could make him suspect in the eyes of PRC officials. His confidential profile, prepared by the Ministry of Education for Party cadres planning to meet with him in 1984, provides two key insights. First, it evinced pride that Chow had clearly chosen to continue working with PRC counterparts, even though the Taiwanese government had allegedly pressured him to pick sides. Second, the document gives little information about Chow's areas of substantive expertise, only describing him as a professor of "political economy"—a term that had a profoundly different meaning in the American context of Chow's professorial title than it did in the Chinese context, in which "political economy" signified Marxian economics. Chow was thus able to appeal to the PRC and even seem palatable on paper to conservatives who, in reading his profile, might have confused him with a fellow "political economist" in the Marxian tradition.[76] In the years to come, Chow would follow up his seminar on microeconomics at Peking University with a seminar on macroeconomics at Renmin University in 1985 and maintain a written correspondence with Zhao Ziyang.[77]

Beyond enterprise reform, the critical policy debate of 1984 focused on the term "commodity economy," a contentious topic since the early 1980s. Zhao Ziyang and Hu Yaobang, who felt strongly that China should endorse a "commodity economy," sought to make a major breakthrough by defining the Chinese system as a "planned commodity economy" at the third plenum of the Twelfth Central Committee scheduled for October 1984. But they knew that substantial ingenuity would be necessary to find an interpretation of this phrase that would placate the conservatives while also advancing the reform agenda. That summer, in each draft report that Zhao, Hu, and the economists on the System Reform Commission produced, they experimented with using the term "commodity economy." Every time that the document was returned after being edited by more conservative leaders, the term "commodity economy" was crossed out.[78] At least rhetorically, despite all they had learned, the Party leaders had reached an impasse.

Wu Jinglian returned to China from Yale in July 1984. Days later, he received a note from Ma Hong asking him to join Ma on a trip to northeastern China, with no further explanation. On the train from Beijing, Ma revealed the reason: Zhao Ziyang had asked him to draft a report to help break the deadlock, and Ma wanted Wu's help.[79] Ma clearly hoped to draw on Wu's greater familiarity

with the workings of a market economy and the latest developments in international economic theory. At a "theoretical level,"
many of the older generation of Chinese economists "supported the
idea of a socialist commodity economy," Xue Muqiao recalled—but
he admitted, "My own understanding was not deep."[80] Drawing on
research by a variety of other scholars, the intergenerational pair of
Wu and Ma agreed to emphasize the necessity of ideological support for urban reform, which they contended could only be provided
by the term "planned commodity economy." Asserting the continued
primacy of the plan, their draft argued that guidance planning (indirect administration), rather than mandatory planning (direct administration), was the key to the next stage of China's "reform and
opening." They concluded, "For both national macroeconomic policy
making and microeconomic enterprise operations, admitting that
the socialist economy is a commodity economy with planning obeys
the law of value . . . and will increase economic efficiency."[81] Ma
submitted their document to Zhao at the end of their northeastern
retreat.[82]

Another contentious issue that reemerged in 1984 was price reform. Economists knew that, because of state subsidies, the urban
consumer price index was artificially low (indeed, after the reforms
were implemented, prices rose by nearly 12 percent in 1985). According to the World Bank, in the mid-1980s the government was
devoting well over 20 percent of its total expenditures to subsidies,
the majority of which went to subsidize daily necessities.[83] The
situation was similar for industrial products and raw materials: in
1985, the prices of raw materials skyrocketed by 18 percent, and ex-
factory product prices rose by 8.7 percent (by contrast, in 1986 they
only rose by 3.8 percent).[84] This suggests that prices in China remained seriously distorted and had been kept artificially low due
largely to state intervention.

Foreign visits contributed further to Chinese reformers' desire to
begin remedying the situation. In late August, the deputy prime
minister of Hungary, József Marjai, visited China, holding meetings
with Zhao Ziyang, the conservative Yao Yilin, his mentee Vice Premier Li Peng, and CASS president Ma Hong, among others. His visit
was closely reported in the Chinese media, with Li Peng quoted as

saying, "Our two countries' overall goals of building socialism are identical" and Zhao saying that he "attached great importance" to the lessons of the Hungarian experience.[85] Zhao and other senior leaders had been interested in Hungary for several years, with Zhao stating in 1983, "Hungarian reform is worthy of research and learning from," and suggesting that it might have direct applications to China. Marjai was widely perceived to be the foremost market reformer in the senior Hungarian leadership at the time, to the point that British prime minister Margaret Thatcher had invited him for a meeting to praise his "independence of action."[86] During his Beijing meetings, Marjai stressed that Hungary's most important error in its reform process had been not to take advantage of the period of rapid growth during the early part of the reform process to implement price reform. According to the recollections of three officials at the System Reform Commission, Marjai's advice built on the impression Šik's visit had created and produced "a greater sense of urgency about reform of the price structure" among China's top leadership.[87]

With this "urgency" in mind, Zhao and Hu turned to a younger generation of economists, born in the 1940s and 1950s, who had more advanced training and greater familiarity with Western economics than their elders (with the exception of middle-aged figures who had studied abroad, such as Wu Jinglian and Zhao Renwei). Many members of this third generation of economists had their educations disrupted by the Cultural Revolution, returned to the cities to complete their studies after Mao's death, and by 1984 were beginning to emerge as independent voices, often mentored by older economists and also influential in their own right. Some of these younger economists joined a new government research organization created during this period, called the Institute for Chinese Economic Structural Reform (Zhongguo jingji tizhi gaige yanjiusuo, abbreviated as Tigaisuo). The new group, led by the more senior Gao Shangquan, who also served on the System Reform Commission, began to draw up proposals targeting price reform as the key to advancing overall reform. One of the younger economists, Chen Yizi, who had moved to this new group from the Rural Development Institute, explained this emphasis was the result of "experts who participated in reform in Eastern Europe" who had "all mentioned that price reform was key."[88]

Beyond the Institute for Chinese Economic Structural Reform, a variety of other young economists attracted attention for bold, sometimes brash proposals. These economists, mostly in their early thirties, began planning a conference at Moganshan—the same resort town where the World Bank–organized conference with Eastern European economists had been held in 1982—to respond to the top Party leaders' requests for new ideas. The conference organizers sifted through more than 1,300 papers submitted by applicants who wanted to attend; 124 participants were chosen, according to the organizers, purely on the basis of the merit of their ideas.[89] At that time, two primary approaches to price reform were receiving the greatest attention. First, officials at the Price Research Center proposed a sweeping recalculation of state-set prices in one large step. Second, young economists adept at computer modeling of the economy, including Tsinghua University graduate student Zhou Xiaochuan and CASS graduate student Lou Jiwei, proposed a series of small, swift recalculations of prices. These two factions initially set the agenda of the price reform debate—until Zhang Weiying, a brash and brilliant graduate student from Xi'an's Northwest University, intervened, insisting that both approaches were unrealistic and calling for prices determined by supply and demand. Although on most days meetings lasted from 8:00 A.M. to 11:00 P.M., that night a ferocious debate raged on into the wee hours of the morning. The thirty-one-year-old CASS graduate student Hua Sheng and several of his peers were inspired. By dawn, the young economists had devised an ingenious approach to reforming China's ossified price system.[90]

What they settled on was called the "dual-track price system." This system required prices for goods within the plan to remain at state-set prices, while permitting goods outside the plan to be sold at market prices.[91] Coal, for example, was priced under the plan at RMB 22 per metric ton, but the market price was over RMB 100.[92] Hua Sheng and his colleagues submitted the report "Consciously Making Use of the Dual-Track System to Reform the Price Mechanism Smoothly" to Zhao Ziyang and in September received approval from the Central Finance and Economics Leading Group.[93] Zhao simultaneously instructed that the Material Supply Bureau, which controlled input allocations, hold constant the size of the central plan, laying the groundwork for the dual-track system to produce sustained increases to output outside the plan.[94] The dual-track system would become a defining—and controversial—feature of China's reforms.

A group of twenty of China's most senior economists also convened in September to hammer out the final draft of the report for the October third plenum of the CCP Central Committee. Ma Hong and Gao Shangquan, the prominent economist who served as the head of the new Institute for Chinese Economic Structural Reform and on the System Reform Commission, both wrote letters to the Standing Committee about the draft. They argued, in Ma's words, that the term "planned commodity economy" should be "explicitly written into the plenum decision."[95] Days later, Zhao Ziyang submitted the version of the plenum decision that Ma Hong had approved. The group of economists endorsed and formalized the document; Zhao then forwarded it to the Politburo Standing Committee on September 9, 1984, noting that the document stated that China was implementing a "planned commodity economy with public ownership as the basic form."[96] Deng Xiaoping approved the document on September 10.[97] Three days later, Chen Yun gave his approval as well.[98] Zhao had won his battle over the "planned commodity economy."

Despite his defeat, Chen had not yet had his final say. At the third plenum, Chen asked his colleagues on the Standing Committee that he be permitted to address the assembled cadres. The elderly man climbed the podium and addressed the decision directly. He admitted that China's problems were far larger and more complex than they were in the 1950s, so the solutions he had developed then could not be "copied indiscriminately"—but he nonetheless defended those decisions as well as his legacy. He emphasized that his economic policy ideas had always been developed "on the basis of the actual situation in China" and had not been "copied indiscriminately" from the Soviet Union or anywhere else. He ended by referring to the need to pursue both "material civilization and spiritual civilization," an idea that recalled both the Campaign to Combat Spiritual Pollution and tracked back at least as far as the thinkers of China's May Fourth movement in 1919, which had brought together much of the group that would subsequently establish the CCP in 1921. He added a final sentence before tottering back to his seat. "We are a socialist country," Chen insisted. "This is the goal toward which we must always struggle."[99]

On October 20, 1984, the CCP Central Committee issued the Decision on Reform of the Economic Structure, formally endorsing the "planned commodity economy."[100] Deng congratulated Zhao, describing the breakthrough as a "new theory of political economy."[101] In a speech two days later, Deng added that some comrades "have been devoted to socialism and communism all their lives" and "are horrified by the sudden appearance of capitalism." But, he promised, "It will have no effect on socialism. No effect."[102]

Triumphant as the market-oriented economists might have been, they knew that the real policy battle was far from over. Although redefining the socialist economy as a "planned commodity economy" signaled progress, the ambiguous formulation promised further debate. How would subsequent economic policies interpret and implement the October 1984 decision? It remained fundamentally unclear, even to economists who participated in the document's drafting, what such an economy would entail in practice.[103] This situation revealed an important emerging characteristic of China's reform process: Because of the compromises necessary to achieve a consensus on an ideological slogan, such slogans often contained components in opposition (in this case, "planned" and "commodity")— and this, in turn, created a situation in which state ideologies were not self-interpreting but, rather, were highly generative and required further interpretation. The challenge for Chinese economists was thus to develop a "best" interpretation of these slogans, a process that often involved the same actors who formulated the phrase in the first place. The ideological signposts may have been vague but certainly were not meaningless.[104]

What was clearest, then, was only what could not work: despite the success of agricultural reforms under Wan Li, Zhao Ziyang, and others, they could not serve as a model for urban and industrial reforms. Stressing that over 80 percent of state revenue came from this sector of the economy, Zhao stated, "We should draw from the rural reform experience on what is common to both and must not mechanically apply the specific forms of operation and management suited only to agriculture to urban industrial and commercial enterprises." Zhao's focus shifted to figuring out how to develop the urban economy and improve the "efficiency" of state enterprises.[105] According to Susan Shirk, this perspective helped to explain his advocacy of the "tax-for-profit" (*li gai shui*) approach to enterprise reform, rather than the profit-contracting approach that had been used in the rural reforms. The tax-for-profit approach transitioned enterprises from remitting profits to bureaucratic superiors to paying taxes, intending to preserve those enterprises in form while making them more self-regulating in practice, but the problems in implementation were myriad. Some reformers, like Hu Yaobang, supported profit contracting, while others felt that the tax-for-profit approach, while useful as an initial reform, would not go far enough or would upset vested interests without adequately improving the fundamentals of the economy.[106] Reformers who hoped to shape the seventh five-year plan to advance their cause were fumbling for answers—and their agitation showed. As Deng Xiaoping put it, Party reformers knew they were finally "daring to touch the backside of the tiger."[107]

Thus, in the early months of 1985, intense debates raged within the reformist camp about how China should proceed. These debates occurred against the backdrop of a takeoff of several key enterprise reforms, particularly an increase in factory manager responsibility, as well as gradual increases in the ability of enterprises to determine their own output. Market prices also increased substantially in scope as enterprises began to conduct transactions outside the plan under the dual-track system.[108] The in-plan price of coal, for example, was raised to RMB 31 per metric ton (from RMB 22, a 41 percent increase), and enterprises were free to sell coal produced beyond the plan quota at market prices. As these changes occurred, gross industrial output boomed; in the first quarter of 1985, it increased by 22.97 percent over the same period in 1984.[109]

Some voices raised concern that the Chinese economy might be overheating, but Zhao urged his lieutenants to "continue reform unflinchingly," drawing special attention to the need for price reform.[110] Privately, he worried about how to stabilize the economy as "overheating got worse," but he knew he needed to forge ahead.[111] This context—a sense of urgency about the need to reform enterprises and the price system, fears of overheating, and Zhao's resolute push for progress—shaped the economic debates of 1985.

Conservative elders even tried their hand at organizing international visits with clear implications for domestic policy debates in China. In December 1984, Chen Yun, Yao Yilin, and others hosted Ivan Vasilyevich Arkhipov, the first deputy on the Soviet Union's Council of Ministers. Arkhipov had been the chief economic adviser sent by Stalin to China in 1950 and had spent much of the following decade there, leading the economic and technical aid the Soviet Union sent to China. He had advised on the design of the first five-year plan and would even call China his "second motherland."[112] At the December meeting at Zhongnanhai, Chen Yun, who could barely walk without assistance, embraced his "old friend," tearfully recalling, "We worked well together."[113] Deng and Zhao, both aware of Chen's well-known affection for the Soviet economic model, worried that Chen would go off-script in the meeting with Arkhipov— but whether because of patriotism or political constraints, Chen toed the line at the meeting.[114] After paying respects to the elderly planners in Beijing, Arkhipov traveled to the Shenzhen SEZ, where he reportedly said he was "moved by what he saw."[115] Chen Yun, in contrast, had never visited an SEZ, despite frequent travel between Beijing and his hometown of Shanghai.

Arkhipov's visit most of all seemed like a nostalgic gesture by Chen Yun and pro-Soviet conservatives who looked back fondly on the first five-year plan—especially during a period when Zhao Ziyang visited Washington, DC, and U.S. president Ronald Reagan visited Beijing.[116] Indeed, numerous delegations of senior leaders traveled abroad during this period, continuing to search for policy alternatives to the much-criticized Soviet planning model.[117] In May and June, Vice Premier Li Peng, accompanied by several vice ministers, including members of the SPC, visited Poland, East Germany, and Hungary. They held meetings with top economic and technical ministers in each country, signing trade agreements for the period 1986–1990 (the same period as the seventh five-year plan then being debated in China) and paying a return visit to Deputy Premier József Marjai, whom Li Peng had hosted in Beijing when Marjai helped spur the CCP to prioritize price reform.[118]

In June 1985, Zhao traveled to the United Kingdom, West Germany, and the Netherlands, accompanied by several senior economic officials from the System Reform Commission and the SPC, primarily to promote trade and discuss the handover of Hong Kong.[119] Meeting with Margaret Thatcher, who had visited China in 1982 and 1984, Zhao listened to the prime minister praise his policies at an official dinner at 10 Downing Street. "We both realize the need to put our resources into what we do well; to raise efficiency; not to spend money we don't have; and to encourage innovation," she said. "I was very struck by a quotation from an early Chinese historian which was carried in *People's Daily* last year: 'The way to govern a country is first to enrich the people.' That principle is guiding you, and it is guiding us."[120]

Thatcher, famed for her certitude, did not know that the future of that principle in China seemed highly uncertain to many of Zhao's closest advisers.

In the first half of 1985, anxiety in Beijing was high. The economy seemed to be ballooning uncontrollably, and reformers knew their victories in the autumn of 1984 would be meaningless if they could not demonstrate that market-oriented policies did not lead to chaos. They competed for influence in a policy environment charged with this concern.

Wu Jinglian, whom Ma Hong had newly appointed to a senior position at the State Council's Development Research Center, emerged as the leader of one group of economists focusing on "coordinated reform" (*peitao gaige*).[121] This group, which included several younger economists who would subsequently rise to prominence, argued for steadily advancing price reform beyond the dual-track system, which they criticized as a temporary holdover at best. They posited that China required comprehensive price reform before the government could develop new policies to use market mechanisms to guide the economy.[122] In February 1985, Wu published an assertive commentary in the *People's Daily* laying out his views. Arguing for the importance of "the experience and lessons of a number of Eastern European countries" in deciding how China should proceed, Wu presented his own views by referencing "many economists in other countries." In the short run, he continued, China should readjust its high-growth orientation, slowing down the growth rate, the rate of investment in capital construction, and increases in wages and bonuses, to ensure the reform did not spiral out of control.[123] Several months later, Wu expanded on his arguments to emphasize the role that macroeconomic policy, particularly with regard to the banking sector, should play in keeping both enterprises and the economy as whole from growing too quickly, or "overheating."[124] Speaking on July 15 about the draft of the seventh five-year plan, Wu argued to China's top economic policy makers that they could not isolate issues like increasing enterprise autonomy from an overall plan that also supported more competitive markets and better indirect control of the economy—in other words, Wu called for the seventh five-year plan to be formulated on the basis of his "coordinated reform" agenda.[125]

Other economists joined Wu's calls to formulate a "comprehensive" vision of reform, including Guo Shuqing, an ambitious twenty-nine-year-old doctoral student at CASS born in Inner Mongolia, whose passion for economics he admitted was "something like an obsession."[126] In summer 1985, Guo Shuqing and two colleagues traveled to Beidaihe to present these arguments to top State Council leaders. After "analyzing Russia's and Eastern Europe's 20 years of experience, and from referencing the latest achievements in modern comparative [economic] research," they stated that the necessity of an "overall plan" for reform was an "urgent need." They contrasted this goal to that in countries like Poland in the 1970s, which had "only attempted to mend the old system," as opposed to innovating and formulating a comprehensive new system. Citing authorities including Brus, Šik, and the World Bank, they concluded the need for coordinated reform was "crystal clear."[127] By mid-1985, the centrality of foreign experience in shaping and supporting the ideas of the "coordinated reform" group was equally "crystal clear."

Wu and his allies would find many opponents in the years ahead, but the most potent in early 1985 were economists who refuted Wu's emphasis on moderating growth and prioritizing price reform. In the circle of younger economists who had risen to prominence around the time of the 1984 Moganshan Conference, the pursuit of rapid growth was a popular view—and it had no more ardent supporter than one of the organizers of the 1984 event, a thirty-five-year-old CASS graduate student named Zhu Jiaming, one of the Four Gentlemen, a group of well-connected young policy advocates. (Another one of the Four Gentlemen was Wang Qishan, currently a member of the Standing Committee of the Politburo overseeing Xi Jinping's anti-corruption campaign.) Zhu was familiar with the 1983 World Bank report and the ideas of international economists that had been discussed in seminars like the lecture series of the Foreign Economics Research Group and a seminar on World Economic Trends that he had attended in 1984.[128] He became fixated on China's poverty and backwardness and believed that, in the course of China's development, it was necessary to follow both developed and developing countries in undergoing a radically "high-speed growth phase"—an economic vision based on what Shirk has called "a version of Keynesianism."[129]

Citing data from economies as diverse as the United States, the Soviet Union, Japan, and Brazil, Zhu contended that during this "high-speed growth phase," inflation was "typical" and not to be feared. He claimed that the high-speed growth phase, however inflationary, would usher in an era of "economic prosperity" and provide an "excellent environment" for systemic reform.[130] Inflation, in Zhu's worldview, was not an insidious force undermining reform; rather, it was a signal that China was booming and catching up with the rest of the world.

That autumn, with funding from the Ford Foundation, Zhu traveled to the United States to conduct research, settling at Columbia University in New York City. The fevered boom time of the American financial sector during the Reagan years matched Zhu's dreams for China. Although he had read exhaustively about the wider world, it was his first trip abroad.[131]

At this juncture, it is important to outline several major factions of reformers who would emerge in the policy debates of the 1980s. As we have seen, one group, led by the middle-aged Wu Jinglian (and including young economists such as Guo Shuqing and Zhou Xiaochuan), argued for "coordinated reform." Another group, led by the middle-aged Li Yining, contended that Wu's emphasis on price reform was fundamentally misguided and that, instead, enterprise reform should be given priority. These were the two most prominent groups during this period, and both were the focus of Zhao Ziyang's favor at various important junctures, with their influence oscillating throughout the second half of the 1980s. A third group of economists, mostly of the young generation identified with the Institute for Chinese Economic Structural Reform, argued for faster results and worried less about the risks of inflation. Chen Yizi organized this institute and maintained close ties to Zhao Ziyang's primary secretary (chief of staff), Bao Tong. Of course, other economists and policy makers did not fit neatly into one of these camps, but these were the predominant factions during the 1980s.

All sides in these debates used foreign ideas—sometimes based on careful study and sometimes taken out of context. Vying for influence over the future of the Chinese economy, the debates did not preclude personal attacks, creating deep and enduring animosities. But each of these groups was composed of serious reformers who deserve accurate historical representation.

To clarify their policy positions, it is also important to emphasize the distinctions between possible positions on macroeconomic policy and economic reform policy, which can sometimes become blurred in the arguments made during this period. One can advocate stable, conservative macroeconomic policy and serious economic reform, as, for example, Wu Jinglian and Liu Guoguang did. One can support stable, conservative macroeconomic policy and oppose reform policies, as Chen Yun did. And one can promote expansionary, inflationary high-growth policy with reforms, a combination associated particularly with Zhu Jiaming and Chen Yizi. (Of course, as the Chinese economy in recent years has shown, there are also advocates for an expansionary policy without reforms, particularly bureaucrats at the local levels who have overseen the country's unbridled development boom.) Thus, advocates of "retrenchment"—that is, policies designed to stabilize the economy and rein in growth—were not necessarily opposed to reform. When Wu Jinglian advanced retrenchment policies, he did so out of a sense that inflation posed dangers to the Chinese economy, not because he had changed his mind about reform; when Chen Yun and his allies favored retrenchment policies, however, they also often intended to slow down the reform policies and to undermine the reformers.

These distinctions are, in retrospect, complicated by the fact that external conditions were changing, and sometimes the economy really *was* overheating. Often economists disagreed not only about the relative risk of an inflationary high-growth policy but also about whether inflation was in fact occurring in the economy. Conservatives were perhaps somewhat more likely to decry perceived overheating because it allowed them to criticize growth-oriented reform policies, but the more realistic reformers were perfectly willing to acknowledge inflation when their research indicated it. Despite angry denunciations to the contrary, reformers who acknowledged the economy was overheating were no less pro-reform than those who denied it was overheating. Yet it is also true that the policy pendulum often swung back and forth in response to the macroeconomic cycles of inflation and overheating. This was particularly evident in the negative case: when inflation soared, conservative influence tended to increase—a dynamic that would be at work, disastrously, in 1988–1989.[132]

Yet in 1984 and 1985, the widespread perception of overheating had another particularly important effect: it spurred reformers to reach out to foreign economic experts who had experience in handling inflationary growth in socialist and capitalist economies. Open inflation was a new phenomenon in the PRC, where state-set prices and the command economy had long repressed inflationary forces. (In 1976, the propaganda book titled *Why China Has No Inflation* called inflation an "incurable disease in capitalist society," while stating that China had "no inflation.")[133] Thus disagreements about inflation—whether it was occurring and, if so, whether it was a serious problem—not only formed one of the major fissures in the reform camp during the 1980s but it also pushed reformers of different stripes to search the world for comparative cases and foreign experts who could help them devise responses to the new and contentious phenomenon of overheating.

*   *   *

In early 1985, as might be expected, Zhu Jiaming's controversial views about the necessity of high-speed growth and the riskiness of inflation generated sharp rebuttals from economists tied to the co-ordinated reform group. A trio of Wu's allies (including Guo Shuqing) argued that pursuit of high-speed growth would actually make it more difficult for China to "break away from the old system." In the past few years, they said, the growth of enterprises had brought with it "blindness" and instability; the overall economy was strained, and lending and investment were difficult to control. As a result, they asserted that the Chinese economy was "in jeopardy," that reforms needed an overall ("coordinated") plan, and they warned that hurtling forward faster, as Zhu Jiaming had suggested, might permanently derail the reforms.[134]

During this same period in early 1985, Edwin Lim and the World Bank reentered Chinese debates with a splash, presenting the Bank's second major study of the Chinese economy, which had been requested by Deng Xiaoping and Zhao Ziyang in 1983. Titled *China: Long-Term Development Issues and Options*, the report provided the World Bank's interpretation of the best future direction for China's "planned commodity economy." It emphasized achieving greater balance by developing services and increasing the efficiency of resource use, while also endorsing the goal of quadrupling the gross value of industrial and agricultural production over the subsequent twenty years.[135] Most importantly, the report provided an even more sophisticated and forward-looking set of multisector economic models, demonstrating applications of econometrics and modeling to the report's readership of Chinese policy makers—many of whom, unlike China's young economists, were still not familiar with these methods.[136] Zhao ordered his economic lieutenants to study the report for both "content and method," according to Wu Jinglian.[137]

However, some conservatives expressed displeasure with the study, which clearly supported the increased use of market mechanisms. One reportedly complained, "We invited a bunch of Western doctors who prescribed many Western medicines. Surely this is going to send China up to the Western sky!"[138] These comments suggested that it was the very notion that the Middle Kingdom was borrowing ideas from the West that was the problem, not just the substance of those ideas. More broadly, economic indicators shaped the contours of conservative criticisms. The continuation of astonishing industrial growth rates in the second quarter of 1985—an increase of 23.4 percent—triggered a new round of attacks on uncontrolled "overheating" from conservative economists and officials.[139]

Importantly, many of these attacks specifically targeted the foreign intellectual influences they believed underlay the 1984 decision. A long article published in May caricatured Wu Jinglian: "Some comrades," wrote the author, "believe that mechanically copying from capitalism can have a miraculous effect on our socialist economy. In fact, this is only an illusion." The article criticized the belief that "investment hunger" was endemic to "socialist public ownership," arguing instead that central planning could overcome these problems by improving controls—exactly the argument Wu Jinglian had witnessed V. R. Khachaturov use to attack János Kornai in Athens.[140] But these arguments were losing ground as the Chinese economy boomed, even if economists in both the conservative and reformist factions acknowledged the risks.

Fears of such risks were never far from the thoughts of Chinese leaders. The spirit of "crossing the river by feeling for the stones" endured, but the current seemed to rush ever faster, surging higher and higher. As China's reformers moved forward more purposefully, with the clearer goal of the "planned commodity economy" in mind, they also recognized how many people expected them to slip and fall. By what means would they keep their balance?

A key next step was to convene a path-breaking weeklong conference in 1985, featuring a most unusual international cast of characters in a scene to match: leading foreign economists and their Chinese counterparts in the deliberately secluded setting of a cruise ship steaming down the Yangtze River. Out on the river, discussing how to advance Deng's ambitious economic agenda, a decisive transmission of economic ideas would occur.

6

Days on the River

◈◈ ON AUGUST 27, 1985, János Kornai and his wife, Zsuzsa Dániel, stepped off the airplane that had carried them on the last leg of a long journey to the blistering heat of Beijing. At the airport, a youthful Chinese man in his early fifties, slightly taller than Kornai, energetically greeted the couple. Speaking in English—a second language for all of them—he introduced himself as Zhao Renwei, deputy director of the Institute of Economics at the Chinese Academy of Social Sciences (CASS), and escorted the pair to their hotel, where seven other foreign economists would join them.[1]

Although Zhao and Kornai had not met before, Zhao already felt acquainted with the Hungarian economist and Harvard professor. Kornai had become internationally famous for his analysis and critique of socialist economics, and, in 1982, as a visiting scholar in the Economics Department at Oxford, Zhao had bought Kornai's *Economics of Shortage* (1980).[2] The book critiqued the socialist system by focusing on the problem of "shortage," which Kornai believed to be "chronic" and characteristic of a planned economy.[3] Among China's leading reformist economists, "poor mild Zhao Renwei" (as one attendee at the conference called him) was not alone in his admiration for Kornai's work.[4] Wu Jinglian, newly appointed executive secretary of the State Council's Development Research Center, felt an even stronger connection to Kornai, having briefly met him at the international conference of economists in Athens, Greece, in 1981. While at Yale University's Department of Economics in 1983–1984, the fifty-three-year-old Wu had read *Economics of Shortage*.[5] Returning to China in 1984, Wu stashed a copy of Kornai's book in his luggage and, at home, excitedly circulated sections of the book among friends and colleagues.[6] In the minds of this small, elite group of Chinese economists, János Kornai seemed like an unexpected friend whose work was, as Wu had said in Athens in 1981, "easy to understand" in light of the "Chinese experience."[7]

Kornai had come to China as part of a distinguished group of economists from Europe and North America who would gather with many of China's leading economists and economic policy makers. The foreigners included Nobel laureate James Tobin, the British economist and official Sir Alexander Cairncross, and Włodzimierz Brus, the Polish exile and Oxford professor who had produced a sensation after his lectures in China in January 1980. The conference took place on direct orders from Premier Zhao Ziyang, who had repeatedly urged China to "make up for our weak points through international exchange," declaring, "We must really strive to learn."[8] The Chinese hosts were the System Reform Commission and CASS, two government agencies tasked with developing the policies of China's "reform and opening." The economists had come together for a week in the deliberately secluded setting of a Yangtze cruise ship to discuss how to advance Deng Xiaoping's ambitious agenda.

"It seems to be a most unusually interesting opportunity," Tobin had written that summer in a letter to his Yale department chair, asking permission to miss the first week of classes to attend the conference. "The idea seems to be to detach the high officials from their desks and phones so they can concentrate on learning some of the unpleasant facts about managing decentralized economies."[9]

And learn they would.

With Kornai, Tobin, and the rest having arrived in Beijing, the group toured the Great Wall—where, one wrote, the excited economists engendered "a great air of fête"—before meeting with Premier Zhao at Zhongnanhai, the leadership compound, on August 31.[10] Zhao laid out what he saw as the main issues facing China. "Urban economic reform is quite a difficult task. After increasing enterprise autonomy, how to manage the macroeconomy and adapt it to our needs requires earnest research and consideration," he said. Despite these challenges, "China's goal of economic reform is unwavering."[11]

This "directness, simplicity, and frankness" stunned Cairncross, who wrote in his diary that it all "seemed quite natural until one stopped to think that the speaker was the Prime Minister of the largest country on earth, canvassing advice from an assorted group of foreign economists, not all of whom could hope for equal attention in their own country"—a comment that perhaps suggests some wistfulness for his own salad days of influence over public affairs in postwar Britain. "Where else," he continued, "would one find a Prime Minister inviting advice from abroad?"[12]

Zhao had good reason to urge both sides to view the conference as crucially important. In early 1985, he had personally requested that the World Bank bring a group of prominent European and North American economists to China for an intensive, broad-ranging discussion of China's "reform and opening."[13] China had initiated important smaller conferences and individual invitations to foreign economists in the early 1980s—including Czech economist Ota Šik and American Milton Friedman—and Zhao clearly hoped for the largest success yet.

In 1985, China's reformers certainly needed it. The previous year, Zhao had made a major breakthrough in official endorsement of market mechanisms within what was called "socialism with Chinese characteristics," rebranding the Chinese economy as a "planned commodity economy" (again, "commodity economy" was a Soviet byword for an economy that permitted some measure of market forces).[14] China's top economic officials held to the pragmatic, experimental mantra that guided reform, "crossing the river by feeling for the stones."[15]

As we have seen, this position produced tremendous receptivity to incorporating market elements into China's socialist system. The debates after the 1984 breakthrough centered on how much market should be allowed and how quickly—with related issues including how to handle the ossified price system, whether a high growth rate posed risks, and how to treat state-owned enterprises.[16] Although

China had successfully transitioned much of its agricultural economy to a market-based system, the commencement of major urban and industrial reforms in 1984 had brought immense difficulties, as Zhao told the delegation. State-owned enterprises, which in 1985 produced 64.9 percent of the gross value of China's industrial output, resisted market-oriented change, and inflation was on the rise.[17] Powerful conservatives asserted loudly that the increased market forces were causing the Chinese economy to "overheat" and that renewed state control was necessary.[18] This conference thus came at a critical moment and was perhaps the single most intensive example of efforts to overcome these challenges.

Zhao sent top economic officials to plan the conference with Edwin Lim of the World Bank, including the State Council's Liao Jili and Hong Hu from the System Reform Commission. Despite persistent conservative attacks on "Western doctors" prescribing "Western medicine" (phrases that recalled the warnings about "capitalist germs" at the height of the Campaign to Combat Spiritual Pollution), Chinese reformers' hunger for new ideas led them to push on undeterred. Lim excitedly began determining the conference's Western participants.[19] He assembled a team that could address the challenges of both socialist transition and managing a market economy. Several of the economists he selected had backgrounds in Eastern Europe. Kornai, one of the most prominent economists critical of socialism, was well known to a small set of China's leading reform economists. Brus was once again called upon to attend.[20] Aleksandr Bajt from Yugoslavia would round out these perspectives.[21]

However, Lim was committed to expanding beyond economists with backgrounds in socialist countries, inviting a majority of experts from market economies in Europe and North America. He immediately thought of his friend Cairncross, who had served in the British government and as the founding director of the World Bank's Economic Development Institute before becoming a professor at the University of Oxford and chancellor of the University of Glasgow.[22] Cairncross had already visited China to help to establish academic relations between the British Academy and China in November 1979, when he had met with Deng Xiaoping for a brief audience.[23]

The lanky, mustachioed, and bespectacled Scottish economist was an archetype of the versatile, technical economic adviser.[24] He had studied with John Maynard Keynes at Cambridge but was avowedly nonideological: "I abominate dogma," he wrote.[25] In his work at the World Bank's Economic Development Institute, he had focused on teaching economic policy makers from developing countries new ways of "thinking about how to run an economy"—a skill he brought with him to China in 1985.[26] Even so, it was clear that Cairncross was a Keynesian, at least as far as British economic policy was concerned. In his book *Years of Recovery*, on the British postwar recovery, Cairncross concluded his study by praising the government's Keynesian policies, calling them "effectively planned" and successful in achieving their key objectives.[27] This praise reveals the substantial consistency in his views between the late 1940s, when he served in government, and the mid-1980s, when he wrote *Years of Recovery* and went to China to talk about the state's role in the economy against the backdrop of Prime Minister Margaret Thatcher's privatization of industry and departure from Keynesian monetary policy.

Talking with Lim about other attendees, Cairncross recommended the German economist Otmar Emminger, who had served as head of West Germany's central bank in the late 1970s.[28] Another internationally renowned participant, Raymond Barre, a French economist who had been prime minister of France, agreed to attend but backed out later that summer; Michel Albert, who had been head of the French Planning Office, replaced him. Lim also invited Leroy Jones, an American specialist in development economics. Finally, most famous of all was James Tobin, the eminent Yale Keynesian who had won the Nobel Prize in 1981 for his work on fiscal and monetary policy. With this impressive set of eight international economists, Lim alerted his Chinese counterparts that the conference could move ahead for early September.[29]

The Chinese officials' response astonished Lim. Zhao and other top Chinese leaders thought the conference seemed so promising that they had decided on an unconventional location: a newly built luxury cruise ship, the S.S. *Bashan*. When Lim asked why they wanted to hold the conference at such an "unusual venue," the Chinese side responded that Zhao wanted the "senior government officials and economists" to be "available fully for a week and not be interrupted by their normal responsibilities."[30] In the frenetic world of Chinese economic policy making in 1985, the leadership clearly believed that the seemingly drastic step of isolating these economists on a boat sailing down the Yangtze would be the best means of ensuring the foreign experts got the full attention of their Chinese counterparts. As a result, the conference became known as the "Bashan Boat Conference" or the "Bashan Conference," in addition to its wordier official name, the International Conference on Macroeconomic Management.

When Lim received the list of Chinese participants, he was delighted. The group included prominent members of all three active generations of Chinese economists. Several of the most distinguished older economists in China were at the top of the list, including Xue Muqiao, CASS president Ma Hong, and An Zhiwen, vice minister of the System Reform Commission (Zhao himself held the title of the commission's minister). A cohort of middle-aged economists formed the bulk of the group, including Gao Shangquan, another top official at the System Reform Commission, and Wu Jinglian. The Chinese participants also included several younger economists, such as Guo Shuqing, a graduate student at the CASS Institute of Economics, and Lou Jiwei, a rising star at the State Council Economic Research Office (they roomed together in Room 233 of the S.S. *Bashan*).[31] The prominent Chinese participants at the conference were not primarily associated with Chen Yun's more conservative faction. Thus, while the Western group was selected for its diversity of viewpoints, it is clear that the Chinese group members were selected for their generally shared beliefs—a decision that seemed designed to maximize not only the group's engagement with and receptivity to the foreign economists' ideas but also their ability to coherently present those ideas to colleagues back in Beijing after the conference.[32]

To prepare for the conference, each side tried to learn more about the other. Wu Jinglian had short excerpts from Kornai's *Economics of Shortage* translated into Chinese and circulated them to the Chinese participants.[33] On August 28, Wu also delivered a speech at CASS on a paper Kornai had recently written for the World Bank, titled "The Dual Dependence of the State-Owned Firm: Hungarian Experience" (1985), both to prepare participants and to inform other colleagues who had not been lucky enough to earn a spot at the upcoming conference.[34] Kornai's paper discussed in detail one aspect of his understanding of the state-owned firm in a mixed or transition economy: the simultaneous "vertical" dependence on the bureaucratic supervisor, who continues to control some of the firm's ability to obtain inputs, and the "horizontal" dependence on consumer demand.[35] Wu said, "Taking the questions discussed in this article and connecting them to China's situation, we can feel a sense of great familiarity. The reason for this is that these questions are in truth the exact topics that we have been intensively discussing for some time."[36] Wu's speech made clear that, in the immediate run-up to the Bashan Conference, he was assertively trying to position Kornai as a leading international thinker with clear and immediate relevance for China's problems.

For the Western economists, Lim, who in July 1985 took up full-time residence in Beijing, prepared an extensive set of briefing materials, focusing mainly on the Chinese economists' writings that he had collected, as well as several World Bank reports on China.[37] Lim also sent out suggested questions for the participants to address in their presentations.[38] To supplement these materials, Kornai consulted with his friend Gregory Chow, the Princeton econometrician active in U.S.-China exchanges, while also closely following news about China in the American press.[39] Newspapers were indeed full of stories on China in the summer of 1985, mostly marveling at its changes. For example, a front-page *New York Times* article in late June shared the fact that China had just acquired a fleet of twenty Cadillac sedans in which newly welcome "capitalist roaders" could "cruise" around Beijing—though Deng Xiaoping was reported to prefer a black Mercedes-Benz.[40] From these readings, Kornai learned the basic situation of China's reform process in 1985. He wrote in his autobiography that he gleaned one major fact from his readings: "The big question after the success with agriculture was what to do with the rest of the economy."[41]

Yet, as they set off for Beijing, Kornai, Tobin, Cairncross, and the other Western participants still thought that they knew little about China.[42] On August 29, 1985, as Kornai, his wife, and several of the other Western participants went on a tour of Beijing with several CASS economists, *New York Times* columnist Anthony Lewis published a piece from Chengdu, the booming capital of Sichuan province. Lewis's essay gave a sense of the larger questions that a first look into the changing China posed to a thoughtful Western observer. "Follow the line of reform," he wrote, "and you begin to see the unraveling of all kinds of rigidities: prices, material allocations, work assignments. Where will it stop? How can it stop?"[43]

Following the meeting with Zhao Ziyang, the group flew south to Chongqing, where they would board the ship for the weeklong conference. The S.S. *Bashan* was luxurious, with accommodations for seventy passengers and amenities including a swimming pool.[44] In the schedule set for the participants, the organizers made sure to build in time for casual conversations, activities for attending spouses, and some afternoon land excursions.[45] However, these trappings of tourism certainly were not intended to override the conference's main purpose, the exchange of ideas and discussion of China's reforms.

On September 2, as the S.S. *Bashan* pulled out of Chongqing, Xue Muqiao faced the distinguished audience and delivered the conference's opening remarks. A grainy photograph shows the octogenarian economist, trim in his official Mao suit, looking up from his prepared materials as he spoke, having set down his glasses. "Convening this international conference on economic planning and macroeconomic management has an exceptionally important significance," Xue declared, "and we are investing great hopes in this conference."[46]

Each day began with lectures on agreed-upon topics by two foreign economists, followed by several hours of discussion. The first full day of the conference focused on international perspectives on macroeconomic management, with Tobin and Kornai both slated to give presentations.[47] Unsurprisingly, the Chinese expressed particular excitement at the prospect of hearing Tobin, whom Wu regarded as "the Keynesian master."[48] Tobin was a genial, soft-spoken figure, described by his friends as careful and observant.[49] He had visited China once before, in September 1972, on an American Economic Association delegation with Wassily Leontief and John Kenneth Galbraith. On that two-week trip, the first formal exchange of American academics following President Richard Nixon's opening to China, Tobin had complained, "Very few macro-economic data were available to us, and we were not able to talk to economists and other responsible officials in the planning and operating agencies of the government."[50] The situation aboard the S.S. *Bashan* could hardly have been more different. It presented Tobin with an opportunity to rectify a problem he had observed in 1972: "Developments in economics in the West in the last thirty years are simply unknown. . . . Their general attitude was that bourgeois economics must be irrelevant."[51]

But rather than focus on contrasts between 1972 and 1985, Tobin, at Lim's behest, gave a long presentation on the basic tenets of macroeconomic policy making in the United States. He outlined the fundamental idea of aggregate demand management, emphasizing three primary goals. First, he told the Chinese audience, macroeconomic policy should seek to maintain a balance between aggregate supply and aggregate demand. Second, it should aim to maintain general commodity price stability. Third, it should promote stability in international economic relations. Tobin described the tools of fiscal and monetary policy, indirect means of macroeconomic control, emphasizing again that avoiding wild fluctuations in aggregate demand should be the goal.[52] Yet Tobin also noted that in a developing country that lacked many of the financial mechanisms through which the central bank manipulates money supply, the government would have to use total credit and outstanding bank loans, as well as income policy, to conduct macroeconomic policy.[53] With numerous caveats, Tobin admitted that he thought China could, in its transition, allow for the continued role of some direct administrative measures, especially concerning the wage rate and exchange controls—conceding that, in the United States and other Western countries, macroeconomic policy never entirely eliminated every form of direct control.[54]

In granular detail, Tobin explained how, as China developed a stronger central bank, it could manipulate the liabilities and assets of the central bank, other banks in the economy, and the assets of the public to conduct monetary policy. He even worked through practice scenarios, beginning with a monetary base of "100 yuan" and demonstrating the multiplier effect.[55] In the middle of his lecture, Tobin pulled out a sheet of statistics about the Chinese economy in the fourth quarter of 1984 and the first quarter of 1985, which Zhao Renwei and Liu Guoguang had prepared for circulation among the participants. Assessing the data, Tobin confirmed that, in his opinion, China's economy was indeed "overheating" and he proposed concretely that China's price inflation rate should aim to fall below 7 percent.[56] To the Chinese participants, Tobin's presentation had an almost theatrical power—after all, they had never before seen an economist in action in this way. One participant recalled that Tobin's seemingly magical ability to make policy recommendations from quickly looking at a set of high-level data astonished him and his peers.[57]

The detail in Tobin's presentation about "overheating" particularly struck some on the Chinese side: They were surprised to hear a Keynesian say that China's extremely high growth rate and high rate of inflation were bad for the economy and that going forward China should aggressively pursue a contractionary monetary policy. To the more widely read Chinese in the audience, this view contradicted what their reading on Keynesian economics had led them to expect. Without realizing it, Tobin also spoke directly to a debate then raging within China over the benefits and risks of "high-speed growth"—the proponents of which, such as Zhu Jiaming, cited the seeming success of Latin American countries to expound on the necessity of expansionary monetary policy in the face of "beneficial inflation."[58] Tobin's views immediately registered with reformers like Wu Jinglian and Guo Shuqing, who advocated reining in the speed of China's growth—promoting deflationary policies so the price reform policies they advocated would not set off serious inflation—as an important weapon in defeating the "beneficial inflation" school of thought.[59]

Although many of the younger Chinese economists were impressed, Tobin's long lecture seemed to confuse many of their elders. Through an interpreter, they struggled to understand the renowned economist's presentation, delivered in the language of the Yale Economics Department rather than the socialist jargon heard in the halls of CASS. At one point, the interpreter burst into tears, frustrated that she simply did not know how to translate many of the newfangled technical terms that had perhaps never before been uttered in mainland China.[60]

After Tobin's lecture, Edwin Lim and Wu Jinglian stepped aside to discuss these challenges. Perhaps more than any Chinese delegate, Wu had the background to understand Tobin's lecture—indeed, he had referred to "Keynesianism" in several academic articles, including one published earlier that year, which had noted changes since World War II in Keynesian macroeconomics as practiced in the United States and parts of Europe.[61] One issue, Lim and Wu decided, was that Chinese lacked a proper term for "macroeconomic management," which Tobin had used repeatedly. The two options, which the interpreter confusingly switched between, were macroeconomic adjustment (*hongguan tiaozheng*), which Lim found too weak, and macroeconomic control (*hongguan kongzhi*), which Wu thought was a holdover from the days of central planning. They decided to invent a portmanteau term for this modern kind of economic "management" that combined "adjustment" (*tiao*) and "control" (*kong*): *tiaokong.* They excitedly told the other participants about their new word, *hongguan tiaokong,* meaning "macroeconomic management." They urged that it be used at the conference going forward.[62]

Kornai's presentation came next, shifting to topics related to the transition from plan to market. The ostensible topic of his presentation was "could Western policy instruments (especially monetary and fiscal policies) be effective in socialist countries?"[63] Kornai's career, built on applying sophisticated economic analysis to the economic problems of socialist countries, clearly suggested an affirmative answer to this question—although this idea was relatively new to China. Since arriving in Beijing, Kornai had been listening carefully to discussions of China's problems, including economic "overheating" and fears of inflation, as well as to the Chinese economists' sense that they did not have in mind a goal model for the reform. Listening to such discussions, he wrote in his memoirs, "I felt . . . that I was at home in China, despite the distance and the historical and cultural differences. All the phenomena that came up and the cares and woes were familiar."[64]

Reminded of Hungary's confusion in deciding what reform path to take—and of his own ideas of "investment hunger," the state's "paternalism toward the enterprises," and enterprise "soft budget constraints," Kornai decided to posit what he thought would be best for China rather than limiting his presentation to a description of Hungary's reform or hewing to the arguments for which he was well-known in Europe and America.[65] This ambitious decision would define the remainder of the conference.

After surveying the many problems of socialism he had studied in *Economics of Shortage*, Kornai presented the Chinese with a choice between what he called the two possible coordination mechanisms in an economy: administrative regulation and market regulation. Each of these, he continued, had two possible incarnations as policy: "IA," direct administrative regulation; "IB," indirect administrative regulation; "IIA," laissez-faire market coordination; and "IIB," market coordination with macroeconomic control.[66] He continued to discuss these models in terms of their alphanumeric labels, allowing the Chinese to follow along more easily.[67] In characterizing the IA and IB models, he hewed closely to his characterizations of the traditional socialist system in *Economics of Shortage*. Emphasizing the role of vertical hierarchical relationships for transmitting information and commands, Kornai pointed out that the primary difference between the two modes of administrative regulation is that in the IA system, input and output directives are given directly by bureaucratic superiors to enterprises, whereas in the IB system, a variety of "interventionary devices" across the economy create additional "horizontal" market-like forces that "compel" the enterprise to make the desired input-output decisions.[68] Hearing this characterization of a IB system, the Chinese economists might have thought back to the lecture Wu Jinglian had given on the concept of "dual dependence" in Hungary's transition at CASS several days earlier—for Kornai's IB model described a generic version of the "dual dependency" situation of Hungarian enterprises, documented in gritty detail in the World Bank paper that was the basis of Wu's speech.

Turning to market coordination, Kornai noted that these mechanisms both emphasized the horizontal flow of information and resources among enterprises. However, in the IIA model, the market mechanism "blindly" governed economic activity, while the IIB system permitted the central authority to play a regulatory role through macroeconomic policy making and regulating economic and legal parameters.[69] Kornai's use of the term "blind" struck a particular chord in the Chinese context, where criticism of reform often described market economies as ruled by the destructive forces of "blind competition."[70] However, in presenting the IIB model, Kornai offered a way out. In this model, the "budget constraint" on enterprises would be "hard," but the state could in exceptional circumstances come to the rescue of the largest enterprises should they encounter serious difficulties and go bankrupt. (This situation contrasted with the "soft budget constraint" that dominated in both the IA and IB models.) In particular, Kornai said the IIB model should be oriented toward creating macroeconomic conditions in which enterprises would shake off their command-economy reliance on vertical relationships and begin responding to market forces. The key measure of success, Kornai noted emphatically, would be the enterprises' "price responsiveness."[71] The IB model could act as a transition device to the IIB model but was not fit to serve as an end goal. Kornai concluded his presentation by declaring that the IIB model of market coordination with macroeconomic control was the only sensible choice as the target model for China's reform.[72]

The reaction to Kornai's proposals from the other Western economists during the discussion period was overwhelmingly positive. Cairncross, Albert, Brus, and Tobin all spoke out in its favor.[73] The immediate Chinese response was more muted, as their guests had come to expect—a few neutral questions, while the younger economists busily took notes.[74] CASS researcher Guo Shuqing praised both presentations, singling out Kornai's analysis as "close to China's realities," but his response was otherwise more formulaic than effusive ("long . . . ," Tobin noted in the margins of his notes next to Guo's name, doodling the Chinese characters for "exit," presumably posted over the door).[75] Yet behind this composure, Kornai's words resonated deeply. Zhao Renwei was immensely impressed with

Kornai's rigorous "dissection" of the socialist economy.[76] Another participant recalled that, as the Chinese economists talked among themselves later that day, they believed that for the first time they had reached a consensus view about the best possible interpretation of the meaning of 1984's "planned commodity economy."[77] To Wu, the moment was one of intense connection—he thought that Kornai had given voice to thoughts long in gestation in his mind, and, he recalled years later, he "concluded" then "that a market with macroeconomic management should be the primary objective of China's economic reforms."[78] That night, a group of the younger Chinese economists excitedly approached Kornai and told him that they were determined to initiate an official Chinese translation of *Economics of Shortage* as soon as they returned to Beijing.[79] Kornai, usually a heavy sleeper, spent the nights onboard sleepless in his cabin, exhilarated by the receptivity he sensed from the Chinese— much to his wife's consternation.[80]

It is important to note that the advice that Kornai offered at the Bashan Conference differed in subtle but significant ways from the views for which he was widely known around the world. In his assessments of the Hungarian reforms, Kornai had offered scathing criticism of "half-way house" market reforms to socialism and was often seen as an advocate of rapid liberalization or "shock therapy" in Eastern Europe.[81] Yet this is simply not what Kornai argued while he was in China, where he realized that the Chinese economists did not see his idea of shortage "as a condemnation of all variants of socialism, but restricted it as a criticism of the command economy. . . . It's a strong perception on my side that China is China, and Budapest is Budapest, and in Budapest I should help to avoid illusions concerning reform . . . but in China I wanted China to go forward." He concluded, "I had in that sense two different faces, one face for Hungary and one other face for China."[82]

The other economists' presentations followed on subsequent days. Cairncross presented remarks on counterinflationary measures during price decontrol in Great Britain after World War II. He emphasized that enterprise profitability and enterprise efficiency were distinct concepts, stressing that enterprise losses in postwar Britain were due to their misplaced objectives, not due to their inefficiency. Calling himself an "ex-bureaucrat" who was "more sympathetic than the other speakers" to the problems of transition, Cairncross stressed that gradual decontrol of prices had been one reason for the success of postwar Britain, because, simply, "some controls are more important than others."

"As aims change," Cairncross said, "so do instruments and their manner of use." He concluded, "Let's not be too *purist*."[83]

Other economists touched on similar themes. Emminger, for example, presented comments on Germany's postwar recovery.[84] He urged the Chinese to focus on indirect controls of the economy through discount rates, reserve requirements, and limits on borrowing from the central bank, rather than open market operations, which he deemed "not now relevant for China." Tobin approved but was frustrated with the Chinese response; during the discussion, he passed a note to another participant, complaining, "It would be good if Chinese central bankers responded to Emminger's provocative remarks about China rather than asking trivial questions about Germany." The note scrawled in response was simply, "I think they completely agree with his diagnosis."[85]

Even so, Kornai loomed over the sessions. Emminger referenced Kornai's presentation, and when Albert spoke on French macroeconomic policy, he explicitly tried to present France's system as an example of Kornai's IIB goal model.[86] Wu Jinglian recalled that Brus (who did not present his own remarks but often commented in the discussions) seemed outdated to him and his colleagues when compared to the Hungarian economist's technical sophistication.[87] Bajt's presentation on Yugoslavia consisted of one main idea, according to a Chinese participant: "My great hope is that you will learn what *not* to do from our experience."[88] Kornai's ideas had carried the day.

Throughout the subsequent talks, the group discussion was not limited only to the subjects the Western delegates raised. For example, the elder Chinese economists consistently asked for input on the appropriate speed of the reforms, presenting for consideration both the so-called *yilanzi* approach, which would reform all sectors of the economy simultaneously in one fell swoop, and a gradualist, sector-by-sector approach. The Chinese economists selected for the

Bashan Conference nearly all already agreed that a gradual approach was best. Nevertheless, over and over again, they asked their foreign visitors to address this question. Although many of the foreign economists initially favored the sweeping approach, the Chinese persuaded them over the course of the conference that a gradual approach would better fit China's circumstances.[89]

Why this talk of *yilanzi* reform when the Chinese participants had clearly already made up their minds? Asking these diverse economists a question to which the Chinese thought they already had an answer can be seen as achieving three aims. First, because they knew that many of the Western economists came to the conference opposed to gradual reform, it allowed them to practice their strongest arguments in favor of gradualism against some of their intellectually strongest foes and attempt to change their minds. In this sense, these interactions can be seen as a rehearsal for the internal debates that would occur within the highest levels of the Chinese economic policy-making leadership. Second, it allowed them to gather evidence for what they already believed and to find better arguments to support their conclusions. Third, at an even more fundamental level, these interactions allowed the Chinese to examine how Western economists thought about problems. To the elder generation of Chinese economists—who had never had the opportunity to study abroad at Yale or Oxford, but who were charged with the massive task of designing China's economic reforms—the conference offered an intense and interactive education in the leading international economists' methods of tackling policy problems.

As the conference participants discussed China's reform, the S.S. *Bashan* steamed past the spectacular scenery of the Yangtze River. The boat frequently docked to allow attending spouses to explore towns along the river while their husbands debated in the banquet hall. For some, this must have been an all too familiar experience—Zsuzsa Dániel, an accomplished economist in her own right, was not invited to the discussions, nor was Elizabeth Fay Ringo, Tobin's wife and a former student of Paul Samuelson. Cairncross, after admiring the "remarkably evocative watercolors" his wife, Mary, had painted during her time alone, bemoaned, "We have rarely seen each other except at meals and bedtime since we got on the boat."[90] Mary

Cairncross, for her part, complained in her diary that she spent her days onboard peering out at only "the black water sliding by at a frightening pace."[91]

Only once did the conference stop entirely for tourism: The whole group spent an afternoon touring the Lesser Three Gorges, famous throughout China for their beauty.[92] In Chinese, they were often described by the phrase *lüshui qingshan* (clear green water, fresh green hills), from the Yuan dynasty dramatist Ma Zhiyuan's description of how a man who had seen everything remembered nature's beauty.[93] Later, the group convened for a photograph on deck. They lined up in three rows, with the senior Chinese and Western members of the delegation seated in the front row. Tobin clasped his hands and grinned into the camera. Kornai, wearing dark sunglasses, sat stiffly in his chair. Brilliant emerald waters stretched out beyond the ship's deck. In the foreground, a corner of the luxury cruiser's swimming pool was visible. Compared to the expanse of river on all sides, it must have seemed a small, controlled thing.[94]

On September 7, as the S.S. *Bashan* pulled into the harbor at Wuhan, Tobin and CASS president Ma Hong delivered the conference's closing remarks. Tobin's speech was lighthearted. "I wish you and the other 999,999,950 Chinese success in the exciting and historic era you are entering," he said.[95] Ma Hong opened by stating that the conference was certain to "actively influence China's economic reforms." He then summarized what he believed to be the major message from the conference. First, showing what he had learned from Tobin, he declared that China must "establish a fiscal, tax, and especially financial system suited to a planned commodity economy, and improve indirect control of the economy through these systems." Second, in a direct reference to Kornai, he said China must "increase the hardness of enterprise budget constraints in order to stimulate their vitality." Third, China must "stabilize the economy in the near term, while also heartily advancing forward with the reform" and increasing the scope of markets and market-supporting institutions like statistical collection. At the same time, Ma admitted he had not understood everything discussed at the conference and he planned to reflect further before drawing final conclusions. "Much of the content we still have not had a chance to digest," he said.[96] With these words, the conference adjourned.

In the coming days, most of the group flew back to Beijing, and the Western economists returned home.[97] The Bashan Conference received almost no media attention in Europe and North America. When the *New York Times* profiled Tobin in October, amid a summary of his daily life at Yale, a brief mention appeared. "His routine is punctuated by frequent travel," the author noted, including a trip to "China late last summer to help the Chinese revise their macroeconomic policies." But the article quickly moved on to topics of greater interest to the *Times*'s readers, like Tobin's "huge black Newfoundland dog, Lola."[98]

Despite claiming that it would take time to "digest" everything said by the Western economists, the Chinese participants immediately began to prepare a report on the conference. While still in Wuhan, several participants hurriedly drafted an initial document, "Several Suggestions with Relevance to China's Reform from the International Conference on Macroeconomic Management," and, under An Zhiwen's name, submitted it to Zhao Ziyang for review on September 10. An's report focused on the goal model of the reform, possible next steps, and the broader methods of moving toward indirect macroeconomic control. He began with explicating the ideas of the "famed economist Kornai," including the importance of "hardening budget constraints" and emphasizing the "innate difference" between Kornai's socialist model and the "Western market economy." He then summarized possible transition steps from direct to indirect administration of the economy that the "foreign experts" had proposed, including their emphasis on the need to make national investment in state-owned enterprises correlate with enterprise profits, once again emphasizing Kornai's views (Kornai had used the term "investment hunger" to name the condition that An urged Zhao to fix). Finally, An shared Tobin's lessons about indirect macroeconomic management, especially the necessity of reforming the price system and creating commodity and financial markets, although he did not mention Tobin's name (only Kornai and Brus were mentioned).[99] Two days later, a revised report was formally submitted to the State Council.[100]

The reason for the rush was clear: In late September, before the upcoming National Conference of Party Delegates,[101] senior economists and economic policy makers would be meeting to make final decisions about China's seventh five-year plan. The new plan would guide the country from 1986 to 1990, and the economists who had attended the conference wanted these ideas incorporated.

The National Conference of Party Delegates, which was held September 16–23, 1985, witnessed serious disagreement on the status of the reforms and the best direction for the next five-year plan. With many of the Bashan attendees in the audience, Chen Yun delivered a speech criticizing the reforms. "From the point of view of national economic work," he said, "the principle of 'the planned economy as primary, with market regulation as supplementary' has not gone out of style."[102] In a speech the next day, Chen further decried the "infiltration" of "decadent capitalist ideology."[103] Chen might have acquiesced in calling China a "planned commodity economy" in 1984, but a year later he still put nearly all his emphasis on the "planned" part of the system, continuing to denounce "capitalist" influences and to relegate the "commodity economy" to a secondary role at best.

Despite this conservative pushback, the proposal published at the conclusion of the National Conference of Party Delegates revealed it had been a resounding success for the reformers.[104] The major significance of the document involved its articulation of "three related areas" that were the keys to the "success" of China's reform, all of which had been discussed at the Bashan Conference: making enterprises bear "complete responsibility for profits and losses" (i.e., hardening their budget constraints), expanding commodity and capital markets, and shifting from direct to indirect management of enterprises and the economy.[105] These core ideas mapped neatly onto Ma Hong's three central lessons that he took from the Bashan Conference, drawing in particular on the presentations by Kornai and Tobin. From these interconnections, it is clear the content shared at the Bashan Conference had directly spoken to the reformers' most important priorities.

Yet would any of this matter? Was the Bashan Conference simply a late-summer junket, a pleasure cruise for an international group of academicians? Cairncross, for one, departed China uncertain about what he had just experienced, however warmly the Chinese welcomed him to the corridors of power. Perhaps because of his years at the World Bank's Economic Development Institute, he sensed that the Chinese would only accept his suggestions as they saw fit. "They are curious about other countries and give no evidence of [an] aggressive nationalism," he wrote in his diary shortly after the 1985 trip. "Yet I have no doubt that they consider what to do very carefully before deciding and do not necessarily *accept* advice."[106]

Those days spent floating down the Yangtze River had opened the eyes of the small, elite group of Chinese economists who attended. Many of them wanted to use what they had learned to push forward China's reform agenda. Would they be able to figure out how to drown out the protests of their enemies and persuade their allies that foreign thinkers like Kornai, Tobin, and Cairncross had something to offer China?

There was an almost immediate answer.

7

In the Wake

PREMIER ZHAO ZIYANG stared down at an auditorium full of senior provincial, municipal, and regional officials, gathered for a meeting that had started on September 23, 1985, on the need to control the scale of investment. Zhao had a message for them: rein it in. Describing China's growth figures in detail and highlighting the problem of expansion of the scale of investment, he used a metaphor to describe this problem. This is "investment hunger," he said, explaining that it was "a common disease in socialist countries."

This language came directly from the work of János Kornai.

Suddenly, Zhao turned from his prepared remarks and began to speak off the cuff. "Investment hunger" had afflicted Poland, Yugoslavia, and Hungary, Zhao warned. "We also more or less have this disease."[1]

He began to generalize. "From a historical perspective, since the founding of the People's Republic of China (PRC), when China has had problems, one [reason] has been 'taking struggle as the key link'; the second [reason] has been expanding the scale of investment, bringing a whole series of dysfunctions. We can talk all we want but it just comes down to these two problems." The analytic tools provided by the concept of "investment hunger" had clearly resonated with Zhao so strongly that they seemed to provide a profound explanation for China's woes both past and present.[2]

"Some foreigners," he continued, "have suggested that China should . . . focus on the operation and management of enterprises, which will greatly improve production efficiency. We always make sure to take care of basic construction but we do not attach importance to the management of existing enterprises. The key is to improve the management level of enterprises."[3]

Having moved through this range of ideas from the Bashan Conference, Zhao returned to his prepared remarks. "Even after several twists and turns, we struggle to accept these lessons," he concluded.[4]

Zhao's speech made it clear that, far from a limited or minor event, the Bashan Conference had an unusual scope—and an unusual focus on the issues most dynamically at play in late 1985. As winter came to Beijing, a core group was assigned to prepare the public report on the conference and to disseminate its ideas. In December, the report, titled "Economic System Reform and Macroeconomic Management" (henceforth, the "Bashan Report"), appeared in full in the year-end issue of *Economic Research*, a leading academic journal; installments were also published in the *People's Daily*.[5] A freestanding booklet followed in 1986. Much more systematic than Ma Hong's closing remarks, An Zhiwen's memorandum, or Zhao's offhand comments, these publications introduced the official interpretation of the Bashan Conference in its immediate aftermath and offered a case study on the transnational influence of ideas about economic development.

The Bashan Report revealed three key dynamics that defined Chinese engagement with international economists and the World Bank. First, the Chinese were not only looking for limited, specialized assistance. They framed the report around a broad question about China's goal model and the ideal relationship between the state and the market:

It should be noted that China's economic circles display considerable flexibility with regard to understanding the term "planned commodity economy." Some people stress the "commodity

economy" aspect, while others stress the "planned" aspect. . . .
What kind of model should be the goal for China's economic
system reform?[6]

This opening made it clear that the team of authors—who included
Liu Guoguang, Zhao Renwei, Chen Jiyuan, and Zhang Zhouyuan,
among others, representing the reform-oriented portion of "China's
economic circles"—were willing to rethink the largest questions of
China's systemic reform with the help of foreign advisers.

Second, some of the ideas the Chinese participants encountered
onboard the ship, especially the presentations by Kornai and James
Tobin, had clearly persuaded the report's authors. The report endorsed concepts like "soft budget constraints," investment hunger,
state "paternalism," and the value of "indirect management of the
economy" as highly relevant to China's situation. These ideas then
prompted the participants to move to self-criticism. "In reforming
China's urban economy, we have focused on enlivening enterprises,"
they wrote, "which has meant that we have overemphasized delegating authority and the incentives of bonuses and rewards, instead
of increasing a sense of responsibility and [fiscal] discipline. In other
words, we provide motivation but do not provide pressure." Kornai's
idea of the soft budget constraint—"pressuring" enterprises to
change their behavior by imposing fiscal discipline—thus provided
them with a critique of China's approach to enterprise reform up
until that point. "Hardening enterprise budget constraints has become the key to strengthening both microeconomic and macroeconomic control," they concluded.[7] By using Kornai's concept to link
microeconomic and macroeconomic policy, the authors of the report
also provided strong support to the conceptual integrity of Kornai's
goal model, giving the Chinese a fuller, more specific vision of how
the country could move toward a system of macroeconomic
management that would allow market forces to govern reformed
enterprises.

Third, they critiqued even the ideas they supported as requiring
further interpretation and analysis to conform to socialism and to
be applied to China's national conditions. "We cannot recklessly
adopt [Kornai's] system as the goal model of China's economic system
reform," they wrote. Elsewhere, they declared: "We must learn from

foreign experiences in light of China's particular experience in order to formulate an overall plan to improve the economic system. But, in the process of reform, we must also 'cross the river by feeling for the stones.'" These statements may have reflected compromise among the authors. This insistence also likely reflected an important presentational concern about preempting conservative critics in China who might be concerned about "Western doctors" prescribing "Western medicine." Even more evocatively, it perhaps also precisely reflected the dissonance many of the Chinese economists experienced when interacting with foreign economic ideas. They were eager to learn from abroad and they were widely receptive to outside influence—but they knew that copying indiscriminately was wrong and that they needed to reconcile foreign advice with a path that reflected China's circumstances. As Zhao Ziyang said plainly in January 1986, "We want to learn from foreign experience, but I'm afraid it won't do to exclusively study the West. . . . We need to make our own way."[8]

This attitude, in turn, reflected the fundamental belief that debates and decision-making about reform policy ought to be guided by the pragmatic spirit of "crossing the river by feeling for the stones," which indicated that China should not reform by following generalized economic or political ideologies but, rather, by learning from each step in the process. In this view, ideas—whether domestic or foreign—were relevant mainly in that they determined which "stones" the Chinese leadership decided to "feel for." Even the best international ideas about the "overall plan" for China's reform would not be permitted to override this experimental spirit. Instead, such ideas would require skillful Chinese navigators to guide and adapt them to "particular experience" as China crossed the river. This usage of the phrase was a far cry from its initial presentation by Chen Yun, but, as with so many things, the reformers had refashioned its possible meanings to support their ambitions.

As his late September remarks showed, Zhao Ziyang had been quick to notice the analytic value of several concepts discussed at the conference. At the same time, the Chinese participants who had spent the week on the river soon moved to apply what they had learned to make policy recommendations.

One of the first to do so was Liu Guoguang, who had been a leading figure in China's engagement with foreign economics at least since he had suggested that Włodzimierz Brus and Ota Šik be invited to visit China. In early November 1985, Liu published an article in the *People's Daily* in which he cited Kornai's concept of "investment hunger," described his own "increased understanding" of the relationship between macroeconomic policy and microeconomic policy and the need to reform both systems together, and called for gradualism in doing so.[9] These proposals were bolstered by a report that a group of economists at the System Reform Commission submitted to the State Council in October 1985 before being published in 1986, which drew on data collected from surveys of 429 enterprises to argue for near-term "bold yet prudent microeconomic reforms."[10]

Heading into 1986, many of the participants at the Bashan Conference were making major plays for influence in the contentious debates over the future of China's economic reform. For example, in December 1985, Wu Jinglian and several of his colleagues at the State Council Development Research Center submitted a report to the leadership on the seventh five-year plan, in which they declared, plainly, "It is necessary to carry out coordinated reform."[11] In 1986, a moment of transformation would occur for both economic thought and policy, in no small part because of the surge of new ideas and analytic tools that entered China in the wake of the Bashan Conference.

One dramatic trend in particular swept through China's economic circles—what was called "Kornai fever" (*Ke'ernai re*).[12] Kornai's ideas, transmitted through diverse channels, flooded into Chinese debates, including the 1986 publication of the Chinese translation of *Economics of Shortage*.[13] Dozens of articles in periodicals introduced an even wider readership to what *Dushu*, then a prominent liberal magazine, called the "enlightening" views of Kornai, whom they dubbed "the economic theorist that the reform cried out for."[14] With its bright aquamarine cover, the two volumes of *Economics of Shortage* [*Duanque jingjixue*] seemed designed to garner attention. "Kornai fever" would go on to fuel sales of over 100,000 copies of the Hungarian economist's book.[15] Kornai was mentioned hundreds of times in academic and research journals in the period 1986–1989, including in regional and provincial journals in areas as varied as

Guangxi, Hubei, Anhui, and Heilongjiang.[16] A group of faculty and graduate students at Peking University even held a seminar devoted to *Economics of Shortage*, at which it was agreed that Kornai had made a major "theoretical innovation." According to a notice in the Peking University newsletter, the participants—who included the dean of the Economics Department—roundly praised the value of Kornai's ideas, although views on how to solve the problems he identified varied widely.[17]

Many responses presented Kornai's ideas with adulation, praising the "soft budget constraint" and Kornai's analysis of the relationship between the economic system and enterprise behavior as "revelatory."[18] The *Dushu* article labeled Kornai as an "innovative" figure in the new era of reform in China. Lauding *Economics of Shortage*, the author cited several specific ways in which China could "borrow from" (*jiejian*) Kornai's works. His "method of researching the socialist system," especially the use of advanced mathematics, were sorely missing in China, where mathematical and model-oriented aspects of economic study were still "relatively weak." At a less instrumental level, the article argued that Kornai represented a synthesis of the best aspects of international economic research, focusing on his "use of the tools of Western economic theory and analysis to study the socialist economic system, combining the scientific elements of Marxian economic theory and Western economic theory." In this formulation, Kornai seemed to provide a methodological correlative to the policy synthesis of the "planned commodity economy," showing how the methods and techniques of Marxist and mainstream Western economics could align and cooperate, much as the plan and the market cooperated in China's mixed system. At the same time, in the context of the Bashan Report, the *Dushu* article's understanding of Kornai pointed toward a particular interpretation of the amorphous "planned commodity economy" concept, which would involve enlarging the scope of the market mechanism, enlivening enterprises, and achieving macroeconomic balance.[19]

Reviews of the translation of *Economics of Shortage* were also exceptionally positive. One reviewer, describing the excited response from Chinese readers interested in reform, acknowledged that the book studied Eastern European experiences but claimed that the similarities and relevance to China of the phenomena it described were incontro-vertible. A researcher at the State Council praised the utterly "unique" quality of Kornai's writings, adding, "Kornai's economic theory is successful . . . because it explores a new method for researching the problems of socialist economies."[20] These authors placed particular emphasis on two related aspects of the book: why the shortage economy was innate to socialism and how enterprise behavior under socialism created shortage phenomena—focusing, as a result, on Kornai's arguments about the "soft budget constraint" and "pater-nalism."[21] These ideas, which the reviewers defined as priorities to address in future reforms in China, would remain the most salient aspects of Kornai's thought for Chinese economists.

In addition to the great attention to *Economics of Shortage*, the most obvious consequence of "Kornai fever" was that Kornai—and, in a related manner, the Bashan Conference—became a central part of economic debates on a diverse range of topics. The primary chal-lenge now facing the participants at the Bashan Conference was to determine how to apply the ideas to China's circumstances, and they processed them in diverse and often divergent ways.

For these individuals, the power of Kornai's ideas to diagnose, name, and clarify China's policy problems did not appear to be fun-damentally contested. For example, the mild-mannered Zhao Renwei argued, in an article the same year, that Hungary (Kornai's arche-typal IB system) may not have had a formal dual-track system in place but "Hungarian state enterprises had a dual dependence, responding to both higher administrative authorities and to the market." (De-spite the similar-sounding names, China's dual-track system and Hungarian-style "dual dependence" were completely different in both structure and economic realities, but Zhao's insight was that in both situations enterprises were forced simultaneously to respond to vertical planning authorities and horizontal market incentives. Zhao, in other words, was looking for echoes between these two systems.) At the Bashan Conference, Zhao added, Kornai had defined the Hungarian IB model as permissible only as a "transitional" device.[22] Similarly, the dual-track system in effect in China should only exist to facilitate China's transition. For many of these economists, Kornai had framed China's policy challenges in such a way that it connected their policy dilemmas to a greater range of international economic debates than ever before.

However, the praise of Kornai's diagnoses did not imply uniformity in their interpretation and application to China. In September 1986, the aging Xue Muqiao delivered a speech in which he called for a "strengthening of macroeconomic control" to help the economy find "balance," an idea Wu Jinglian had advocated in 1984 and 1985.[23] Xue presented the need for China to develop a mode of "macroeconomic regulation" that differed from what "Western capitalist countries" used, asserting, "We are not the same as them."[24] Xue then turned to Kornai, relying on his analysis but suggesting a different conclusion:

> It seems from these cases [in *Economics of Shortage*] that "investment hunger" is a disease that socialist countries cannot cure. I am not so pessimistic, as long as the whole country from top to bottom, and especially Party leaders, develop a deep understanding of this widespread disease . . . and strictly and consciously use macroeconomic controls to avoid this problem.[25]

Thus Chinese-style "macroeconomic controls" would differ from their "Western capitalist" equivalent principally with regard to the goals of such macroeconomic controls—goals that Xue found defined in Kornai's work, such as curing "investment hunger."[26] Yet Xue's disagreement with Kornai's "pessimism" ran deeper, because he was fundamentally disagreeing with Kornai's implicit condemnation of socialism itself. Within the framework of foreign ideas presented at the Bashan Conference, Xue articulated a Chinese vision of a "cured" socialism—using a medicine, macroeconomic controls, adapted to suit China's needs.

Other participants seemed to agree that investment hunger was an affliction that could be "cured" within the context of the socialist system, while giving greater credence to Kornai's proposals for China's future path and not just his diagnosis of China's problems. For example, referencing the many theories propounded by "foreign scholars and domestic theorists," Liu Guoguang asserted the most important was Kornai's new classification from the Bashan Conference.[27] He dismissed the laissez-faire IIA model as "capitalist" and "incompatible with socialism" because it had no central control, but he praised the IIB system as having attributes that allow it to "play a leading role" as a theoretical foundation for formulating the goal model for the reform.

In this context, Liu Guoguang voiced a question that dominated Chinese economic debates in the mid-1980s: "What exactly is a 'planned commodity economy'?"[28] Each economist's answer, of course, seemed designed to nudge this officially accepted ideology in the direction of his favored policies. Liu's definition stressed "enlivening" enterprises while also increasing macroeconomic management, with an eye toward curing "investment hunger" and prioritizing "adjustment of supply and demand."[29] "We are demolishing the formerly paramount vertical relationships between government and enterprises," he declared proudly.[30] In another speech delivered the same year, Liu elaborated on these ideas, using the Bashan Report to argue that moving beyond the dual-track system and the use of indirect administrative controls as quickly as possible was necessary to develop a system of macroeconomic controls with market adjustments (Kornai's IIB model).[31] Thus, for Liu, international knowledge was indispensable to determine both the meaning of the "planned commodity economy" and the means of managing such an economy— all while maintaining socialism.[32] As Liu elaborated elsewhere, these reform ideas would not overtake the country's specific conditions and commitment to socialism because China's economists would promote "continuity" and respect for the "legacy" of the old system.[33] Liu was a savvy and politically minded operator, and his conceptualization of China's economic reform deployed elements from the Bashan Conference to address what he saw as China's distinct circumstances and to define the Party's stabilizing role in exercising macroeconomic control.

Outside the circle of participants, the Bashan Report and the ideas shared at the conference became a standard reference for framing many issues facing China. This touchstone function was evident at a Nanjing conference in October 1986 on the "goal model of the reform," sponsored by Nanjing University, two economic institutes at the Chinese Academy of Social Sciences (CASS), and the Jiangsu Academy of Social Sciences. Approximately one hundred delegates attended the meeting, including senior economists and many younger scholars.[34] After Liu Guoguang's opening lecture, the second speech at the session focused exclusively on the Bashan Conference.[35] Its report has garnered "universal attention," the industrial economist Zhou Shulian declared, pointing to Kornai's goal model of market coordination with macroeconomic controls as the idea of greatest interest.[36] Without directly endorsing the report, Zhou presented engagement with Kornai's ideas as indispensable for any Chinese economist who hoped to devise an alternative "goal model." Kornai had "captured the core problem of economic system reform," which was the relationship between enterprises and the state and the "core" goal of "transforming socialist enterprises into real enterprises." Zhou wove Tobin's ideas into this tapestry, saying that the Bashan Conference also demonstrated that indirect economic management through monetary and fiscal policy was possible and desirable.[37] What emerged was a synthesis of the ideas of Kornai and Tobin, framed in terms of China's national conditions (although Tobin, perhaps because he was an American of "bourgeois liberal" tendencies, did not receive the same explicit acknowledgment that the Chinese accorded to Kornai, who had come up through a socialist system and maintained his Hungarian Academy of Sciences affiliation).

Many of the subsequent papers presented at the Nanjing conference alluded to the Bashan Conference and to Kornai's proposals. For example, Kornai's categorizations appeared throughout one economist's paper on an important emerging interpretation of the "planned commodity economy," as meaning that "the state manages the market, and the market guides the enterprises" (*guojia tiaojie shichang, shichang yindao qiye*). The paper asserted this new ideological interpretation closely resembled Kornai's theoretical goal model but was "more in keeping with Chinese characteristics." In addition, "under China's conditions," the author wrote, "It is first necessary to develop toward [indirect administrative control], and then later [we] can move toward the mechanism of the plan guiding the market."[38] This paper thus used Kornai to describe both the theoretical underpinnings and the implementation challenges of the emerging concept of "the state manages the market, and the market guides the enterprises"—a concept that would become critically important to the future of the Chinese system.[39] At this elite economic research meeting, the message was clear: The Bashan Conference, especially Kornai's ideas, had become threads woven through the Chinese discourse on reform, even though many possibilities remained open for interpretation and application.[40]

In short, just over a year after the participants disembarked the S.S. *Bashan* at Wuhan, Kornai's reputation in China had grown to an astonishing level. Attending a conference in New York, Zhao Renwei and Wu Jinglian spoke with Yale professor John C. H. Fei, who closely followed the latest trends in Chinese economic thought. He allegedly exclaimed to Zhao and Wu, "Some mainland economists have raised up Kornai too high, as if putting him on par with Marx! But how can you compare Kornai to Marx?"[41]

How can we understand the extraordinary interest in Kornai's work by such a wide range of Chinese economists? The most prominent reason, of course, was intellectual: the broad appeal of his ideas lay in the precision of his identifying, naming, and interpreting the problems of China's socialist economy. But "Kornai fever" was not only an intellectual craze. Even more than Brus and Šik, Kornai represented a kind of counterfactual life that China's economists had not been able to live. He was born and educated in the socialist world but he produced work that earned him acclaim and respect on both sides of the Iron Curtain. His writings were grounded in Hungary's experience, but he had attained, for his Chinese audiences, a thrilling universality. In a recent essay, a prominent Fudan University professor wrote, "When Yu Guangyuan died, I was reading Kornai's autobiography, and suddenly I thought: What would have happened if Yu and Kornai could have switched the environments in which they lived?"[42] Reflecting on the older generation of Chinese economists, the Fudan professor realized that, despite that generation's immense capacities and the historic transformation they had lived through, there was no "Kornai-type character" among them—and they knew it. In this sense, Kornai was at once a foreign expert who descended from a distant land and almost—only *almost*—became one of them.

This possibility is mirrored by Kornai's own understanding of his influence in China. Writing with his wife, Zsuzsa Dániel, in 1986, Kornai attributed the success of his ideas to his personal history. "We think that French or American authors, lacking personal experience, can hardly understand and interpret the Chinese events of the last decade. . . . With Hungarians, empathy comes much more naturally."[43] Writing from Cambridge, Massachusetts, as a Hungarian, about what he learned on the Yangtze River, Kornai suggested that he believed his influence in China had both personal and intellectual bases.[44]

The prominence of the Bashan attendees and the dense networks of China's leading economists during this period allowed the contestation of these ideas to extend far beyond the publications by the conference's immediate participants. Their disagreement on how to apply the ideas to China did not limit their influence. To the contrary, this spread may, in part, have been the result of how contestable the ideas were. Because the ideas had great diagnostic precision but ambiguous application to China's policy dilemmas, they acted as newly cleared ground on which a wide selection of China's reformers could hash out their disagreements.

Across the intellectual spectrum, this moment in 1986 was one of extraordinary openness—to the point that the thirtieth anniversary of the Hundred Flowers campaign, an abortive attempt under Mao to encourage dissenting opinions from Chinese intellectuals, was celebrated as the beginning of what the *New York Times* called "a new 'Hundred Flowers' drive." Deng Xiaoping had helped lead the crackdown on the original Hundred Flowers campaign after Party leaders decided that the openness they had encouraged had gone too far, but Deng promised that the 1956–1957 fiasco would not be repeated in 1986.[45] In the heady atmosphere of 1986, Chinese intellectuals felt free to make bold claims, clearly demonstrating their sense of empowerment due to the encouragement of Zhao Ziyang, Hu Yaobang, and even Deng.

In this context, Kornai may have resonated with reformers worried about perceived problems in the transitional economy, but widespread disagreements about whether his ideas could solve problems or simply identify them soon cooled the "Kornai fever" into a more critical approach. The ideas introduced to China at the Bashan Conference became protean, invoked to support the contending policies of China's reformist economists, who fought fiercely as power, ego, and the future of China all hung in the balance.

Wu Jinglian's "coordinated reform" group had largely defined their positions before the Bashan Conference, but they used the arguments of Kornai, Tobin, and others to bolster their ideas about the need for immediate reform of the macroeconomic system, aiming to increase the economy's responsiveness to market incentives while simultaneously developing stronger mechanisms for macroeconomic management during periods of economic instability. They began to stress the urgency of price reform in new terms that reflected growing sophistication. Their emphasis on the fact that price reform had lagged behind other reforms under the dual-track system now shifted to assertions that price reform was the "key link" between macroeconomic and microeconomic reform. Wu Jinglian made these arguments in a report on "coordinated reform" to the State Council in January 1986.[46] That summer, in an important article, Wu and several allies drew on the Bashan Report to bolster their related assertions that in China aggregate demand exceeded aggregate supply, despite some economists' claims to the contrary.[47]

Wu's opponents within the reformist camp, however, argued that reform of the enterprise ownership system should come first. Five economists from CASS and State Council research units wrote an article criticizing the Bashan Report and attributing "shortages under the traditional socialist system" to the problems of enterprise ownership, rather than Wu's theory that rigid pricing was the problem.[48] They criticized Kornai's "overgeneralization of the problem," which prevented him from "coming up with a solution" to the problems he had identified. Kornai's inadequacies, and those of his Chinese followers, became an opening for their own proposals for "restructuring of the microeconomic base starting with the reform of ownership."[49] They proposed an "asset management responsibility system" as the goal of restructuring, in which "returns on assets" would be the only metric of enterprise success, solving the problem of "investment hunger" by creating market incentives driven by the pursuit of profit.[50]

Not all was smooth sailing, however. In early March, Xinhua News Agency circulated an editorial titled "Marxian Economics Has Great Vitality." It attacked the ideas of an author named Ma Ding (a pseudonym used by the writer Song Longxiang) for "fawning on foreign theories." In late 1985, Ma Ding had written an essay on Chinese economics that stated, in no uncertain terms, that Marx was holding China's economists back: Chinese economists "must free themselves of Marxist books . . . and establish a new branch of economics in building socialism" explicitly incorporating beneficial insights from Western economics, including Keynesian proposals for monetary and fiscal policy. Although many reformist economists agreed with Ma Ding's assessment, conservatives led by the ideologues Deng Liqun and Hu Qiaomu soon attacked the article's eager embrace of Western economics and its criticisms of Marxian economics.[51] Yet Zhao Ziyang wrote a letter to Hu on March 3 that included a clear warning about those sorts of statements: "You should be cautious when criticizing the liberalization of economic theory." Deng Liqun later said he would never forget those words.[52] A series of periodicals subsequently republished Ma Ding's article in full or released comments praising his ideas.[53]

Amid these disagreements, Zhao Ziyang made comments at a mid-March 1986 meeting of the Politburo Standing Committee that suggested he was leaning toward Wu Jinglian's proposals. Praising the previous year's research efforts and demonstrating his detailed knowledge of the competing reform proposals, Zhao emphasized the goal of reforming three key interrelated systems: the taxation system, the financial system, and the price system. Of these three, he said price reform was "primary," but the three sets of reforms "must be *coordinated*" (emphasis added).[54]

For opponents of "coordinated reform," there was no time to waste. Li Yining, the Peking University economist who had helped lead the Foreign Economics Lecture Series and coauthored *The English Disease*—in which he discussed the history of British industrialization and the perils of nationalized enterprise as a way of writing about "the stagnation of Chinese industry" when it was otherwise "too sensitive" to do so in 1982—had clearly decided the moment had come to make a dramatic play for influence.

He came out swinging. In April 1986, Li Yining delivered a speech at Peking University that made his viewpoint clear in its title: "Ownership Reform Is the Crux of Reform." In May, Li published a searing article in the *Beijing Daily*, calling the emphasis on price reform wrong and demanding that leaders in the Chinese Communist Party focus on reforming the ownership system of China's enterprises. Li wrote what one scholar of the period has called "perhaps the best-known sentence to be penned in the course of debate over economic reform": "Economic reform can fail because of the failure of price reform but cannot succeed because of the success of price reform alone; that will take reform of the ownership system."[55] (In a later interview, Li Yining said he had found Kornai's "paternalism" concept helpful in clarifying his own views of the necessity of enterprise reform.)[56] Li's article became the buzz of Beijing—and his ideas soon caught the eye of Zhao Ziyang. Wu and his allies spent many late nights in Wu's home, agonizing over how to push back and struggling to craft language that equaled Li's powerful prose.[57]

Amid the schism among reformers over whether price reform or ownership reform should come first, Kornai remained a touchstone. Some economists even believed it was necessary to argue that China would get nowhere unless its economists explicitly decided to disregard Kornai. One professor at Fudan University deployed Kornai's "soft-budget constraint" and "investment hunger" concepts to critique the continuing problems of the state's relationship with enterprises under the dual-track system, but he voiced concern about the popularity of Kornai's IIB model. "Many comrades are advocating Kornai's 'IIB model' as the future goal model of our system reform," the professor wrote, but it "is too vague and uncertain to serve as the goal model and will pose a large risk to China's reform."[58] Another Shanghai-based economist echoed these criticisms but framed them in different terms, declaring that *Economics of Shortage* hewed too closely to "contemporary mainstream Western economics" to apply to China's conditions. Citing China's status as a developing country, this author suggested that Kornai's ideas did not actually match the realities of China's situation. Kornai inspired goals such as the hardening of enterprise budget constraints, which "can only be the result of the ongoing reform of the socialist economic system" but "cannot be the starting point of the structural reform."[59] Thus these authors both concluded that adherence to Kornai's ideas as a guide to reform would lead China down the wrong path.[60]

Despite these intellectual divides, reformers made concrete progress. Their longer-term goals were made more systematic when the State Planning Commission convened a meeting on macroeconomic management in September 1986, endorsing the slogan "the state manages the market, and the market guides the enterprises," which had been discussed in Nanjing earlier that year. Although disagreements persisted over whether to use "manage" (*tiaokong*) or "grasp" (*zhangwo*, in the sense of "control") to define the state-market relationship, this slogan was a substantial step in the direction of a market-oriented interpretation of the 1984 redefinition of China's system as a "planned commodity economy."[61]

Indeed, many economists wrote of this period as a turning point, with the flourishing of both "Western microeconomic market theory" and Kornai's "Eastern European shortage theory," in the words of a 1988 article on industrial reform (one of the coauthors of which, Liu He, is currently the vice chairman of the National Development and Reform Commission and chief of the Leading Group for Financial and Economic Affairs).[62] For reformers of all stripes, the ideas introduced at the Bashan Conference played a major role in informing their interpretations of the 1984 "planned commodity economy" and their competing proposals for China's next steps. Another group of economists, citing the Bashan Report as they discussed a new emphasis on China's "microeconomic base," characterized this as "transformative knowledge." They put its importance somewhat more poetically: "It can be said that 1985 was like bamboo shoots sprouting after a spring rain, especially with respect to research into enterprise behavior, the market for labor and capital, ownership, and the microeconomic foundations of market operations."[63] These bamboo shoots were growing in Chinese soil, but they had been grafted from plants with roots beyond China's shores.

It is clear that if this knowledge was "transformative," it was also transforming. Aboard the ship, Cairncross had urged his listeners "not [to] be too *purist*"—and they certainly followed this advice when it came to interpreting the ideas of Kornai, Tobin, and others.

Research and theoretical debate flourished in the wake of the Bashan Conference, and the ideas introduced there informed many different policy proposals. But it remained uncertain whether these ideas would lead to improved results in the Chinese economy.

Would these ideas endure to become more than only an intellectual craze? The conditions in late 1985 had been good for growing bamboo, but, sooner or later, that bamboo would have to be harvested and put to use.

Participants at the Bashan Conference, 1985. Photo courtesy of Edwin Lim.

Zhao Ziyang (right) speaks with Deng Xiaoping (left), 1987. Forrest
Anderson/The LIFE Images Collection/Getty Images.

Xue Muqiao at work, 1978. Photo courtesy of Xue Xiaohe.

Ma Hong (front, third from left), Xue Muqiao (front, center), and other senior economists at Zhongnanhai, 1980. Photo courtesy of Xue Xiaohe.

Chinese leaders vote "yes" to the economic report submitted by Premier Zhao Ziyang (first row, lower left), at the National People's Congress in Beijing, 1981. In the second row, left to right, are Hu Yaobang, Deng Xiaoping, Li Xiannian, Chen Yun, and Hua Guofeng. AP Photo/LHS.

Zhao Ziyang (right) shakes hands with János Kornai as Edwin Lim (center left) looks on, 1985. Photo courtesy of János Kornai.

陈云同志

Propaganda image portraying Chen Yun, 1983. Stefan R. Landsberger Collection, International Institute of Social History (Amsterdam).

János Kornai delivers his presentation at the Bashan Conference, 1985. Photo courtesy of János Kornai.

János Kornai and Zsuzsa Dániel enjoying Chinese cuisine, 1985. Photo courtesy of János Kornai.

Xue Muqiao, Ma Hong, Li Kemu, and Wu Jinglian (left to right) during the Bashan Conference, 1985. Photo courtesy of Wu Jinglian.

James Tobin, Xue Muqiao, and an unidentified woman on deck during the Bashan Conference, 1985. Photo courtesy of Xue Xiaohe.

János Kornai, Zsuzsa Dániel, Xue Muqiao, and others on a riverboat during
the Bashan Conference, 1985. Photo courtesy of János Kornai.

Gregory Chow (left) meets with Zhao Ziyang (right). Photo courtesy of Gregory Chow.

Milton Friedman (left) meets with Zhao Ziyang (right), 1988. Box 114, Folder 14, Milton Friedman Papers, Hoover Institution Archives, Stanford, California.

Zhao Ziyang meets Milton Friedman as Wu Jinglian (center left) looks on, 1988. Box 189, Folder 4, Milton Friedman Papers, Hoover Institution Archives, Stanford, California.

Milton Friedman (left) speaks alongside Pu Shan in Shanghai, 1988. Box 114, Folder 14, Milton Friedman Papers, Hoover Institution Archives, Stanford, California.

Xue Muqiao (left) is honored by Zhu Rongji (right), 1994.
Photo courtesy of Xue Xiaohe.

János Kornai (left) and Wu Jinglian (right) celebrate their birthdays, 2008.
Photo courtesy of János Kornai.

8

A Tempestuous Season

❦❪ FOR SOME CHINESE economic policy makers, the Bashan Conference had piqued their interest, but they wanted to flesh out what they had read in the report before they could make concrete policy recommendations based on the new ideas. Spurred on by the presentations of János Kornai and Aleksandr Bajt at the Bashan Conference, a delegation of prominent younger economists organized a trip to Hungary and Yugoslavia in May–June 1986, aiming to conduct further research. The group included Gao Shangquan at the System Reform Commission and his colleague Chen Yizi, the important younger economic adviser who had transitioned from rural policy to the Institute on Chinese Economic Structural Reform, as well as Ma Kai, a rising official in Beijing. The goal of the trip was explicit and, by now, characteristic: to find ideas and experiences that would "provide reference points and lessons for designing reforms" in China.[1]

The delegation arrived in Belgrade on May 26 where they met with top economic officials before moving on to Budapest. In both cities, they asked detailed questions about those countries' economic reforms and about the mistakes they had made in the past. They had 111 meetings with a dizzying array of officials, scholars, business leaders, and others. For many Chinese members of the delegation, it was their first time abroad. Like Xue Muqiao in Paris, Chen Yizi recalled they were impressed by the rich range of goods individuals could choose among in Hungary and Yugoslavia compared to in China. Of course, it was not all work: the group had several nights of wild drinking with their Eastern European counterparts, the liquor washing away the stresses of designing policies that would affect the lives of a billion people.[2]

When the delegation members returned to China, they prepared the publication of a report on Hungary's and Yugoslavia's reforms. This document can be read as an attempt to supplement and elaborate on the Bashan Report, enlarging on the insights that Kornai and Bajt had brought to China with details harvested from a voyage into the state economic apparatuses of both countries.

In the case of Hungary, the report analyzed the challenges of that country's bungled enterprise reform, illustrating that by the early 1980s the subsidies granted to state-run enterprises once again exceeded the enterprises' profits. This showed that the failed reforms had "further softened the enterprises' budgetary constraints" and created what one official at the Planning Bureau reportedly called the "Bermuda Triangle" of price, subsidy, and taxation, in which endless funds mysteriously vanished. The situation supported the authors' arguments in favor of sweeping enterprise reform: The only way to escape this "Bermuda Triangle" was for "enterprises to be made responsible, by themselves, for profits and losses," they wrote. "Without abolishing the monopoly status of enterprises and letting loss-making enterprises close their doors, the market economy did not have even the bare minimum required to be effective."[3] They made similar arguments based on the Yugoslav case, in which comprehensive price reform had been completed, but, because of the failures of enterprise reform, price reform had not fundamentally changed the incentive structure of the economy.

This report fed directly into a meeting of System Reform Commission officials held shortly after the delegation's return from Eastern Europe to discuss with Zhao Ziyang the best future direction for the reforms. On June 11–12, 1986, the commission's administrator, An Zhiwen (who had attended the Bashan Conference and had submitted the summary report to Zhao at its conclusion), laid out the major options on the table, citing Li Yining's emphasis on enterprise ownership reform—as did Ma Hong, the former president of the Chinese Academy of Social Sciences (CASS), who now led the Development Reform Center, where Wu Jinglian now worked. This prompted a lively two-day discussion among Zhao Ziyang, An Zhiwen, Ma Hong, and Yao Yilin about enterprise autonomy, owner-ship, management, and the possibilities of price reform. Zhao was clear about his eventual goals—to "shrink the portion [of the economy] governed by planning and increase the portion under market prices," but he was still grappling with the sequencing and timeline. When Yao Yilin spoke up in favor of "coordinated reform," Zhao showed he understood what was at stake, citing the proposals of the coordinated reformers and acknowledging that "market prices" offered "the best information" about supply and demand in the economy. However, the main thrust of Zhao's response once again emphasized the critical problem of enterprise autonomy and, further, hypothesized about enterprise reforms that would "gradually pro-duce market prices." Although the meeting concluded with Zhao calling for further research on the questions discussed, it was clear that Zhao, who at the beginning of 1986 had called for "coordinated reform," was now demonstrably leaning toward the ideas of the en-terprise reform group, due in part to strong arguments that well-placed economists had developed by studying the experiences of Hungary and Yugoslavia.[4]

Other Chinese economists continued to deepen their partnerships with academics in the United States and to gain exposure to the U.S. economy. In October 1986, Bruce Reynolds, an expert on the Chi-nese economy at the University of Virginia, organized a conference at Arden House, the sprawling former estate of railroad mag-nate E. H. Harriman. Surrounded by the ornately carved wood-work and lushly upholstered furnishings of the mansion, Reynolds brought together many of the leading U.S.-based scholars of Chi-na's economy and of socialist transition with a team of prominent Chinese counterparts from State Council research institutes, CASS, and Peking University. Attendees included Gregory Chow, Dwight Perkins, Béla Balassa, and János Kornai from the United States, and Wu Jinglian, Zhao Renwei, Zhou Xiaochuan, Qian Yingyi, and others from China.[5]

Wu Jinglian and Zhao Renwei were already familiar faces, but the Arden House conference was notable because it introduced the Western economists to several extraordinary talents in the younger Chinese generation. Wu Jinglian had urged Reynolds to invite Zhou Xiaochuan, who had recently received his doctorate from Tsinghua University and had taken up a position as a researcher at the State Council, becoming a frequent collaborator with Wu and other members of the "coordinated reform" group.[6] At the conference, Zhou presented a paper on the Chinese banking system as of late 1985, predicting that China would face a "destabilizing cycle between easy and tight [monetary] policies" until it could develop strong institutions for conducting macroeconomic policy. (Zhou is currently serving as governor of the People's Bank of China [PBOC], China's central bank, a position he has held since 2002.) Zhou and his coauthor asked, "What should banking reform aim for?" In answering, Zhou showed he had deeply internalized the lessons James Tobin had taught at the Bashan Conference, which had been so important to his mentor, Wu Jinglian. Zhou stressed that the central bank "should be freed from the responsibility" to finance sectoral reforms (which should be the job of fiscal policy) and he highlighted the need to "mainly use guidance regulation instruments and use direct quantity controls as auxiliary supplements." China should "gradually form a financial market compatible with China's conditions of economic reform," Zhou and his coauthor declared.[7]

It was a memorable debut. Zhou was, Reynolds stated, "incandescently brilliant."[8] The Arden House conference introduced Western economists to the man who would help to build—and eventually lead—China's central banking system, and Zhou Xiaochuan's arguments revealed his deep familiarity with the ideas of neo-Keynesian macroeconomists.

In addition to the journeys abroad, Chinese economic officials also invited more economists from the "capitalist" West, including from West Germany and Switzerland, to visit China and offer input on reform policy making. The German experience had been of interest to Chinese economists since the early 1980s because of the "German economic miracle" that followed World War II under the guidance of Ludwig Erhard, who soon became West Germany's economics minister. The elimination of price controls in 1948 and the subsequent reduction in tax rates had led to extraordinary rapid economic growth.[9] Chinese thinkers saw potential lessons in the large effects of price decontrols on the German economy and had invited several German experts to China, including Armin Gutowski in 1979 and the former central banker Otmar Emminger in 1985. Yang Peixin, a Chinese central banking expert who supported the contract responsibility system for enterprises and the expansion of government investment in the economy, met with a former West German official in October 1986 to discuss Germany's fiscal and monetary reforms.[10] A week later, reporting to Zhao Ziyang, Yang Peixin said that despite postwar price decontrols, the West German experience actually indicated that emphasis should not fall on price reform but, rather, on developing enterprise production. China did not need to fear deficits as long as deficit spending was used productively, said Yang, noting that these proposals were very similar to the views of Li Yining, one of Yang's allies in the larger reform debates during this period—a similarity that Zhao Ziyang also observed in his response to Yang's presentation.[11]

This international support for the arguments of the enterprise reform group—of which Li Yining was the most prominent intellectual leader—helped sway Zhao Ziyang, who had been leaning toward prioritizing enterprise reform as early as June of 1986. In early November, Zhao listened to a report on several possible methods for reforming national commodity prices. His response was firm: although commodity prices were extremely important and deserved attention, "enlivening the enterprises must first be resolved." He added, "Reform is precisely the rationalizing of [economic] relationships. The old ideas won't do."[12] Zhao had made up his mind that enterprise reform would be his priority, but he knew that Chinese economists still needed to search far and wide for new ideas if this latest goal were to succeed.

As this search continued, the intellectual ferment of the period produced several new policies that pointed toward longer-term reform goals. In 1986, the State Council introduced a set of regulations to define the ambiguous relationship of the PBOC, established 1948, to specialized banks, credit cooperatives, and new financial institutions, such as trust and investment companies. Nicholas Lardy has written that this was an important step on the bank's path to assuming "the supervisory and regulatory roles usually associated with central banks."[13] That autumn, the Party leadership also introduced a new law to regulate enterprise bankruptcy, a step toward creating a system in which the softened enterprise budget constraints could be hardened more effectively. Further, showing strong interest in modernizing China's financial system, several major cities reportedly began to experiment with the creation of small-scale capital markets, and state-owned firms received authorization to sell bonds. The leadership also made reforms to the labor system and lifted price controls on some consumer goods.[14] During this period of transition and turbulence after the 1984 Decision on the Reform of the Economic Structure, the incremental adjustments showed the near-term policy implications of the fierce intellectual debates and set the stage for more sweeping changes to come.

In 1986, Zhao Ziyang also spearheaded another important initiative that signaled China's efforts to join the international economic community: China applied to regain its membership in the General Agreement on Tariffs and Trade (GATT), of which it had been a founding member in 1947. The predecessor to the World Trade Organization (WTO), the GATT had requirements that were far more stringent than China was able to meet only ten years after Mao's death—but, as Wu Jinglian has written, "this very act signified China's determination to further open itself to the outside world."[15] China had been sending officials to attend GATT-run policy courses since 1980 and in both 1984 and 1985 China had invited the GATT legal adviser to run a seminar in China. In January 1986, Arthur Dunkel, director-general of the GATT, visited China to discuss what it would take for China to become a full member. During a meeting with Dunkel, Zhao Ziyang vigorously argued that China's "planned commodity economy" could fit with what Harold K. Jacobson and Michel Oksenberg called "the market-oriented principles of GATT." On July 14, 1986, China formally announced its intention to become a full member in the GATT.[16] Not until 2001 would China join the WTO.

The World Bank also remained central to Zhao's plans for China. As a result, 1986 was a banner year for Edwin Lim, the World Bank's first resident chief of mission in China. He had already enjoyed high standing in Beijing as a result of the success of the two major World Bank reports on China that had preceded the Bashan Conference and that remained frequently cited texts.[17] Lim's reputation received a considerable further boost as a result of the success of the Bashan Conference, and he continued to develop a close personal relationship with the premier.

On June 21, 1986, Lim was honored with an afternoon meeting at the Diaoyutai State Guesthouse in what the *People's Daily* described as "an amiable discussion in an unconstrained atmosphere" and a formal dinner. Zhao praised the bank's work and peppered Lim with questions on a wide range of topics, from wages to enterprise reform, making reference to Eastern Europe, Germany, South Korea, France, and the United Kingdom.[18] Lim sat with Zhao for four hours, as the pair talked in embroidered overstuffed chairs. At one point during their animated conversation, Zhao, in midsentence, illustrated a comment by pointing upward with his index finger, in a gesture reminiscent of Plato in Raphael's *School of Athens*, as Lim beamed. A camera clicked, capturing the moment. After the meeting, Zhao escorted Lim to the door, drawing astonished looks from Zhao's retinue—after all, the premier usually remained in place as his visitors departed. The next day, the photograph of Lim and Zhao talking appeared on the front page of the *People's Daily*.[19] The stature of this World Bank economist had risen to the level of a foreign dignitary and a personal friend of the primary guide of reform policy.[20]

The Bashan Conference became an important component of the bank's rising stature in China during the second half of the 1980s, but a tremendous amount of money was also at stake in this relationship. During the period of China's sixth five-year plan, 1981–1986, the World Bank provided over US$3 billion in loans to thirty projects in China, in addition to technical consultation on many projects.[21] By 1989, the number of approved projects would grow to sixty-nine, totaling over US$7.25 billion; in 1987–1988 alone, the World Bank committed to fourteen new projects in China at a total cost of US$1.42 billion, nearly 9 percent of the bank's total global lending in that year.[22] Pieter Bottelier, chief of the World Bank mission in China in the mid-1990s, noted that during this period, "The World Bank became China's largest single source of foreign capital, and China became the Bank's largest borrower."[23]

The World Bank provided the Chinese government with intellectual, technical, and financial support for reform. Of course, providing technology and financing was hardly unusual, but this variety of intellectual support was unique. In 1989, when the economist John Williamson would coin the term "Washington Consensus" to describe policies the World Bank (along with the International Monetary Fund and the U.S. Treasury Department) endorsed to deal with crises in developing countries in Latin America, the World Bank became seen as a bastion of neoliberalism, often with damaging results.[24] However, it is clear that in China, under Lim's guidance, the World Bank's intellectual support was offered primarily in response to specific Chinese requests for guidance and in accordance with China's needs and conditions; in Lim's words, it was "demand-driven."[25] Of course, the World Bank supported market reforms, and much of its policy input bolstered Chinese reformers. But rather than advancing an a priori or one-size-fits-all agenda, as the caricature of the Washington Consensus might suggest, the bank's recommendations for China were flexible and context-specific.

Yet this flourishing of international exchange, the shifts in Zhao's thinking it had helped to create, and the numerous policy implications did not mean that the reforms were progressing smoothly. Instead, intellectual turbulence on China's university campuses had reached a new peak of intensity in late 1986, cohering around frustrations at the lack of political reforms to accompany the economic reforms. Fang Lizhi, a prominent astrophysicist and university administrator, toured the country delivering speeches that called for democracy and education reform and he urged students to "look to the West for new models of intellectual commitment," as Orville Schell wrote in *The Atlantic* in 1988. In a November 1986 speech at Tongji University in Shanghai, Fang declared, "We must remold our society by absorbing influences from all cultures."[26] He continued, "The change in many people's outlook, including my own, came from seeing the outside world. . . . We discovered our backwardness and were enlightened." He declared China's socialist system a "failure."[27]

In early December, students at Fang's university in Hefei staged a series of short protests, which quickly spread to Beijing, Shanghai, and other major Chinese cities.[28] The Shanghai protests received particular attention after December 19, when students marched to the municipal government offices. According to one eyewitness, during the march, there were "abortive attempts at choruses of the 'Internationale,' to which few people appeared to know all the words."[29] Instead, the students had memorized slogans such as "Give me liberty or give me death."[30] At the same time, according to interviews, the majority of students did not want to strengthen the hand of the opponents of reforms or to undermine the progress of Deng Xiaoping, Hu Yaobang, and Zhao Ziyang. Instead, they sought to make clear that their views were based on liberal values and that they wanted to add their voices to calls for reforms, especially reforms of the political and education systems.[31]

In a speech in late December 1986, Bo Yibo, who had become closely allied with Chen Yun (holding at least three private tête-à-têtes in 1986, no small number for two ailing gerontocrats who were in and out of the hospital[32]), took a strong stance on these matters. He saw the unrest as directly linked to the students' fixation on foreign ideas and values, facilitated by intellectuals like Fang Lizhi. Chinese thinkers should not "consider all things foreign to be better than those in China. We must not think that the moon in foreign countries is fuller than in China. This is tantamount to forgetting historical factors and our own origins."[33] Several days later, Deng Xiaoping delivered a speech criticizing "bourgeois liberalization," giving these attacks his imprimatur.[34]

Bo Yibo had made clear that he believed any successful proposal on the future direction of the reforms needed to operate within the discourse not only of reform and economic development but also of Chinese "historical factors" and "origins." China's conservative elders seemed to believe that the student protesters in 1986 had lost touch with such "origins." A subsequent speech by Deng Liqun affirmed that these elders believed, with Deng Xiaoping's support, that "bourgeois liberalization" was behind the unrest. The protests gradually subsided as leaders of the Chinese Communist Party (CCP) made clear that participating in the protests would damage students' futures—but someone was going to have to pay.[35] In a private conversation in October, Deng Xiaoping had criticized the dogma-defending Deng Liqun for slanting Party documents "to the left" and undermining Hu Yaobang and Zhao Ziyang. But now the situation had changed.[36] Deng Xiaoping was completely "shocked" by the protests, Zhao Ziyang recalled, and he assembled a "Party life" meeting to assign blame. In addition to criticizing the intellectuals who had stirred up discontent, Deng placed the blame on Hu Yaobang. It was clear to the assembled leaders that Hu's days as general secretary were numbered.[37]

On January 2, 1987, Hu made an internal announcement that he was resigning as general secretary. But before publicly taking down Hu, the Party leadership first targeted certain intellectuals perceived to have instigated the students' discontent, most prominently Fang. He was accused of having "disseminated many erroneous statements reflecting 'bourgeois liberalization'" and "denying socialism, calling for complete westernization, and advocating the capitalist road." On January 12, 1987, he was fired from his job and expelled from the CCP. Four days later, on January 16, the Politburo publicly "accepted the resignation" of General Secretary Hu, who had held back from criticizing the student protesters and had refused to authorize Fang's dismissal. One senior leader, Xi Zhongxun, protested the decision— "Don't repeat what Mao did to us," he is alleged to have said—but the decision was final. The conservative leaders who had decried the protests as the result of "bourgeois liberalization" forced Hu to resign and designated Zhao Ziyang as his successor.[38]

According to some reports, Hu Yaobang's ouster had been a long time coming. Several accounts, including Zhao Ziyang's memoirs, claim Deng Xiaoping saw Hu Yaobang as responsible because, in 1984, at the fourth congress of the Chinese Writers' Association, he had allowed open elections without guidance from the Organization Department; the liberal "slate" elected in 1984 railed against Deng's policies to eliminate "bourgeois liberalization," anger that Deng evidently suspected had been festering until this episode in late 1986 due to Hu Yaobang's permissiveness.[39] As early as the summer of 1986, Deng Xiaoping had told the Party elders gathered for the annual conclave at the seaside resort of Beidaihe that he had made "a big mistake: he had misjudged Yaobang," recalled Zhao Ziyang, who believed this statement rendered Hu's fate inevitable—a matter of when, not if. (Some rumors suggested that Zhao had attempted to orchestrate or accelerate Hu's fall, a charge he vehemently denied.)[40] Conservative elders had also attacked Hu's interest in foreign ideas and foreign partners, saying, "A Communist Party's General Secretary should not be so enthusiastic about visiting capitalist countries."[41] Hu had mismanaged the crisis in late 1986 and the student protests, but he had also been guilty of the ideological failing of thinking that, as Bo Yibo had said, "the moon in foreign countries is fuller than that in China." Deng's "big mistake" had been to misjudge both of these qualities.

Zhao Ziyang was swiftly named general secretary and would serve as both general secretary and premier in the coming months. His power had increased, and he set about trying to limit the conservative tide attacking "bourgeois liberalization." Mirroring his strategy during the Campaign to Combat Spiritual Pollution earlier in the decade, Zhao insisted in remarks delivered on January 19 that these attacks should be limited to "political and ideological" work and should not involve economic work. On January 29, he went even farther, stating that opposing bourgeois liberalization should remain internal to the Party and focus mainly on political theory, rather than on policy. Even so, the conservative elders did not see Zhao himself as above attack. Li Xiannian sent a warning through Yang Shangkun, another Party elder: "Ziyang has learned too much foreign stuff. Continuing in this is unacceptable. You should tell him that."[42]

Learning "foreign stuff" had been an essential component of Zhao's policy-making process as premier. After purging Hu Yaobang, would conservatives next come after Zhao?

In early 1987, Deng was willing to let Hu fall, but he stepped in to curb criticism of Zhao and to support Hu's new apparent successor. In February, Deng drew attention to the Party congress scheduled for the end of that year and signaled his intention to continue on a reformist path. Speaking to leading members of the Central Committee, Deng said that, despite the "student disturbances," he believed that the Party leadership had been "much too cautious" in advancing reform:

> Why do some people always insist that the market is capitalist and only planning is socialist? Actually they are both means of developing the productive forces. So long as they serve that purpose, we should make use of them. If they serve socialism they are socialist; if they serve capitalism they are capitalist.[43]

This emphatic statement made plain Deng's frustration with Party conservatives. Although he had agreed that Hu had to go, Deng wanted to stress that his overall goals remained intact. He went even further, announcing a break with Chen Yun's economic ideology. Historically, Deng said, "We said that in a socialist economy planning was primary. We should not say that any longer."[44] This favorite phrase of Chen Yun's—emblematic of the overall ideological agenda of the conservative wing of the Party leadership—was no longer operative.

Reformist officials quickly moved to fill the space Deng and Zhao had cleared. In March, An Zhiwen of the System Reform Commission and Fang Weizhong, a leader in the State Planning Commission, presented a report to Zhao based on their consultations with a wide variety of Chinese economists. Calling for a transformation of China's "undeveloped" commodity economy, they drew attention to the diverse range of ideas then in circulation about for how to define the relationship between the plan and the market, prominently including a model of the economy in which "the state plan adjusts and controls the market through a variety of economic means, and, through the market, guides the enterprises."[45] This idea had gained attention at the Nanjing conference on the "goal model of the reform" in October 1986, where it had been debated in connection with Kornai's proposals. On March 21, 1987, following a discussion with Bo Yibo, Hu Qiaomu, and other senior officials, Zhao sent a memorandum to Deng Xiaoping on the drafting of the main work report for the Thirteenth Party Congress. On March 25, Deng approved the plan.[46]

Zhao Ziyang and his network of economists got to work crafting the Thirteenth Party Congress's work report and policy proposals. In April, Ma Hong and his staff at the Development Research Center (DRC) submitted a report (drafted by Wu Jinglian) to Zhao. They contended that a consensus had emerged that China's fundamental problem was an overexpansion of demand, although opinion remained divided on which "transitional symptoms" were most dangerous to the overall health of the Chinese economy. Assessing problems such as overissuance of currency and rises in commodity prices, the DRC report offered a long series of policy possibilities for Zhao to consider.[47]

Zhao's comments in response to the DRC report simultaneously referenced foreign economic ideas, revealing his familiarity with them, and declared that China's situation was unprecedented. Assessing the situation of China's enterprises, consumption, and wages, and wondering aloud whether it was investment or consumption that had been driving up China's inflation, Zhao explicitly referred to Bashan as a touchstone. But China would have to chart its own course based on "actual results," because no number of outside experts could prescribe policy remedies for China's distinctive problems.[48] Zhao's reference to the Bashan Conference in the intensive internal debates leading up to the Thirteenth Party Congress showed that these ideas were at the front of his mind as he planned China's reform strategy—and he was both drawing on this knowledge to formulate his proposals and pushing back against some of what the foreign economists argued in order to define what was unique about China's situation.

Despite the momentum of the reformers during this period, some conservative officials—deeply troubled by the student protests and emboldened by the purge of their longtime antagonist, Hu Yaobang—refused to fall into line. As news of Deng's statements dismissing the leftist notion of "planning as primary" spread throughout the Party, Deng Liqun, Hu Qiaomu, and others attacked both "speaking liberalism" and "doing liberalism," suggesting that the Chinese leadership should go after individuals whose actions were "doing liberalism," regardless of their outward ideological affiliations, in addition to punishing individuals such as Fang Lizhi, who had explicitly promoted liberal ideas.[49] Even more dramatically, that summer Zhao received a confidential letter from the Propaganda Department revealing that Deng Xiaoping's statements had led some of the department's bureau chiefs to realize they were facing a renewed focus on opposing the left and to cry out, "We must hold out and resist!" and "There is still no telling who will win!"[50]

Ideological conservatives were on the warpath, and it would take even more decisive action by Deng Xiaoping to put a stop to their resistance. On July 7, 1987, Deng summoned the top Party leadership to his home and said he had decided to remove one of China's most powerful conservative ideologues, Deng Liqun, from his positions at the Propaganda Department and in the Secretariat, because his opposition was undermining reform.[51] The man Deng Xiaoping had once called stubborn "like a Hunan mule" had seen his staunch resistance to reform become his undoing. Chen Yun continued to protect his close ally, ensuring that he still lived the luxurious life of a high official, but even Chen could not maintain his friend's influence on Chinese policy.[52]

With Deng's support, Zhao had reined in conservatives, solidified his power, and was calling for continued learning from abroad while staking out an ambitious agenda for the Party congress.[53] In policy terms, it was clear that over the previous year Zhao had begun to shift toward supporting the primacy of enterprise reform. But his ambitions for reform were large, and he realized that his newfound power would not, on its own, legitimate the sweeping agenda he hoped to usher in with the Thirteenth Party Congress. First, he needed to make an ideological breakthrough that would solidify Deng's dismissal of "planning as primary" and support a new wave of market reforms, without undermining China's socialist system and the CCP. "There had been no explanation" of the "theoretical basis for reform," Zhao recalled, and it was time: "Reform needed to be powerfully backed up with theory."[54]

After exhausting discussions, Zhao and his advisers devised an ingenious solution: Zhao would take a phrase that had been percolating among Chinese intellectuals for years and declare China was in the "initial" or "primary" stage of socialism. By embracing this idea, Zhao would not visibly undercut China's commitment to socialism but would shift the emphasis to the notion that China's historical moment—its current "stage"—was preliminary and evolving. As a result, increasing production became the indisputable and critical task so that China could in the future move to a more "advanced" stage of socialism. This "initial stage of socialism" thesis provided ideological justification for further market-oriented reforms without "sparking major theoretical debates," because it did not endorse capitalism or fundamentally question the basic tenets of China's system.[55] Deng used this phrase publicly on August 29, 1987, announcing, "The Thirteenth National Party Congress will explain what stage China is in: the primary stage of socialism."[56]

This conciliatory ideological proposal was especially important, given the serious distortions that emerged as a result of the reform policies. The dual-track price system had been a success, but tensions were high as production of key industrial commodities had climbed steadily even as the in-plan requirements remained basically unchanged; for example, production of steel increased by nearly 10 million metric tons between 1984 and 1987 (an increase of over 25 percent), essentially all of which was produced outside the plan.[57] Enterprise management remained a serious challenge, as attempts to boost autonomous decision-making foundered. A 1987 survey of 2,000 enterprises conducted by the Institute for Chinese Economic Structural Reform and the State Statistical Bureau (later renamed the National Bureau of Statistics) revealed that less than 5 percent had implemented the new management structure that Party officials had encouraged. This more competitive structure would have determined how the enterprise and its superiors divided up profits, selected managers, and compensated workers.[58] It was clear that hard choices would have to be made in the time ahead if the reform were to advance.

In the face of these challenges, the Chinese leadership continued to demonstrate interest in learning from European and North American economists. The Ford Foundation, for instance, received formal approval from the State Council to open a Beijing office in April 1987. A Ford Foundation official, Peter Geithner, who had built close relationships with Chinese economic officials like Chen Yizi, would lead the office. "According to CASS, we are the first foreign private foundation to be authorized to open an office in China," Geithner wrote proudly.[59] The Ford Foundation had provided millions of dollars to fund expert exchanges and academic study, and this new feather in its cap indicated that the Chinese had long-term plans for its role in the country.

Lim and the World Bank also organized seminars in 1986 and 1987 at Zhao Ziyang's request. These sessions, planned with the System Reform Commission, addressed specific functional issues (rather than the expansive scope of the Bashan Conference), targeting "financial system reform" and "state-owned enterprise reform," respectively.[60] The July 1987 seminar, also known as the Diaoyutai conference, discussed the modern corporation in the context of Chinese enterprise reform. The main Western participant was Peter Drucker, the management consultant and sociologist of the corporation; Chinese participants included Wu Jinglian, Zhou Xia-ochuan, and Guo Shuqing.[61] Drucker, for one, was not impressed with what he learned about Chinese enterprises—writing in the *Wall Street Journal* after he returned, "I doubt there is a single Chinese business that is actually in the black."[62] The seminars were clearly designed to follow up on particular issues raised at the Bashan Conference that the Chinese hoped to learn more about; although they did not play the transformational role of the 1985 conference, the simple fact that China's leading economic policy makers continued to reach out to the World Bank to organize formal exchanges of ideas with foreign economic experts attested to their sense of the usefulness of these interactions. As the 1987 International Seminar on State-Owned Enterprise Reform made clear, the problems of China's enterprises remained paramount in the minds of the country's economic policy makers.

That summer, Zhao Ziyang traveled to five Eastern European countries, including Hungary. Accompanied by several of his top aides, including An Zhiwen from the System Reform Commission and Wen Jiabao, the director of the CCP's General Office, Zhao was delighted to have the opportunity to display his detailed knowledge of the Hungarian reform process and to see for himself whether Hungary had "accomplished fully" the program of reforms that its leaders had laid out.[63] A Chinese Foreign Ministry official then stationed in Budapest recalled that Zhao believed the country to have "a better approach" and conditions "closer to ours" than other Eastern European countries.[64] Later that year, János Kádár, Hungary's leader, would return Zhao's visit, indicating the quick progress in the two countries' relations in the span of less than a decade since the first delegation of Chinese economists had traveled to inspect Hungarian socialism.[65]

During the same busy summer of 1987, at Zhao's direction, the CCP introduced an important new policy designed to harden budget constraints and diminish what Kornai termed the state's "paternalism": State-owned enterprises began to implement a contract responsibility system. Under this system, enterprises and the state set contractual obligations, guaranteeing the state a certain portion of the enterprise revenue but otherwise generally allowing enterprises to make independent operational decisions. Enterprise managers and government agencies would negotiate the terms of the contracts, an arrangement intended to eliminate "ratchet effects," in which enterprises produced at minimum levels and lowballed any estimates of their capacity so that planners set lower, easier-to-fulfill production targets. The new model of a contract responsibility system, which Hu Yaobang had advocated in the early 1980s, went beyond any previous management reform; it came closer to pleasing Li Yining than Wu Jinglian, although it did not target the more basic issue of ownership. By July 1987, over 50 percent of state-owned enterprises had adopted the system.[66]

Economists associated with Li Yining's enterprise reform group were frustrated. One of these reformers, Zhang Xuejun, launched an attack on Wu Jinglian in August 1987. He presented "János Kornai's theory of shortages" as already canonical and wrote, "As everyone knows, shortages, or a sellers' market, is a chronic illness of our traditional structure."[67] However, he positioned his fundamental disagreement with Wu in terms of Wu's reliance on the example of Hungary. Accusing Wu of a misguided emphasis on "price reform, or, to be more exact, on price readjustment as part of a 'package,'" Zhang attributed this error to a fixation on lessons from Hungary, because "Hungary is a typical case of [economic] structural change occurring through a package deal." In China, however, Zhang claimed such a "package deal" (meaning the "coordinated reform" beginning with the price reform that Wu Jinglian advocated) would not actually heighten competition among enterprises, but would only raise prices.[68] Zhang thus suggested that Wu's fixation on Kornai had led him down the wrong path with respect to China's reform.

Wu fired back, but not against allegations that he had learned too much from Hungary. Rather, he responded that Zhang had distorted the Hungarian experience:

> In order to undermine the importance of the price reform to the overall success of the reform, Comrade Zhang Xuejun informs his readers that Hungary, at the initial stage of its reform, "abolished all mandatory plans and even, on the basis of the price system already being fundamentally straightened out,

delegated to the enterprises the power to set the prices of most products." This conclusion . . . has absolutely no proof in history. It is only Comrade Zhang Xuejun's fabrication. . . . [On the contrary,] the excessive "compromises" Hungary made in its price reform, and the resulting delay in the formation of a reasonable price system, were one of its principal errors in making strategic choices about reform.[69]

Wu boldly asserted that intellectual support for his proposals for China could be found in the "history" of Hungarian reform. He blasted Zhang's suggestion that the Hungarian experience did not apply to China's circumstances, suggesting that Zhang had deliberately distorted Hungary's experiences; by implication, Wu proposed that his critics needed to understand international ideas of reform better in order to present proper criticisms of his proposals for China. In other words, the debate between these two men, each representative of the country's major reform-oriented factions, took shape in part around conflicting claims about Hungarian ideas and experiences.

The acrimonious tone of the argument between Wu and Zhang revealed, more than anything else, that both groups of reformers realized they were at a crucial period of ideological and political transformation, in which successful ideas could have a tremendous and swift impact on official policy. The "initial stage of socialism" thesis was having exactly its desired effect. By the eve of the Thirteenth Party Congress, Zhao and Deng had cleared the path for a major event.

Advances by Chinese reformers in the 1980s culminated in a series of breakthroughs articulated at the Thirteenth Party Congress in October 1987.[70] The CCP elite gathered from around the vast country, assembling in orderly rows in the Great Hall of the People, a massive hammer and sickle hanging over the rostrum, where the Party's new leadership sat together surveying the crowd.[71]

The top leadership group that emerged made one area of the congress's significance obvious: many of the oldest members of the Politburo retired, replaced by a new generation of leaders, in-

cluding Shanghai's mayor, the sixty-one-year-old Jiang Zemin.
Deng Liqun had made a last-ditch bid for membership on the Politburo, but he was not selected. All of the CCP's "Eight Immortals" were now officially retired from the Politburo Standing Committee, though Deng Xiaoping retained his post as chairman of the
Central Military Commission, which allowed him to wield continued influence.[72]

Despite these personnel changes, the true breakthrough of the
1987 congress was ideological, oriented toward mapping out reform
policy. Zhao's work report, the congress's primary policy document,
revealed how far Party views about the proper relationship between
the state and the market had come since the codification of the
"planned commodity economy" in 1984.[73] As the congress convened
on October 25, 1987, Zhao began his report by setting out a new
characterization of the Chinese economy, framed by the "initial stage
of socialism" thesis. "We must gradually shrink the scope of com-
pulsory plans and gradually transform to a management system of
primarily indirect management," he declared. Then, in a sweeping
gesture, Zhao redefined the goal of the reforms: "Overall, the new
system must be one in which 'the state manages the market, and the
market guides the enterprises.'" By endorsing this slogan, Zhao established an expansive and pro-market interpretation of the "planned
commodity economy." After years of debate, Zhao and the network
of economists he supported had achieved a landmark change that solidified the central role of the market.[74]

Zhao elaborated on the meaning of the initial stage of socialism.
The three key goals endorsed in Zhao's report were that the economy
should move toward giving full play to "market forces," that enterprises of all ownership types should be fully "guided" by the market,
and that macroeconomic controls should be "primarily indirect." Remarkably, these conclusions directly mirrored the three main policy
lessons described in the Bashan Report. At the same time, it was clear
that the meaning of the slogan in the 1987 document had been developed and refined, in part through debates over the meaning of the
Bashan Conference and Kornai's ideas, especially his goal model of
macroeconomic management with microeconomic marketization,
which it closely resembled. With a full-throated endorsement of the

essential role of the market, Zhao solidified the reformers' gains and, ideologically, pushed beyond what many had thought possible.

Possible—or desirable. Not everyone was pleased with Zhao's report. Chen Yun, in particular, was evidently dismayed. As Zhao took the stage to read the text aloud, Chen stood up from his seat and, hobbled by age and illness but resolute as ever, walked straight out of the room.[75] The fight over China's future was far from over.

9

The Narrows of the River

⟨⟨⟩⟩ On November 1, 1987, the Thirteenth Party Congress came to an exuberant close. Zhao Ziyang had triumphed in introducing a new ideology that would legitimate the next phase of economic reform. That day, the sixty-eight-year-old Zhao spoke to the press corps. One participant recalled that he was "preternaturally tranquil" and "beamed with a relaxed confidence." Flanked by his leadership team, including the new acting premier, Li Peng, Zhao wore a natty double-breasted pinstripe suit—albeit one proudly "made in China." All the members of the Politburo's new Standing Committee wore Western attire; the Mao jackets always worn by Deng Xiaoping, Chen Yun, and members of the elder generation were notably absent.[1]

But this did not mean the elders planned to stand by idly. In his new job as Party general secretary, Zhao had less direct control over economic policy than as premier. He reportedly believed he would be able to dominate his much less experienced replacement, Li Peng, but, even at the time, Zhao's view probably ignored the fact that Li was the handpicked protégé of Chen Yun and Yao Yilin, who opposed many of the reforms—and events would certainly demonstrate that Zhao had underestimated the consequences of Li's appointment.[2] At a mid-November meeting of economic officials from the System Reform Commission and other government agencies, Zhao said he believed price reform would take "a long time" and he emphasized carrying out enterprise reforms.[3] This policy orientation was consistent with the views he had espoused earlier in 1987 before the congress.

At the same time, Zhao and his reformist lieutenants were searching for ways to make good on the ambitions of the Thirteenth Party Congress. Shortly after the conclusion of the congress, Zhao invited eight prominent economists, including Liu Guoguang, Li Yining, and Wu Jinglian, to organize research teams to design their own "1988–1995 Medium-Term Reform Proposals," which would provide a buffet of concrete options to help him flesh out the policy direction set in 1987.[4]

The newest bold idea Zhao endorsed was what came to be known as the "coastal development strategy." Beginning in June 1987, a researcher at the State Planning Commission (SPC) named Wang Jian had begun to publish articles that argued China should take advantage of a "beneficial international cycle," in which the coastal areas would lead the country by developing export-oriented industry, using international markets both to purchase inputs and to sell finished products. As these coastal industries accumulated foreign exchange, they could attract foreign capital and technology to speed up the development of China's domestic industry, which would in turn produce funds the government could spend on fostering rural development.[5]

In essence, this idea took what was already happening in China's special economic zones (SEZs), which had their roots in Gu Mu's 1978 trip to Western Europe, and systematized that successful model into a framework for economic development in the period ahead. As early as 1984, Zhao had called for the faster development of the coastal regions, which he believed could serve as both a model and an engine for the whole country's growth. In September, just before the Party congress, Zhao ordered a research group to further investigate the feasibility of the coastal development strategy.[6] At an early November meeting designed to set the agenda for 1988, Zhao cited Wang Jian's idea by name; he ended the meeting by praising it as "very reasonable" and calling for additional investigation, although Zhao would later claim that he had devised the idea himself.[7] In the winter of 1987, Zhao went on "inspection tours of the coastal regions," as he recalls in his memoir, where he concluded that the "coastal development strategy" could propel China to extraordinary economic growth and become a signature agenda of his tenure as general secretary.[8]

The coastal development strategy—in particular, its "two ends extending abroad" strategy, which stressed importation of raw materials that could be turned into manufactures and sold abroad—revealed how Chinese economists had studied the experiences of the four Asian tigers (Singapore, Taiwan, South Korea, and Hong Kong).[9] These countries had used an export-led growth strategy to industrialize rapidly in the decades after World War II, earning worldwide acknowledgment for astonishingly rapid transformations. This "takeoff" was particularly appealing to Chinese officials, who, in Deng's memorable phrase, wanted to see "several more Hong Kongs" emerge on the mainland.[10] Chinese attention focused on Singapore and Hong Kong, "drawing on their experience" to design policies that could work in China. However, Zhao stated clearly that the coastal development strategy, with its focus on driving nationwide progress using the coastal regions as an engine, should not be viewed as mimicking the Asian tigers: "They are small, and we are big," he said in February 1988. "They are capitalist, and we are socialist."[11]

While the coastal development strategy united the lessons of Western European export zones that had laid the intellectual foundations for the SEZs with the experiences of the Asian tigers, conservatives voiced their displeasure with references to these small capitalist countries. "We cannot compare ourselves to the 'four little dragons,'" Chen Yun maintained. "We have over 800 million peasants; this is always our starting point in considering a problem." Chen noted that he had never been to an SEZ but said he had taken a "keen interest" in them and would follow their progress closely.[12] Perhaps with this end in mind, Chen's ally Deng Liqun traveled to inspect the Shenzhen SEZ in 1988.[13]

Meanwhile, Chen's protégés Yao Yilin and Li Peng criticized the risk of "overheating" as a result of the rapid takeoff that would accompany export-led development.[14] Indeed, the appeal to some reformers of rapid development tapped into wider and longstanding controversy about the perils of inflation, which other countries that had attempted export-led growth models (particularly in Latin America) had encountered. A delegation of Chinese economists would travel to Latin America later that year for further study.

Zhao began a full-scale rollout of the coastal development strategy at the beginning of 1988. After a laudatory front-page interview with Wang Jian was printed in the *Guangming Daily*, the *Economic Daily* ran a front-page article on Wang's ideas on January 5, 1988, accompanied by support from other economists.[15] Zhao submitted a detailed report on the strategy to the rest of the central leadership. On January 23, Deng indicated that he "completely supported it."[16] When Zhao traveled to Davos, Switzerland, to attend the World Economic Forum's annual conference in early February, he prominently featured both the coastal development strategy and Wang's "beneficial international cycle" during a televised address.[17] Only a few days later, on February 6, the Politburo formally adopted the "coastal development strategy," presenting it as a crucial means of eventually developing "self-reliant national construction."[18]

The characterization of the coastal development strategy as a step on the path toward "self-reliance" (a strategy Zhao had used earlier in the 1980s to justify international exchanges) mirrored Zhao's ploy with the "initial stage of socialism" formulation. In both cases, he allowed important conservative goals—"socialism" and "self-reliance"— to remain unchallenged in theory, even as he innovated new ideas and policies that might be at odds with these goals. By lengthening the time frame and arguing that his policies were merely necessary deviations on the overall path that conservatives wanted to follow, Zhao gave himself space to experiment without provoking sufficient conflict to kill the newborn projects that were not yet producing good results.

As Zhao promoted the coastal development strategy in the early months of 1988, prominent reformist economists enjoyed a sense of great possibility. Xue Muqiao, speaking at a January forum of economists, praised the "initial stage of socialism" thesis as capable of "eradicating dogmatism and the ossified economic pattern" of "counterposing planning to market," while also maintaining China's commitment to Marxism. In Xue's view, Zhao had helped to forge a new synthesis of plan and market.[19]

Xue also made clear that his study of capitalist countries had contributed to a significant reappraisal of the condition of workers under capitalism: "Globally speaking, today's capitalist world has changed a lot since Marx's writing," Xue said. It is now possible "for workers under a capitalist system to considerably improve their living standards." However, China remained a socialist system, and Xue emphasized that Zhao's "breakthrough" was primarily conceptual.[20] It remained to be seen whether Zhao would succeed in reworking China's system along the lines he had promised in 1987.

Opponents of these policies were closing ranks. For one thing, many Party officials thought that the timing was not right. In mid-January 1988, officials from the Ministry of Finance and planning agencies delivered reports to Li Peng that raised concerns that rising prices were negatively affecting the entire financial system.[21] Shortly thereafter, the State Price Office submitted a memorandum declaring it was "already not possible to control the rise in commodity prices to be capped at approximately 6 percent," the planned goal, which might mean that the economy was on the verge of overheating. In a discussion responding to these reports, Yao Yilin admitted he was "nervous" about China's policy direction.[22] Yet reform-oriented leaders disputed the negative assessments by Yao and others. Tian Yuan, who led the State Council Research Center on Economic, Technological, and Social Development, was dismissive of these concerns, saying, "The conditions are very good." Tian's view came from a study of China's price system he and his State Council research team had conducted and would subsequently publish; in their assessment, partial reforms would doom the process unless dramatic reforms moving beyond the dual-track price system were quickly implemented.[23] It is important to note that for reformers like Tian, their disagreement had two dimensions: first, they disagreed with the conservatives' analysis of data suggesting that the risk of inflation was high; second, they more generally disagreed with the view (held by both conservatives and many reformers) that inflation was dangerous, so either way they were not seriously concerned about the risk of overheating. Their arguments sometimes blurred the distinction between the two viewpoints, but as we saw earlier, one of the most substantial disagreements within the reformist camp was over the relative risks of inflation. This debate became more acute in 1988 than ever before.

When the SPC relayed these disagreements to Zhao in a late January presentation, he fundamentally did not support the attitude Li Peng and Yao Yilin had taken. He emphasized that only focusing on a rise in commodity prices was "missing the forest for the trees."[24]

These skirmishes continued into February, when Yao warned that if
the inflation that China was experiencing was not firmly controlled,
"malignant inflation will be unavoidable." Privately, Li and Yao argued that the coastal development strategy and its emphasis on
speeding up development was risky because it might trigger economic
overheating, which Zhao had told them was a "needless" concern.
The rapid growth of industry was basically "healthy," Zhao said
firmly, and would not produce an overheated economic situation
like the 1985 episode.[25] Conservatives led by Li and Yao hoped to see
some form of retrenchment, but Zhao and his allies fundamentally
disputed their diagnosis of the risks of inflation and instead sought
to forge ahead.

However, the pushback on Zhao's assessment of the economy continued. At the second plenum of the Thirteenth Central Committee, held March 15–17, 1988, Liu Guoguang openly disagreed
with Zhao's report.[26] In response to Zhao's sunny assessment, Liu
said the rise in prices that China was experiencing was in fact inflationary and not just a matter of an imbalance in supply and demand
of a few goods that could be addressed by tweaking prices. Rather,
Liu saw an excess supply of currency and a concomitant fall in the
value of currency.[27] These arguments, even if based on a genuine
professional assessment and not political motivations, were exactly
what the conservatives hoped to hear. At a meeting of the National
People's Congress in March, Li Peng and his allies continued to
argue for their interpretation that China's economy was facing a period of serious inflationary risks, which would mean that the timing
was not right for an aggressive reform push.[28]

The disagreement underway was, however, not only over interpreting indicators like price rises. Although he had expressed cau-
tion about excessively rapid growth rates earlier in the decade, Zhao
now began to signal that he did not regard inflation as a serious
risk. In an environment in which several of his advisers, including
Tian Yuan and Zhu Jiaming, had portrayed inflation as benign or
even as a positive sign that growth policies were working correctly,
Zhao's view can be understood as a direct outgrowth of the policy
advice he was receiving. On April 2, meeting with senior economists to discuss price reform, Zhao said he believed that if com-

modity prices and wages were to rise significantly as the economy developed, "I think that doesn't seem so terrible."[29]

Zhao's suggestion that inflation might not be "so terrible" was bold in the context of socialist economics, but he knew it was not anathema in the experience of other developing countries. In particular, Chinese reformers (especially the economic official Zhu Jiaming) had previously cited the experience of the Latin American countries, which were apparently successfully enduring high rates of inflation alongside high rates of growth, although this view about "beneficial inflation" had been out of vogue in China since the Bashan Conference in 1985. As he pushed forward the high-growth coastal development strategy in an already inflationary environment, Zhao Ziyang began to show interest in Zhu Jiaming's views—and, in late April 1988, Zhu Jiaming and Chen Yizi set out for Latin America to learn more.

It is important to note that the Chinese Communist Party's (CCP's) ideological justification for learning from developing countries such as Brazil and Argentina was different from its engagement with developed capitalist partners like the United States and the United Kingdom. When Deng Xiaoping met with President João Baptista de Oliveira Figueiredo of Brazil on May 29, 1984, Deng observed that China "shares a common destiny with all Third World countries. China will never seek hegemony or bully others, but will always side with the Third World."[30] These comments echoed the Party's three worlds theory—including the "first world" countries of the United States and the Soviet Union and the "second world" of other developed countries, as well as China and its "third world" compatriots—which was usually attributed to Mao but had been forcefully explicated to an international audience by Deng at his 1974 speech to the United Nations.[31] Thus, Chinese reformers were using the legacy of Mao's worldview to argue for a distinctly non-Maoist market-led growth policy. This offers another excellent illustration of the strategy of leaving a Party doctrine unchallenged in theory, such as Zhao had used with the "initial stage of socialism," even as reformers innovated new policies that seemed at odds with those goals.

Zhu Jiaming, Chen Yizi, and their delegation left Beijing on April 26, 1988. The level of development they saw in Rio de Janeiro,

Brasília, and São Paolo astonished them, Chen Yizi recalled. In Brasilia, they met with Antônio Delfim Netto, often called "the father of the Brazilian economic miracle"; Delfim Netto described how foreign investment had helped power Brazil's economic growth. In Chile, Chen observed widespread satisfaction with the economic governance of Augusto Pinochet's authoritarian regime, because, he noted with admiration, the dictator had said, "Whoever can earn a doctorate from a famous European or American university can be a minister."[32] As they traveled, the delegation actively debated what they were learning. From the Chinese consulate in São Paolo, they sent a telegram back to Beijing that, as Zhu recalled, informed the Beijing leadership that they believed Brazil's experience definitively proved that inflation was not necessarily harmful and would not always lead to economic crisis.[33] Zhu, it seemed, had found what he was looking for.[34]

Upon returning to China, Chen and Zhu both sought to publicize what they had learned. Chen briefed Zhao on the trip, focusing on Delphim Netto's views on foreign investment and inflation. "Inflation will exist in any country that undergoes rapid economic development, and this includes socialist countries. The currency inflation caused by the rise in investment and consumption is especially hard to avoid, especially when the issue of enterprise property rights has not been resolved," Chen told Zhao. "Of course, we are not encouraging inflation, but rather we are recognizing its reality and its extent," he added. In Brazil and Argentina, "People are accustomed to this. In contrast, because our prices have remained the same for decades, people are less willing to accept any increased prices."[35] Zhu put it in plainer terms: "It seems impossible to have both low inflation and high economic growth."[36] Yet other reformers fired back, attacking Zhu and his allies as dangerously eager to pursue rapid growth in an inflationary environment.

To make these arguments, Guo Shuqing, the protégé of Wu Jinglian who had been one of the youngest attendees at the Bashan Conference, returned to what he had learned on the river. He wrote that a wide range of Eastern and Western European policies during the period since World War II had demonstrated that "one-sided pursuit of a high-speed growth policy is detrimental—even devastating—to the economic system." "China's reform was launched after the accumulated bitter lessons of Eastern Europe," and because China was particularly eager to avoid economic losses, "a significant group of Chinese officials and scholars kept in mind what our Eastern European colleagues had told us and vigilantly watched out for [those problems]." Even though China's growth had taken off much more quickly than in those comparative cases, Guo made it clear that he believed Zhu's favored cases in the Latin American developing countries were not applicable to China, which had learned much more from countries transitioning from socialism.[37]

To better understand the substance of the disagreements over inflation, two historical factors are important to keep in mind. First, the CCP leadership never forgot that inflation had helped facilitate the collapse of the Guomindang (Nationalist Party) in 1948 and 1949 and the success of the Chinese revolution, a lesson in the serious risks that inflation posed to political stability.[38] Second, most Chinese economists had lived through decades with state-set prices and had little experience with markets in which inflation was not systematically repressed by government fiat. China's economists believed that this problem of "repressed inflation" was a distinctive problem that socialist economies faced—but they disagreed on the fundamental question of whether inflation was caused by excess money supply or by imbalances between aggregate supply and aggregate demand.[39] As Zhu and Chen's case made clear, Chinese economists also disagreed about whether inflation was beneficial or harmful for economic growth. Zhu was clearly in the minority; most Chinese economists believed that inflation created shortages of resources and social problems, and had long-term "corrosive" effects on the economy.[40] Yet all sides had little recent evidence from China upon which to draw because the country's price and fiscal systems had only recently been reformed.[41] Economic "overheating" was one thing, but Chinese economists were divided over whether the country's economy had experienced a major period of inflation since the "reform and opening" had begun, one of many reasons they repeatedly turned to foreign experts and foreign experiences for diagnosis and advice.

By May 1988, however, two countervailing forces from a high level of the economic policy-making apparatus overtook the economists' debates about inflation. Deng Xiaoping, still the paramount leader and increasingly aware that market reforms would define his legacy, had begun to call for implementing a major round of price and wage reforms. "It is better to endure short-term pain than to endure long-term pain," he said.[42] Deng's push for quick, painful price reform butted up against CCP conservatives who wanted to slow the progress of reform and focus on consolidating central control. That same May, Premier Li Peng downgraded the role of the System Reform Commission, shrinking its ability to participate in the policy-making process and increasing its "advisory" function.[43] Yao Yilin's status as a CCP Cassandra seemed confirmed that month when consumer prices in Beijing rose by at least 30 percent.[44] But Deng continued his calls for rapid price reform.

Zhao was under pressure from all sides. He attempted to continue business as usual, meeting with the Central Finance and Economics Leading Small Group to formulate policies that would flesh out the 1987 Thirteenth Party Congress document and calling for "the establishment of the new order of a socialist commodity economy," but pressure on him continued to grow.[45] On May 12, Chen Yun made widely publicized remarks from Zhejiang province, criticizing an excessive focus on "fast results" and opining that China's leaders needed to do a better job of studying Marxist philosophy.[46] Zhao, long criticized as an insufficiently orthodox Marxist, was clearly among Chen's intended audience.

The day after Chen's comments, Zhao held a meeting with some of his senior economic advisers, including Ma Hong and An Zhiwen. He revealed that he was still struggling to decide how to view the situation with commodity prices and how to handle price and wage reforms. Admitting that "this year commodity prices are too high," Zhao said he now understood, "If commodity prices rise, then you also have an income problem." His orders followed a familiar pattern: "Research how this problem has been approached internationally," he said.[47]

As his researchers got to work, Zhao spoke to the Politburo Standing Committee, attempting to preempt a new wave of criticism by endorsing Deng's calls for price reform. "A socialist commodity economy is our program, and market adjustments are mandatory," he said, "but without rationalizing prices, market adjustments are just empty talk." In this way, "Yugoslavia, Hungary, and Poland all put the cart before the horse," Zhao said.[48] He thus framed his call for "rationalizing prices" as a way to avoid the costly errors of the socialist transition in Yugoslavia, Hungary, and Poland—about which China had learned from the likes of Aleksandr Bajt, János Kornai, and Włodzimierz Brus—comparative cases that showed the dangers to CCP authority that could come from unsuccessful economic reform efforts.

With the Politburo scheduled to meet on May 30, Zhao saw his chance to make a case for pushing forward with reforms, even in the face of rising prices. He called for taking risks, saying the economy was in good enough shape and waiting would lead to a missed opportunity. "The Eastern European experience demonstrates that if you miss a good opportunity and wait for the speed [of growth] to come down before moving ahead with reforms," problems including political instability might emerge, he said. Shifting geographies, Zhao continued, "[Our prices] go up 15 percent, and our debates become horribly mixed up. In Brazil, they go up 15 percent in one month, and they get through it."[49] Advancing the role of the market under the framework of the "socialist commodity economy" was the only permanent solution to China's woes, Zhao reiterated; other options were merely "temporary."[50]

Some officials at the May 30 Politburo meeting made even stronger claims, following from Zhao's call for risk taking and emboldened by Deng's statements. According to one participant, Li Tieying contended that sweeping price reform would create a smoothly functioning market economy, even without private ownership. Zhao raised concerns about Li's argument, especially because no feasibility studies had been conducted.[51] Xue Muqiao urged that price reform commence the following year and be carried out over three years, and An Zhiwen evidently agreed.[52] Zhao's call for risk taking signaled to the entire Politburo that he was planning to forge ahead with his agenda in the summer of 1988, and his references to a remarkably wide range of other countries' economies—from those in Eastern Europe to Brazil—showed that he intended to draw on international experience in defining his policies.[53]

Yet Zhao's calls for confidence in the future were met with a mixed reception, even among reformers. In particular, the atmosphere of ideological openness his leadership had fostered also allowed for unprecedented speculation about the underlying causes of the country's economic woes. In June 1988, a shatteringly iconoclastic perspective exploded into these discussions. China Central Television (CCTV), the state-run broadcaster that was primarily the domain of propaganda, broadcast a six-part television documentary called *River Elegy*, which scoured China's millennia-old civilization—usually the recipient of reverential treatment—and found it wanting. Using the slow-flowing, loess-filled Yellow River as a symbol of China's backwardness, the narrator intoned, "We must create a brand new civilization, one which cannot flow from the Yellow River. . . . [Our civilization] needs a good scrubbing by the great flood," which arrived from the West in the form of "industrial civilization." This new "civilization" was unabashedly capitalist. "Only healthy markets can link opportunity, equality, and competition," it said, praising Zhao and his decisions at the Thirteenth Party Congress. Suggesting that Karl Marx's predictions of the death of capitalism were flatly wrong, the documentary voiced optimism that reform could advance in China if the Chinese people turned away from the "backwardness" that the Yellow River symbolized and embraced the market- and Western-oriented values represented by the "blue ocean."

Indeed, in addition to indicting Chinese civilization as fundamentally flawed, *River Elegy* called for entrusting more of China's fate to two particularly pro-reform groups: intellectuals and entrepreneurs. It praised the SEZs, especially Shenzhen, as the forefront of ending China's backwardness, turned to the literal and symbolic sea. Even so, *River Elegy* voiced uncertainty about whether success would be possible. "Even if the great Lord [John Maynard] Keynes were to come back to life, he could do nothing" about China's economy, the narrator noted. With more than 200 million viewers, *River Elegy* exposed an extraordinarily large audience to ideas previously confined to relatively rarified circles in the policy debates of the period.[54] "It may be the single most-watched documentary in the history of television," writes historian Rana Mitter. Embracing capitalism and denigrating the value of "Chinese characteristics" at a moment of perilous inflation and possible price reform, *River Elegy* offered a substantial challenge to China's official ideology and the emergent official narrative about the goals of the reforms. Zhao evidently enjoyed the documentary and recommended that others view it.[55]

Around the same time that *River Elegy* was first broadcast, the eight teams of economists Zhao had assigned to prepare the "1988–1995 Medium-Term Reform Proposals" presented their results. All endorsed the goals of Zhao's 1987 report—and "none of them supported the policy to start radical reform [of prices] immediately," recalled one former official.[56] Wu Jinglian worked with his frequent collaborator Zhou Xiaochuan to devise a proposal that strongly advocated price reform as the key link in the overall reforms, but they did not say that price reform should begin immediately because of the inflationary environment then prevalent. Li Yining agreed on the postponement, but argued that his enterprise shareholding reform should precede price liberalization. Liu Guoguang, meanwhile, proposed a three-year agenda of economic stabilization, a strikingly cautious and middle-of-the-road proposal clearly intended to be maximally politically palatable.[57]

Wu recalled, "There were no principal differences among the economists on the basic issues regarding establishing a market economy in China. However, each person had a different understanding of how markets operate," as well as "the required steps and sequence of implementation."[58] Li Yining took a different view of the matter. In a furious article attacking Wu's proposed "required steps" toward price reform, he wrote, "Those economists who advocate price reform as the main line do not understand China's conditions but, rather, are indiscriminately copying from the market and price theories of Western economics." He also attacked the same economists' reliance on Kornai—they "only say whatever he says."[59] Li leveraged his ostensible commitment to "China's conditions" to denounce his policy opponents for advocating Westernization. In the heat of a domestic political debate, Li—who had been and would continue to be an important channel for introducing Western economic knowledge to China—introduced an ideological posture in a vehement attempt to win his argument. However, attacks by Li and the consensus among the economists against immediate price reform failed to sway Deng Xiaoping, who ramped up his calls for price reform, urging CCP leaders to move boldly.[60]

Yet at this critical juncture in China's economic reforms, Yao Yilin, the cautious conservative and ally of Chen Yun, was given the task of leading the State Council group dedicated to formulating a price reform plan—rather than Zhao, who was now too senior, or Li Tieying, who might have been perceived as too enthusiastic. One former State Council policy maker recalled that the conservative staff on Yao's group largely excluded reformist economists—and alleged that Chen Yun, who had remained on the sidelines throughout the debates, secretly had the SPC simultaneously prepare an austerity plan that would be ready if the price reform did not succeed.[61] Zhao, for his part, perceived that Yao Yilin was making decisions behind his back and trying to sideline him.[62] Meanwhile, in his usual fashion, Deng remained distant from the gnarled policy details, simply expressing an attitude that he expected his lieutenants to follow loyally.[63] However, in this crucial case, it was clear that Deng did not have the wholehearted support of his economic policy-making apparatus.

Indeed, that summer Zhao continued to worry out loud about Deng's inclination to favor price reform without simultaneously implementing large-scale enterprise reforms. Zhao issued a warning at a meeting of the Central Finance and Economics Leading Small Group on July 11 and repeated it again on July 20, stating that some comrades mistakenly believed "a market system would appear after a price reform without reform of the public sector," but this was impossible.[64] As the Chinese leaders gathered at the seaside resort of Beidaihe, they had not reached any clear substantive agreement about when and how to carry out price reform.

At this summer conclave, ensconced between the low sandy beaches of the Bohai Sea and the cypress-covered slopes of Lianfeng Mountain, Deng made his case for price reform. The meetings encountered such serious disagreement that they briefly ended on July 28, as heated tempers cooled and policy makers conducted "further research."[65] From August 5 to 9, Li Peng hosted a State Council meeting with Politburo members that included presentations by top officials from the SPC, the Ministry of Finance, and People's Bank of China (PBOC), among other government organs, striking a decidedly cautious note about the near-term prospects for the Chinese economy.[66] After the Politburo assembled in Beidaihe and the meetings resumed from August 15 to 17, Yao Yilin presented his research group's report on prices and wages. Yao talked about a multiyear time frame for price reform, projecting that 1989 would be a "new start" and discussing a strategy that included freeing steel prices and raising consumer prices.[67] Intense debates continued during the August session, with Zhao stressing that the CCP needed to "prevent the circumstances that had occurred in Eastern Europe" when those countries had failed to carry out lasting price reform. Yet Zhao allegedly voiced his optimism that the reform could succeed, saying that China's economy was "more vibrant, with clearer theoretical guidance for reform" than the economies in the Eastern European countries. Still, he warned that inflation would be the "biggest hurdle" and he worried aloud about the potentially "significant" consequences if the reform failed.[68]

Deng demonstrated his continuing authority by prevailing over any internal disagreements, and, by August 19, the Politburo had decided to support a plan for immediate, sweeping price decontrols. Although some leaders at the Beidaihe meetings had underlined the need for "prudent" news reporting, in the words of Xi Zhongxun (the former Guangdong leader and father of current President Xi Jinping), that same day the Xinhua News Agency announced the decision in bold language, with prominent items published in the *People's Daily* and broadcast on television.[69]

A crisis immediately followed. As consumers faced the prospect of soaring prices and pent-up inflation exploding throughout the economy, fear drove an extraordinary spate of bank runs and panic buying. One such scene broke out at the Qingshan Friendship Store in Wuhan, which sold gold. It was a cinematic tableau: crowds of consumers crashed against the store's tightly sealed metal gate, their fingers forced through the gaps, rattling the bars and grasping for the gold inside. Their hands waved thick wads of RMB bills, urgently withdrawn from bank deposits, and shouts came from all directions as they clamored for attention. Outside, men fought violently to the front of the mob, climbing on top of others, stepping on people's heads with their shoes, and gripping the doorframe for support. The frantic saleswoman inside grabbed their cash as quickly as she could, doling out as much 24-karat gold as the shop possessed. The price of gold had risen, almost overnight, to RMB 140 per gram and it was expected to rise even higher as people tried to convert their cash into precious metal.[70]

Scenes like the gold frenzy in Wuhan were replicated throughout the country, pushing China to the brink. One woman in Shanghai, interviewed in front of a crowd lining up at a department store, said, "I took my money out of the bank and bought a bed. . . . I already have a bed at home, I really didn't need to buy a bed [but] everyone is buying them, and I'm afraid that prices will rise."[71] Other reports described frantic consumers buying "enough matches to last twenty years," as well as cotton shirts and soap, and a "toilet paper crisis" in Beijing, where some people bought as many as fifty rolls at once.[72] Bank runs and spending sprees for electronics in the northern city of Harbin led, according to local authorities, to the largest bank withdrawals since the founding of the People's Republic of China (PRC) thirty-nine years earlier.[73] Rather than evincing confidence in the regime, Chinese consumers responded to the news of price reform with a show of extreme anxiety about the prospects for the economy.

The panic buying led to a further inflationary spike. A survey of thirty-two large and medium-size cities revealed a 24.7 percent price increase in the month of August.[74] An atmosphere of crisis descended on Party leaders. On August 30, Li Peng chaired a meeting of the State Council, at which the direction once again shifted dramatically, this time away from the radical reforms announced only eleven days earlier. The State Council decided not to implement the plan for major price adjustments that year and to focus on restoring public stability and confidence by "curbing price hikes and panic buying." It was a rare admission of substantial error. Price reform, meanwhile, was characterized as a goal that would take five or more years to achieve. The document released after the August 30 meeting shifted emphasis to "stabilizing the economy while deepening reform," Premier Li Peng's favored slogan. Due to the disaster of the price reform, Li had solidified control over economic policy making and even ideology.[75]

At the September 2 Politburo meeting, General Secretary Zhao acknowledged the many problems in the economy that had emerged as a result of the radical price reform plan; Li followed him and made clear that the "environment" had changed and the ideas endorsed at Beidaihe would no longer work. Li and Zhao disagreed explicitly, and the tone soured quickly as they traded conflicting timelines and interpretations of events.[76] Li's August 30 decision to abandon price reform and begin a period of "stabilizing the economy" received the Politburo's official endorsement, and he began to position Zhao as the senior leader most likely to take the fall for the error. Zhao, too, realized that as general secretary responsibility naturally fell at his feet, and that conservatives would now more openly seek to exclude him from economic policy making.[77]

Most fundamentally, the CCP leadership had been burned: the most ambitious and radical reform attempt to date, personally spearheaded by Deng, had ended in failure and a complete policy reversal. It was, according to Ezra Vogel, "perhaps the most costly error of his [Deng's] career."[78] On September 12, Deng called a meeting at his home with Zhao, Li Peng, Bo Yibo, Hu Qili, Wan Li, Qiao Shi, and Yao Yilin. In the fractious discussion that followed, Zhao was frequently interrupted, and Deng supported Yao Yilin when he spoke.[79] Deng affirmed his commitment to "deepening reform" (without pairing the phrase with "stabilizing the economy," as in Li Peng's formulation) and held out hope that the leadership could still eventually create a "good environment" to implement price reform. Although Zhao, Yao, and Li all made comments reflecting their divergent interpretations of what "deepening reform" would entail in 1988 and 1989, Deng did not decisively resolve their disagreements.[80] As Li Peng and his allies promoted a narrative that reckless market-driven pursuit of high growth had permitted inflation to get out of control, Zhao saw his control over economic policy making vanishing and he realized that his position might be imperiled.[81] The 1987 Thirteenth Party Congress had marked the high point of Zhao's reform agenda. By the autumn of 1988, that agenda had fallen apart.

At this moment of crisis, Zhao made a characteristically bold decision: he would meet with a leading foreign economist to seek advice.

Yet the economist he chose—Milton Friedman—was, on the surface, an extremely unlikely candidate, especially given how poorly Friedman's 1980 visit had gone. In the years since, Friedman had maintained correspondences with a range of the Chinese economists whom he had met. Several prominent figures, including Li Yining and Liu Hongru, deputy governor of the PBOC, wrote to him to recommend students. Friedman also received an increasing quantity of fan mail from ordinary Chinese readers who obtained copies of *Free to Choose* and *Capitalism and Freedom.* They included an earnest English teacher at Ji'nan University who wrote to Friedman in 1985 and a loquacious finance student at Xiamen University who initiated a correspondence with Friedman after starting a translation of *Milton Friedman's Monetary Framework* in the mid-1980s. In his letters, Friedman sought acolytes, sending additional copies of his books and encouraging the students to seek "a broader group of readers" for his works.[82]

Unaware of the fraught context but eager to return to spread his message in the world's most populous country, Friedman accepted an invitation to speak at a September 1988 conference on economic reform in China, hosted in Shanghai by the Cato Institute and Fudan University. The seventy-six-year-old economist lectured to a crowd of 400 students at Fudan University, where he received an honorary professorship. At lunch with Shanghai Party secretary Jiang Zemin, who had just attended several of the key meetings in Beidaihe and in Beijing, Friedman argued for the importance of privatization and free markets, that is, "liberalizing in one fell stroke." Jiang responded by stressing the "political difficulties" of such an idea.[83] Despite this pushback, Friedman returned to these themes for his presentation at the Cato conference, advocating "free private markets" rather than dwelling on inflation per se.[84]

The response came from an economist named Pu Shan, a leading Party expert on "world economics," who wore a tightly buttoned Mao jacket and sharp-cornered military crew cut.[85] Pu attacked the distinguished visitor: "The direction of China's economic reform is toward the development of a planned commodity economy based on socialist public ownership and not what Professor Friedman calls 'free private markets.'" In addition to this rebuttal of Friedman's relevance for China, Pu pushed back against Friedman's entire worldview.

"Judging from actual evidence," it seems "unwarranted" to conclude that "an economic system based on 'free private markets,'" is superior to "the planned commodity economy based on Chinese-style public ownership," he said pointedly.[86] With characteristic confidence, Friedman dismissed the critique as political correctness.[87] However, in the context of Chinese debates at the time, Pu's response indicated that Friedman's evangelizing message about the end of state authority over the economy had not found as many converts as he might have hoped.

From Shanghai, Friedman traveled to Beijing, where he stayed at the Diaoyutai State Guesthouse, the residence of state guests, a great improvement from the shoddy hotel where he stayed during his 1980 trip. Amid its tranquil ponds and elegant villas, Friedman lectured to officials, calling on China's leaders not to "fool yourselves" about the urgency of the problems with rising inflation. He emphasized the importance of free private markets with regard to remedying the failings of the dual-track system, which he called "an open invitation to corruption and inefficiency."[88]

In what was the trip's most dramatic development, Friedman received word that Zhao had requested to meet with him. Zhao and his network of economists, struggling to right the tilting ship of reform and regain influence in the policy-making process, were in need of new proposals—and even though Friedman had proved unpredictable, they seemed to believe his monetarism might offer necessary insight into how China could control its inflationary woes.[89]

At the suggestion of his Chinese hosts, Friedman submitted a memorandum to Zhao, which laid out his views on the best direction of China's reform.[90] Friedman began the document with a direct refutation of the central Chinese idea during this period that China's experiences were exceptional and that "Chinese characteristics" were an aspect of every problem the country faced. "Every country always believes that its circumstances are special," Friedman wrote, but the acceptance of free-market principles is necessary regardless. Attacking the dual-track system, Friedman advocated that China decontrol prices in "one bold stroke" and "end" inflation by tightening money and limiting the government deficit financed by money creation and credits granted to enterprises. Above all, he called again for China to move ahead with establishing true "free private markets," not just "markets," although he did not elaborate on this distinction. "Beware of getting stuck partway through the process," Friedman warned.[91]

When this unlikely pair met, Zhao Ziyang thanked Friedman for his memo but attempted to set the discussion on his own terms. He laid out how he and other top Chinese leaders conceptualized the challenges facing China's economy.[92] Zhao explained that Party leaders were working to reform enterprises so that they would "take responsibility for their profits and losses." Regarding enterprise reform, Zhao admitted, "Naturally, on this point I was inspired by the West." Although he acknowledged difficulties in realizing the goals, Zhao referenced the Party's 1987 decision to establish an economy in which "the state manages the market, and the market guides the enterprises." Zhao stressed, "The direction of the reform will not change."[93]

Zhao asked for Friedman's input, in particular on China's "difficult problems, especially sizable inflation." He asked, "Can the people take such a shock, both economically and psychologically?" Furthermore, Zhao raised the most fundamental question of all: "Why did inflation occur in China?"[94]

Friedman's response was highly critical, as he believed the 1987 decision was "impossible": "The state is organized from the top down; the market, from the bottom up. The two principles are incompatible."[95] He asserted that the dual-track system was making goods "more expensive, not less," because, although prices were still held down, the costs of queuing, shortage, and other negative effects were high. Thus inflation would persist as long as the dual-track system remained in place, Friedman argued.

Zhao responded by asking Friedman to understand China's special circumstances: "The reform of the Chinese banking system has only just begun, so it is very difficult for banks to follow the Western practice where you can control inflation by tightening up the money supply," Zhao said, rendering the dual-track system necessary.[96] Yet Friedman seemed unconvinced, and the conversation ended abruptly. However, Zhao concluded the meeting with an extraordinary gesture of friendship, walking Friedman to his car and opening the door for the American economist.[97] Rumors began spreading throughout

Beijing about the close connection forged between the two men. Despite the inconclusive tone of the meeting, this final gesture provided Beijing's networks of policy makers and scholars, used to finding meaning in such seeming minutiae, with a definitive image of Friedman's visit.[98]

Before leaving China, Friedman gathered for a lavish banquet with several of his hosts. Wearing a red plaid shirt and a white linen jacket, and tanned from his city tour, the American economist grinned broadly and clinked small glasses of liquor with his Chinese counterparts.[99] Indeed, despite the frictions, Friedman highly rated his meeting with Zhao, praising the Chinese leader for possessing "a sophisticated understanding of the economic situation and of how a market operated," a stark contrast to the "unbelievably ignorant" officials he had disparaged after his 1980 trip.[100] The *People's Daily* buoyantly summarized their meeting, concluding with Friedman praising Zhao for having "the temperament of a professor." The paper subsequently also released an interview with Friedman, translated into Chinese, which ended on a similarly cheery tone.[101] Friedman's radically pro-market ideas had been transformed into views that cohered with CCP reformers' goals for the economy; his visit was presented in the state-run media more as a public relations boost for Zhao than as a meaningful intellectual exchange.

In both China and the United States, word of Friedman's supposed bond with Zhao spread quickly. Some Chinese reformers moved to align themselves with Friedman's ideas, like Yang Peixin, now an economic official at the State Council, who that same month wrote directly to Friedman to declare their affinity: "You are against inflation in Western countries and I am against inflation in China."[102] In the United States, meanwhile, Gregory Chow confirmed to his American colleagues that Friedman's meeting with Zhao had received "wide publicity."[103]

Friedman also worked to publicize his grand reception in China in articles and interviews.[104] He had been fiercely attacked in the 1970s for his "responsibility" for supporting the repressive military junta in Chile, where, the *New York Times* opined, "The Chilean junta's economic policy is based on the ideas of Milton Friedman. . . . Friedman himself has visited Santiago and is believed to have suggested the

junta's draconian program to end inflation."[105] Announcing his return from China in the *Stanford Daily* that October, the always-
provocative Friedman wrote, somewhat facetiously: "Under the circumstances, should I prepare myself for an avalanche of protests for
having been willing to give advice to so evil a government?"[106] None
came, and in an interview with *Forbes* after returning to the United
States, Friedman predicted that major pro-market changes were im-
minent in the PRC.[107]

Just days after Zhao's meeting with Friedman, the State Council formally launched a retrenchment program, which was the main focus
of the third plenum of the Thirteenth Party Congress convened on
September 26, 1988. This meeting was a disaster for Zhao. Other top
Party leaders attacked him for having permitted inflation to get out
of control, making clear Zhao would take the public fall for the economic problems of the summer of 1988.[108] (Deng's image was dam-
aged, too, but he remained the paramount leader and thus above
direct criticism.)[109] Zhao's speech at the 1988 plenary session admitted that inflation had not been properly controlled, characterizing
the economy as "overheated" and citing excess aggregate demand.
Zhao then said, "If in the early part of this year we had firmly
grasped and resolved this problem, things would be a bit better now."
He still maintained, "The path we have taken over the past few years
was correct." Even so, when Zhao turned to explicitly discuss price
reform, it was clear how much ground the reformers had lost: Zhao
sounded more like Li Peng, stressing that price rises should be
strictly controlled, giving a time frame of "five or more years" for
rationalizing commodity prices, endorsing the continued existence
of the dual-track price system—and, finally, deferring to Yao Yilin
to present the details of the new plan for price and wage reforms.[110]

The coming months saw China's economic policy move more
sharply toward the "rectification" and retrenchment policies Li Peng
and Yao Yilin supported. On September 27, 1988, for example, the
State Council issued a decision on "strictly controlling" money and
loans to produce financial stability.[111] Although prominent economists
like Li Yining warned retrenchment would only produce "stagflation,"
and enterprise managers voiced fears that the "achievements of the
reform will be destroyed in a day," the agenda moved forward.[112]

In pushing for reversals of Zhao's policies, senior conservative leaders specifically targeted Zhao's engagement with foreign ideas. On October 8, Chen Yun said pointedly, "In a socialist country like ours, studying the methods of Western market economies made our difficulties seem numerous" and led policies astray. Predictably, Chen demanded that the retrenchment affirm the core role of planning and strengthen the economic center in response to the "current difficulties." This theme informed much of China's economic policy agenda over the subsequent months. On October 24, 1988, the State Council released a report on strengthening "strict control" over rises in commodity prices and an influential report on "Party discipline," which called for "ideological unanimity" in "cleaning up the economic environment and improving the economic order."[113]

Yet Zhao continued to search out new ideas and hold frank discussions with foreign experts. In November, he met with Stanley Fischer, the chief economist and vice president for development economics of the World Bank (and currently the vice chairman of the U.S. Federal Reserve System). Zhao announced that he would speak with Fischer as "an economist who has done much research on controlling inflation," rather than strictly as a World Bank official, and their conversation swiftly moved to the details of policy. After a question from Zhao about whether prices should be liberated quickly or gradually, Fischer responded that he was aware of Zhao's meeting with Milton Friedman in September and assumed that Friedman had advocated for a rapid liberalization. However, looking at the condition of the Chinese economy in late 1988, Fischer was adamant that changes needed to be made gradually. "China can't reform its economy overnight," he said.[114]

Even so, Zhao would later insist he had not believed the situation in late 1988 posed serious, systemic risks to the Chinese economy. But his views were no longer steering policy. Only a few days later, on December 5, Li Peng delivered a major address to the National Planning Conference in which he issued a series of jeremiads about the "harmfulness of the overheated economic situation and inflation," warning cadres that they should not underestimate how difficult and time consuming it would be to salvage the economy. Stating that CCP leaders would cut down on excessive demand by curbing investment and instituting other administrative measures and direct interventions, Li reimposed broad price controls.[115]

At subsequent official commemorations of the tenth anniversary of the 1978 third plenum that had symbolically launched Deng's "reform and opening," some reformers, like the prominent theoretician Su Shaozhi, attempted to call for further reform. An Zhiwen wrote that the lesson of the past ten years was that "reform should not be allowed to remain as 'half cooked rice' or to be delayed indefinitely." But Bo Yibo and other high-level leaders supportive of retrenchment made it clear that those calls would not translate into policy during the year ahead.[116] As 1988 came to a close, Zhao was under attack from his critics and some of his erstwhile allies, who were likewise under immense pressure to fall into line with the intensifying retrenchment.

As economic policy in late 1988 and early 1989 moved to curtail inflation, some leading Chinese economists reflected on the status of the reforms and attempted to formulate lessons from China's experience. As one element of such reflections, some reformist officials and economists sought to defend the reforms from the problems that had emerged over 1988. The *World Economic Herald*, a boldly reform-oriented publication in Shanghai, published an essay by two senior policy researchers that agreed substantively with Zhu Jiaming's arguments about inflation, saying that China's rate of inflation, though high, was not serious and that inflation was a common experience among successfully developing countries. In the same issue, another senior economist used the example of British Prime Minister Margaret Thatcher to argue that Zhao should persevere with his reform agenda even in the face of criticism. To these thinkers, China's experience was defensible and exemplary. Articles with titles such as "To Gain Intellectuals Is to Gain Everything, and to Lose Intellectuals Is to Lose Everything" suggested that China's reformist thinkers were best positioned to make this case.[117]

These confident intellectuals also wanted to defend China's newly crystallized reform policies on a global stage. In March 1989—shortly after U.S. president George H. W. Bush visited Beijing and met with Deng, Zhao, and others in late February[118]—Dong Fureng, who had just completed his tenure as director of the Institute of Economics at CASS, attended an International Economic Association (IEA) conference in Moscow on "Market Forces in Planned Economies." With János Kornai and Włodzimierz Brus presenting papers and Edwin Lim of the World Bank attending as an observer, Dong made a bold decision: he would inform the Western participants about China without referencing any international economists or economic ideas—an unusual decision in Chinese economic writing at this time, especially in writing aimed at engaging international audiences.[119] (By contrast, Wu Jinglian and Zhao Renwei's coauthored article for the *Journal of Comparative Economics* in 1987 referenced Czech price reforms, quoted Brus, alluded to Kornai, and cited the American economist Gene Tidrick.)[120] Although Dong had referred to Kornai and had repeatedly invoked the Hungarian experience in a major 1988 article on the reform of enterprise ownership and the economic system, here he made no mention of Chinese absorption of international ideas, strenuously avoiding even widely used terms like "shortage" and "budget constraint."[121]

In this setting, why did Dong make this decision? Perhaps, attending as a presenter on an equal level with figures of towering stature in China like Kornai and Brus, Dong realized that international economists were beginning to regard China's reform as possessing the kind of emulative value China had seen in Eastern Europe. Perhaps he thought that avoiding the recognizable idiom of Kornai's views in the presence of the Hungarian economist would help bolster the appearance of China's achievements. Or perhaps Dong believed that China had diverged substantially from the international ideas that had helped Chinese reformers make their case in the 1980s and thought that those ideas had already received sufficient credit. Either way, Dong's decision to omit any references to international ideas marked a shift in how Chinese economists discussed their country's reforms on the global stage.

At the same time, international intellectual exchanges were continuing, as Chinese economists traveled to glean new knowledge that could address China's inflationary economy and help reformers put their policy agenda back on track. "Through international exchange, we can overcome difficulties [and] promote development," Zhao Ziyang said in the spring. "The past decade's development has proven this point."[122] Gregory Chow at Princeton organized a rare encounter: a meeting between leading PRC and Taiwan economic officials, held in Hong Kong in March 1989. The meeting was held in secret, with System Reform Commission leader An Zhiwen, deputy central bank governor Liu Hongru, and other reformers spending several days with senior Taiwan economists, including Sho-Chieh Tsiang, a renowned senior adviser to the Taiwan government. Tsiang proposed that the Chinese economists "raise the interest rate to ensure a positive real return to bank deposits," as Chow recalled, a strategy Taiwan had used in the 1950s.[123] An and Liu characterized the Taiwan economists as criticizing Keynesian expansionary monetary policy and stating that government policy should "as far as possible be in line with market forces." The PRC's inflation rate of 18.5 percent was a problem but not a "very serious" one, they wrote, noting that inflation in Taiwan had been significantly higher in the 1950s. The Taiwan economists also urged that China move forward with bold price reform.[124] Immediately after the conference, the Chinese attendees submitted a report directly to Zhao Ziyang and Li Peng outlining their impressions. Some of the contents may have reflected Liu Hongru's strong interest in American monetarists (he had written several letters to Friedman during the 1980s)[125]—but, most of all, the report reflected the seeming consistency of views among international experts that China's inflationary environment could be cooled down if the leadership promulgated further market reforms. Addressed to both the CCP's leading reformer and leading advocate of retrenchment, the report implicitly challenged the leadership not to cower in the face of inflation and, instead, to push on with market reforms. After reading the report, Zhao sent it to Deng Xiaoping and gave orders to the System Reform Commission to conduct further research.[126]

Other reform-oriented Chinese economists drew directly from the 1987 decision to formulate some of the boldest proposals yet. The influence of Kornai and the Bashan Conference remained prominent in these arguments. One economist who had attended the conference, Guo Shuqing, cited Kornai to propose a shift away from administrative controls of any kind, arguing that dragging out reliance on indirect administrative controls over large swaths of the economy and over a long period would only make it more difficult to turn the economy over to market coordination. "Indirect administrative controls are a trap," Guo wrote.[127]

Most remarkably, some economists began to openly advocate for political reform. In doing so, they were responding to top-level signs of support, including comments that Deng Xiaoping had made in 1986 encouraging political reform. Zhao's report to the Thirteenth Party Congress endorsed greater separation between the Party and the government, broadening intraparty democratic mechanisms, creating an independent judiciary, and reforming the handling of personnel issues within the Party, among other reforms. Bao Tong, Zhao's secretary (chief of staff), evidently wrote these proposals.[128] Working with many individuals who had cut their teeth on economic reform, Zhao had created a Political Reform Office, organized by Bao and with staff members including Chen Yizi.[129] Other officials, including senior members of the System Reform Commission and the Development Research Center, discussed the necessity of reforming the political structure if economic reforms were to make next-stage breakthroughs.[130]

The literature on the successes and failures of Chinese political reform in the Deng era is vast. Here I focus on the economists who wrote on political reform at the critical juncture in 1988–1989. They often used criticism of the corruption and rent seeking that had emerged under the dual-track system—phenomena in which political and economic factors became inextricable—as a way to present their proposals.[131] The political reforms advocated by people working within the system were cautious and, as Andrew Nathan has written, certainly did not pose "any challenge to the Party's monopoly on power."[132] Zhao and his top aides argued that political reform was necessary to achieve continued economic progress—a key connection that was an important contribution to Chinese reform debates as a whole. Yet in the early 1990s, after the disaster at Tiananmen, the CCP would shift its line and ensure that economic reform and political reform were conceptually separated.

Within this framework, the experiences of Hungary, Poland, and Czechoslovakia—the homelands of Kornai, Brus, and Šik—provided fodder for the economists' calls for political reform.[133] In an April 1989 article in *Economic Research*, Zhao Renwei and two coauthors assessed the changing relationship of the "state" to the "enterprise" as "marketizing reform"—referencing several of Kornai's works, including his 1986 article on his trip to China.[134] They concluded with a simple statement of the inevitability of political reform. "Market-oriented reforms are bound to change some noneconomic factors, and they are especially connected to political system reform," they wrote.[135] By April 1989, it was clear that the belief among many leading reformist economists that political reform was an urgent necessity had derived at least in part from reading the work of figures like Kornai. The shift is particularly remarkable because Kornai and other scholars of socialist transition were viewed as major advocates of political reform at home, even though they had not advocated those views in China. Increasing calls for political reform by Chinese economists showed their rising awareness of the kinds of arguments being made by colleagues abroad, including some of the partners and role models they most admired, as well as of the deep and persistent inequities in China's political system.[136]

All these developments—Dong's paper, further international exchanges, and domestic debates—revealed the extent to which the new conception of state-market relations, which stressed market guidance of enterprises with the state guiding the market through indirect macroeconomic regulation, had crystallized among China's reform-oriented elites. Even in an environment of policy retrenchment and conservative pushback, these thinkers demonstrated a firm belief that reform should continue in the direction that Zhao had laid out in 1987.

However, events far beyond the rarified confines of research organizations and policy institutes would knock the plans of Chinese reformers farther off course. After collapsing from a heart attack at a Politburo meeting, Hu Yaobang died on April 15, 1989. The sudden death of the sympathetic Hu—a popular reformer stripped of his power—triggered outpourings of grief among university students around the country. On the evening of April 17, three thousand students marched from Peking University to Tiananmen Square, the center of Beijing, where they camped out overnight. By the time of Hu's funeral on April 22, their numbers had allegedly swelled to one hundred thousand. The crisis escalated, with the students calling for comprehensive democratic political reform.[137] The causes, tragedy, and consequences of the spring 1989 student democracy movement have received and will continue to receive in-depth treatment. Here I provide only a compressed account of this horrifying event and moment of political upheaval to show how the tragedy of Tiananmen was an important juncture in the way subsequent CCP narratives would treat two key subjects: Zhao's reform policies and Western influences on China.[138]

The student movement had clear antecedents. As noted earlier, smaller-scale student protests had led to Hu's purge in early 1987. In the early months of 1989, urban society bubbled with democracy salons and liberal-minded petition movements, including one calling for the release of political prisoners, most prominently Wei Jingsheng of "Fifth Modernization" fame. At the same time, criticism of the retrenchment policies implemented after the failed price reform attempt of 1988 was coming from many quarters, including angry managers whose enterprises were suffering from slowing growth following the adoption of the new state industrial policy in March.[139] At a meeting with foreign leaders on March 23, Deng acknowledged that China's problems with inflation continued despite the strict retrenchment policies.[140]

As the streets of Beijing filled with students in April 1989, the combination of student protests, persistent inflation, and angry interest groups turned Deng's mind to the Polish case, which he had watched with great interest and concern.[141] On April 4, 1989, Solidarity—which had emerged in Poland as a trade union in the summer of 1980, survived the ruling Polish Communist Party's attempts at repression, and forced it to the negotiating table after sweeping workers' strikes in 1988—produced the so-called Roundtable Agreement, which effectively dissolved the position of Communist Party general secretary and set the stage for a large-scale electoral victory for its coalition in the upcoming national elections. The Polish Communist Party's days were numbered.[142] On April 6, Zhao Ziyang said, "Some places are experiencing very obvious problems in public order. We must attach great importance to this." CCP leaders were determined not to meet the same fate as their Polish counterparts; the lesson Deng drew was that "concessions" would fail and a forceful response was necessary.[143] One senior Chinese official told Egon Krenz, the number-two official in East Germany, that the Chinese leadership believed that "legalizing the opposition would be the beginning of the end of socialism in China" because of the Polish experience with Solidarity. As Mary Sarotte has argued, in addition to closely watching events such as the Polish (and Hungarian) liberalization, China's leaders "wanted to prevent similar contagion from spreading to their territory," and they were prepared to take extreme measures to stop it.[144]

This belief in the necessity of a forceful response took several forms. As the student protests began to engulf Beijing, Premier Li Peng's faction solidified its rise as a distressed Deng authorized the publication of the infamous "April 26 Editorial" on the front page of the *People's Daily*, calling for a "clear-cut stand against the disturbances," intending to intimidate the students.[145] The leaders of the protests did not back down; instead they reacted by hardening their stance and intensifying their criticisms of Li and Deng, with a new wave of protests occurring the following day.[146] Both in the editorial and at internal meetings, top officials suggested that foreign "black hands" and domestic "provocateurs" were behind the demonstrations, turning their attention to the intellectuals whom, they asserted, were manipulating the student protesters.[147]

Top officials thus put immense pressure on thinkers, writers, and reformist publications to support the CCP leadership. In Shanghai, the *World Economic Herald*, a paper that reformist leaders including Zhao Ziyang had been reading and referencing since the early 1980s, was the focus of this pressure. In 1989, the *Herald* had been publishing a spate of articles that criticized senior conservative leaders by name—including an April 3, 1989, article that railed against Li Peng's "serious mistakes in overlooking the importance and urgency of political reform"—and it organized conferences on "Democracy, Science, and Modernization" and "Hu Yaobang lives in our hearts," which aligned with the claims of the student protesters.[148] By late April, Jiang Zemin, the Party secretary of Shanghai, decided that the newspaper had gone too far. He suspended the newspaper's chief editor and, despite an angry statement of "attitudes and demands" from the *World Economic Herald*'s editorial board on May 1, shuttered the paper.[149] In the coming weeks, the *World Economic Herald* would be condemned as part of a "conspiracy" with the students and even as the "trumpet" of an international "cantata" of forces allied against the Party and socialism.[150]

Another battleground for officials was the seventieth anniversary of the 1919 May Fourth movement, a student movement that had criticized imperialism, called for a strengthened China, and high-lighted the value of science and democracy in rejuvenating the Chi-nese nation. Intellectuals who had played a role in the May Fourth movement founded the CCP shortly thereafter, in 1921; independent-minded Chinese intellectuals in the 1980s thus looked to the May Fourth movement as a source of inspiration. The official commemo-rations in 1989, led by Li Peng, highlighted the movement's patrio-tism. Reformers and intellectuals, however, emphasized the scientific and democratic ideas of the 1919 student protesters; Fang Lizhi even went so far as to criticize patriotism and the government's constant emphasis on "Chinese characteristics," saying, "You can't go tip-toeing around for fear of challenging anything that is labeled 'Chinese.' . . . Truth doesn't distinguish between localities."[151] Matters came to a head after Zhao Ziyang delivered several speeches that carefully walked the line between these two positions, including a speech on May 4, 1989, at a meeting of the Asian Development Bank, where his tone was markedly warmer toward the students than Li Peng had been in the preceding days. Zhao came under immediate fire from Li, Bei-jing mayor Chen Xitong, and others for going off message and for using an international venue to pressure his CCP colleagues.[152] The rift between reformist intellectuals and the Party leadership was ob-vious and widening—as was a rift within the Party leadership.

In the coming days, the increasingly isolated Zhao unsuccessfully urged Deng to retract the April 26 editorial, deepening the gulf be-tween the two men and causing Deng to more often look to Li Peng for input. On May 13, two days before Soviet president Mikhail Gor-bachev was scheduled to arrive in Beijing for a highly anticipated meeting, the first Sino-Soviet summit since 1959, the students launched a hunger strike. As Deng made clear to Zhao that he would not retract the April 26 editorial and as the senior leadership decided to declare martial law, Zhao repeatedly attempted to resign from his post as general secretary. Yet it was allegedly an error by Zhao that finally cost him his standing with Deng. In his meeting with Gorbachev on May 16, Zhao reportedly made a comment explicitly confirming that Deng remained the paramount leader, with final say on all decision-making; this comment infuriated Deng, who evidently found it inappropriate to tell foreigners and thought it might push him into a head-on confrontation with the protestors.[153] Zhao wrote him a letter, frantically trying to explain he had not intended to shift blame onto Deng, but he received no reply.[154]

On May 18, the final day of Gorbachev's visit to Beijing, 1.2 million people had massed in Tiananmen Square, according to a Ministry of State Security estimate.[155] That same day, leaders of the student protests and hunger strikes, including Wu'er Kaixi and Wang Dan, met with Li Peng, Chen Xitong, and other senior officials at the Great Hall of the People, with Wu'er Kaixi interrupting Li Peng's prepared remarks to criticize China's leadership before suddenly fainting in his chair.[156]

As Party leaders began to implement Deng's decision to impose martial law to quell the protests, Zhao finally decided to resign regardless of whether Deng wanted him to or not. Zhao refused to see troops enter Beijing on his watch. In the early morning of May 19, Zhao walked to the square to speak to the students directly. Urging them to call off the hunger strike for the sake of their health, Zhao—his voice filled with emotion as he held a small megaphone— told the students, "We have failed you."[157] The next day, on May 20, the imposition of martial law began. Li Peng read out the decree announcing that China had entered a state of emergency—and on the dais where the Politburo Standing Committee members sat, Zhao's chair remained empty.

But as the troops attempted to enter the city, Beijing residents joined forces to block them from advancing, preventing them from moving into the heart of the city for at least fifty hours; then, on the morning of May 22, the troops received orders to withdraw. Galvanized, workers began to join the students in the square, expressing anger over economic issues and official corruption, though not endorsing democracy and other liberal ideals that seemed to motivate the intellectuals and students who had been protesting since April.[158] The participation of urban workers was, to Deng and other Party elders, a frightening echo of events in Poland and elsewhere in Eastern Europe. Equally threatening was the nature of their complaints, which criticized Deng's pragmatism as insufficient. "It's not

enough to say that you are 'feeling for stones as you cross the river,' "
one worker clamored at the time. "What about those of us who fall
in and drown?"[159]

After the withdrawal of the troops, Deng, Li, and their allies prepared an even stronger military response that would be able to subdue
any attempts to prevent troops from entering Beijing. On May 28,
Zhao was formally placed under house arrest, where he would remain for the rest of his life.[160] The next evening, the students in the
square unveiled a statue called the Goddess of Democracy, positioned
to stare directly at the portrait of Mao hanging over the Gate of
Heavenly Peace. Although the number of students was evidently declining, a large group remained committed to staying in the square.[161]

To justify the decision to crack down on the student movement,
internal reports sought to portray the protests as an existential threat
that sought to depose the communist regime. On June 1, the Ministry
of State Security reportedly submitted a document to the Politburo
justifying its belief that "ideological and political infiltration" from
"Western capitalist countries" had advanced to the point of immense
danger for "the big socialist country of China." The report alleged
relationships between the U.S. Central Intelligence Agency and officials at the System Reform Commission. Painting a terrifying picture of the "murderous intent" of "international monopoly capitalists and hostile, reactionary foreign forces," the ministry argued
that the student movement represented a life-or-death struggle with
enemies that sought to "annihilate" the CCP.[162] Reacting to this document, Li Xiannian purportedly connected this account to the
"turmoil in the Soviet Union and all the socialist countries of Eastern
Europe," to which Deng responded, "Comrade Xiannian is correct."[163] It seemed as if their nightmare of the Polish scenario was
on the verge of unfolding—driving the leadership to decide the moment had come to clear the square.

Meanwhile, nearly 150,000 troops began to enter the city in small,
secret groups, gradually moving into Beijing so that they could not
again be blocked by the crowds. The army also readied weaponry, including tanks and armored vehicles. On the night of June 3, the troops
received orders to assemble in Beijing and march toward the square.[164]

Sitting in the courtyard of what had become both his home and
his prison, Zhao could hear gunfire.[165]

10

At the Delta

⌘ **B**Y THE MORNING of June 4, 1989, Tiananmen Square had been emptied of the students who had camped out for weeks. They left behind only a few blood stains on the stones, newly scarred with the tread marks of tanks. In the imperial city that spread out below the empty gaze of Mao's official portrait, an unknown number had been killed and wounded. The clearing of the square took less than twelve hours.[1]

Because of China's openness to the outside world in the 1980s, the international media (already in Beijing for Gorbachev's visit) documented this extraordinary episode—the feverish student movement and the authoritarian violence that terminated it—in real time and in great detail, focusing the attention of the world on Beijing. The U.S. government, under President George H. W. Bush, closely monitored the tumult.[2] Even to foreign government observers, it was clear the crackdown would directly affect the reformist economists who had driven China's intellectual innovation under Zhao Ziyang. A recently declassified telegram sent on June 4 cited Chen Yizi's Institute for Chinese Economic Structural Reform, which had authored a "declaration supporting the students," cosigned by the Beijing Society of Young Economists, among other economic organizations—and the telegram predicted the Chinese Communist Party (CCP) leadership would crack down on economic research. "Researchers have been told not to leave the country," the U.S. ambassador to China warned.[3]

Some of these "researchers," including Chen Yizi, were able to flee the country.[4] But others ran into trouble—the most prominent among them Fang Lizhi, who sought asylum at the U.S. embassy as the mass arrests began. "We had no choice but to take him in," wrote Bush in his diary, "but it's going to be a real stick in the eye to the Chinese." Fang and his wife would remain at the embassy for over a year before being allowed to leave China, amid a diplomatic standoff that brought intense global attention to the precarious and sometimes captive position of Chinese intellectuals after the crackdown at Tiananmen.[5]

Yet in the days after Deng Xiaoping had authorized the violent termination of the student movement, he attempted to signal internally that his commitment to economic reform remained paramount. On June 9, he made his first appearance since the crackdown, meeting with military officials—whose loyalty had allowed the suppression of the protests and whose continued fealty Deng needed. Deng affirmed his commitment to the work report of the Thirteenth Party Congress, even though that era's general secretary, Zhao Ziyang, had been sidelined. "Not even one character can be changed," Deng declared. "We must stick with a combination of planned economy and market economy," he said, using the formulation associated with the reformist thinkers under Zhao. However, because Hu Yaobang was now dead and Zhao was under house arrest, conservatives dominated the remaining senior Party leadership after Tiananmen. When Deng's remarks were made public in early July, his phrase a "market economy" (*shichang jingji*) had been changed to a "market-regulated economy" (*shichang tiaojie jingji*). The substantial demotion in status presented the market as less important than the "planned economy," contrary to Deng's original intentions.[6]

A week later, on June 16, Deng made public comments reaffirming "reform and opening to the outside world will not change."[7] However, Chen Yun, Li Peng, and other conservatives, who had prevailed on sending in troops, ensured that the retrenchment policies of 1988 would be deepened. With Deng's permission, the Chinese leadership implemented a new and far-reaching thirty-nine-point economic retrenchment program, slated to last for three years, which aimed to recentralize planning, implement macroeconomic austerity, and strengthen the position of state-owned industrial enterprises. Pushing down domestic consumption and investment was particularly important to Li Peng and his allies because, in the face of international sanctions and embargos on foreign credit, China's trade deficit (previously allowed to grow to help deal with the rising inflation in 1988) would have risen rapidly if demand were not held down.[8]

At the fourth plenum of the Thirteenth Central Committee, which convened on June 23–24, 1989, the Party leadership not only solidified its policies of retrenchment but also ended a month of uncertainty about Zhao and the position of general secretary.[9] Zhao was formally dismissed, along with his ally Hu Qili. The Politburo Standing Committee brought in several new members under the leadership of Jiang Zemin, who was promoted from Shanghai Party secretary to CCP general secretary.

Zhao, who attended the meeting but was cut off when he tried to defend himself, came under attack for what was presented as his political betrayal. "He made the mistake of supporting turmoil and splitting the Party, and he bears unshirkable responsibility for the formation and development of the turmoil," Li Peng's report trumpeted, while he declared that Zhao had "accommodated, encouraged, and supported bourgeois liberalization."[10] Party elder Peng Zhen even allegedly accused Zhao of "attempting to topple the Communist Party and wreaking havoc with the socialist system in coordination with hostile powers at home and abroad."[11] Another elder purportedly attacked Zhao as having "turned socialism into something that nobody could define."[12] Yao Yilin, meanwhile, was said to have called for "breaking out of Zhao Ziyang's policy influence" and he directly attacked the 1987 Party congress tenet, "the state manages the market, and the market guides the enterprises."[13] In this way, conservatives were able to include Zhao's reform agenda as part and parcel of his alleged goal of undermining socialism and the Party's authority. Although Deng had called for the Central Committee to avoid "opening up some sort of discussion on ideology" at the fourth plenum, the attacks on Zhao showed that Deng's advice had gone unheeded.[14]

Conservatives directly indicted Zhao for his engagement with Western economists as a component of their attack on his broader relationship with "hostile powers at home and abroad." The mayor of Beijing, Chen Xitong, read his report on the "quelling of the counterrevolutionary riots" to the Standing Committee meeting of the Seventh National People's Congress (NPC) on June 30, 1989, alleging that Zhao had sought to overthrow the socialist order in China and replace it with a liberal capitalist system. Yet the evidence for these accusations was unusual. "Especially worth noting," Chen wrote, "is that last year on September 19, Comrade Zhao Ziyang met with one American 'extreme liberal economist,'" the report declared damningly.[15] September 19, 1988, was the date of Zhao's meeting with Milton Friedman.

The anti-Western message was clear. What the report called Zhao's "brain trust" had been enamored with the ideas of many Western economists, and the "long-term strategy" of those foreigners was insidious: pushing China to abandon socialism, a lethal endeavor Zhao had encouraged.[16] In this conservative vision, the toxic spread of foreign ideas, especially Friedman's pernicious influence, had undermined the Party at Zhao's instigation—and was emblematic of the insidious intellectual tendency to seek out foreign economists who would allow dangerous "liberal" ideas to infiltrate China.

Almost as quickly, the status of partnerships with foreign economists, some of whom had been identified as the source of the ideological pollution that had corrupted Zhao and his "brain trust," went from precarious to worse. Friedman, for one, became persona non grata. Plans for a Chinese edition of his *Price Theory*—already translated by the summer of 1989, with a special foreword written by Friedman—came to a sudden halt. At the same time, Friedman was inundated with pleas for help from young economists who had become targets in the wake of the crackdown and who now saw Friedman as emblematic of the future that had been forcefully prevented in China. One young man named Fan Di (a doctoral student under Li Yining), wrote fearfully, "I am told that I have been listed on a blacklist by China's government since I am an executive member of the Beijing Young Economists Association, which is believed to be loyal to Zhao Ziyang and has been announced [as] a counterrevolutionary organization." He pleaded for Friedman to take him on as a student, "in order to do further studies and survive as well."[17] It is unclear what role Friedman, who had no active graduate students as a senior research fellow at the Hoover Institution at Stanford University, might have played in helping Fan Di—but within several months, Fan was a visiting scholar at the University of California at Berkeley, helping to found the 1990 Institute that was dedicated to collaborative programs between the United States and China.[18]

Yet the optimism about China's future that Friedman had voiced only a few months earlier vanished with Zhao. Friedman wrote in 1990, "The tragedy has not changed the underlying economic realities facing China, but it has made far more difficult the task of achieving a successful transition."[19] For Friedman, who had argued in *Capitalism and Freedom* that economic freedom and political freedom were inextricably connected, the Tiananmen tragedy demonstrated the danger of conducting economic reforms without a concomitant opening of the political system.

In the days and weeks ahead, the political and social trauma of Tiananmen would be paralleled by a further rolling back of the reform policies as well as the introduction of new policies of economic retrenchment. But, as we will see, when the hard-liners' influence eventually waned and the reformers returned to power in the early 1990s, remarkable continuities in policy would emerge. Some changes were nonnegotiable: Zhao had been purged in 1989, so official accounts would fastidiously omit mention of his influence and the role of his Western advisers. However, after this period of retrenchment, reformers would bring back many of the substantive policies he had advocated for the Chinese economy in the 1980s and for which he and his Western-influenced "brain trust" had been attacked—albeit without full acknowledgment of their supposedly treacherous origins.

As the fallout over the crackdown at Tiananmen broadened from attacks on Zhao, Chinese leaders consistently blamed foreign infiltration and interference in domestic Chinese affairs, with a particular focus on the United States. Friedman fit into this narrative, but it extended far beyond him. Even as the administration of George H. W. Bush made secret overtures to the Chinese regime, Deng and other top CCP officials painted the West as an antagonist that had played a leading role in causing the student "rebellion." On July 2, 1989, Brent Scowcroft, the U.S. national security advisor, and Deputy Secretary of State Lawrence Eagleburger traveled to Beijing, despite the administration's public position of not engaging with China, and met with Deng.[20] Scowcroft and Eagleburger had flown clandestinely in a military cargo plane, landing at a Chinese base and stealthily hustling to their meeting at the Diaoyutai State Guesthouse. There, Scowcroft recalled, Deng said that the United States "on a large scale has impinged upon Chinese interests. . . . It is up to the United States to cease adding fuel to the fire."[21] Even at the highest levels of secret interactions between the two countries, the Chinese leadership espoused this attitude and rejected Western overtures.

Thus, in the aftermath of the summer of 1989, the official line of the CCP leadership became, in some ways, more firmly anti-Western than it had been since the Mao era. Importantly, unlike the Campaign to Combat Spiritual Pollution in 1983, the target of this anti-Western attitude now encompassed a more comprehensive range of interactions with the West—political, ideological, economic, and intellectual—that, together, had allegedly fomented a popular movement that promoted "Western" values as a means of criticizing China's authoritarian leadership.

Global developments gave additional support to this interpretation. The anti-communist contagion spreading throughout Eastern Europe, which had powerfully informed Deng's response to the student protests in June, continued to proliferate. The turmoil that soon engulfed the Soviet Union and the communist states of Eastern Europe ensured that conservative Chinese leaders would keep a tight grip on both economic and ideological policy. "Stability" became the key priority, in both the economy and politics.[22]

This emphasis on stability occurred just as an important leadership change was underway: Deng told a small group of Party elders at Beidaihe in mid-August 1989 that he would transfer his last remaining official position, the chairmanship of the Central Military Commission, to Jiang Zemin, thereby retiring and allowing

Jiang to fully succeed him. Determined to avoid destabilizing the careful balance he had crafted, Deng planned to formalize his retirement in November 1989 at the fifth plenum.[23]

In this search for stability, the strongly anti-Western, anti-capitalist line that had become prominent after June 4 persisted. On November 7, the ideologue Deng Liqun—again empowered after Zhao's fall—held a meeting that openly blamed the reforms for the June "disorder." As early as October 1986, he had said bluntly to Deng Xiaoping that he believed Zhao was an "arrogant bully" who was fond of "sophistry" and "had read few of Marx's and Lenin's works"—and, worst of all, Zhao was "obsessed with transplanting Western capitalism" to China.[24] Although at the time Deng Xiaoping had rebuked him sharply for this vitriol, in November 1989 Deng Liqun found a ready audience.

Deng Liqun's main argument was that the reforms under Zhao and Hu Yaobang had pursued a "capitalist orientation," seeking to eliminate the plan and supplant it with the market, rather than a "socialist orientation." As a result of this Western, capitalist "orientation," Deng Liqun posited, the reforms had led China to the brink of chaos. The fifth plenum released a document that implicitly critiqued Zhao's policies and praised Chen Yun's vision for the Chinese economy.[25] That winter, other conservative ideologues delivered speeches and published articles along the same lines, indicating a major conservative push to define the reform project of the 1980s as inherently "capitalist" in nature and dangerous for China.[26]

Yet the Chinese leadership was also willing to entertain overtures from Western governments, international institutions, and economists who sought to resume engagement that had been stopped in the public furor over the Tiananmen crackdown. As early as August 23, 1989, the American economists Gregory Chow, Dwight Perkins, and Lawrence Lau traveled to Beijing to "assess the impact of recent events on the academic environment at China's universities." The National Academy of Sciences (NAS) had suspended its dealings with China, but, according to a memorandum, Perkins and several other members of the NAS-organized Committee on Economics Education and Research in China thought that "the benefits of continuing our programs in China outweigh the potential political costs."[27] In Beijing, the American economists were evidently pleased by what their Chinese interlocutors told them: "In spite of the unfortunate political events in June, Chinese economics education and economic exchanges with foreign countries have remained essentially unchanged," Chow claimed, making it clear that he intended to continue his work in China.[28]

At the diplomatic level, Deng Xiaoping met with former Secretary of State Henry Kissinger on November 10 and hosted a public visit from National Security Advisor Brent Scowcroft in early December.[29] At a glittering banquet in his honor, above the soft glow of candlelight, Scowcroft delivered a toast calling for "new impetus and vigor" in the U.S.-China relationship, deriding "irritants in the relationship" and stating, "It is important that we not exhaust ourselves in placing blame for problems that exist," which can be "isolate[d]" and dealt with "another time."[30] Similarly, Shahid Javed Burki, who served as head of the World Bank's China Department from 1987 to 1994, flew to Beijing shortly after the crackdown. While there, he decided that the bank should remain in China. "My efforts to keep the Bank's program going," he wrote, "created an enormous amount of trust for me, as well as for the Bank, in Beijing."[31] The American economists' visit, Scowcroft's toast, and Burki's outreach functioned as both pleas and promises: if China resumed dealings and softened its anti-Western line, the Bush administration might stop "placing blame" for the tragedy of June 1989 and the World Bank would continue its work in China.

Yet dramatic events in Eastern Europe disrupted Scowcroft's plans. The CCP's anxieties about the collapse of communism in Eastern Europe, beginning with Poland and Hungary, reached a heightened pitch with the fall of the Berlin Wall in November and the Velvet Revolution in Czechoslovakia. Most of all, it was the Romanian revolution—and the execution of Nicolae Ceauşescu on December 25, 1989—that particularly shocked CCP leaders. After the Tiananmen crackdown, the Romanian ambassador to China had been one of the few international officials who publicly criticized the student protestors and supported the CCP.[32] Senior Party leader Qiao Shi had visited Romania in both August and late November of that year, and the *People's Daily* had earlier printed comments by Ceauşescu that cooperation between the CCP and the Romanian regime was "extremely important."[33] Following a crisis meeting on December 20, Party leaders launched a volley of attacks on Mikhail Gorbachev and Soviet revisionism as the root causes of the changes sweeping Eastern Europe. These comments were perhaps somewhat confusing to Chinese audiences, because the fall of the Berlin Wall had not been reported in major Party outlets—but, as Li Peng told Scowcroft at their December meeting, the Chinese leadership saw a direct connection between what Li Peng called "the resolute measures on June 4" and the CCP's ability to avoid the fate of the communist rulers in Eastern Europe. Although the meetings between Scowcroft and Chinese leaders had been positive and left the American delegation optimistic about the prospects of re-normalizing relations, Scowcroft believed that Ceaușescu's fall had caused China's leadership to "panic" and become "absolutely inflexible." The possibility of normalized U.S.-China relations suddenly faded away.[34]

The effect of Ceaușescu's fall on Chinese engagement with the wider world was similarly immediate. "The entire picture has changed because of Romania," a Chinese scholar said at the time. A liberal student added: "We were so happy about Romania. But who dares to go out on the streets, with martial law still in effect? We can't show our pleasure."[35] The ramifications were clear to observers around the world, as a headline in the *Chicago Tribune* blared, "China Loses Its Favorite Socialist Archetype."[36] An era was coming to an end in Eastern Europe, and China's leaders—who had long reached out to both Party leaders and ardent reformers in those countries— maintained a hard grip on the levers of power in Beijing.

Eager to ensure a more direct transmission of state-sanctioned ideology to the Chinese universities and intellectuals who had spearheaded the 1989 student movement, conservative leaders in China launched a new Patriotic Education Campaign, which proved a remarkable success—thanks in part, no doubt, to the continuation of martial law. The Propaganda Department disseminated images portraying a morally decadent West that hypocritically attacked China, a strategy that Geremie Barmé has shown successfully produced outraged anti-Western reactions even from Chinese liberals.[37] Books such as Yuan Hongbing's *Wind on the Plains* (1990), which criticized the search for "Western solutions to China's problems" (although in a firebrand style and with radical ideas unpalatable to the CCP), became popular reading on the same university campuses where the 1989 protests had begun.[38] In contrast to the worldview presented in *River Elegy*, these texts—and the Patriotic Education Campaign that helped bolster their success—focused on the glory of China's traditions and envisioned a future for China in which the West played, at most, an ancillary role. In an environment that combined strict political control with economic incentives to those who complied with government strictures, it is easy to imagine how the propaganda campaign was so successful.

Outside China, many of the economists who had partnered with their Chinese peers in the 1980s voiced anger and disappointment. The survival of the CCP after the collapse of communist parties throughout Eastern Europe also caused shifts in the writings of some of these economists. János Kornai was the clearest example. In the world transformed after the fall of the Berlin Wall, he made attempts to unify what he described as his "two faces" in Hungary and China and to fit China's system into his overall arguments about the fate of socialism and the goals of "a real change of system." Writing that China was not an "exception" to his critical analysis of the mixed "socialist-market" system on the pathway to transition, Kornai argued that this mode of economic, political, and social organization was fundamentally unstable and predicted its internal contradictions would cause a collapse, calling the post-Tiananmen system in China "incoherent."[39] These views were widespread after 1989, with figures ranging from Alec Cairncross to Milton Friedman suggesting that the socialist system in China might have entered its endgame.[40]

In Beijing, the newly elevated general secretary Jiang Zemin allowed reform to continue in small ways while also emphasizing "stability" and a turn away from the West. Chinese economists were permitted to continue their work as long as they did so silently. We "may be less animated than before the June storm," wrote one reformer, "but [we] are still thinking."[41] Those who did publish—like the eighty-five-year-old Xue Muqiao—largely did so in highly regulated environments such as the *People's Daily* and hewed closely to the official line about the need for rectification and "consolidation" (*zhengdun*) under the control of the central government.[42] Even after Li Peng lifted martial law in Beijing on January 10, 1990, the dominant theme of Jiang's first years in office followed the emphasis on "patriotic education" and "consolidation." A Production Commission under the State Planning Commission (SPC) was created in January 1990, once again heavily involving the state in the affairs of hundreds of "key enterprises," including the allocation of materials, the setting of production targets, and budgeting.[43] Celebrating the anniversary of the May Fourth movement in 1990, Jiang delivered an address to an audience of 3,000 students at the Great Hall of the People. The distance China had traveled from Zhao Ziyang's 1989 speech on the same anniversary to Jiang's 1990 speech was on extraordinary display. Jiang defined "patriotism" as the "mission" of Chinese intellectuals, adding, "Because we neglected ideological and political work and our excellent educational traditions, some young intellectuals were, to varying degrees, influenced by the system of values of Western bourgeois life."[44] A front-page editorial in the *People's Daily* on June 2, 1990, on the anniversary of the Opium Wars that marked the beginning of China's "century of humiliation," persisted with this theme, declaring, "We cannot advocate total Westernization and we must resist pressure from the West." Chinese television stations were authorized to broadcast scenes of the chaos in Eastern Europe, as visual evidence of what would happen when the central control of a Communist Party eroded.[45] The connections were unmistakable: intellectuals received Western influence, undermining the control of the "patriotic" Communist Party, which in turn led to complete disaster.

Yet reformers, buffeted though they may have been, decided to fight back in the summer of 1990. As China's relations with the wider world warmed—with U.S. president George H. W. Bush renewing China's most-favored-nation status in May 1990, despite maintaining sanctions[46]—a narrow window seemed to open for reformers to create momentum against the conservatives who held the reins of power in Beijing. That month, Xue Muqiao sent a letter to the SPC that argued, "Whether it is a capitalist country or a socialist country, if you want to develop a commodity economy, [the strategy of] controlling money and freeing prices is an objective law for the smooth functioning of the market mechanism that must be observed."[47] It was a subtle signal from China's most distinguished economist that reformers still had the stamina to fight future battles.

They also seized the opportunity presented by the friendly overtures by Gregory Chow and others during the previous year. In June 1990, the Chinese Academy of Social Sciences (CASS) partnered with the Ford Foundation and the United Nations Development Programme to organize a conference celebrating the tenth anniversary of the workshop on econometrics that Lawrence Klein had led at the Summer Palace in 1980. From June 24 to 28, almost exactly one year after Zhao's formal purge, Chow, Klein, Lawrence Lau, Albert Ando, and several other economists traveled to China for the celebration hosted by Liu Guoguang and the leadership of the CASS Institute of Quantitative and Technical Economics.[48] Chow wrote a jubilant update to his colleagues upon returning to the United States, reiterating his message that China's intellectual partnerships with foreigners remained on track. But not everyone agreed. "I do miss any account" about Tiananmen, wrote Nobel laureate Kenneth Arrow, proposing that "critical remarks, if appropriate, would not cause any trouble in future relations."[49] However, even if Chow could have been more "critical," the conference in June 1990 helped to resurrect an emphasis on economics and lend at least a modicum of support to Chinese economists who had been sidelined since the crackdown.

Reformers soon had other opportunities to demonstrate their renewed verve. On July 5, 1990, at a meeting convened by Deng Liqun, three economists—Wu Jinglian, Xue Muqiao, and Liu Guoguang—represented the reformist position against Deng Liqun and another conservative ideologue.[50] Wu argued that individuals who wanted to recentralize and carry out structural readjustment under strict administrative controls actually "feel that reform has had a mistaken orientation from the beginning." Wu declared that such views were wrong: "Theoretical inference and international experience both prove that a commodity economy with market allocation as the basic operational mechanism is an appropriate system for large-scale production that can guarantee effective growth"—and, most of all, this was "a historical tide that cannot be turned back." Where conservatives saw ideological poison, Wu saw the possibility of "a fresh form of socialist enterprise" that would produce a system that could avoid "the pain and sacrifice of 'shock therapy'" and, in time, in which "market forces can create stability and a prosperous economy."[51]

What advantage did Wu see in making such strong claims in this setting? Perhaps he simply sought to persuade—or perhaps he was using a more unconventional strategy suited to a time of constraint, in which he and other reformers could make claims just brash enough to push the conservatives to stop veiling their initiatives in language about "patriotism" and "stability" and to come down openly against Deng Xiaoping's "reform and opening" policies. If this was the plan, though, conservatives did not take the bait. Rather than directly rebutting the charges that they believed "reform has had a mistaken orientation from the beginning" or overtly criticizing Deng, they held up an old patron for lionization: Chen Yun. That summer, Chen, sickly but still wily, challenged Deng in a variety of small but significant ways. In particular, Chen criticized Deng's two unsuccessful choices for CCP general secretary—both Hu Yaobang and Zhao Ziyang—perhaps as a means of casting broader aspersions on Deng's judgment.[52] Chen seemed to be actively distancing himself from his longtime colleague and sometime rival and, in the process, becoming a symbol of an alternative path China could have taken in the 1980s.

Chen's allies were quick to support their patron's resurgence. That autumn, Deng Liqun and Liu Guoguang both praised Chen's "prescience" and "theoretical contributions," which were also the subject of a series of events that summer and fall.[53] By October, Premier Li Peng was sidelining Deng's belief in prioritizing reform and asserting, with references to Chen Yun, that central planning and slow, balanced growth needed to remain China's economic priorities. According to some reports, Li Peng even criticized several major policies from the 1987 Party Congress, including Zhao's formulation of China's economy as one in which "the state manages the market, and the market guides the enterprises."[54]

It seems to have been this attempt to roll back the reforms beyond the 1987 breakthrough that caused Deng to spring into action. Perhaps he had been willing to allow the 1988 retrenchment to continue longer than expected because of the crises of 1989 but, ultimately, he was not willing to lose substantial ground beyond what had been achieved by the end of 1987. In September, when disagreement broke out between pro-reform provincial officials and conservative centrists at an economic work conference, Deng sent word to the regional leaders Ye Xuanping (the son of Marshal Ye Jianying) in Guangdong province and Zhu Rongji in Shanghai that he supported their point of view, rather than Li's.[55] Reformist economists also gave signs that the environment was warming: on October 10 Xue Muqiao delivered a speech in which he criticized policies that "abandoned the law of value" and caused distorted prices, a cautious public step toward reviving a reformist ideology.[56] Deng said that advancing with reform had been "delayed" long enough: "We can no longer afford a wait-and-see attitude."[57]

To make good on these statements, Deng looked to Zhu Rongji, who, as mayor of Shanghai, had managed to continue the reforms, even under the watchful eye of Chen Yun. Once branded a rightist in 1957, the self-confident Zhu—with his arching eyebrows, high cheekbones, and affable public manner—would become a central figure during the next stage of China's reforms, eventually serving as premier. Zhu was a technocrat well versed in modern economics and in Zhao's reform policies of the 1980s. Before rising through the official ranks beginning in 1979, he had briefly been deputy director of the CASS Institute of Industrial Economics. He had also worked intensively with the World Bank, serving as part of the Chinese team that partnered with the bank's team in China on its initial report, which Zhao had praised highly.[58]

Zhu had a flair for dramatic decisions that made his reformist intentions extremely clear. On December 19, 1990, he announced the launch of the Shanghai Stock Exchange, a development with potent symbolic value—even though two years later the government would still hold at least 62 percent of the share value of all listed joint stock corporations, with much of the rest being held by state-owned enterprises.[59]

On December 24, five days after Zhu Rongji's announcement of the opening of the stock exchange, Deng held a meeting at his house with General Secretary Jiang, Premier Li Peng, and President Yang

Shangkun—China's top leadership—to discuss his satisfaction with the stock exchange and the need for more new market-oriented initiatives. Deng repeated one of his central injunctions from the reform era: "Socialism also involves a market economy, just as capitalism does not do away with government planning. Adopting some market principles is not equivalent to embracing capitalism."[60] In effect, he was making clear that he refused to be sidelined even during a period of retrenchment and conservative ascendancy. Traveling to Shanghai and meeting with Zhu Rongji that February, Deng reiterated these comments, stressing the importance of finance in a modern economy.[61] Shortly thereafter, in 1991, Deng designated Zhu the senior official who would lead China's economic restructuring, appointing him vice premier and bringing him to Beijing, where he was better positioned to serve as an advocate of reform in the central government.[62] Deng would later say, "The current leaders do not know economics. Zhu Rongji is the only one who understands economics."[63]

This turn to Zhu showed Deng's sense of urgency. Several months later, citing slow growth figures, Deng held another meeting with Jiang and other senior Politburo members, at which he framed the challenge in unvarnished terms. "Many nations in this world have fallen, and the root cause has always been poor economic performance," he said, adding that a growth rate above 5 percent would be necessary to preserve Party rule—and that for China to reach this growth rate, it would be necessary to give greater play to the market.[64] In 1990, the gross domestic product (GDP) grew by only 3.9 percent; annual net losses at state-owned enterprises increased by a staggering 57 percent, and the size of total losses at state industrial firms surpassed 2 percent of GDP.[65] Zhu clearly had his work cut out for him.

With Zhu's promotion and Deng's strong statements, economists and intellectuals on both the conservative and the reformist sides sprang into action. In early 1991, a series of editorials under the pen name Huangfu Ping appeared, asserting boldly that markets were not inherently capitalist; these were published with Deng's authorization and edited by Deng's daughter, Deng Nan, and Zhu Rongji.[66] An internal report circulated within the System Reform Commission fleshed out these views, asserting that China's developing mechanisms of macroeconomic management (*tiaokong*) would "for the most part follow the path that many market economy countries have taken and are currently taking."[67] Meanwhile, one conservative thinker directly contradicted Deng in the *People's Daily*, portraying socialism and capitalism as Manichean opposites struggling for primacy and stating flatly: "A market economy means eliminating public ownership and is effectively capitalism, which negates the CCP's leadership and the entire socialist system."[68] A battle over the fundamental meaning of China's guiding ideology had reached a new stage, with both Deng's authority and the fate of the market in China teetering in the balance.

In the summer and fall of 1991, Jiang treaded carefully in negotiating the line between Chen Yun and Deng Xiaoping.[69] Commemorating the seventieth anniversary of the founding of the CCP in July, Jiang used ideas both elders had endorsed—the "initial stage of socialism" thesis balancing the "supplementary" role of the private economy, and the need to "enliven" state-owned enterprises balancing his commitment to "stability" and "rectification." Although articles reporting on Jiang's speech made no explicit mention of the market, one comment showed his continuing openness to engagement with the wider world and learning from the capitalist West. Praising the "reform and opening," Jiang used a classical Chinese expression: "Stones from other hills can be used to carve jade." In other words, Jiang explained, ideas from abroad "can allow us to develop faster."[70] (Jiang had experience learning from abroad, having studied in the Soviet Union in the 1950s. He also had experiences of a humbler variety: in the early 1980s as a midlevel official Jiang had traveled to Chicago, where he studied the sanitation and public works system in order to solve no less a challenge than "the problem of littered watermelon rinds," he recalled self-deprecatingly years later.)[71] Even as Jiang balanced the competing agendas of Deng Xiaoping and Chen Yun, he signaled his commitment to incorporating ideas from abroad into China's reforms.

Although Foreign Minister Qian Qichen had visited Hungary in March—his first trip to Eastern Europe since the collapse of communism in 1989—political events in the Soviet Union reminded CCP elders that turmoil in the region had not completely died down and that the divide among senior leaders held risks.[72] In August 1991, an attempted coup by hard-liners in the Communist Party of the Soviet Union against the reformist Gorbachev led to the dissolution of the Soviet Union, an event that rocked the world and sent shudders among CCP leaders, forcing them to confront in stark terms the risks of unsuccessful reforms and factional strife. Deng's warning from earlier that year must have echoed in Jiang's ears: "Many nations in this world have fallen, and the root cause has always been poor economic performance." Others in China's leadership saw opportunity. Three senior reformist officials purged after Tiananmen—Hu Qili, Rui Xingwen, and Yan Mingfu—were all rehired as vice ministers that summer, and a group of "princelings" (children of prominent CCP elders) campaigned for a "neo-conservative" agenda.[73] Led by Chen Yun's son, Chen Yuan, this neo-conservative group tolerated some role for markets but criticized the pre-1989 reforms as dangerously decentralizing and stressed the importance of the continued centralization of economic policy.[74]

Most of all, Zhu Rongji seized this moment to assert his role as an economic czar with the skills to replace Chen Yun and the reformist credentials to please Deng. On September 3, 1991, Zhu delivered a speech at a conference on cleaning up "triangular debt," the situation that had emerged when manufacturers remained unpaid for their products, rendering them unable to pay their suppliers, who in turn were unable to pay their own suppliers. This complex problem had been Li Peng's challenging first assignment for Zhu, which some analysts have claimed was evidence that Li was setting Zhu up for failure.[75] In his speech, Zhu showed ambition and expertise, endorsing the market mechanism but stating he would fight fire with fire: "There has to be administrative intervention—we must order [debtor state-owned enterprises] to borrow" from banks to repay their debts, creating a multiplier effect throughout the economy as those suppliers in turn pay back their own suppliers.[76] A year later, Zhu deployed this "administrative intervention" to great effect, reducing the net debt of China's state-owned enterprises by RMB 300 billion.[77]

"I feel that triangular debt actually touches on all aspects of the deep contradictions," Zhu said in his September 1991 speech, and resolving it, he suggested, would allow a major breakthrough.[78] His remarkably successful and swift resolution of this previously intractable problem was no doubt aided by his study of Western economics.[79] As James Tobin had discussed at the Bashan Conference in 1985, the multiplier effect was a fundamental principle of modern macroeconomic policy making and a bedrock concept in central banking. But as Tobin and other Western economists had stressed throughout their interactions with their Chinese counterparts, one marker of a modern economic technocrat is knowledge of when administrative intervention is necessary and valuable—when it can, as Zhu said, begin to resolve the "deep contradictions" and lead to a breakthrough that will allow the market to flourish. Zhu had learned these lessons well.

When conservatives saw the reformers' results-oriented efforts, they ratcheted up their ideological claims. That October, both Deng Liqun and Bo Yibo delivered addresses attacking reform, continuing to call the "reformist road" the "capitalist road."[80] Deng Liqun, in particular, seemed to sense that his efforts to condemn market-oriented reforms to a position of ignominy were on the verge of permanent failure. "Intellectuals who engage in liberalization," he reportedly shrieked, "should be smothered to death!"[81]

This fever pitch seemed to arise from the conservatives' perception that the Party leadership's ideological commitment was once again weakening. On October 23, 1991, Deng Liqun published an article in the *People's Daily* that called for resolving the contradictions in China's system by turning away from the "anti-communist West."[82] The decision would, ultimately, fall to Jiang Zemin, who had vacillated between the reformist and conservative lines since his rise to the position of general secretary.

In the coming months, Jiang Zemin made a significant decision that would have the effect of strengthening the hand of reformers. He convened eleven discussions on three clearly defined topics: "Why had the capitalist system showed renewed vitality instead of collapsing? What were the reasons for the dissolution of the system in the Soviet Union and Eastern Europe? Given the foregoing, how should we proceed with our economic reforms going forward?"[83] He also devoted himself to studying Western economic texts from Adam

Smith on, seeking to "understand how the market works."[84] As Jiang consolidated his power, his focus on a diverse range of economies and economic theories offered a significant opportunity to appraise the prospects for China's economic reforms—and, with that, an explicit return to the contributions Western economists had made and might continue to make to Chinese thinking about its economic development.

These eleven meetings assembled a range of China's boldest reformist economists who had been "thinking" in silence since the Tiananmen crackdown in 1989 (including Liu Guoguang, Wu Jinglian, Zhou Xiaochuan, Justin Yifu Lin, and Guo Shuqing).[85] Given the stringent political constraints on open discussion, Zhou Xiaochuan recalled that the economists all prepared extremely cautious written statements, but Jiang's probing questions pushed them to speak more openly and make bolder proposals.[86] Wu Jinglian called for "a clarification of the authorized expression of a 'combination of planned economy and market adjustment,'" which Deng had used on June 9, 1989, and had been the subject of considerable contention since then.[87] Wu advocated a more market-oriented interpretation of Deng's June 9 formulation by arguing that Western countries had actually achieved the much-discussed goal of "stability" by embracing the market and not by returning to wholesale planning. "Contrary to a popular view in today's China, it is not the case that the postwar capitalist economy became stable because government intervention replaced the market mechanism," Wu said. "Even the expansion of planning," he continued, "was directed toward the improved functioning of the market mechanism," including the adoption of freer trade policies, global markets for both factors of production and products, intensified de-monopolization, and technological progress that led to the entry of many new competitors—all policies he advocated for China. Socialism in Eastern Europe and the Soviet Union had failed because of "unclear objectives and mistaken methods" in implementing reforms; China should learn from those mistakes in crafting its own reform plans.[88] Guo Shuqing, meanwhile, directly attacked the Soviet-bloc countries, which, he argued, had too long continued "meddling in economic affairs" under reforms and had "dogmatic views of public ownership," while Zhou Xiaochuan described in depth how a market could provide incentives and efficiently allocate resources. Jiang Zemin responded to the presentations by setting out an important goal: "The Fourteenth Party Congress should articulate very clearly the contents of a 'planned commodity economy.'" In the course of the discussion, Zhou recalled, one idea repeatedly came up: clarifying those "contents" as a "socialist market economy." This term, "socialist market economy," was a way of expressing a greater role for the "market" (rather than euphemistic "commodity" relations), but without undermining the primacy of the "socialist" system. It was not clear, however, that this particular term had gained any traction.[89]

Jiang Zemin seemed open to a moment of ideological reckoning. He was evidently pleased by what he had learned at these eleven internal meetings, and transcripts of the discussions were circulated among party cadres nationwide.[90] As Jiang familiarized himself between October and December with the details of what a market economy actually entailed, he also built relationships with reformers who had been associated with Zhao Ziyang and had not had the ear of China's top leaders since Zhao's fall.

In view of these developments and seeing that Jiang's mind-set had become more open to reform, Deng Xiaoping decided that the time was right for a dramatic bet. On January 17, 1992, he traveled to southern China for what was supposedly a family vacation. Putting all his accumulated credibility on the line, the eighty-eight-year-old Deng gave a series of informal, unexpected speeches that urged the resumption of intensive reforms.[91] Although acknowledging the risk of "the right," Deng declared that the "primary" risk in China was "the left." He added, "The proportion of planning to market forces is not the essential difference between socialism and capitalism. . . . A planned economy is not equivalent to socialism, because there is also planning under capitalism; a market economy is not capitalism, because there are also markets under socialism."[92] To illustrate these comments, Deng returned to a vivid metaphor he had been using since the early 1960s: "It doesn't matter whether a cat is black or white, so long as it catches the mouse."[93] But Deng had far more than aphoristic felines on his mind and he was prepared to take a harsher tone. In both Wuhan and Zhuhai, he declared bluntly, "Whoever is against reform must leave office." As he rode in his car, Deng reportedly denounced his conservative opponents in Beijing, voicing hope that this trip—which became known as his Southern Tour (*nanxun*)—could force their hands.[94] On the Southern Tour, Deng gave a definitive signal that he believed the period of retrenchment needed to end.

Deng's bold gambit soon triggered the response he had hoped for in Beijing. At a Politburo meeting on February 12, 1992, as an indication of support Jiang Zemin relayed Deng's remarks.[95] (There was reason to believe that Deng might have tried to replace Jiang if he had not supported the Southern Tour; in addition to comments about opponents of reform needing to "leave office," Deng had seemingly made a jab at the slow-moving and tentative Jiang when he said, "We should not act like women with bound feet.")[96] In March, the Politburo endorsed an initiative to oppose "leftism," and Jiang delivered a self-criticism for his "passivity" over the previous years in advancing the reform agenda.[97] Deng had won his gamble.

Only days after Jiang's self-criticism, a large group of prominent economists and economic policy makers convened in Beijing a conference sponsored by the magazine *Reform*, where they called for a rapid return to market-oriented growth policies. Conservative efforts to revert to central planning had "sacrificed reform for the sake of stability," according to one participant, who added, "Deng's words have saved China's life." According to newspaper reports at the time, "enthusiastic applause broke out" when the economists promoted the idea that China should "critically inherit and draw on the experience of capitalism."[98] These ideas were coming back into vogue, receiving vocal support in an editorial by a Renmin University professor who called for absorbing "capitalist" economic theories to allow China to grow.[99] Wu Jinglian made clear that he believed Chinese reformers had reached a crucial turning point: "I don't think the leftists will be able to obstruct reforms, especially in coming months," he told the *Christian Science Monitor*. "In coming years, if we do not make mistakes, I think the changes will go forward."[100]

As such gatherings showed, Deng's Southern Tour allowed Chinese thinkers, forced to keep quiet in the years following the

Tiananmen crackdown, to burst back onto the scene. Even at the elite political level, reformist officials moved quickly to use Deng's remarks to advance their own agendas. On March 25, at a meeting of the seventh NPC, Zhu Rongji delivered a speech he characterized as his "personal" lessons from Deng's talks on the Southern Tour. "The present international conditions are favorable to us," Zhu said, and "our national economy is moving in a truly positive direction," the direction of reform. Worrying about whether something is "capitalist" or "socialist" was in the past, according to Zhu. For example, the Shanghai stock market—which Zhu had helped to launch, bolstering his meteoric rise—was "socialist" and not "capitalist." (This particular nod to the "noncapitalist" stock markets was also a protective gesture from China's new economic czar, coming at a time when these young markets were clearly overheating.) Even though the "truly positive direction" Zhu was advocating involved policies that had long been discussed by reformist economists, he was willing to give the credit to Deng's latest speeches in order to advance market ideas. "Deng Xiaoping's talks caused us to suddenly see the light," Zhu said. "[We have to] graft the good things from capitalist countries onto our socialist system"[101] In April Zhu returned to these themes in a speech in which he further strengthened his endorsement of the market, stating that if China wanted to reform enterprises and improve the quality of its products, its leaders should "combine market mechanisms with stronger government oversight" and "first and foremost rely on market competition."[102] After years of beating around the bush, Zhu and a phalanx of Chinese reformers finally could wholeheartedly and publicly praise the market.

Even relatively conservative thinkers felt empowered to write in a more relaxed style, which sometimes included direct references to Western economists. In a spring 1992 article, Chen Yuan—who had become the standard-bearer for the centralizing but market-tolerating agenda known as "neo-conservatism"—published an essay on China's economic research and policy agenda, which began by discussing the 1985 Bashan Conference.[103] Chen had been a graduate student at CASS under Ma Hong (at the same time as Zhu),[104] but he broke with the dominant interpretation of the conference participants, erroneously citing Kornai's presentation as exemplifying the views of those who believed the plan and the market were irreconcilable. (These views were Kornai's arguments with his Budapest "face," not his Beijing "face"; Kornai became an even more ferocious international advocate of these views after 1989, but Chen incorrectly attributes them to the Bashan Report.) "As for our country," he continued, reformulating the significance of Kornai's ideas, "there do not exist purely planned or purely market models"; instead, the relation between the two is "symbiotic."[105]

However, in the final section of Chen's essay, titled "The Revelation of Western Economics," he praised John Maynard Keynes as "a revelation" for "clearly showing that conducting macroeconomic management cannot solely rely on the market, but can only be accomplished by the state." Chinese reformers who claimed that "the state should be driven out of the economy and only become a passive 'referee'" were both out of step with China's "national conditions" and "out of date" with developments in Western economics. Chen continued to say that Milton Friedman and others of the "monetarist school" had useful insights for China about "currency stability, keeping aggregate demand low, and increasing supply," but they were dangerous because some Chinese acolytes admired "their laissez-faire philosophy" more than these policy positions. "If we can rectify these errors," Chen wrote, "we will discover that we can use Western economics for our construction of socialism." Skillful deployment of Western economics, together with careful attention to China's "national conditions," would allow for the emergence of balanced fiscal policy, prudent monetary policy, and effective state intervention to achieve currency stability—thus creating the best macroeconomic environment for the reforms. "This is proven by both Chinese and foreign history," Chen concluded.[106] The two criteria—"Chinese" and "foreign"—were back on the table. Even for the son of Chen Yun, the goal of making China rich allowed China's leaders once again to "use Western economics for our construction of socialism."

As a result of the immense reopening enabled by Deng's Southern Tour, leading economists began to call for an official, permanent endorsement of the role of the market in the Chinese economy. Although Zhao Ziyang's 1987 formulation had given the market a central position, those views—and policies such as the coastal development strategy that were closely associated with Zhao—had become uncomfortable and uncertain territory since his purge. Anticipating the Fourteenth Party Congress scheduled for October 1992, reformers saw a window of opportunity to turn Deng's statements into official ideology.

Early that spring, Wu Jinglian submitted a policy memo to the Politburo that called for the Fourteenth Party Congress to "formally adopt a clear and well-defined authorized expression [*tifa*] for our economic system," which could redefine the Chinese economy to reflect Deng's statements. Wu believed China had only two options: a "socialist commodity economy" (using the Soviet byword for market forces that had been acceptable in China since at least 1984) or a "socialist market economy." The second term had appeared in the 1987 report to describe specific sectors (as a "socialist market system") but had not previously been accepted as a description of the entire economy. Wu found the term "commodity economy," primarily used in Russian, "too confusing" and thought calling China a "socialist market economy" was vastly preferable.[107]

The breakthrough of the Southern Tour also allowed concrete reforms to be implemented. The State Council issued a set of Regulations on Transforming the Operational Mechanisms of Publicly Owned Industrial Enterprises, marking a substantial step forward in expanding the autonomy of state-owned enterprises by granting increased rights to managers. The leadership also approved construction of the Pudong Development Zone in Shanghai and other related activities, including welcoming a large rise in foreign investment. Price reform, which had caused such a crisis in 1988, resumed without turmoil: sixteen provinces launched pilot programs to decontrol grain prices, and, on July 1, 1992, the central government raised the prices of rail transportation, coal, and natural gas and decontrolled production materials "to a considerable extent," such that the number of categories of production and transportation goods under state price control was reduced from 737 to 89. Momentum was building, and Deng's gamble was having swift, tangible effects on the Chinese economy.[108] This process would continue in the years ahead, and, by 1999, 95 percent of retail commodities and

approximately 85 percent of both agricultural commodities and producer goods would be sold at market prices.[109]

As these policies went into effect, Jiang Zemin began to build consensus around redefining the Chinese economy's guiding ideology
at the Fourteenth Party Congress. On April 1, he telephoned Chen
Jinhua, who had taken over the top post at the System Reform Commission, and reportedly told him, "Reform and opening up has
reached a crucial turning point, and everyone is anxiously waiting.
They want to know what the next step will be. . . . I want the commission to research this matter and make a proposal to the Central
Committee." Chen tasked his deputy Lou Jiwei—a rapidly rising
technocrat who had attended the 1985 Bashan Conference and had
become an active voice in the debates under Zhao Ziyang—to organize an internal conference on this subject and to produce the
proposal that Jiang requested. Following this conference, the commission wrote a report submitted directly to Jiang that promoted
the goal of "establishing a socialist market economy." Using this bureaucratic endorsement of the "socialist market economy" concept,
Jiang reached out to Zhu Rongji, confirming his support. Shortly
thereafter, at a June 9 speech at the Central Party School, Jiang
publicly acknowledged his backing of the term, which he praised as
"clear-cut" and "explicit," although he admitted that an internal debate was continuing over the exact wording that would be endorsed at the Fourteenth Party Congress.[110]

On June 12, 1992, Jiang gave the term its final test: he asked Deng
Xiaoping whether he liked it. Deng said yes, adding, "In fact, this is
just what we've been doing. Shenzhen has a socialist market
economy."[111] The ailing Chen Yun, almost ninety years old, did not
put up a significant fight, despite what he once might have thought of
China's embrace of the market; in a July speech, Chen, acknowledging he had never visited a special economic zone, suggested his
support for Zhu Rongji and conceded, "Many effective measures in
the past are no longer appropriate."[112] Within a few short months, the
"socialist market economy" had gone from an unthinkable heresy
to a phrase on the verge of becoming the official designation of
China's booming economy.

*   *   *

The Fourteenth Party Congress, which opened on October 12, 1992, was an event of great fanfare. It doubled as a debut for Jiang and his new reform ideology and a farewell to Deng.[113] Jiang's report to the congress confirmed that the period of conservative retrenchment was over. Citing the initial stage of socialism thesis, Jiang declared, "What we want to establish is a socialist market economic system." He elaborated that a "socialist market economy" would involve:

> [M]arket forces, under the macroeconomic management [*hong-guan tiaokong*] of the state, serving as the basic means of regulating the allocation of resources; to subject economic activity . . . to the changing relations between supply and demand; and to make use of pricing and competition to distribute resources to those enterprises that yield good economic returns . . . so that the efficient ones will prosper and the inefficient ones will be eliminated.

The vision of reformers throughout the 1980s—a system in which market forces would be the "basic means" of running China's economy and the state would engage in indirect "macroeconomic management" of the economy—had, at last, received a full-throated endorsement that pointed directly toward sweeping reform of enterprises and the price system.

As China continued to "give full play to market forces," it would be necessary to continue with the full spectrum of policies that had helped China's economy grow, including learning from unlikely partners. "To achieve superiority over capitalist countries, socialist countries should not hesitate to adopt [ideas] from abroad, including from the developed capitalist countries," Jiang stated—a direct articulation from China's new leader of the role of international influences in developing "socialism with Chinese characteristics."[114]

The congress also endorsed Deng's pragmatic, development-oriented views as an ideological contribution labeled "Deng Xiaoping Theory." Calling Deng the "chief architect of our socialist reform," Jiang repeatedly deferred to the elder statesman's ideas and praised the Southern Tour as a "great breakthrough." As Ezra Vogel has argued, although Deng was not a theoretician, "for Jiang Zemin, elevating Deng's views to a theory strengthened their importance, making them comparable to 'The Thought of Mao Zedong' and making it as easy to focus on the four modernizations as on making revolution."[115] Importantly, however, some of Deng's supposed ideological contributions were taken wholesale from the purged Zhao. For example, Deng received credit for the "initial stage of socialism" thesis that Zhao had championed. Five years after Zhao's 1987 report to the Thirteenth Party Congress, Jiang showed the enduring relevance of many of Zhao's ideas, from the "socialist market" to the "primary stage of socialism," although they were stripped of any reference to their origins. Most fundamentally, Jiang's interest in "elevating Deng's views to a theory" underscored the crucial role Jiang believed ideology would continue to play in debates over China's economic future. As Jiang cleansed China's market-oriented ideology of the taint of Zhao's legacy, he was also sharpening the weapons he and his reformist lieutenants would use in battles to come. Many of his lieutenants walked onstage when, at the end of the congress, a new Politburo Standing Committee was appointed, including Zhu Rongji, who was quickly becoming the country's indispensable economic leader.[116]

Jiang's reformist allies began to sketch out their next steps shortly after the conclusion of the congress. On October 20, Zhu made comments on "the current economic situation" to a large group of central and provincial officials. Highlighting the "very rapid growth" in investment and production, Zhu cited "international financial organizations, globally authoritative research institutes, well-known economists, and businessmen" to contend that "China's economy is already overheating, and inflationary pressures are increasing." To address these problems, Zhu detailed an agenda centered on strengthening macroeconomic control over investment and credit, which would be necessary before price reform could accelerate and investments could come to fruition. Admitting that he was using "mainly administrative measures," Zhu defended his decisions as necessary, because "it would be very hard for economic measures to produce timely results," and, most importantly, "even in developed countries with a market economy, the use of administrative measures when needed is not precluded."[117] Zhu argued that firmly intervening to cool down China's economy was a necessary step to achieve the larger market-oriented goals of his administration.

As Zhu's invocation of "international financial organizations, globally authoritative research institutes," and "well-known economists" acknowledged, China's reformers had also renewed their commitment to learning from foreign economic experts—albeit in less grandly publicized style than during the 1980s. The Ford Foundation resumed its substantial giving to China, providing the CASS Institute of Quantitative and Technical Economics with US$178,000 in 1991.[118] That same year, Franco Modigliani, an expert on household and firm behavior who had won the Nobel Prize in 1985, held seminars at the People's Bank of China (PBOC) attended by Chen Yuan.[119] The following year, Lawrence Klein became a "technical consultant" to the SPC, the kind of position Zhao had hoped Ota Šik would hold a decade earlier.[120] Sir Alec Cairncross also returned to China, this time at the invitation of the re-empowered System Reform Commission. In addition to traveling to western China, Cairncross held meetings in Beijing. His travel diaries from 1992 show how quickly Chinese reformers had returned to their work after Deng's Southern Tour. Significantly, Cairncross encountered tremendous optimism about the prospects for China's growth, with Guo Shuqing—whose passion for economics was a self-described "obsession" and whom Cairncross had brought to Oxford after the conference onboard the S.S. *Bashan*—excitedly citing reports in the *Independent* and the *Guardian* "forecasting that by 2020 China would be the pivot of the world economy," as Cairncross recalled.[121]

Pricing remained a central issue for China's leaders to resolve, but they continued their quick progress without triggering the kind of crisis that had marred previous attempts at price reform. State plans, cut back over the course of 1992, ceased to cover the prices of many key industrial commodities in a transition that economist Barry Naughton has called "remarkably smooth": over 200 million tons of coal were sold at market prices in 1992, and only 20 percent of output at China's largest steel producer was sold under price controls in 1993, down from 80 percent the previous year.[122] Although consumer prices in thirty-five major cities rose by 15.7 percent between January and March 1993, Jiang and Zhu continued to push their reform agenda and avoided another major episode of panic buying.[123]

Zhu's policies, as outlined the previous year, were designed to control inflation without necessitating wholesale retrenchment or undermining longer-term "market vitality." At the same time, the changes in pricing were connected to Zhu's signals that he personally intended to tackle long-standing problems in the reform of state-owned enterprises, calling for "genuine separation of government and enterprises."[124] His rise over a few short years was proof of the need for skillful technocratic leadership at the top rungs of the Party apparatus. A combination of age and strife had eliminated the roles of many of China's savviest economic leaders, from Chen Yun to Zhao Ziyang, and Zhu Rongji was functionally becoming their successor. Due to Zhu's promotion, he was also able to recruit a team of economists he had encountered during the 1980s, including Zhou Xiaochuan, Wu Jinglian, Lou Jiwei, Guo Shuqing, and Wang Qishan (the reformist son-in-law of Yao Yilin). When Li Peng unexpectedly had a heart attack in the spring of 1993 and withdrew to convalesce, Zhu Rongji became acting premier—completing his astonishing rise to the top.[125]

In a step with major ideological significance, the concept of a "socialist market economy" was codified into the Chinese constitution at the eighth NPC in late March 1993. Reformers seized the opportunity to further solidify their gains, replacing a "planned economy on the basis of socialist public ownership" with the new concept. The justification for this change came from another amendment, stating that China was in the "initial stage of socialism." Further, this new "socialist market economy" was formally defined as requiring "macroeconomic management" (*hongguan tiaokong*), the term coined at the Bashan Conference in 1985. These concepts were inextricably connected, and now they were chiseled into the cornerstone of the Chinese state. It had been a long journey from the days on the river in 1985 to the inclusion of new language that redefined the Chinese system in 1993.[126]

Zhu quickly moved to further strengthen the central government's control over the inflationary economic environment. In the morning of June 9, he met with senior economists from the World Bank and the International Monetary Fund, and later that day he chaired a State Council meeting, hearing presentations from the SPC and the System Reform Commission. At the conclusion of the meeting, he proposed a draft of thirteen measures (three more would be added later by the SPC, producing Document No. 6, often referred to as the "Sixteen Articles"; see below). Zhu called for China's leaders to stop "arguing" and face "the hard facts": China needed to impose a sophisticated austerity policy—including curbing the issuance of currency, limiting bank lending, and imposing order on "chaotic" investment. But, in contrast to the 1988 retrenchment, Zhu was adamant that "deepening the reforms"—rather than rolling them back—could achieve these goals and cool down China's overheated economy. These "emergency measures" were set for final review later that summer.[127]

The policies received praise from China's re-empowered economists. Wu Jinglian and Zhou Xiaochuan—both policy advisers to Zhu—coauthored a major statement of their goals for the Chinese economy in the magazine *Reform*. They called for a much more powerful central bank that would strengthen its control over the economy through indirect instruments and gradually move toward conducting open market operations. They also proposed State Council–led fiscal reforms, including the introduction of a value-added tax, transforming state-owned enterprises into "legally defined" joint-stock corporations, and completing price reform. These ideas, developed in tandem with Zhu's "emergency measures," helped to fit these measures into a broader reform plan. At the same time, they acknowledged clear "influences" from other market economies, including "the German-style market economy," Japan, and the "Anglo-American-style market economy." In making reform policy, Wu and Zhou wrote, "We should make a conscious choice among models and design a market economy system with Chinese characteristics."[128]

Zhu, like Zhao Ziyang before him, was eager to seek input from foreign economic experts on his plans. He had given orders for the System Reform Commission, the Ministry of Finance, and the World Bank to organize a conference to think through urgent questions in China's economic reforms, particularly the overheating of the economy that had returned with the relaxation of some of the 1988–1989 retrenchment policies. The conference, convened in mid-June in the northeastern city of Dalian, brought several internationally renowned economists to China, including Kwoh-Ting Li, the Taiwanese official who had led the island's economic transformation from 1965 to 1976; Stanford professor Lawrence Lau; the American expert on the Chinese economy Nicholas Lardy; and Nicholas Stern, a British scholar of development economics who had a close working relationship with the World Bank.[129] Chinese attendees included a number of economic officials who had participated in key exchanges during the 1980s—including Guo Shuqing, Gao Shangquan, and Zhou Xiaochuan—as well as a number of new faces promoted in the years after Tiananmen. Proposed reforms to the governance of China's banks and Zhu's plans for macroeconomic policy making were intensively discussed, with Chinese economists presenting papers on which the foreign economists could comment. This structure was an indication of how much the sophistication and confidence of China's economists had grown since 1985; once largely passive listeners who only offered comments, they were now presenting original research. The foreign economists recommended that China raise bank deposit and loan rates while putting caps on bank lending. They also advised that the government resume its plans, put on hold in 1988, to liberalize price controls, while also strengthening its central bank and taking steps to join the International Monetary Fund.[130] At the conclusion of the conference, the final conference document was submitted directly to Zhu's office.[131]

The ideas of the Chinese and international experts helped Zhu promote an aggressive agenda to cool the economy, reform the tax system, and strengthen macroeconomic controls. In the midsummer heat, Zhu took a series of dramatic steps that left no doubt about his intentions. He appointed himself governor of the PBOC, giving him tremendous personal control over the reforms he hoped to promulgate.[132] At the same time, he unveiled a sixteen-point austerity plan—enlarged and developed from the June draft, drawing heavily on Zhao's "tax for profit" (li gai shui) concept—to cool the economy and create a new tax system. These "Sixteen Articles" worked quickly: by October, the growth rate of money supply (M1) had fallen by more than one-half, and the growth rate of investment in the state sector had fallen from the sky-high 74 percent to 58 percent.[133] In regaining control over the money supply and imposing discipline on China's financial system, Zhu made it clear that he had high expectations for his economic officials, but promised that China was near a breakthrough in bringing about a socialist market economy.[134] The CCP implemented a raft of new policies that were designed to encourage the growth of private businesses by removing restrictions and reforming the accounting and registration systems—leading to a boom in private business that helped keep the economy growing. In 1993, real industrial growth rose by more than 20 percent and GDP increased by 13.4 percent.[135]

Even the "extreme liberal economist" who had been cited in the 1989 report attacking Zhao Ziyang and his relationship with "hostile powers at home and abroad" was welcomed back to China. A Chinese translation of Milton Friedman's *Capitalism and Freedom* was published in 1993 and, that same year, Friedman received and accepted a formal invitation from the System Reform Commission to visit China once again. He traveled to Shanghai and Beijing in October and was astonished at the rapid pace of development. He met with officials and business leaders from both state-owned enterprises and private joint ventures, many of whom said they were trying "to follow the course that Zhao [Ziyang] had commended."[136]

Meeting with economic officials, Friedman issued a challenge that reflected his excitement and bemusement: "The economist who is able to provide an analysis of China's economic development and reform is qualified for a Nobel Prize." At the end of his trip, he was summoned to the Great Hall of the People to meet with Jiang. He repeated his arguments about the necessity of absolutely free private markets.[137] But, unlike Zhao, Jiang did not engage with Friedman; instead, he delivered what Friedman perceived as a pro forma speech about the successes and challenges of CCP management of the Chinese economy. "I conjecture that Jiang did not really want to hear what we had to say," Friedman wrote after the meeting.[138]

The public response to the meeting was muted. A short article in the *People's Daily* described how Jiang had "introduced China's economic system reform" to Friedman and had "welcomed" his "research."[139] In this official forum, it was as if the memory of Friedman's tumultuous role in the 1980s had been erased from history.

Yet, in reviewing the array of major decisions made in the months and years after reform resumed, two crucial dynamics become visible. First, these new leaders were committed to a resumption of consultations with Western economic advisers. Second, Zhu, Jiang, and other economic leaders were clearly returning to a pre-1989 playbook without identifying it as such, drawing on ideas, strategies, and policies that had been developed under Zhao Ziyang. Many of these were the type of Western-influenced, market-oriented proposals for which Zhao had been criticized in June 1989. While under house arrest, Zhao reflected on this fact: "The strategy was no longer mentioned by name, but in reality it continued," he wrote about the coastal development strategy, a comment that can also apply to many other reform policies.[140] Taken together, these two dynamics reveal a substantial continuity between the Zhao era and the early 1990s, even as any explicit references to Zhao and Western economists' influence were erased or downplayed.

In fact, China's leadership moved to set in stone the new ideology and economic policies that owed their origins to Zhao's initiatives. In mid-November 1993, the third plenum of the Fourteenth Party Central Committee convened with the goal of setting out a series of decisions and policy steps about establishing the "socialist market economy" that Jiang Zemin had endorsed in October of the preceding year. The Decision issued at the plenum reiterated many of the key concepts from Jiang's address—embracing the market, advancing enterprise reform, transforming government management of the economy into a system of indirect macroeconomic management—but it broke new ground by offering a thorough, operational blueprint for realizing those goals.

In internal debates among the policy makers tasked with drafting this "Decision," it was precisely in fleshing out Jiang's goals from the previous year that contentious issues emerged. As had been the case in the 1980s, fighting over how to interpret a slogan or phrase was often as intense as the strong-arming needed to garner official consensus to endorse that slogan or phrase in the first place. In the 1993 debates, Jiang's commitment to revitalizing public ownership was a particularly contentious topic, according to participants. Jiang repeatedly asked his team to come up with proposals for creating a corporate governance structure that could integrate public ownership and a market system. Wu Jinglian and Qian Yingyi, a Chinese doctoral student in economics at Harvard, formulated a plan for transitioning "noncorporate" state-owned enterprises into "legal corporate entities" which Jiang approved. But this was not enough, because the broader decision about how to define China's system of enterprises remained unresolved—until, after further debate, Party leaders decided to name "transparency in asset ownership, clear-cut responsibilities of management, 'scientific' economic management, and the separation of party politics from enterprise management" as the key criteria.[141] These items, as well as Wu and Qian's idea, appeared in the section of the Decision on enterprise reform, which stated that achieving these goals would allow for "a modern enterprise system that meets the requirements of the market economy"— requirements that involved having the market become "unified, open, competitive, and predictable."[142] They were lofty goals, but they had not previously been articulated as clearly or as forcefully in a document with the weight of a Decision.

The goal of making the "socialist market economy" a functioning reality underlay the 1993 Decision. The Decision identified specific areas that needed to change for progress to occur. "It is necessary, on the one hand, to inherit our fine traditions and, on the other, to break away from outmoded conventions," the Decision read. One "outmoded" target was the controversial dual-track price system; the Decision called for shifting fully to "a system in which the market sets the prices"—a process already largely underway. Overall, the Decision named "five pillars" of the new socialist market economic system: corporate governance, giving full play to market forces, macroeconomic management, a market-based resource allocation system (including labor, land, and capital), and a continued commitment to social welfare. The Decision concluded with a call to "overcome" the "contradictions and problems" in China's reform process, which were "due to the shortcomings of the old system and the fact that the new system is not yet completely formed." The failures of the "old system"—and the importance of the now clearly defined "new system"—were no longer up for debate.[143]

Western economists were not directly acknowledged or addressed in this blueprint, though they had played a crucial role in shaping its goals and content. That role had sometimes taken the form of direct influence on specific policies, but more frequently their influence was indirect—shaping the ideas and strategies of key CCP economists and policy makers and providing a rising cohort of Chinese experts with techniques and inspiration. Without the participation of the foreign economists, China would not have reformed as quickly, innovatively, and successfully.

By the end of 1993, with a compelling blueprint and Jiang and Zhu leading the charge, China was poised to begin a new era of sweeping economic reform. There was no going back.

Conclusion: Arrivals and Departures

THE IMPORTANCE of this story extends beyond the end point just reached—indeed, its importance extends very much to today and into the future. After the momentous decisions of 1992 and 1993, a new generation of leaders under Jiang Zemin put the crystallized "socialist market economy" concept into practice—and this conceptual underpinning endures. China's global economy today demonstrates the remarkable continuity of two framing dualities: state and market, Chinese and foreign. Yet, although the past and present are continuous, the dominant narratives of the reform era in today's China sideline the international intellectual exchanges at the heart of this book. Indeed, "foreign influences" of all sorts are viewed with open distrust and, at times, even hostility. This distortion of the past not only is wrong but also ignores an important lesson: China is stronger, on its own terms, when it welcomes and acknowledges foreign influence.

In the months and years after the November 1993 Decision, the new generation of reform-oriented leaders that Deng Xiaoping had helped to install in power—including Jiang Zemin, Zhu Rongji, and their economic lieutenants—made large strides toward achieving its goals. On New Year's Day of 1994, a sweeping slate of reforms went into effect, creating a new fiscal and tax system overnight. This "all-around

reform" aimed to solve the problems of the failing fiscal responsibility system and was, in the assessment of present-day analysts, an
"existential necessity."[1] In one dramatic action, Zhu and his lieutenants created a new unified tax system that divided authority between
the central and local governments and established a simpler tax structure, including a value-added tax on manufactures that would substantially boost central government revenue and impose policies
designed to control the fiscal deficit using long- and short-term
government bonds.[2] At the same time, the Chinese leadership over-
hauled the country's foreign exchange system, devaluing the ren-
minbi, eliminating the system of certificates that had previously
governed foreign exchange, and bringing all foreign exchange revenue and expenditures under the control of the state banks that Zhu
was working to strengthen.[3] The new tax system, writes economist
Barry Naughton, "resemble[d] the Western system in many ways."[4]
In 1994, central government revenue would more than double.[5]

As a testament to the continued role of foreign expertise in crafting
China's reform policies, Zhu welcomed a delegation of foreign econ-
omists to Beijing in late August 1994. The conference on "Next
Steps in the Reform of China's Economic System" focused on mi-
croeconomic reforms, which had not moved forward with the bold-
ness of the fiscal reforms. The participants included China expert
Nicholas Lardy and Stanford economists Lawrence Lau, Ronald
McKinnon, and Masahiko Aoki. On the Chinese side, economic officials and advisers in attendance included Wu Jinglian and Zhou
Xiaochuan (who were co-leading the Task Force on the Overall
Design of Economic System Reform) and Lou Jiwei (who was leading
the Task Force on Reforming China's Public Finance and Tax
System). The visiting economists argued that China's state-owned
enterprises should be reformed to become modern multi-shareholding
companies and that China should implement a stronger corporate
governance structure. They also stressed these points in their
meeting with Zhu Rongji, as well as offering suggestions on how to
handle the large debt burden that many enterprises, even profitable
ones, continued to carry.[6]

In 1999, the fourth plenary session of the Fifteenth Party Congress issued a "Decision on Several Important Issues Regarding

Reform and Development of State-Owned Enterprises," which emphasized corporate governance and mandated that state-owned enterprises be transformed into multiple equity-holding entities to end their monopolies. The following year, the Shanghai Stock Exchange issued China's first corporate governance guidance, which Wu Jinglian described as drawing heavily on "the experiences of other countries," especially the "Anglo-American model . . . to enhance the shareholders' value and strengthen the control of the company," and, in January 2002, the China Securities Regulatory Commission made these principles a legal requirement of the country's socialist market economy.[7]

Over this same period, China's economic policy makers moved to develop institutions that would allow the central leadership to make effective macroeconomic policy interventions in the economy—the kind of system that had been a goal since James Tobin introduced it to the attendees of the Bashan Conference in 1985 but that had long seemed out of reach. In January 1996, as a result of recommendations from economists, including Wu Jinglian and Zhou Xiaochuan's task force, China created a unified interbank lending market and, in April, it began to conduct trial runs of open market operations. In 1997, a Monetary Policy Committee was established to provide policy guidance as China's leaders developed these institutions.[8]

A series of promotions the following year confirmed China's commitment to these policies. On March 7, 1998, Zhu Rongji—who had been running the economy in a variety of roles for five years, including as a member of the Politburo Standing Committee—became the country's premier, completing his rise to the top. He brought his favorite economic policy makers with him: Lou Jiwei was promoted to vice minister of finance and Zhou Xiaochuan and Guo Shuqing were made vice governors of China's central bank, the People's Bank of China (PBOC). These decisions ensured that the technocrats who had studied and helped to design these systems from the beginning would also run them.[9]

Those years also saw the passing of some of the last members of the generation that had helped to lead the PRC since its founding. Yao Yilin died in December 1994, followed shortly thereafter by his ally and mentor Chen Yun in April 1995.[10] Their lives had spanned the vast transformations of their homeland's tumultuous twentieth century. Chen, born during the last throes of the Qing dynasty, had fought in the communist revolution that took power in 1949, had been denounced during the Cultural Revolution, had argued with Deng about the direction of China's reforms, and then lived to see China's GDP surpass half a trillion US dollars.

Deng Xiaoping himself died on February 19, 1997, following years without a public appearance. Hailing him as a "great Marxist and the true architect of China's socialist reforms and modernization," news reports noted that his death did not disturb the daily routines of Beijing residents—a stark contrast to Mao's death over twenty years earlier. In contrast to the historic transformation after Mao died, Deng's death portended continuity: the continuation of the policies of "reform and opening" and of China's market-oriented economic boom under the rule of the Chinese Communist Party (CCP).[11]

When the CCP held its official funeral for Deng a week later, ten thousand cadres dressed in black attended. Jiang Zemin wept as he delivered an hour-long eulogy in the Great Hall of the People, adorned only with austere garlands of cypress and evergreen. The speech praised Deng's "most precious legacy" of the "socialist market economy" and looked forward to the continuation of reform. Deng's ashes rested in an urn draped with the CCP flag's hammer and sickle. Audiences all around China watched the funeral on television. A young woman scarcely old enough to have lived in China before Deng—and now working at the Beijing Commodities Exchange, an unimaginable place before the "reform and opening"—wiped a tear from her eye as news cameras rolled.[12]

In September 1997, seven months after Deng died, Jiang presided over the Fifteenth Party Congress. It had been a year of historic changes: in addition to Deng's death, Hong Kong had been returned to the People's Republic of China (PRC) on July 1, an event that not only had enormous practical and financial benefits but also symbolized China's resurgence over a former imperialist menace. Jiang's report to the congress reaffirmed the Party's commitment to Deng Xiaoping Theory and to "building socialism with Chinese characteristics." While he called for "keeping public ownership as the mainstay of the economy," Jiang encouraged "diverse forms of ownership to develop," and stated, "Even if the state-owned sector accounts for a smaller proportion of the economy, this will not affect the socialist nature of our country." An era of booming private business had arrived, and Jiang, with Zhu Rongji at his side, was willing to assert that "nonpublic sectors are organic components of a socialist market economy," a claim that was intended to legitimate the status of the private sector and was codified as an amendment to China's constitution in the following year.[13]

As financial crisis spread throughout Asia in the second half of 1997, causing demand for Chinese goods to fall, Zhu Rongji and his lieutenants determined that they had a critically important opportunity to develop macroeconomic policies that could increase aggregate demand. These policies went into effect beginning in early 1998. Although GDP growth slowed in 1998 and 1999, the Asian financial crisis was more of a warning (what Nicholas Lardy termed a "wake-up call") than a disaster for China. The crisis in Asia had been precipitated in large part by weak banking systems and highly leveraged industrial investment in the countries where it originated. Seeing this encouraged the leadership to prioritize cleaning up and improving China's banking system and making progress with industrial reform—persistent issues that the 1997–1998 crisis demonstrated could threaten to undermine the large strides China had made over the preceding twenty years.[14]

During the period that followed, China's economy truly became the global superpower that Deng, Zhao Ziyang, and their colleagues had labored to create. One of the most significant achievements of Zhu's tenure came in November 2001, when China celebrated its accession to the World Trade Organization (WTO). Zhao Ziyang had led China's application to rejoin the General Agreement on Tariffs and Trade (GATT) in 1986. In the 1990s, Zhu aggressively moved to lower tariff barriers, remove import quotas, open up the banking and financial sectors, and reform China's enforcement system so that the country could meet WTO standards and, in the words of Wu Jinglian, "be integrated into the world economic system" and accept "the rules of globalization to some extent." At the same time, Zhu vigorously negotiated the terms of China's accession to protect his country's interests and facilitate the transition.[15] President Bill

Clinton called it a "once in a generation" opportunity.[16] Zhu also "used the WTO accession to promote domestic reforms," in the words of scholar Yang Jiang. In order to meet WTO standards and enable China to be "integrated into the world economic system," Zhu beat back resistance by various domestic interests and forced reforms in China's financial policy, currency valuation, and the treatment of state-owned enterprises.[17]

Thus, China's WTO accession can be understood in two ways: first, as bringing a huge rise in trade and investment, reshaping the Chinese economy through global flows of goods and services; and, second, as joining an international institution that required new standards for the domestic economy, translating global requirements into Chinese policies. As with the savvy economists of the Zhao era, but with a new twist, Zhu Rongji used international ideas and norms to shape and support his agenda at home—showing how powerful those norms continued to be when Chinese leaders saw them as aligned with their own reform objectives. At the end of 2002, China surpassed the United States as the largest market for foreign direct investment (FDI) in the world.[18] In 2005, during the early years of President Hu Jintao's and Premier Wen Jiabao's tenures, some Chinese economists were estimating that the private sector accounted for as much as 70 percent of China's GDP.[19] Growth has continued since. In 2015 alone, China attracted over US$126 billion in FDI. Its trade with the world has boomed: the total value of exports and imports in 2015 were approximately RMB 24.59 trillion, or US$3.8 trillion—and fluctuations in its economy are felt in markets across the world.[20] Even as it faces clear uncertainties about its future growth prospects, China now has a truly global economy and is a driving force in the global economic system.

In the midst of all this growth, on January 17, 2005, Zhao Ziyang—one of the key figures who had made this economic transformation possible—died after more than fifteen years under house arrest. A brief official announcement referred to Zhao only as a "comrade," not mentioning that he had served as premier and Party general secretary. No further coverage of his death was allowed in the PRC.[21] Later that year, the CCP rehabilitated Hu Yaobang on what would have been his ninetieth birthday, despite his alleged "bourgeois tendencies."[22] But no change has been made to Zhao's status in the ten years since he died, although Zhao's family announced in April 2015, after many years of arguments with authorities, that it had received permission to bury his ashes.[23] Zhao has not been rehabilitated, despite the fact that the Party and country enjoys the fruits of his labor to remake China's economic system.

At this writing, despite tremendous transformations in China's economy and society, the two dualities of state and market, Chinese and foreign, remain as central as ever. In part, of course, this is because they are large, enduring themes at the heart of modern Chinese history. But it is also because the ideology that governs the world's most populous country has been evolving in ways that are continuous with the period from 1976 to 1993—and because the individuals at the center of the action today continue both to debate and to enact these same dualities.

Many of the junior figures in this book have taken up the reins of power. Zhou Xiaochuan, who coauthored numerous articles with Wu Jinglian and advocated "coordinated reform," has been governor of China's central bank since 2002 and is widely credited with modernizing China's monetary policy system and maintaining macroeconomic stability.[24] Lou Jiwei, the young advocate for reforms to China's fiscal system in the 1980s, has assumed top positions in the financial field: in 2013, he became China's minister of finance, leaving behind China's sovereign wealth fund (which he had led since 2007) with US$575.2 billion in assets under its management.[25] Guo Shuqing, another member of Wu Jinglian's "coordinated reform" group in the 1980s, has served as chairman of the China Construction Bank (the second-largest bank in the world by market capitalization) and the country's chief securities regulator, and was subsequently promoted to the governorship of Shandong province (population of nearly 100 million and GDP of approximately US$800 billion). In Shandong, he has advanced an ambitious, experimental program of market reforms that a leading Chinese newsmagazine dubbed "Guo's New Deal."[26] It is particularly remarkable to recall that Lou Jiwei and Guo Shuqing shared a room aboard the S.S. *Bashan* in 1985.

These economists fill out the ranks of President Xi Jinping's policy-making apparatus, steering the state-market relationship forward as the world watches their every move. The transformation of the Party's technocratic elite is clear, with a new generation of senior CCP policy makers who were educated in modern economics and, in some cases, in the West. Premier Li Keqiang and Vice President Li Yuanchao both earned graduate degrees in economics at Peking University under the supervision of Li Yining, the skillful advocate of enterprise reform who played a consistent role as an economic adviser in the 1980s.[27] Liu He, who runs the Central Leading Group for Financial and Economic Affairs and is widely believed to be Xi's closest economic adviser, received a graduate degree in public administration at Harvard.[28]

These Chinese leaders regularly consult with foreign economic experts to help devise new policies. After all, they grew up at a time when their predecessors were calling for "learning to do economic work from all who know how, no matter who they are," and many of them have continued in this spirit. For example, Premier Li Keqiang, while he was still vice premier, commissioned a report from the World Bank, titled *China 2030*, coauthored with the Development Research Center of the State Council. The report set out long-term development goals, including avoiding falling into a "middle-income trap"; it received praise from many quarters, as well as the pushback that marked many of the World Bank's activities in China in the 1980s, with one Chinese economist calling the document "mainly garbage."[29] Edwin Lim, the former World Bank chief of mission in Beijing, has partnered with Nobel laureate Michael Spence to create the China Economic Research and Advisory Program.[30] Other annual conferences for providing policy advice to Chinese policy makers include the Bo'ao Forum for Asia and the China Development Forum, which have become institutionalized venues for consultation and exchange.

Chinese economists have also joined the professional ranks of their peers around the world. For example, Justin Yifu Lin, who received his PhD in economics from the University of Chicago, served from 2008 to 2012 as the first non-Western World Bank chief economist, and Qian Yingyi, dean of Tsinghua's School of Economics and Management, received his PhD in economics from Harvard and was a professor at the University of California at Berkeley.[31] Career paths such as these represent the culmination of a process that began in the late 1970s with calls for "observing objective economic laws" and subsequently led to the formation of training programs in modern economics led by figures such as Lawrence Klein and Gregory Chow.

To a remarkable degree, current debates over the future direction of China's economic reforms have the same pivot points as the debates of the preceding decades. In 2013, the communiqué of the third plenum of the Eighteenth Central Committee, presided over by Xi Jinping, stated, "We must deepen economic system reform by centering on the decisive role of the market," which Xi called the "major theoretical viewpoint in this plenum resolution."[32] The release of this document signaled the perennially ambiguous standing of reformers as Xi came to power. The new word "decisive" (*juedingxing*) was clearly inserted to signal a greater pro-market emphasis, but Xi asserted, "We have consistently sought new scientific positions concerning the relationship between government and market," and it remained unclear how far the new leadership will actually push the possible meanings of "decisive." Even as he was emphasizing the central importance of the "decisive role" of the market, Xi pointed to what he termed a global "competition with capitalism" and further stated:

> Now, our country's socialist market economic system has basically been established, and the extent of marketization has risen substantially, our understanding of market laws and our ability to control them is incessantly rising. . . . [W]e still must persist in giving rein to the superiorities of our country's socialist system, and give rein to the positive role of the Party and the government. The market has a decisive function in resource allocation, but it does not have the total function.[33]

Xi also emphasized the continuing role of the state-owned sector, including enterprises and asset management, as well as a role for the "nonpublic economy," including private companies and foreign joint ventures, with the "public" economy and "nonpublic" economy as the "organic component parts of the socialist market economy."[34] In the years ahead, the government-market balance in the Chinese system will surely be the subject of ongoing debate, contestation, and movement.

Within academic economic circles in China, debates about the state and the market rage on. In the summer of 2014, two leading economists—Justin Yifu Lin and Zhang Weiying—clashed over how to interpret the "decisive" role of the market at a Shanghai conference, with Lin calling for a greater role for the government and Zhang promoting freer markets. The prominent financial news outlet Caixin called this "a debate reminiscent of the clashes between John Keynes and Friedrich Hayek that shaped major developed countries' economic policies for most of the last century."[35] The comparison is a reminder that debates about "the relationship between government and market"—Xi's phrase—remain a perennial subject within the West as well as in China.

Beyond the realm of economics, of course, China's reform is far from complete, with particular progress needed in the realm of political and social organization. In 2010, János Kornai asked insistently in an interview with the Chinese newsmagazine *Caijing:* "How long will it be possible to sustain, without change or reform, a political system that guarantees the present macroeconomic situation and the present ratio of consumption to investment?" He added, "The spread of private ownership, free enterprise, and market coordination provides favorable conditions for political reform, but it does not guarantee automatically that the reform will be accomplished."[36] Chinese leaders have asserted that they understand the need for political reform to improve governance, reduce corruption, and take account of public opinion, but their ideas about democracy and political rights are contested by many inside China as well as outside, and rightly so. Xi Jinping's political style seems fundamentally authoritarian, as he consolidates titles and power in his person and develops his public persona as "Papa Xi," and his actions have demonstrated a low tolerance for political dissent and a broadened role for the state in everyday life.[37]

Whatever changes lie ahead, it seems prudent to try to understand China's evolving state-market relationship in terms of its own lineage. In the economic realm, the evolution of the meaning of "socialist market economy" is likely to reflect the same generative contradictions that have shaped the entire history of the reform period: rising understanding of market forces enmeshed with rising ability to control them, and a "decisive" but not "total" role for the market within a "socialist system." In the future, of course, it is possible that the Chinese concept of a "socialist market economy" might change into a genuine "market economy" with various "social" constraints on the market, such as social safety nets, considerable government regulation, government-mandated economic redistribution policies, and even some government ownership—that is, something more closely resembling the mixed system of markets and government that characterize many economies around the world that are considered "market systems." In other words, the phrase "socialist market economy" is tremendously malleable in terms of both the "socialist" and the "market" dimensions. As long as the CCP remains in power, the relationship between the socialist state and the competitive market will continue to be the pivotal duality and the perpetual ground of contestation over further reform.

A related, equally important, but less certain dynamic is how these economic ideas and the resulting practices will cause the global China of today to interact with the West and the international order. The United States has the world's largest economy by nominal GDP, and China has the world's second-largest economy by nominal GDP.[38] In 2013, the WTO ranked China as the world's largest exporter of goods and the second-largest importer, and its total volume of imports and exports made it the world's largest trading country, with the European Union and the United States its largest trading partners.[39] China's foreign exchange reserves increased from US$610 billion in 2006 to US$3.23 trillion in February 2016, the largest holdings of any country in the world.[40] Of course, in the realm of trade and investment, China and other economies will continue to compete for advantage—that much is a given.

But beyond these regular competitive economic activities, President Xi has also referred to the "competition with capitalism," as we have seen—and also "the protracted nature of contest over the international order." In an important foreign policy speech at the end of 2014, he stressed, "The growing trend toward a multipolar world will not change."[41] Such statements imply that China still views itself as pitted against the West in more fundamental ways: in the realm of economic ideas and political models and in the developing international order, including economic organizations as well as broader regional, geopolitical, and military arrangements. In considering these prospects, however, the themes remain remarkably persistent, pivoting around the two dualities of state and market, Chinese and foreign. Of course, in the decades ahead, these issues will also continue to evolve. Will China join a global order that it believes Western capitalist countries have built? Will it seek adjustments to that order? Will it seek to overturn that order?

The continuities between the debates this book has chronicled and those in the present are clear. Why does it matter that we tell these stories? And why have they been sidelined in the dominant narrative of China's transformation?

One of the great achievements of the reformers in and around the Chinese leadership was a willingness to engage with international economists and ideas and to bring them to bear on China's reforms—an approach that identified the most relevant ideas, like iron filings in sawdust, using the magnet of China's "national conditions" and needs. Put another way, Chinese reformers displayed considerable skill in exploring, learning from, interpreting, applying, and presenting these foreign ideas for Chinese audiences, and these skills were one reason for the success of China's transition from socialism, compared to the experiences of so many other countries that stumbled. The engagement was not a sign of failure or submission to foreign hegemony but, rather, a signature achievement that helped to define a "golden age" of openness and intellectual flexibility in China.

Yet these stories of international engagement are uncomfortable terrain for the Chinese leadership, largely because its dominant narrative identifies China's "socialist market economy" as the CCP's major post-Mao ideological innovation, a wholly Chinese product of the Party's leadership that brought China to a position of global power. China's rulers have justified and explained the country's transformation using the ideology of the "socialist market economy"—which was, in Foreign Minister Wang Yi's words, "grown out of the soil of China." In contrast to a history of humiliation at the hands of foreign imperial powers, China's enormous economic success is a critical component of the "rejuvenation" (*fuxing*) of the Chinese nation. In the face of this patriotic narrative, it could be seen as a slight to shine a light on the role of foreign ideas and individuals. If anything, official Chinese organs are stressing "Chinese characteristics" and voicing greater resistance to the ideas and influence of "hostile foreign powers."[42] In early 2015, following a series of announcements about the need to emphasize ideological purity on Chinese university campuses, Education Minister Yuan Guiren issued a set of rules designed to eliminate the influence of "Western values" from the education system, starting with translated textbooks: "By no means allow teaching materials that disseminate Western values in our classrooms." The pungent irony of these decisions by no means rests solely on the influence of Marx and Lenin on Mao's revolutionary China. Just as central is the reality that the economic theories that guided China's post-Mao economic policies were often developed after consulting influential foreign ideas and partners. The irony becomes even greater when one recalls that the current premier, Li Keqiang, not only was a doctoral student under Li Yining but devoted a substantial portion of his graduate studies in both economics and law to translating and studying foreign texts. ("We should convene a conference to study how Premier Li Keqiang disseminated Western legal theories," the controversial liberal law professor He Weifang told the *New York Times*, with more than a hint of sarcasm.)[43] Leaders who rule a country that boomed due in part to intellectual engagement with the West now seek both to marginalize those historical stories and to repress their continuation in the present.

The CCP undoubtedly deserves credit for its decision to embark on China's "reform and opening." The policies have reduced poverty and produced much greater prosperity for the Chinese people and, through trade, countless others around the world. But we have an obligation to tell the fuller story. The CCP has invested a great deal of effort to maintain an identity for "socialism with Chinese characteristics" that conforms to what the Party wants today. Just as

Zhao Ziyang has been erased from the history of the reforms he led because of his alleged "betrayal of the Party," so, too, are the partnerships between Western experts and Chinese policy makers too often sidelined. This disconnect is also regrettable for those who seek to give credit for the success of China's reforms to the CCP's leadership, because if they do not acknowledge this history they cannot even fully praise China's leaders for bringing the best ideas in the world to China, negotiating among complex competing viewpoints, and developing a system that could work in China.

This disconnect between the actual historical role of foreign advisers and the present-day denunciations of "Western influence" is also troubling for much broader reasons. China advances more rapidly and becomes more successful when it is open to the outside world. That openness brings risks and challenges, to be sure, but it has been a consistent guide to the positive development of the Chinese system since 1976. China's economy has flourished through partnership with foreigners.

Do President Xi Jinping and Premier Li Keqiang truly believe that foreign influences have been "hostile" to China's achievement of wealth and power on a global scale? If they do, they are, paradoxically, undercutting the potent and pervasive theme of Chinese agency in shaping and reshaping foreign influences throughout the entire reform era. And they are dramatically misinterpreting the recent history of the country that they rule. The choice is not between wholesale importation and total refusal. The process of influence is not one of "infiltration" or rejection. The full spectrum of partnering dynamics—picking and choosing, reformulating, occluding, and disguising influence—remains open to the Chinese leadership, and the success of a prior generation of leaders who saw the value of these forms of openness and engagement should guide China's leaders today.

The episodes in this book are seldom discussed in the West, which also deserves explanation. One reason may be that they call into question the received assumptions about how Western countries influence the developing world—and, indeed, how economic development occurs. Instead of an inevitable teleology toward Western-defined "development," these stories show the negotiated acceptance of market ideas and global norms—by Chinese leaders, on Chinese terms. As countries around the world from Hungary to Cuba to South Africa openly praise the Chinese system as a seemingly viable alternative to the liberal capitalist model of many Western countries—and as China "goes global" and attempts to spread its influence[44]—it is critical for our policy makers and opinion leaders to rethink what they take for granted about what "Western influence" can and cannot do in other countries. It is especially important that they do so when, as in China's case, the country in question rejects the wholesale importation of foreign proposals and sees itself as an equal partner in interpreting and implementing economic ideas from abroad and in shaping new ones.[45]

However, as always, the choice about how to view this history and whether to continue these partnerships will ultimately fall to the Chinese. It will be deeply regrettable if the current leadership continues to sideline international engagements as one of the signature achievements of the reform era in China. And it will be worrying indeed if these leaders and their policy advisers turn inward and break with the tradition of beneficial openness, which Deng Xiaoping—the "chief architect of China's socialist reform and opening," as Xi Jinping called him in a major speech in 2014[46]—embraced throughout his tenure and that had a proven track record of success in the period 1976–1993 and beyond. As the Chinese propaganda apparatus goes into overdrive promoting Xi's "China Dream" for the future of his country, even declaring that President Xi is the "new architect" of China's reforms, we must hope that one of the new architect's innovations will not be to close the gate to foreign ideas that Deng opened for a prior generation.[47] Openness to the outside world has served China well for more than three decades, and it still can help China address the daunting problems it faces today.

For all these reasons, it is my hope that the theme of partnership explored in this book will become a central part of the narrative of China's ongoing economic transformation. This shift is long overdue—and it must happen to build a more positive future for China's relationships with Western countries.

What we emphasize about the past shapes what we are likely to do in the present. At a moment when "strategic distrust" between

Western countries (especially the United States) and China is running high, the ways we choose to conceive of our shared history matter more than ever.[48] The *Wall Street Journal* reported in June 2015, "As tensions with China rise, U.S. foreign policy thinkers are dusting off ideas from the Cold War—and questioning the long-standing consensus for engagement with Beijing."[49] As China rises and projects its newfound power in Asia and globally, taking a more resolute stance toward Beijing will often be necessary. But this is another area in which historians can offer a broader perspective. If we emphasize the conflicts between the Western systems of economic organization and China's, then these examples of conflict are likely to breed more of the same. But if we can focus on the stories of partnership and exchange between China and the wider world, then we may be able to push back against Chinese jeremiads about "hostile foreign influences" and American warnings about the unmitigated "threat" of China's "influence" around the globe.[50]

The same is true of helping to advance the cause of reformers in China today, who want to make Chinese society freer, fairer, and more sustainable. In recent years, Wu Jinglian has written, "It is clear that the reform is far from complete" in the PRC, and he has called on international economists to make "common efforts" with their Chinese peers "to build a better world."[51] The spirit of cooperation and partnership is a part of China's shared history with the rest of the world, certainly on matters like the development of its economic system but also on challenges on many other fronts, and we should hope that our experts and leaders take up the challenges with that spirit in mind.

Economic development is a more complex process of transnational interactions than is often assumed. This book has focused primarily on transnational interactions that take place in the realm of ideas and experts. Because those ideas had real-world consequences, some attention has also been given to transnational interactions that take place on the practical terrain of economic activity, such as the trading relationships between China and the rest of the world. But another element also deserves mention: the people-to-people relations that create complex webs of personal relationships between millions of ordinary individuals across countries.[52] In fact, history may increasingly be made by the personal interactions of millions of ordinary individuals connecting with others across national borders, through travel, work, the Internet, and so forth. In the case of the United States and China, a generational sea change is underway on this front. Hundreds of thousands of Chinese study in the United States every year, and the number is growing. In a more recent development, tens of thousands of American high school and college students are studying or working in China, expanding their knowledge of China and the Chinese on an unprecedented scale and at an earlier and more formative stage.[53] The dynamics of these person-to-person interactions are as complex as the dynamics in the realm of economic ideas I have discussed—with crosscutting lines, in both directions, of influence, curiosity, resistance, and the full range of other dynamics that make up human relationships. For now, it is sufficient to say that these relationships are not simply part of individuals' personal histories. Cumulatively, they are in fact shaping, expressing, and even enacting the world's public history.

Today a socialist market system governs the world's second-largest economy, with a GDP of more than US$10 trillion as of 2016. And although their stories and "common efforts" are hardly acknowledged in China or the West, the achievements of the partners whose stories are told in this book have endured, as have the relationships built in this process. In January 2008, the year the Beijing Olympics celebrated China's ascension to a truly global stage, Wu Jinglian and János Kornai celebrated their birthdays, only a few days apart, together in Beijing. Despite the winter cold, the city was bustling and booming, a testament to China's growth. Kornai had come to China to lecture but made sure, as always, to see his "dear friend" Wu. Surrounded by admirers, Kornai and Wu spent the party reminiscing about old times and discussing the current state of China's reforms. The hot September days aboard the S.S. *Bashan* must have seemed a world away. A birthday cake was brought out as the pair beamed. The two men rose from their chairs, as if to give a speech. Then, together, they blew out the candles.[54]

Abbreviations in the Notes

CYNP   Zhu Jiamu 朱佳木, ed., 陈云年谱: 一九〇五–一九九五 [*Chronology of Chen Yun: 1905–1995*], 3 vols. (Beijing: Zhongyang wenxian chubanshe, 2000).

DXPNP   Leng Rong 冷溶, ed., 邓小平年谱 *1975–1997* [*A Chronology of Deng Xiaoping, 1975–1997*], 2 vols. (Beijing: Zhongyang wenxian chubanshe, 2004).

GSJTL   Committee on Historical Manuscripts of the People's Republic of China 中国人民共和国史稿委员会, ed., 邓力群国史讲谈录 [*A Record of Deng Liqun's Talks on the History of the Country*], internal manuscript (7 volumes, 2000–2002).

JJYJ   经济研究 (*Economic Research*), journal.

LXNNP   李先念年谱 [*Chronology of Li Xiannian*], 6 vols. (Beijing: Zhongyang wenxian chubanshe, 2011).

RMRB   人民日报 (*People's Daily*), newspaper.

SWDXP   *Selected Works of Deng Xiaoping, 1975–1982* (Beijing: Foreign Languages Press, 1984).

SWDXP-3   *Selected Works of Deng Xiaoping, Vol. III* (Beijing: Foreign Languages Press, 1994).

XMQHYL   薛暮桥回忆录 [*Memoirs of Xue Muqiao*] (Tianjin: Tianjin renmin chubanshe, 1996).

XMQNP   薛暮橋年谱 [*A Chronology of Xue Muqiao*], unpublished document, no pagination.

ZFLZQJ   Fang Weizhong 房维中, ed., 在风浪中前进: 中国发展与改革编年记事 [Forward in the Storm: Chronology of China's Reform and Development, 1977–1989], unpublished 2004 document. Available in the Fairbank Collection, Fung Library, Harvard University.

ZZYWJ   赵紫阳文集 *1980–1989* [*Collected Works of Zhao Ziyang,*
                 1980–1989], 4 vols. (Hong Kong: Chinese University
                 Press, 2016).

ZZYYZZGG   Wu Guoguang 吴国光, 赵紫阳与政治改革 [*Zhao Ziyang and
                 Political Reform*] (Hong Kong: Taipingyang shiji chu-
                 banshe, 1997).

Notes

INTRODUCTION

1. National Bureau of Statistics, 中国统计年鉴 2009 [*China Statistical Yearbook 2009*] (Beijing: Zhongguo tongji chubanshe, 2009).

2. Deng Xiaoping, "Uphold the Four Cardinal Principles" (March 30, 1979), in *Selected Works of Deng Xiaoping, 1975–1982* (Beijing: Foreign Languages Press, 1984) (cited hereafter as SWDXP), 174.

3. See Chen Yun 陈云, "经济形势与经验教训" [The Economic Situation and Our Experiences and Lessons] (December 16, 1980), in 陈云文选 [*Selected Works of Chen Yun*] (Beijing: Renmin chubanshe, 1995), 3:279.

4. Zhao Ziyang, *Prisoner of the State: The Secret Journal of Zhao Ziyang* (New York: Simon & Schuster, 2009), 113.

5. Chen Yizi 陈一谘, 陈一谘回忆录 [*Memoirs of Chen Yizi*] (Hong Kong: Xin shiji chuban ji chuanmei youxian gongsi, 2013), 312; Zhang Weiying 张维迎 [Shaan Ren 陕仁], "中国的经济改革与经济学家" [Chinese Economic Reform and Economists], 知识分子 [*The Chinese Intellectual*] 3, no. 2 (Winter 1987): 23–28.

6. Deng Xiaoping 邓小平, "实行开放政策, 学习世界先进科学技术" [Implement the Reform and Opening, Study the World's Advanced Science and Technology] (October 10, 1978), in 邓小平文选 [*Selected Works of Deng Xiaoping*] (Beijing: Renmin chubanshe, 2nd ed., 1994), 132–133.

7. Gu Mu 谷牧, "小平同志领导我们抓对外开放" [Comrade Xiaoping Led Us to Pursue Opening to the Outside World], in 回忆邓小平 [*Remembering Deng Xiaoping*], ed. China Central Party Literature Research Center 中国中央文献研究室 (Beijing: Zhongyang wenxian chubanshe, 1998), 1:155–156.

8. Hu Yaobang, "Speech at the Second National Congress of the Chinese Scientific and Technical Association (Excerpts)," *Beijing Review*, no. 15 (April 14, 1980): 13–16.

9. Deng Xiaoping, "There Is No Fundamental Contradiction between Socialism and a Market Economy" (October 23, 1985), in *Selected Works of Deng Xiaoping, Vol. III* (Beijing: Foreign Languages Press, 1994) (cited hereafter as SWDXP-3), 152. The connection between "markets" and "capitalism" is a

controversial element of reform socialism. Although it is grounded in the writings of Karl Marx and Friedrich Engels, some commentators, discussing "the extensive markets in many precapitalist societies and the strong element of monopoly and state interference with markets throughout the history of capitalism," have claimed this "familiar equation" has no "historical or theoretical basis." See Benjamin Kunkel, "Paupers and Richlings," *London Review of Books* 36, no. 13 (July 3, 2014): 17–20.

10. Li Lanqing, *Breaking Through: The Birth of China's Opening-Up Policy* (Oxford: Oxford University Press, 2009), 5.

11. Mao Zedong, "We Must Learn to Do Economic Work" (January 10, 1945), in *Selected Works of Mao Tse-tung* (Peking: Foreign Languages Press, 1965), 3:191. See also Stuart Schram, *The Thought of Mao Tse-tung* (Cambridge: Cambridge University Press, 1989), 92–93; Alexander V. Pantsov and Steven I. Levine, *Mao: The Real Story* (New York: Simon & Schuster, 2012).

12. Constitution of the People's Republic of China (adopted December 4, 1982 and amended March 29, 1993), Article 7, accessed March 1, 2013, at http://english.peopledaily.com.cn/constitution/constitution.html.

13. I define ideology as a system of beliefs people hold to motivate political action—or, to use a metaphor, "ideology takes an undifferentiated visual field and brings it into focus, so that objects appear in a predetermined relation to each other" (Mark Lilla, "Our Libertarian Age," *The New Republic* [June 17, 2014], at https://newrepublic.com/article/118043/our-libertarian-age-dogma-democracy-dogma-decline).

14. I use the term "Western" to refer to figures from Eastern Europe as well as Western Europe and North America, a usage that comes from Chinese sources, where both sides of the Iron Curtain are often grouped together. When the source material makes a distinction, I have noted it. Usage of the term is not intended to be reductive or Procrustean; the spectrum of identities the term "Western" could encompass was varied, but it was a central and pervasive concept in the writings by senior Chinese policy makers and economists.

15. See Joseph Fewsmith, *Dilemmas of Reform in China: Political Conflict and Economic Debate* (Armonk, NY: M.E. Sharpe, 1994), 169; Ezra Vogel, *Deng Xiaoping and the Transformation of China* (Cambridge: Belknap Press of Harvard University Press, 2011), 461; and Harold K. Jacobson and Michel Oksenberg, *China's Participation in the IMF, the World Bank, and GATT* (Ann Arbor: University of Michigan Press, 1990), 141. Treatment of the weeklong 1985 Bashan Conference with participation by China's top economists and an extraordinary group of leading foreign economists demonstrates this tendency. Fewsmith gives it one paragraph, calling the conference "the turning point" but saying little else. Because his project is primarily political and biographical, Vogel devotes three paragraphs suggesting the importance of the Bashan Conference but he does not provide intellectual context for that claim. Jacobson and Oksenberg's study makes only deprecating mention of the World Bank's intellectual influences. Many other works addressing this period ignore the Bashan Conference entirely.

16. See, for example, Wu Jinglian, "Economics and China's Economic Rise," in *The Chinese Economy: A New Transition*, ed. Masahiko Aoki and Jinglian Wu (New York: Palgrave Macmillan, 2012), 13–33; Zhao Renwei 赵人伟, "1985 年'巴山轮会议'的回顾与思考" [Remembering and Reflecting on the 1985 'Bashan

Conference'], 经济研究 [*Economic Research*] (cited hereafter as JJYJ), no. 12 (2008): 17–28. One study that makes use of some of these connections, focusing on neoliberalism and pension reform, is Aiqin Hu, "The Global Spread of Neoliberalism and China's Pension Reform since 1978," *Journal of World History* 23, no. 3 (2012): 609–638.

17. Daniel H. Bays, *China Enters the Twentieth Century: Chang Chih-tung and the Issues of a New Age, 1895–1909* (Ann Arbor: University of Michigan Press, 1978); William Ayers, *Chang Chih-tung and Education Reform in China* (Cambridge: Harvard University Press, 1971); Paul Trescott, *Jingji Xue: The History of the Introduction of Western Economic Ideas into China, 1850–1950* (Hong Kong: Chinese University Press, 2007); Y. C. Wang, *Chinese Intellectuals and the West, 1872–1949* (Chapel Hill: University of North Carolina Press, 1966); Benjamin Schwartz, *In Search of Wealth and Power: Yen Fu and the West* (Cambridge: Belknap Press of Harvard University Press, 1964).

18. Benjamin I. Schwartz, *Chinese Communism and the Rise of Mao* (Cambridge: Harvard University Press, 1951); Rana Mitter, *A Bitter Revolution: China's Struggle with the Modern World* (Oxford: Oxford University Press, 2004), 135–137, 143–145; Tony Saich, "The Chinese Communist Party during the Era of the Comintern (1919–1943)," prepared for Juergen Rojahn, "Comintern and National Communist Parties Project," International Institute of Social History, Amsterdam, 5–6.

19. See Timothy Cheek, ed., *A Critical Introduction to Mao* (New York: Cambridge University Press, 2010); Stuart Schram, *The Political Thought of Mao Tse-tung* (New York: Praeger, 1963), 70. This dynamic—a kind of "anxiety of influence" (Harold Bloom, *The Anxiety of Influence: A Theory of Poetry* [Oxford: Oxford University Press, 1973])—appears in many such cases. For example, during the Nanjing Decade, Chiang Kai-shek's experiments with fascism often directly connected to Western ideas, but his Blue Shirts were self-conscious not to be perceived as simply copying Western fascist ideas, writing, "Many comrades believe that our organization was founded just at the time that European fascism was rising . . . and that our ideology therefore is fascism," a charge they vehemently denied. See Frederic Wakeman, Jr., "A Revisionist View of the Nanjing Decade: Confucian Fascism," *China Quarterly*, no. 150 (June 1997): 395–432. Even during the period of isolation under Mao, several well-documented examples can be found. Scholars have shown that the uprisings in Eastern Europe in the 1950s influenced Mao's launch of the 1957 anti-rightist movement, which Deng oversaw; Mao referenced the Hungarian revolution of 1956 on several occasions; see Zhu Dandan, *1956: Mao's China and the Hungarian Crisis* (Ithaca, NY: East Asia Program, Cornell University, 2013).

20. Jonathan Spence, *To Change China: Western Advisers in China, 1620–1960* (New York: Penguin, 1980). On the book's last page, Spence speculates as to whether Western advisers could still attempt to "change China": "The Chinese, in their turn, seem strong enough now to ensure that if the Westerners come to China as advisers, they will do so on strictly Chinese terms and will not insinuate unwanted values in the pursuit of extrinsic goals" (293).

21. Rong Jingben 荣敬本, "忆改革开放三十年中的一段往事" [Remembering One Episode in the Thirty Years of Reform and Opening], 经济学家茶座 [*Teahouse for Economists*], no. 37 (2008): 45–46.

22. W. W. Rostow, *The Stages of Economic Growth: A Non-Communist Manifesto* (Cambridge: Cambridge University Press, 2nd ed., 1971), xlvii, 6; John Williamson, "What Washington Means by Policy Reform," in *Latin American Adjustment: How Much Has Happened?* ed. John Williamson (Washington, DC: Institute for International Economics, 1990); James C. Scott, *Seeing Like a State: How Certain Schemes to Improve the Human Condition Have Failed* (New Haven: Yale University Press, 1998).

23. Matthew Hilton and Rana Mitter, "Introduction," *Past and Present* 218, Supplement 8 (2013): 25; Odd Arne Westad, *The Global Cold War: Third World Interventions and the Making of Our Times* (Cambridge: Cambridge University Press, 2005).

24. Works that informed my understanding of the process of reception of ideas, both in China and beyond, tend to focus on the process of translation rather than policy interpretation. These include Schwartz, *In Search of Wealth and Power*; Lydia Liu, ed., *Tokens of Exchange: The Problem of Translation in Global Circulations* (Chapel Hill: Duke University Press, 1999); Sophus A. Reinert, *Translating Empire: Emulation and the Origins of Political Economy* (Cambridge: Harvard University Press, 2011). Liu's emphasis on "confrontations" between texts, languages, and traditions is important for giving greater agency to Chinese translators and readers. But using the language of "confrontation" itself assumes a stance on the part of the readers that does not ring wholly true when the readers in question are figures like the Chinese economists Wu Jinglian and Zhao Renwei, who were fluent in English and played a crucial mediating role between the Western texts and Chinese audiences. In particular, the focus on textual "confrontation" deemphasizes their intense hunger to search out valuable elements within the texts and to appropriate them for the Chinese context.

25. This book draws on the *Collected Works of Zhao Ziyang, 1980–1989* (赵紫阳文集 *1980–1989*, 4 vols. [Hong Kong: Chinese University Press, 2016]), a landmark collection of four volumes of internal documents that were smuggled out of mainland China and published in Hong Kong by the Chinese University Press in July 2016. It will take scholars years to fully analyze and reflect on these four volumes. For now, it is sufficient to say that this publication, like other sources cited in this book, will help restore Zhao Ziyang to his rightful place at the center of the history of China's reform era. These documents offer important insights into the political reforms of the late 1980s, the evolution of the economic reforms, Zhao Ziyang's diverse interests and policy initiatives, and leadership dynamics. Many of these documents had previously been available in unpublished, internal compilations, such as the twelve volumes edited by Fang Weizhong, but many are new—and thanks to this new publication, all are now more widely accessible than they have ever been before.

The gaps to fill are numerous. See, for example, Contemporary China Research Office 当代中国研究所, ed., 中华人民共和国史稿 1976–1984 [*History of the People's Republic of China, 1976–1984*] (Beijing: Renmin chubanshe, 2012), which elides Zhao's role (even praising the reforms implemented when he was Party secretary of Sichuan province without naming him, while Wan Li, the equally reformist leader of Anhui province, is named on p. 127), except for a buried mention of Zhao becoming premier in 1980 in its timeline appendix (p. 368) and Wu

Guoyou 伍国友, ed., 中华人民共和国史 1977–1991 [*History of the People's Republic of China, 1977–1991*] (Beijing: Renmin chubanshe, 2010), which barely mentions or credits Zhao Ziyang with any initiative; for two exceptions, see pp. 354 and 408. Western news outlets reported, for example, when "a Chinese magazine has published a memoir praising purged Communist Party leader Zhao Ziyang, making a rare break with the official taboo about the leader ousted in the bloody and still-sensitive upheavals of 1989. . . . recount[ing] Zhao's time as Party chief of southwest Sichuan province from the late 1970s, when Zhao was one of the first provincial leaders to experiment with economic liberalisation. . . . not mention[ing] Zhao's career as a central leader or the tumult of 1989. That time remains too sensitive to broach." See "Chinese Magazine Breaks Zhao Taboo," Reuters, July 8, 2010, at http://www.smh.com.au/business/world-business /chinese-magazine-breaks-zhao-taboo-20100708-1022g.html.

26. Even international commentators publishing in China suffer from these constraints. For example, Edwin Lim's (林重庚) introduction, "中国改革开放过程中的对外思想开放" [The Opening of Thinking to the Outside World in the Process of China's Reform and Opening], to 中国经济: 50 人看三十年 : 回顾与分析 [*China's Economy: Fifty People on Thirty Years: Reflections and Analysis*], ed. Wu Jinglian 吴敬琏, et al. (Beijing: Zhongguo jingji chubanshe, 2008), refers to Zhao Ziyang only once, not by name but, rather, through one of his least-known titles, director of the System Reform Commission. (This fact was brought to my attention by Edwin Lim in our interview, Barnstable, Massachusetts, September 14, 2012.)

27. "王毅部长在第二届世界和平论坛午餐会上的演讲" [Minister Wang Yi's Luncheon Speech at the Second World Peace Forum], June 27, 2013, at www .mfa.gov.cn/mfa_chn/zyxw_602251/ t1053901.shtml; Zeng Peiyan 曾培炎, "伟大的历程、辉煌的成就、宝贵的经验" [Great Process, Glorious Achievements, Precious Experience], 求是 [*Seeking Truth*], no. 11 (June 2012): 10–14.

28. Some commentators have described this goal—to "develop, maintain and defend a state capitalist system" while "explicitly rejecting the liberal capitalist model of the West"—as one of China's "core national interests." See Kevin Rudd, "An Address at the Launch of the Zbigniew K. Brzezinski Institute Convened by the Center for Strategic and International Studies," October 1, 2014, at https://www.yumpu.com/en/document/view/36137215/kevin-rudd -brzezinski-address-bi-lingual-2014-10-1.

29. Fourth Plenary Meeting of the Eighteenth Party Central Committee 中国共产党第十八届中央委员会第四次全体会议, "中共中央关于全面推进依法治国若干重大问题的决定" [Decision of the CCP Central Committee on Major Issues Pertaining to Comprehensively Promoting the Rule of Law], Xinhua News Agency, October 23, 2014, at http://news.xinhuanet.com/politics/2014-10/23 /c_1112953884.htm.

30. Nicholas Dynon, "China's Ideological 'Soft War': Offense is the Best Defense," *China Brief* 14, no. 4 (February 20, 2014), at http://www.jamestown .org/programs/chinabrief/single/?tx_ttnews[tt_news]=41985&tx _ttnews[backPid]=25&cHash=7cc753436d0a57b3a9216e66c39da3e0# .U69FiaiH-EM/; Chris Buckley, "China Takes Aim at Western Ideas," *New York Times*, August 19, 2013, A1, at 13/08/20/world/asia/chinas-new-leadership -takes-hard-line-in-secret-memo.html?_r=0.

31. "Document 9: A ChinaFile Translation: How Much Is a Hardline Party Directive Shaping China's Current Political Climate?" *ChinaFile*, November 8, 2013, at http://www.chinafile.com/document-9-chinafile-translation/.

32. Peter Ford, "China Targets 'Hostile Foreign Forces' in Crescendo of Accusations," *Christian Science Monitor*, November 9, 2014, at http://www.csmonitor.com/World/Asia-Pacific/2014/1109/China-targets-hostile-foreign-forces-in-crescendo-of-accusations/.

CHAPTER ONE   *The Great Helmsman Departs*

1. "化悲痛为力量继承毛主席遗志把无产阶级革命事业进行到底" [Turn Grief into Strength, Carry out Chairman Mao's Behests and Carry the Proletarian Revolutionary Cause through to the End] (Shanghai: Shanghai renmin chubanshe, September 1977), at http://chineseposters.net/gallery/pc-1976-l-001.php.

2. Hua Guofeng's reputation has been the subject of a substantial scholarly reappraisal in recent years. The predominant narrative in official Chinese Communist Party politics generally reduces Hua to the "two whatevers" slogan and holds up Deng's triumph over him by the time of the December 1978 third plenum as the beginning of the era of "reform and opening." Hua's interregnum is, in many ways, viewed as wasted time. However, a 2010 biography by Robert Weatherley (*Mao's Forgotten Successor: The Political Career of Hua Guofeng* [Basingstoke, UK: Palgrave MacMillan, 2010]) shows, as Lowell Dittmer wrote in a review, that Hua was "a true radical" during the Mao period, but, as Mao's successor, "he was not an ideological polemicist like the Gang of Four but a policy generalist with experience in agriculture and science policy." Dittmer praises: "his arrest of the Gang, cessation of incessant campaigns, refocus on the economy—yet his Maoist legacy did not permit a clean break with his past, making him an almost tragic (if minor) transitional figure" (Lowell Dittmer, *China Quarterly*, no. 205 [March 2011]: 174–176). However, the contention that Hua was "minor" and "transitional" soon came under scrutiny, with Australian historian Warren Sun and political scientist Frederick Teiwes arguing "on all key dimensions—the overambitious drive for growth, a newly expansive policy of openness to the outside world, and limited steps toward management reform—Hua and Deng were in basic agreement," and rehabilitating Hua's reputation from what they term the "systematic distortion" of his ideas and accomplishments. See Frederick C. Teiwes and Warren Sun, "China's New Economic Policy under Hua Guofeng: Party Consensus and Party Myths," *China Journal*, no. 66 (July 2011): 1–23.

3. "Chinese Mourning Mao Zedong's Death in 1976," chinaSMACK, last modified December 21, 2011, at http://www.chinasmack.com/2011/pictures/chinese-mourning-mao-zedongs-death-in-1976.html; S.L. James, "China: Communist History through Film," Internet Archive, last modified August 2, 2010, at https://archive.org/details/china-communist-history/.

4. Hua Guofeng, "Speech by Hua Guofeng, Premier and Acting Chairman of the CPC at the Memorial Rally in Tian'anmen Square in Beijing on 18 September 1976," *China Report* 31, no. 1 (January–March 1995): 170.

5. Jiang Qing had attempted to keep Mao's personal papers in her possession, but eventually ceded them to Hua. She also called a Politburo Standing

Committee meeting to discuss the documents, which scholars believe she intended to alter in support of her bid for leadership of the Party, but her efforts were unsuccessful. Vogel, *Deng Xiaoping and the Transformation of China* (Cambridge: Belknap Press of Harvard University Press, 2011), 176–177. See Fan Shuo 范硕, 叶剑英在关键时刻 [*Ye Jianying at the Crucial Moment*] (Shenyang: Liaoning renmin chubanshe, 2001), 363–370.

6. "Secret Telegram No. 3239/III—From Moscow to Warsaw," September 24, 1976, History and Public Policy Program Digital Archive, Archives of the Polish Ministry of Foreign Affairs (AMSZ), s-Depesze, Moscow, 1976, trans. for the Cold War International History Project by Malgorzata K. Gnoinska, at http://digitalarchive.wilsoncenter.org/document/113570.

7. Alexander C. Cook, "Unsettling Accounts: The Trial of the 'Gang of Four': Narratives of Justice and Humanity in the Aftermath of China's Cultural Revolution" (PhD dissertation, Columbia University, 2007), 36–37. See also Zhang Gensheng 张根生, "华国锋谈粉碎'四人帮'" [Hua Guofeng Talks about Smashing the 'Gang of Four'], 炎黄春秋 [*Chinese Annals*], no. 7 (2004): 1–5.

8. Fan, *Ye Jianying at the Crucial Moment*, 377–383; Cook, "Unsettling Accounts," 40–42; Vogel, *Deng Xiaoping*, 178–180.

9. Richard Baum, *Burying Mao: Chinese Politics in the Age of Deng Xiaoping* (Princeton: Princeton University Press, 1994), 42, citing Tony Saich's eyewitness account; Vogel, *Deng Xiaoping*, 180. Cook, "Unsettling Accounts," cites Li Kuaicai 李魁彩, ed., 文革秘档 [*Secret Files of the Cultural Revolution*] (Hong Kong: Hong Kong Chinese Culture Press, 2003), 6:2023–2025.

10. Baum, *Burying Mao*, 28.

11. Lowell Dittmer, *China's Continuous Revolution: The Post-Liberation Epoch, 1949–1981* (Berkeley: University of California Press, 1987), 134; Baum, *Burying Mao*, 38.

12. See Wu Guoguang, "'Documentary Politics': Hypotheses, Process, and Case Studies," in *Decision-Making in Deng's China: Perspectives from Insiders*, ed. Carol Lee Hamrin and Suisheng Zhao (Armonk, NY: M. E. Sharpe, 1995).

13. Mao Zedong, "On the Ten Major Relationships" (April 25, 1956), in *Selected Works of Mao Tse-tung*, vol. 5 (Beijing: Foreign Languages Press, 1977), 284–307.

14. See Hua Guofeng, *Continue the Revolution under the Dictatorship of the Proletariat to the End: A Study of Volume V of the* Selected Works of Mao Tse-tung (Beijing: Foreign Languages Press, 1977).

15. "愤怒声讨'四人帮'反党集团篡党夺权的滔天罪行!" [Angrily Denounce the Monstrous Crime of Usurping the Power of the Party by the "Gang of Four" Anti-Party Clique!] (Shanghai: Shanghai renmin chubanshe, October 1976), at http://chineseposters.net/posters/g2-34.php.

16. Barry Naughton, *Growing out of the Plan: Chinese Economic Reform, 1978–1993* (New York: Cambridge University Press, 1995), 42–50.

17. David Granick, *Chinese State Enterprises: A Regional Property Rights Analysis* (Chicago: University of Chicago Press, 1990), 117–123.

18. Teiwes and Sun, "China's New Economic Policy under Hua Guofeng," 7; Huang Yibing 黄一兵, 转折: 改革开放启动实录 [*Turning Point: The True Record of the Beginning of Reform and Opening*] (Fuzhou: Fujian renmin chubanshe,

2009), 22; For Hua's speech on December 25, 1976, see *Peking Review* 20, no. 1 (January 1, 1977): 41–42.

19. Cyril Chihren Lin, "The Reinstatement of Economics in China Today," *China Quarterly*, no. 85 (March 1981): 39.

20. Alexander Pantsov and Steven Levine, *Deng Xiaoping: A Revolutionary Life* (Oxford: Oxford University Press, 2015), 222–223, on the "black cat, yellow cat," and 296–298, on Deng's rehabilitation in 1976.

21. Leng Rong 冷溶, ed., 邓小平年谱 *1975–1997* [*A Chronology of Deng Xiaoping 1975–1997*], 2 vols. (Beijing: Zhongyang wenxian chubanshe, 2004) (hereafter cited as DXPNP), 141–144.

22. Baum, *Burying Mao*, 27–39.

23. Vogel, *Deng Xiaoping*, 192.

24. Meng Kui and Xiao Lin, "On Sun Yefang's Reactionary Political Position and Economic Program," 红旗 [*Red Flag*], no. 10 (1966), in *The People's Republic of China: A Documentary Survey, 1949–1979*, ed. Harold C. Hinton (Wilmington, DE: Scholarly Resources, 1980), 3:1372.

25. Xue Muqiao 薛暮桥, 社会主义经济问题: 告读者 (打印稿) [Economic Problems of Socialism: To the Reader (Printed Version)] (January 1977), quoted in 薛暮桥年谱 [*A Chronology of Xue Muqiao*], unpublished document, no pagination (hereafter cited as XMQNP). On Xue's background, see Naughton, *Growing out of the Plan*, 100.

26. I have defined these "generations" to reflect both birth dates and levels of seniority before and after the Cultural Revolution. The eldest generation was born between 1900 and 1920; the middle generation between 1920 and 1940; and the youngest generation was born in 1940 or later (see Liu Hong 柳红, 八〇年代: 中国经济学人的光荣与梦想 [*The Eighties: Chinese Economists' Glory and Dreams*] [Guilin: Guangxi shifan daxue chubanshe, 2010]).

27. Ma Ya 马雅, 大风起兮: 马洪传 [*A Great Wind Blows! A Biography of Ma Hong*] (Hong Kong: Mirror Books, 2014). Ma Ya is Ma Hong's daughter. See also Ma Hong, *Collected Works of Ma Hong*, ed. China Development Research Foundation (London: Routledge, 2014), xii–xiii. The chairman of the State Planning Commission from 1952 to 1954 was Gao Gang.

28. Geremie Barmé, "History for the Masses," in *Using the Past to Serve the Present: Historiography and Politics in Contemporary China*, ed. Jonathan Unger (Armonk, NY: M. E. Sharpe, 1993), 264.

29. The differences between Mao and Liu Shaoqi were clearly ideological as well as personal; one Cultural Revolution poster showed the sharp tips of fountain pens plunging into a battered copy of Liu's essay "How to Be a Good Communist." "彻底批判大毒草《修养》" [Thoroughly Criticize the Great Poisonous Weed of "How to Be a Good Communist"] (Shanghai: Shanghai renmin chubanshe, April 1967), at http://chineseposters.net/posters/pc-1967-008.php.

30. Lawrence R. Sullivan, *Historical Dictionary of the Chinese Communist Party* (Lanham, MD: Scarecrow Press, 2011), 81–82. See Liu Shaoqi, "How to Be a Good Communist" (July 1939), in *Selected Works of Liu Shaoqi* (Beijing: Foreign Languages Press, 1984), 1:107–168.

31. Deng Jiarong 邓加荣, 中国经济学杰出贡献奖获得者: 刘国光 [*Liu Guogang: Awarded the Chinese Economics Prize for Exemplary Contributions*] (Beijing: Zhongguo jinrong chubanshe, 2008), 85–100, 163–177; "Liu Guoguang interview

with Heng Ling," Chinese Academy of Social Sciences, 2007, at http: //casseng .cssn.cn/experts/experts_1st_group_cass_members/201402/t20140221_969619 .html.

32. Catherine H. Keyser, *Professionalizing Research in Post-Mao China: The System Reform Institute and Policymaking* (Armonk, NY: M. E. Sharpe, 2003), 27.

33. "学好文件抓住纲" [Study the Documents Well and Grasp the Key Link], 人民日报 *(Renmin Ribao)* (cited hereafter as RMRB), February 7, 1977. See also Zhu Jiamu 朱佳木, ed., 陈云年谱: 一九〇五–一九九五 [*Chronology of Chen Yun: 1905–1995*], 3 vols. (Beijing: Zhongyang wenxian chubanshe, 2000) (cited hereafter as CYNP), 3:206.

34. CYNP, 3:207. Deng Xiaoping would submit a letter pledging support to the Party center on April 10, which was circulated on May 3. See Vogel, *Deng Xiaoping*, 192–195.

35. Fan, *Ye Jianying at the Crucial Moment*, 386–387.

36. Yu Guangyuan, "Speech at the Opening Ceremony of the Fourth Symposium on Theory of Distribution According to Work" (October 1978), in Yu Guangyuan, *Chinese Economists on Economic Reform: Collected Works of Yu Guangyuan*, ed. China Development Research Foundation (London: Routledge, 2014), 1–10.

37. Xue Muqiao, "A Letter to Comrades Deng Xiaoping and Li Xiannian" (April 18, 1977), in Xue Muqiao, *Chinese Economists on Economic Reform: Collected Works of Xue Muqiao*, ed. China Development Research Foundation (London: Routledge, 2011), 16–21.

38. Roderick MacFarquhar, "The Succession to Mao and the End of Maoism, 1969–1982," in *The Politics of China: The Eras of Mao and Deng*, ed. Roderick MacFarquhar (Cambridge: Cambridge University Press, 1997), 248.

39. Ma Hong 马洪 and Sun Shangqing 孙尚清, eds., 中国经济结构问题研究 [*Research into the Problems of China's Economic Structure*] (Beijing: Renmin chubanshe, 1981), 3. They estimate that this led to a loss of RMB 75 billion in output.

40. Teiwes and Sun, "China's New Economic Policy under Hua Guofeng," 8, quoting RMRB, April 19, 1977, 1.

41. Fang Weizhong 房维中, ed., 在风浪中前进: 中国发展与改革编年纪事, 1977–1989 [Forward in the Storm: Chronology of China's Reform and Development, 1977–1989], unpublished 2004 document. Available in the Fairbank Collection, Fung Library, Harvard University (cited hereafter as ZFLZQJ), 1977–1978, 28–31.

42. "毛主席论反对经济主义" [Chairman Mao Discusses Anti-Economism], 光明日报 [*Guangming Daily*], January 18, 1967.

43. "Long Live the Great Proletarian Cultural Revolution," 红旗 [*Red Flag*], no. 8 (June 1966), cited in *The People's Republic of China*, ed. Hinton, 3:1304.

44. Su Shaozhi, "The Structure of the Chinese Academy of Social Sciences and Two Decisions to Abolish Its Marxism-Leninism-Mao Zedong Thought Institute," in *Decision-Making in Deng's China: Perspectives from Insiders*, ed. Hamrin and Zhao, 114. See also Vogel, *Deng Xiaoping*, 209; Joseph Fewsmith, *Dilemmas of Reform in China: Political Conflict and Economic Debate* (Armonk, NY: M. E. Sharpe, 1994), 60; and Lin, "Reinstatement of Economics," 39.

45. Ma, *Chinese Economists on Economic Reform: Collected Works of Ma Hong*, ed. China Development Research Foundation, xiii.

46. Su, "The Structure of the Chinese Academy of Social Sciences," 114–115.

47. Meng and Lin, "On Sun Yefang's Reactionary Political Position," 3:1372; Barry Naughton, "Sun Yefang: Toward a Reconstruction of Socialist Economics," in *China's Establishment Intellectuals*, ed. Carol Lee Hamrin and Timothy Cheek (Armonk, NY: M. E. Sharpe, 1986), 147.

48. Lin, "Reinstatement of Economics," 40.

49. Yao Yilin 姚依林, "同心协力做好经济改革的调查研究" [Work Together to Conduct Successful Economic Reform Research], 金融研究动态 [*Journal of Financial Research*], no. 13 (1986): 1–8; Xue Muqiao 薛暮桥, 薛暮桥回忆录 [*Memoirs of Xue Muqiao*] (Tianjin: Tianjin renmin chubanshe, 1996) (cited hereafter as XMQHYL), 360–363. Susan Shirk provides a persuasive argument about the role of institutions and networks in determining the success of the reform policies (*The Political Logic of Economic Reform in China* [Berkeley: University of California Press, 1993], 7–11).

50. Zhang Jun 张军, "于光远与科尔奈的不同际遇" [The Differing Receptions of Yu Guangyuan and Kornai], 东方日报 [*Eastern Daily*], November 12, 2013.

51. Zhang Zhanbin 张湛彬, 改革初期的复杂局势与中央高层决策 [*The Complex Situation in the Early Reform Period and Policy Making in the Top Ranks of the Central Government*] (Beijing: Zhongguo guanli kexue yanjiuyuan bianji chuban yanjiusuo, 2008), 1:399.

52. "把经济理论展现解批'四人帮'的斗争径行到底" [Expose and Criticize the "Gang of Four" on the Economic Theory Front], 经济研究 [*Economic Research*] (hereafter cited as JJYJ), no. 1 (1978): 2. In November 1977, Xue Muqiao would take to the pages of *Red Flag*—the same journal that had vociferously criticized the "black line in economic circles" a decade earlier—to decry the Gang of Four as "political impostors" who had claimed to be "Marxist theoreticians" with coherent economic views. Xue Muqiao 薛暮桥, "批判'四人帮'在资产阶级法权问题上提反动谬论" [Criticism of the "Gang of Four's" Reactionary Theory on the Question of Bourgeois Rights], 红旗 [*Red Flag*], no. 11 (1977)]: 8.

53. Shen Baoyang, "Lecture Notes: July 4, 1977," in XMQNP.

54. For differing classifications of the strands of Chinese economic thought during this era, see Lin, "Reinstatement of Economics," 6, and Robert C. Hsu, *Economic Theories in China, 1979–1988* (Cambridge: Cambridge University Press, 1991), 7.

55. DXPNP, 159–161; Deng Xiaoping, "The 'Two-Whatever' Policy Does Not Accord with Marxism" (March 24, 1977), *Beijing Review* 26, no. 33 (August 15, 1983): 14–15.

56. DXPNP, 162–163; Vogel, *Deng Xiaoping*, 199, 205–207; Joel Andreas, *Rise of the Red Engineers: The Cultural Revolution and the Origins of China's New Class* (Stanford: Stanford University Press, 2009), 224–226.

57. "认真组织好出国考察工作, 主义出国人员的政治条件和技术水平, 要派熟悉业务的人去" [Organize Delegations Seriously, Mind the Political Backgrounds and Technical Proficiency of the Delegations, Send Those Familiar with the Work], in ZFLZQJ, 1977–1978, 33. Previous trips to the United States and capitalist countries had not been so investigatory in spirit. When Deng traveled to New York City in 1974 to speak at the United Nations, he returned with

what Vogel describes as "a doll that could cry, suck, and pee," which proved to be "a great hit" with his colleagues (Vogel, *Deng Xiaoping*, 86).

58. "学习外国经验与探索中国自己的建设道路: 访袁宝华同志（三）" [Learning from Foreign Experience and Exploring China's Own Path to Construction: Interview with Comrade Yuan Baohua, Part 3], 百年潮 [*Hundred Year Tide*], no. 11 (2002): 11–19; He Yaomin 贺耀敏, "扩权让利: 国企改革的突破口: 访袁宝华同志" [Expanding Rights and Giving Profits: Breakthroughs in the Reform of State-Owned Enterprises: Interview with Comrade Yuan Baohua], 百年潮 [*Hundred Year Tide*], no. 8 (2003): 4–11.

59. Teiwes and Sun, "China's New Economic Policy under Hua Guofeng," 14.

60. See the discussion in the Introduction.

61. DXPNP, 181–182; ZFLZQJ, 1977–1978, 37–38. See Fewsmith, *Dilemmas of Reform*, 90–96. The phrase "Seeking Truth From Facts" (实事求是) in CCP discourse originated in Mao's October 14, 1938 speech "中国共产党在民族战争中的地位" [The Role of the Chinese Communist Party in the Ethnic Struggle], at https://www.marxists.org/chinese/maozedong/marxist.org-chinese-mao-19381014.htm. It reappeared in "To Reform Our Way of Learning" in May 1941 during the Communist Party's rectification campaign. It initially originated in the classic *History of the Han*, from 111 CE.

62. Mao Zedong, "Speeches at the Second Session of the Eighth Party Congress, 8–23 May, 1958," in *Miscellany of Mao Tse-tung Thought (1949–1968)* (Arlington, VA: Joint Publications Research Service, JPRS, 61269-1, February 20, 1974), 91–118; "The Soviet Leading Clique Is a Mere Dust Heap" (October 25, 1966), in *Selected Works of Mao Tse-tung*, vol. 9 (Secunderabad, India: Kranti Publication, 1981), at https://www.marxists.org/reference/archive/mao/works/1966/leadcliq.htm#1. (Note: These volumes contain many documents published by Red Guards and other sources. Although the material was not officially published by the Chinese Communist Party, it has important historical significance.) Yet even during the Mao period, there was interest in understanding Yugoslavia on the part of China's economic policy makers, as demonstrated by the internal records of a series of high-level economic meetings in 1958 and 1959. See "经济问题座谈会第九次会谈情况" [The State of the Ninth Meeting of the Conference on Economic Problems] and "经济问题座谈会三十二次以记录" [Record of the Thirty-Second Meeting of the Conference on Economic Problems], in 五十年代经济问题座谈会 [Conferences on Economic Problems in the 1950s], including comments by Yao Yilin, Xue Muqiao, Yu Guangyuan, and others. Unpublished manuscript. Available in the Fairbank Collection, Fung Library, Harvard University.

63. Zhu Liang 朱良, "铁托与华国锋互访: 对改革开放带来启迪的外事活动" [Visits between Tito and Hua Guofeng: Diplomatic Activities That Brought Inspiration to Economic Reform], 炎黄春秋 [*Chinese Annals*], no. 8 (2008): 8–10, quoted in Liu Hong 柳红, "探索与选择: 对南斯拉夫、匈牙利的历史性考察" [Exploration and Choice: Historical Observations of Yugoslavia and Hungary], 经济观察报 [*Economic Observer*], June 7, 2010.

64. *Beijing Review*, no. 20 (May 19, 1980): 4.

65. Lin, "Reinstatement of Economics," 41.

66. CYNP, 3:215. See Li Honglin 李洪林, "按劳分配是社会主义原则还是资本主义原则"[Is Distribution According to Labor a Socialist or a Capitalist Principle?], RMRB, September 27, 1977; Chen Yun 陈云, "坚持实事求是的革命作风" [Firmly Uphold the Revolutionary Style of Seeking Truth from Facts], RMRB, September 28, 1977.

67. Lin, "Reinstatement of Economics," 42.

68. CASS Institute of History Research Office 中国社会科学院历史研究所, 中国社会科学院编年简史 *(1977–2007)* [*Brief Chronology of the Chinese Academy of Social Sciences (1977–2007)*] (Beijing: Shehui kexue wenxian chubanshe, 2007), 6; "薛暮桥同志在世界经济讨论会上的讲话" [Comrade Xue Muqiao's Speech at the Conference on the World Economy] (December 5, 1977), in XMQNP.

69. The line comes from V.I. Lenin's 1899 *Our Programme*. "薛暮桥同志在世界经济讨论会上的讲话" [Comrade Xue Muqiao's Speech at the Conference on the World Economy] (December 5, 1977), in XMQNP. The translation of the quotation that Xue used was "社会主义者如果不愿意落后于实际生活, 就应当在各方面把这门科学推向前进."

70. ZFLZQJ, 1977–1978, 55–56.

71. Michael Schoenhals, "The 1978 Truth Criterion Controversy," *China Quarterly*, no. 126 (June 1991): 243–268, quoting Wu Jiang 吴江, "关于实践标准问题讨论的情况" [Facts Surrounding the Debate on the Practice Criterion], in 真理标准问题讨论文集 [*Collected Articles from the Debate on the Truth Criterion*], ed. Theory Research Unit of the Central Party School of the Communist Party 中共中央党校理论研究室 (Beijing: Zhongyang dangxiao chubanshe, 1982), 165.

72. Tan Zongji 谭宗级 and Ye Xinyu 叶心瑜, 中华人民共和国史录 [*Historical Record of the PRC*], vol. 4, part 1: 5, cited in Teiwes and Sun, "China's New Economic Policy under Hua Guofeng," 10–11.

73. Ibid., 13.

74. Fewsmith, *Dilemmas of Reform*, 57–58. Fewsmith notes that, under Deng's protection, between 1973 and 1976 the "Petroleum Group" advocated similar policies.

75. Hua Guofeng, "Unite and Strive to Build a Modern, Powerful Socialist Country," *Beijing Review* 21, no. 10 (March 10, 1982): 7–40; Chris Bramall, *Chinese Economic Development* (London: Routledge, 2009), 167–168.

76. Wu Jinglian, *Understanding and Interpreting Chinese Economic Reform* (Mason, OH: Thomson/South-Western, 2005), 3, 293.

77. Xue Muqiao, in his memoirs, recalls some of his colleagues wondering, "Isn't this doing 'the Great Leap Forward' again?" (See XMQHYL, 263.) Vogel acknowledges that Hua, not Deng, initiated and advocated loudly for China's engagement with the Western economies (see Vogel, *Deng Xiaoping*, 190).

78. "It Is Imperative to Make Research in Social Sciences Prosper as Never Before," RMRB, March 11, 1978, and "Social Scientists Formulate Development Plan at Peking University," trans. in Foreign Broadcast Information Service (FBIS), November 8, 1978, E10, quoted in Keyser, *Professionalizing Research in Post-Mao China*, 41.

79. DXPNP, 288–289; ZFLZQJ, 1977–1978, 1:91–93.

80. Reference from "' 薛暮桥在 1978' 解说词" [Explanatory Note for "Xue Muqiao in 1978"], on the television show 大家 [*Everyone*], CCTV, December 2015.

81. "前往南斯拉夫、罗马尼亚进行访问 李一氓同志率党的工作者访问团离京 耿飚同志等到机场送行" [Heading to Yugoslavia and Romania to Conduct Interviews, Comrade Li Yimang Leads Party Delegation and Departs from Beijing; Comrade Geng Biao Accompanies and Sends Them off at the Airport], Xinhua News Agency, March 11, 1978; Rong Jingben, author interview, Beijing, China, September 3, 2013.

82. Yu Guangyuan, "I Return from a Visit to Yugoslavia," in Yu, *Chinese Economists on Economic Reform: Collected Works of Yu Guangyuan*, ed. China Development Research Foundation, 11–18.

83. From Teiwes and Sun, "China's New Economic Policy under Hua Guofeng": Yu Guangyuan 于光远, 我亲历的那次历史转折 [*That Historical Turnaround That I Personally Experienced*] (Beijing: Zhongyang bianyi chubanshe, 1998), 69.

84. *Beijing Review*, no. 20 (May 19, 1980): 5. Sun Yefang and the delegation, organized by CASS, were in Yugoslavia from November 1978 to January 1979. It also stopped in Romania, the same itinerary of Yu Guangyuan's delegation. Several Yugoslav scholars said that they had read Sun's works and they praised his contributions.

85. "薛暮桥同志在全国职工思想政治工作座谈会上的讲话" [Comrade Xue Muqiao Speaks at Political Thought Seminar for National Workers] (July 25, 1980), in XMQNP.

86. Otto Juhász, formerly Hungary's ambassador to China. noted: "For a period we treated each other as reform partners." Otto Juhász's comment is quoted in Xiaoyuan Liu and Vojtech Mastny, eds., *China and Eastern Europe, 1960s–1980s: Proceedings of the International Symposium Reviewing the History of Chinese–East European Relations from the 1960s to the 1980s* (Zürich: ETH Zürich, 2004), 115.

87. Since Xi Jinping came to power, he has devoted substantial time to official veneration of his father's accomplishments. On the centenary of Xi Zhongxun's birth in 2013, a six-part television series, statues in his hometown, and a new collection of postage stamps commemorated the former leader of Guangdong (Barbara Demick, "Chinese President's Father Is Getting a Postmortem Revival," *Los Angeles Times*, October 15, 2013, at http://articles.latimes.com/2013/oct/15/world/la-fg-china-xi-father-20131016; Chris Buckley, "China Venerates a Revolutionary, the Father of Its New Leader," *New York Times*, Sinosphere Blog, October 15, 2013, at http://sinosphere.blogs.nytimes.com/2013/10/15/china-venerates-a-revolutionary-the-father-of-its-new-leader/). See also Vogel, *Deng Xiaoping*, 395–399.

88. "实践是检验真理的唯一标准" [Practice Is the Sole Criterion of Truth], 光明日报 [*Guangming Daily*], May 11, 1978. The editor was Wu Lengxi 吴冷西. According to Deng Liqun, at the Chinese Academy of Social Sciences some people wondered if "practice as the sole criterion" meant that China would no longer take Marxism as its fundamental theory. See Committee on Historical Manuscripts of the People's Republic of China 中国人民共和国史稿委员会, ed.,

邓力群国史讲谈录 [*A Record of Deng Liqun's Talks on the History of the Country*], internal manuscript (7 volumes, 2000–2002) (hereafter cited at GSJTL), 3:352. See also Schoenhals, "Truth Criterion," 245, 259–262, quoting Tao Kai 陶铠, Zhang Yide 张义德, and Dai Qing 戴晴, 走出现代迷信: 真理标准讨论始末 [*Leaving Modern Superstition Behind: The Beginning and End of the Truth Criterion Debate*] (Changsha: Hunan renmin chubanshe, 1988), 3:18–19; and Vogel, *Deng Xiaoping*, 211.

89. Schoenhals, "Truth Criterion," 269, citing "分清两条思想路线 坚持四项基本原则" [Distinguish between the Two Ideological Lines, Adhere to the Four Cardinal Principles], RMRB, May 11, 1979.

90. Schoenhals, "Truth Criterion," 263–265; Li Lanqing, *Breaking Through: The Birth of China's Opening-Up Policy* (Oxford: Oxford University Press, 2009), 34–35.

91. DXPNP, 305; Gu Mu 谷牧, "小平同志领导我们抓对外开放" [Comrade Xiaoping Led Us to Pursue the Opening to the Outside World], in 回忆邓小平 [*Remembering Deng Xiaoping*], ed. China Central Party Literature Research Center 中国中央文献研究室 (Beijing: Zhongyang wenxian chubanshe, 1998), 1:155–156; Zhang, *Complex Situation*, 1:157. See also Vogel, *Deng Xiaoping*, 221–226, for his analysis of Gu Mu's trip.

92. Gu Mu 谷牧, 谷牧回忆录 [*Memoirs of Gu Mu*] (Beijing: Zhongyang wenxian chubanshe, 2009), 293–294.

93. 李先念年谱, 6 vols. [*Chronology of Li Xiannian*] (Beijing: Zhongyang wenxian chubanshe, 2011) (cited hereafter as LXNNP), 5:621–622; Gu, *Memoirs of Gu Mu*, 295–296; ZFLZQJ, 1977–1978, 121–130.

94. Gu, *Memoirs of Gu Mu*, 305; ZFLZQJ, 1977–1978, 126; Research Center for Contemporary China 当代中国研究所, ed., 中华人民共和国史稿 *1976–1984* [History of the People's Republic of China, 1976–1984] (Beijing: Renmin chubanshe, 2012), 43–44.

95. Teiwes and Sun, "China's New Economic Policy under Hua Guofeng," 15–16; 赵紫阳文集 *1980–1989* [*Collected Works of Zhao Ziyang, 1980–1989*] (Hong Kong: Chinese University Press, 2016) (cited hereafter as ZZYWJ), 1:200. The official was Duan Yun, vice chairman of the SPC in 1984. According to the Chen Yun chronology, he did not attend the meeting with Gu Mu—his absence perhaps fed into his later opposition to the SEZs (CYNP, 3:221)—and he shortly thereafter derided Gu Mu by name for bringing the wrong ideas back from abroad (CYNP 3:223; see more on this criticism in Chapter 2). See also George T. Crane, "'Special Things in Special Ways': National Economic Identity and China's Special Economic Zones," *Australian Journal of Chinese Affairs*, no. 32 (July 1994): 77, in which Crane writes that the SEZs were "modelled loosely on export processing zones in other developing countries."

96. GSJTL 4:146.

97. Teiwes and Sun, "China's New Economic Policy under Hua Guofeng," 18.

98. Hu Qiaomu 胡乔木, "按照经济规律办事" [Act in Accordance with Economic Laws] (delivered on July 28, 1978), RMRB, October 6, 1978, trans. in Foreign Broadcast Information Service, FBIS-CHI-78-197, October 11, 1978, E1–E23.

99. Xue Muqiao 薛暮桥, "再接再厉 乘胜前进: 关于价值规律作用问题讨论会闭幕词" [Persevere with Vigor, Advance with Victory: Closing Remarks at the

Conference on the Question of the Application of the Law of Value] (1978), in 社会主义经济中计划与市场的关系 [*The Relationship between Planning and the Market in a Socialist Economy*], ed. CASS Institute of Economics Research Materials Office 中国社会科学院经济研究资料室, State Planning Commission Research Materials Office 国家计划委员会资料室, and Jiangsu Province Joint Philosophy and Social Sciences Research Materials Office 江苏省哲学社会科学界联合会资料室 (Beijing: Zhongguo shehui kexue chubanshe, 1980), 10; Xue Muqiao 薛暮桥, "就当前需要研究的经济理论问题给胡乔木的信" [Letter to Hu Qiaomu on the Problems of Economic Theory That Need to Be Studied Presently] (1978), in 薛暮桥文集 [*Works of Xue Muqiao*] (Beijing: Zhongguo jinrong chubanshe, 2011), 7:48. See also XMQNP.

100. Teiwes and Sun, "China's New Economic Policy under Hua Guofeng," 14. The quotation comes from V. I. Lenin, "The Importance of Gold Now and after the Complete Victory of Socialism," *Pravda* 251 (November 6–7, 1921).

101. DXPNP, 339–340; Vogel, *Deng Xiaoping*, 322.

CHAPTER TWO   *Pushing Off from the Shore*

1. Frederick C. Teiwes and Warren Sun, "China's New Economic Policy under Hua Guofeng: Party Consensus and Party Myths," *China Journal*, no. 66 (July 2011): 9.

2. Joseph Fewsmith, *Dilemmas of Reform in China: Political Conflict and Economic Debate* (Armonk, NY: M. E. Sharpe, 1994), 58.

3. "Note from the Conversation with the Politburo Member of the CC CPS, Minister of Foreign Affairs of the USSR, Comrade Andrei Gromyko," September 1978, History and Public Policy Program Digital Archive, Archive of Modern Records, Warsaw (AAN), KC PZPR, XIA/598, translated for the Cold War International History Project by Malgorzata K. Gnoinska, at http:// digitalarchive.wilsoncenter.org/document/113249/.

4. Teiwes and Sun, "China's New Economic Policy under Hua Guofeng," 19–20, citing a "well-placed former State Planning Commission official." See also Yang Rudai 楊汝岱, "中国改革初期的四川探索" [Sichuan Explorations during the Early Period of China's Reform], 炎黄春秋 [*China Annals*], no. 7 (2010): 25. Many of the ideas of the first five-year plan were themselves imported, as Deborah A. Kaple has shown: "The Chinese communists consciously studied and attempted to adopt Stalin's recovery model of the immediate postwar period, 1946 to 1950" (*Dream of a Red Factory: The Legacy of High Stalinism in China* [Oxford: Oxford University Press, 1994], 5). Kaple writes that this model was, in the Chinese vision of it, "idealized" (vii) and "optimistic" (ix) because the Chinese drew what they knew largely from propaganda "campaigns, slogans, and worker competitions" (10).

5. David L. Shambaugh, *The Making of a Premier: Zhao Ziyang's Provincial Career* (Boulder, CO: Westview Press, 1984), 90.

6. Fang Weizhong 房维中, ed., 在风浪中前进：中国发展与改革编年记事 [Forward in the Storm: Chronology of China's Reform and Development, 1977–1989], unpublished 2004 document. Available in the Fairbank Collection,

Fung Library, Harvard University (cited hereafter as ZFLZQJ), 1977–1978, 155–156.

7. Xiao Donglian 肖冬连, "中国改革初期对国外经验的系统考察和借鉴" [Observations of and References to Foreign Economic Systems during the Early Reform Period in China], 中共党史研究 [*Chinese Communist Party History Research*], no. 4 (2006): 23; Committee on Historical Manuscripts of the People's Republic of China 中国人民共和国史稿委员会, ed., 邓力群国史讲谈录 [*A Record of Deng Liqun's Talks on the History of the Country*], internal manuscript (7 volumes, 2000–2002) (cited hereafter as GSJTL), 1:398.

8. Vogel discusses Deng's "opening to Japan" at great length (Ezra Vogel, *Deng Xiaoping and the Transformation of China* [Cambridge: Belknap Press of Harvard University Press, 2011], 294–311). During this period, economists were continuing to press for decisions based on "objective economic laws" like the formerly verboten "law of value." On October 19, the same day that Deng departed for Japan, Xue Muqiao delivered a report entitled "Use the Law of Value to Serve Economic Construction," in which he called for using fewer administrative methods and more economic methods to manage enterprises: "We must learn to use the law of value and to use market mechanisms" (薛暮桥年谱 [*A Chronology of Xue Muqiao*], unpublished document, no pagination (cited hereafter as XMQNP).

9. Shang-Jin Wei, "Foreign Direct Investment in China: Sources and Consequences," in *Financial Deregulation and Integration in East Asia*, ed. Takatoshi Ito and Anne O. Krueger (Chicago: University of Chicago Press, 1996), 81; Ezra Vogel, *Japan as Number One: Lessons for America* (Cambridge: Harvard University Press, 1979).

10. For a perspective on Japan's contributions to Deng's plans, see Vogel, *Deng Xiaoping*, 462–463.

11. Leng Rong 冷溶, ed., 邓小平年谱 *1975–1997* [*A Chronology of Deng Xiaoping, 1975–1997*], 2 vols. (Beijing: Zhongyang wenxian chubanshe, 2004) (cited hereafter as DXPNP), 450–452. For a lengthier analysis, see Vogel, *Deng Xiaoping*, 241–245.

12. Deng Xiaoping, "Emancipate the Mind, Seek Truth from Facts, and Unite as One in Looking to the Future" (December 13, 1978), in *Selected Works of Deng Xiaoping, 1975–1982* (Beijing: Foreign Languages Press, 1984) (cited hereafter as SWDXP), 156–163; ZFLZQJ, 1977–1978, 157–168. "Many business practices that are commonplace nowadays were entirely new to us in the early days of opening up," recalled former vice premier Li Lanqing (*Breaking Through: The Birth of China's Opening-Up Policy* [Oxford: Oxford University Press, 2009], 386).

13. Zhu Jiamu 朱佳木, ed., 陈云年谱: 一九〇五－一九九五 [*Chronology of Chen Yun: 1905–1995*], 3 vols. (Beijing: Zhongyang wenxian chubanshe, 2000) (cited hereafter as CYNP), 3:230–232; DXPNP, 454–456.

14. Chen Yizi 陈一咨, 中国: 十年改革与八九民运 [*China: Ten Years of Reform and the 1989 Pro-Democracy Movement*] (Taipei: Lianjing chuban shiye gongsi, 1990), 1–15.

15. Teiwes and Sun, "China's New Economic Policy under Hua Guofeng," 17; Yu Guangyuan 于光远, "我亲历的那次历史转折"[That Historical Turnaround

That I Personally Experienced] (Beijing: Zhongguo bianyi chubanshe, 1998), 71–72, 272.

16. Zhao Ziyang, *Prisoner of the State: The Secret Journal of Zhao Ziyang* (New York: Simon & Schuster, 2009), 113.

17. Chen Yun 陈云, "经济形势与经验教训" [The Economic Situation and Our Experiences and Lessons] (December 16, 1980), in 陈云文选 [*Selected Works of Chen Yun*] (Beijing: Renmin chubanshe, 1995), 3:279.

18. "East German Report on the Tenth Interkit Meeting in Havana, December 1978," particularly item III.3 (pp. 7–8), History and Public Policy Program Digital Archive, included in the document reader for the international conference "China and the Warsaw Pact in the 1970–1980s," held by the Cold War International History Project and the Parallel History Project in Beijing, March 2004, at http://digitalarchive.wilsoncenter.org/document/118520/. See also "Evaluation of Chinese Policies toward Eastern Europe by the Central Committee of the Communist Party of the Soviet Union," March 10, 1980, History and Public Policy Program Digital Archive, included in the document reader for the same conference, at http://digitalarchive.wilsoncenter.org/document/114834/.

19. "Joint Communiqué of the United States of America and the People's Republic of China," January 1, 1979, released on December 15, 1978. See also https://history.state.gov/milestones/1977-1980/china-policy/.

20. Vogel, *Deng Xiaoping*, 396–397.

21. DXPNP, 475–486; "Teng Hsiao-Ping, Man of the Year," *Time*, January 1, 1979, at http://content.time.com/time/covers/0,16641,19790101,00.html; Odd Arne Westad, "The Great Transformation: China in the Long 1970s," in *The Shock of the Global: The 1970s in Perspective*, ed. Niall Ferguson, et al. (Cambridge: Belknap Press of Harvard University Press, 2011), 77; Vogel, *Deng Xiaoping*, 333–348; quotation from Vogel, *Deng Xiaoping*, 347.

22. Merle Goldman, "Hu Yaobang's Intellectual Network and the Theory Conference of 1979," *China Quarterly*, no. 126 (June 1991): 230, 232. On the question of international influences, Goldman notes these intellectuals were "not so much influenced by Western ideas at this time as by ideas on reform and revisions of Marxism being debated in Eastern Europe, particularly Yugoslavia, Hungary and Poland," although she does not substantially develop this assertion (ibid., 219).

23. Su Shaozhi 苏紹智 and Feng Lanrui 冯兰瑞, "无产阶级取得政权后的社会发展阶段问题" [The Question of the Stages of Social Development after the Proletariat Comes to Power], 经济研究 [*Economic Research*] (cited hereafter as JJYJ), no. 5 (1979): 14–19; see Goldman, "Hu Yaobang's Intellectual Network," 234.

24. Kwok-sing Li, comp., *A Glossary of Political Terms of the People's Republic of China* (Hong Kong: Chinese University Press, 1995), 400. See the discussion of this term in Chapter 8.

25. The description of Deng Liqun is given in Zhao, *Prisoner of the State*, 9.

26. Goldman, "Hu Yaobang's Intellectual Network," 230–231. Sun Yefang's memorable speech at the conference called for "rehabilitating the word

'criticism'" from its struggle-session "defiling" during the Cultural Revolution; rather than thinking of "criticism" as a unidirectional process of attack and acceptance, Sun praised the "Western European" usage of the term (i.e., to signify so-called critical thinking) and he urged his colleagues to move toward such an understanding of "criticism." See Sun Yefang 孙冶方, "在理论工作务虚会上的发言" [Speech at the Theoretical Work Conference], 炎黄春秋 [*Chinese Annals*], no. 3 (2011): 86–88, at www.21ccom.net/articles/lsjd/jwxd/article_2011032732331.html.

27. Yihong Pan, *Tempered in the Revolutionary Furnace: China's Youth in the Rustication Movement* (Lanham, MD: Lexington Books, 2002), 53, 230; Goldman, "Hu Yaobang's Intellectual Network," 228.

28. ZFLZQJ, 1977–1978, 11–13; Chen Yun, *Selected Works of Chen Yun, Vol. III (1956–1994)* (Beijing: Foreign Languages Press, 1999), 244–247; CYNP, 3:238.

29. 李先念年谱 [*Chronology of Li Xiannian*], 6 vols. (Beijing: Zhongyang wenxian chubanshe, 2011) (cited hereafter as LXNNP), 2:538–539 and 6:21–22.

30. Teiwes and Sun, "China's New Economic Policy under Hua Guofeng," 22; the original quotation, which is in CYNP, 3:223, comes from comments that Chen made to Li Xiannian on July 31, 1978.

31. CYNP, 3:240; Zhang Zhanbin 张湛彬, 改革初期的复杂局势与中央高层决策 [*The Complex Situation in the Early Reform Period and Policy Making in the Top Ranks of the Central Government*] (Beijing: Zhongguo guanli kexue yanjiuyuan bianji chuban yanjiusuo, 2008), 2:414–415.

32. Xiao Donglian 肖冬连, 中华人民共和国史, 第 10 卷: 歷史的轉軌 從撥亂反正到改革開放, 1979–1981 [*History of the People's Republic of China, vol. 10: The Turning Point of History: From Bringing Order out of Chaos to Reform and Opening, 1979–1981*] (Hong Kong: Dangdai Zhongguo wenhua yanjiu zhongxin, Zhongwen daxue, 2008), 474, cited in Frederick C. Teiwes and Warren Sun, "China's Economic Reorientation after the Third Plenum: Conflict Surrounding 'Chen Yun's' Readjustment Program, 1979–80," *China Journal*, no. 70 (July 2013): 169.

33. Nicholas R. Lardy and Kenneth Lieberthal, eds., *Chen Yun's Strategy for China's Development: A Non-Maoist Alternative* (Armonk, NY: M. E. Sharpe, 1983), 3–23.

34. Chen Yun 陈云, "计划与市场问题"[Problems Concerning Planning and the Market] (March 8, 1979), in 陈云文选 [*Selected Works of Chen Yun*] (Beijing: Renmin chubanshe, 1995), 3:220–223.

35. Fewsmith, *Dilemmas of Reform*, 11–12.

36. Ibid.

37. David M. Bachman, "Differing Visions of China's Post-Mao Economy: The Ideas of Chen Yun, Deng Xiaoping, and Zhao Ziyang," *Asian Survey* 26, no. 3 (March 1986): 292–321; Barry Naughton, *Growing out of the Plan: Chinese Economic Reform, 1978–1993* (New York: Cambridge University Press, 1995), 75; Susan L. Shirk, *The Political Logic of Economic Reform in China* (Berkeley: University of California Press, 1993), 224–226.

38. CYNP, 3:253.

39. GSJTL 1:259 (lecture on February 3, 1994).

40. Yao Jin 姚锦, 姚依林百夕谈 [*Talking with Yao Yilin for One Hundred Nights*] (Beijing: Zhonggong dangshi chubanshe, 2008), 183–187, 219–228; Cyril Chihren Lin, "The Reinstatement of Economics in China Today." *China Quarterly*, no. 85 (March 1981): 38, citing 红旗 [*Red Flag*], no. 9 (September 1970): 26–33, and no. 2 (February 1971): 39–47.

41. David M. Bachman, *Chen Yun and the Chinese Political System* (Berkeley: Institute of East Asian Studies, University of California, 1985), viii, 33–34. Vogel has written an article on Chen Yun's career: see Ezra Vogel, "Chen Yun: His Life," *Journal of Contemporary China* 14, no. 45 (November 2005): 741–759.

42. Xue Muqiao, "A Practice-Based Review of More Than Two Decades of Economic Work" (March 1979), in Xue Muqiao, *Chinese Economists on Economic Reform: Collected Works of Xue Muqiao*, ed. China Development Research Foundation (London: Routledge, 2011), 36.

43. Xue Muqiao 薛暮桥, 经济工作必须掌握经济发展规律 [*Economic Work Must Master the Laws of Economic Development*] (Beijing: Xuexi cankao ziliao, 1979), manuscript. Available in the Fairbank Collection, Fung Library, Harvard University. These comments were published in edited form as Xue Muqiao 薛暮桥, "经济工作必须掌握经济发展规律" (Report to the State Economic Enterprise Management Seminar, March 14, 1979) [Economic Work Must Master the Laws of Economic Development], in 当前我国经济若干问题 [*Current Problems in Our Country's Economy*] (Beijing: Renmin chubanshe, 1980), 3–29. Xue spoke out against further copying the Soviet economy in the 1950s; regarding the delegations to Yugoslavia, he said, "思想却是解放了, 但南斯拉夫的情况和我们距离比较远, 很难照抄照变" [Thought is liberated, but the Yugoslav case is quite different from ours, and very difficult to simply imitate]. The preceding was deleted from the openly published version.

44. Xue, "A Practice-Based Review of More Than Two Decades of Economic Work," 34. During the same period, CASS economist Liu Guoguang published an article attacking China's "excessively centralized" and "badly uncoordinated" economic management system and contended that the accumulation rate had been far too high, so China needed to "get capital construction under control," implement retrenchment, and "raise returns on investment." See Liu Guoguang 刘国光, "关于国民经济综合平衡的一些问题" [Some Problems about Synthesis and Balance in the National Economy], JJYJ, no. 3 (1979): 36–44.

45. Deng Xiaoping, "Uphold the Four Cardinal Principles" (March 30, 1979), in SWDXP, 174, 177, 188; DXPNP, 501–503.

46. Xue Muqiao 薛暮桥, "坚持百家争鸣, 坚持理论联系实际" [Uphold a Hundred Contending Schools of Thought, Uphold Linking Theory to Reality], in 社会主义经济中计划与市场的关系 [*The Relationship between Planning and Market in the Socialist Economy*] (Beijing: Zhongguo shehui kexue chubanshe, 1980), 1–14. "A hundred schools of thought contending" is a classical Chinese phrase for intellectual debate; "linking theory to reality" is connected to Deng's principle of "seeking truth from facts." See also He Jianzheng 何建章, "我国全民所有制经济计划管理体制存在的问题和改革方向" [Problems in China's System of Public Ownership and Planned Economic Management and the

Direction of the Reform], JJYJ, no. 5 (1979): 35–37. See also ZFLZQJ, 1977–1978, 54–58; Fewsmith, *Dilemmas of Reform*, 62–68.

47. Liu Guoguang 刘国光 and Zhao Renwei 赵人伟, "论社会主义经济中计划与市场的关系" [On the Relationship between Plan and Market in a Socialist Economy], JJYJ, no. 5 (1979): 46–49.

48. CYNP, 3:243. See Deng Liqun 邓力群, "正确处理计划经济和市场调节之间的关系" [Correctly Handle the Relationship between the Planned Economy and Market Regulation], 经济学周报 [*Economics Weekly*] (February 22, 1982): 79. These changes, according to Deng Liqun, would be implemented through "the integration of planned adjustment and market adjustment, with planned adjustment as primary but simultaneously giving full weight to the role of market regulation." In this socialist formulation, it is important to note that the market is the *mechanism* of regulation, not the target of regulation as it is in a market economy.

49. GSJTL, 1:419.

50. Teiwes and Sun, "China's New Economic Policy under Hua Guofeng," 1, 23, citing [Li] Shengping, ed., 胡耀邦思想年谱 1975–1989 [*Chronology of Hu Yaobang Thought 1975–1989*] 2 vols. (Hong Kong: Taide shidai chubanshe, 2007) 1:355–356. On economic expertise more generally, see Andrew Watson, "Social Science Research and Economic Policy Formulation: The Academic Side of Economic Reform," in *New Directions in the Social Sciences and Humanities in China*, ed. Michael B. Yahuda (London: Macmillan, 1987), 79.

51. LXNNP, 6:49 and ZFLZQJ, 1979, 80–132, particularly 122. See also Fewsmith, *Dilemmas of Reform*, 70–74; and 经济问题研究资料 [*Research Materials on Economic Problems*] (Beijing: Zhonggong zhongyang shujichu yanjiushi jingjizu, 1979), vol. 4.

52. Xiao, "Observations" 30.

53. Ibid., 24; Yao Yilin 姚依林, "同心协力做好经济改革的调查研究" [Cooperate to Complete Survey Research on Economic Reform], 金融研究 [*Financial Research*], no. 13 (1979): 1–8.

54. LXNNP, 6:49. Fang Weizhong, Liao Jili, and Liu Mingfu were the other deputy heads.

55. The speakers were Bo Yibo and Li Xiannian; XMQNP, citing: Research Office of the General Office of the Central Committee of the Chinese Communist Party 中共中央办公厅研究所, ed., 经济问题研究资料 [*Research Materials on Economic Problems*], no. 4 (August 3, 1979) and 薛暮桥工作笔记 [*Working Notes of Xue Muqiao*], provided by CASS, among other documents.

56. David Barboza, "Interviews with Wu Jinglian, Shelley Wu, and Wu's Biographer," *New York Times*, September 26, 2009, at www.nytimes.com/2009/09/27/business/global/27spy-text.html.

57. Mary Jingyu Wu, *Indelible Red: Memories of Life in the Mao Era* (Singapore: Lingwei Guan, 2013), 283, 329.

58. Barboza, "Interviews"; Wu Jinglian 吴敬琏, "顾准之死" [The Death of Gu Zhun], in Wu Xiaobo 吴晓波, 吴敬琏传: 一个中国经济学家的肖像 [*Biography of Wu Jinglian: Portrait of a Chinese Economist*] (Beijing: Zhongxin chubanshe, 2010); Wu Xiaolian 吴晓莲, 我和爸爸吴敬琏 [*Me and My Father Wu Jinglian*] (Beijing: Zhongguo dangdai chubanshe, 2007), 80–84, 92–95.

59. Xu Jing'an 徐景安, "我所经历的经济体制改革决策过程" [My Experience in the Policy-Making Process of the Economic Reform] (2008), in 改革开放口述史 [*Oral History of the Reform and Opening*], ed. Ouyang Song 欧阳淞, Gao Yongzhong 高永中, et al. (Beijing: Renmin daxue chubanshe, 2014), 306–316.

60. Office Files of F. X. Sutton, International Division, Box 58, Folder 12, Ford Foundation Archives, Rockefeller Archive Center, Sleepy Hollow, New York.

61. State Commission for the Reform of the Economic System 国家经济体制改革委员会, ed., 经济体制改革文件汇编: 1977–1983 [*Collected Documents on Economic System Reform: 1977–1983*] (Beijing: Zhongguo caizheng jingji chubanshe, 1984), 182–188.

62. By the end of 1979, the enterprises implementing these reforms constituted 60 percent of output and 70 percent of the profit of "state factories under the state budget" (Naughton, *Growing out of the Plan*, 100; Shirk, *The Political Logic of Economic Reform in China*, 200–204). Profit retention in state industrial firms would further expand in September 1980. One reason was what this policy actually entailed, as demonstrated by the astonishingly simple profit retention equation that was used: $R = aP_{t-1} + b(P_t - P_{t-1})$, where R was profit retained by the enterprise, P_t was profit in the current year, P_{t-1} was the previous year's profit, and the coefficients a and b were calculated based on the previous year's performance (usually set so that a was equal to b, to minimize any ratchet effects). As Naughton has noted, this decision meant marginal retention equaled average retention, thus raising incentive problems: In 1980, the average retention for in-budget industrial enterprises was 12.6 percent, meaning, "an enterprise that increased its profits by one dollar would only retain an additional 12.6 cents on average" (Naughton, *Growing out of the Plan*, 103).

63. Ma Hong, " 'China-Style' Socialist Modernization and Issues of Economic Restructuring" (August 1979 and 1980), in Ma Hong, *Chinese Economists on Economic Reform: Collected Works of Ma Hong*, ed. China Development Research Foundation (London: Routledge, 2014), 11.

64. "Chinese Society of Quantitative Economics Founded," Xinhua News Agency, July 27, 1979, trans. in Foreign Broadcast Information Service, China Daily Report (FBIS-CHI), July 27, 1979, L16, quoted in Catherine H. Keyser, *Professionalizing Research in Post-Mao China: The System Reform Institute and Policymaking* (Armonk, NY: M. E. Sharpe, 2003), 187.

65. Xiao, "Observations," 25.

66. Lin, "The Reinstatement of Economics," 48. See also Zhou Shulian 周叔莲, Wu Jinglian 吴敬琏, and Ma Shufang 马树方, "关于作为政治经济学对象的生产关系问题的讨论" [Discussions on Production Relations as the Object of Political Economy], JJYJ, no. 12 (1979): 67–69.

67. Xinhua General Overseas News Service, September 30, 1979, 1–22; Fan Shuo 范硕, 叶剑英在关键时刻 [*Ye Jianying at the Crucial Moment*] (Shenyang: Liaoning renmin chubanshe, 2001), 398–399. See DXPNP, 554–555, 558, 562–563; Vogel, *Deng Xiaoping*, 355–357. On the CCP's attempts to control the parameters of reversing verdicts and rehabilitation, see Geremie Barmé, "History for the Masses," in *Using the Past to Serve the Present: Historiography and Politics in Contemporary China*, ed. Jonathan Unger (Armonk, NY: M. E. Sharpe, 1993), 261.

68. "*Guangming Daily* Reports Beijing Economic Discussion," 光明日报 [*Guangming Daily*], October 21, 1979, trans. in Foreign Broadcast Information Service, FBIS, November 14, 1979, 7, quoted in Keyser, *Professionalizing Research in Post-Mao China*, 40.

69. Song Yangyan, "A Discussion on the Starting Point and Main Basis for the Reform of the Economic Structure," *Chinese Economic Studies* 14, no. 4 (Summer 1981): 30–37.

70. Ibid., 36.

71. Wang Zheng, "Some Questions on Right and Wrong in Statistics Work Must Be Clarified," *Chinese Economic Studies* 15, no. 1 (Fall 1981): 60.

72. Richard Baum, *Burying Mao: Chinese Politics in the Age of Deng Xiaoping* (Princeton, NJ: Princeton University Press, 1994), 68–69; Shambaugh, *The Making of a Premier*, xv.

73. Hua Sheng, Xuejin Zhang, and Xiaopeng Luo, *China: From Revolution to Reform* (Basingstoke, UK: Macmillan, 1993), 38–53; Naughton, *Growing out of the Plan*, 76–77, 144–148.

74. Fewsmith, *Dilemmas of Reform*, 20–25.

75. Hua, Zhang, and Luo, *China: From Revolution to Reform*, 45–46.

76. Shirk, *The Political Logic of Economic Reform*, 35; Shambaugh, *The Making of a Premier*, 75–76.

77. "Obituary: Zhao Ziyang," BBC News, January 17, 2005, at http://news .bbc.co.uk/1/hi/world/asia-pacific/2989335.stm.

78. See, for example, Frederick C. Teiwes and Warren Sun, *Paradoxes of Post-Mao Rural Reform: Initial Steps toward a New Chinese Countryside, 1976–1981* (London: Routledge, 2016); Jean Oi, *Rural China Takes Off: Institutional Foundations of Economic Reform* (Berkeley: University of California Press, 1999); Yasheng Huang, *Capitalism with Chinese Characteristics: Entrepreneurship and the State* (Cambridge: Cambridge University Press, 2008); Dali L. Yang, *Calamity and Reform in China: State, Rural Society, and Institutional Change Since the Great Leap Famine* (Stanford: Stanford University Press, 1996). For a valuable new selection of translated writings by Du Runsheng, one of the chief economic advisers who oversaw rural reform, see Du Runsheng, *Chinese Economists on Economic Reform: Collected Works of Du Runsheng*, ed. China Development Research Foundation (London: Routledge, 2014).

79. This statement is cited in Fewsmith, *Dilemmas of Reform*, 29.

80. The group was named 中国农村发展问题研究组 [Research Unit on Development Issues in Rural China]. See Chen Yizi 陈一咨, 陈一咨回忆录 [*Memoirs of Chen Yizi*] (Hong Kong: Xin shiji chuban ji chuanmei youxian gongsi, 2013), 192–196, 236–239; Liu Hong 柳红, 八〇年代: 中国经济学人的光荣与梦想 [*The Eighties: Chinese Economists' Glory and Dreams*] (Guilin: Guangxi shifan daxue chubanshe, 2010), 177–182.

81. Fewsmith, *Dilemmas of Reform*, 41–42.

82. "Chinese State Visits to the U.S.," BBC News, January 18, 2011, at www .bbc.co.uk/news/world-asia-pacific-12172292/.

83. Joan Robinson, "Reminiscences" (1957), in *Reports from China: 1953–1976* (London: Anglo-Chinese Educational Institute, 1977), 39. Robinson was the guest of two Western-educated propagandists, Ji Chaoding and Solomon

Adler. She enjoyed what she called a "magnificent tour" of China with Ji and Adler, both trained economists who would later be revealed to have served as secret intelligence agents for the CCP. See John Earl Haynes and Harvey Klehr, *Venona: Decoding Soviet Espionage in America* (New Haven, CT: Yale University Press, 1999), 144.

84. Joan Robinson, *Letters from a Visitor to China* (Cambridge: Students' Bookshops, 1954), 7–8, 13, 32; George R. Feiwel, ed., *Joan Robinson and Modern Economic Theory* (London: Macmillan, 1989), xxxvi–xxxvii; Prue Kerr and Geoffrey Colin Harcourt, eds., *Joan Robinson: Critical Assessments of Leading Economists* (London: Routledge, 2002), 1:76–77.

85. Robinson, *Letters from a Visitor to China*, 32, 35; Feiwel, *Joan Robinson and Modern Economic Theory*, 868. The "three antis" and "five antis" campaigns aimed to eliminate capitalist behavior and opposition to the CCP regime (the "three antis" were anti-corruption, anti-waste, and anti-bureaucratism; the "five antis" focused on bribery, tax evasion, and private business activities). According to one estimate, these campaigns led to hundreds of thousands of coerced and voluntary suicides (Philip Short, *Mao: A Life* [London: Holt, 2001], 437).

86. Official CCP estimates state that the famine caused deaths of 17 million people. Prominent estimates include 36 million deaths from starvation (Yang Jisheng), 43 million to 46 million (Chen Yizi), and 45 million (Frank Dikötter). Yang Jisheng 杨继绳, 墓碑: 中国六十年代大饥荒纪实 [*Tombstone: The True History of the Great Famine in China in the 1960s*], 2 vols. (Hong Kong: Tiandi tushu youxian gongsi, 2008); Yang Jisheng, *Tombstone: The Great Chinese Famine, 1958–1962*, trans. Stacy Mosher and Guo Jian (New York: Farrar Straus, and Giroux, 2012), especially 406–430; Frank Dikötter, *Mao's Great Famine: The History of China's Most Devastating Catastrophe, 1958–1962* (New York: Walker, 2010). Chen Yizi's estimate, recalled in an interview with Jasper Becker, is based on a 1979 survey of rural China in which he participated at the request of Zhao Ziyang. See Jasper Becker, *Hungry Ghosts: Mao's Secret Famine* (New York: Free Press, 1996), 271–272.

87. Joan Robinson, *Notes from China* (Oxford: Blackwell, 1964), 3, 26–27.

88. Roderick MacFarquhar and Michael Schoenhals, *Mao's Last Revolution* (Cambridge: Belknap Press of Harvard University Press, 2006), 251–252, 262; Andrew G. Walder and Yang Su, "The Cultural Revolution in the Countryside: Scope, Timing, and Human Impact," *China Quarterly*, no. 173 (March 2003): 95–96.

89. Joan Robinson, *The Cultural Revolution in China* (Middlesex, UK: Penguin, 1969), 24, 28; Joan Robinson, "Cantab 2 Shorthand Book 1972," JVR xi/9.3, and "For Shorthand Notebook," JVR xi/6.2, Papers of Professor Joan Violet Robinson, King's College Archive Centre, University of Cambridge, Cambridge, UK. Among British leftists, Robinson was far from alone in her support for Mao's regime. Robinson's Cambridge colleague Joseph Needham, a historian of Chinese science, led the Society for Anglo-Chinese Understanding and openly sided with China against the Soviet Union in 1963, earning him derision from many other British Marxists. In partnership with his friend "Joan," Needham continued to lead exchange efforts to China, writing in

December 1967 that he was "prepared to approve of" the Cultural Revolution, but, as a lifelong lover of traditional Chinese culture, he added that he had "reservations." See Tom Buchanan, *East Wind: China and the British Left, 1925–1976* (Oxford: Oxford University Press, 2012), 144, 164, 176, 197. Needham had also been a central player in an earlier episode during the Korean War, when he supported since-discredited claims, made by Chinese scientists under pressure from the CCP, that the American military had used "germ warfare" in China during the conflict. See Ruth Rogaski, "Nature, Annihilation, and Modernity: China's Korean War Germ-Warfare Experience Reconsidered," *Journal of Asian Studies* 61, no. 2 (May 2002): 381–415.

90. Her support of Mao and North Korea's Kim Il-sung "may have lost her the Nobel Prize," writes George R. Feiwel; see Feiwel, *Joan Robinson and Modern Economic Theory*, xxxv–xxxvi. See also "Joan Violet Robinson," in *The Concise Encyclopedia of Economics*, ed. David R. Henderson, Library of Economics and Liberty, available at http://www.econlib.org/library/Enc/bios/Robinson.html.

91. On Joan Robinson in China, a further irony emerges. One of China's most brilliant economists, Gu Zhun, had been purged during the anti-rightist campaign but, thanks to the patronage of his close friend Sun Yefang, he returned to work in 1962, beginning a series of translations. including a translation into Chinese of several of Joan Robinson's best-known essays. But as the Cultural Revolution took off in 1965–1966, Gu was once again labeled "reactionary" and was ferociously persecuted. His wife committed suicide several months later. The year before Gu died from back-breaking "reeducation" in 1974, he recorded in his diary in March 1973 that he continued to read the early works of Joan Robinson. See Wu, *Biography of Wu Jinglian*; Luo Yinsheng 罗银胜, 顾准传 [*Biography of Gu Zhun*] (Beijing: Tuanjie chubanshe, 1999), 450, 455. His most significant translation was Joseph Schumpeter's 1942 treatise *Capitalism, Socialism, and Democracy*; Gu Zhun, 顾准日记 [*Diary of Gu Zhun*], ed. Chen Minzhi 陈敏之 and Ding Dong 丁东 (Beijing: Jingji ribao chubanshe, 1997), 290, 436.

92. Xue, "Economic Work Must Master the Laws of Economic Development." The comments on the Great Leap Forward statistics are omitted from this openly published final text. See also Deng Liqun 邓力群, 我为少奇同志说些话 [*My Words on Behalf of Comrade Shaoqi*] (Beijing: Dangdai Zhongguo chubanshe, 1998), 107–108; Wang Guangmei 王光美, Liu Yuan 刘源, et al., 你所不知道的刘少奇 [*The Unknown Liu Shaoqi*] (Zhengzhou: Henan renmin chubanshe, 2000), 90; Yang, *Tombstone*, 15.

93. Joan Robinson, *Aspects of Development and Underdevelopment* (Cambridge: Cambridge University Press, 1979), 141–142; Joan Robinson, "Mao Tsetung on Soviet Economics," JVR/ii/53, Papers of Professor Joan Violet Robinson, King's College Archive Centre, University of Cambridge, Cambridge, UK.

94. Yang Deming 杨德明, "琼·罗宾逊谈西方资产阶级经济学和资本主义经济危机" [Joan Robinson Discusses Western Bourgeois Economics and the Crisis of Capitalist Economies], 世界经济 [*World Economy*] (February 1978): 75–77. These comments cohered neatly with a propagandistic discourse in China that derided the capitalist economies as "in turmoil": "Ordinary people and their families are haunted daily by inflation," which is an "incurable disease in capi-

talist society," one Chinese propagandist wrote. In China, meanwhile, there was "no inflation." See Peng Kuang-hsi, *Why China Has No Inflation* (Beijing: Foreign Languages Press, 1976).

95. "China 1978," JVR/ii/55, Papers of Professor Joan Violet Robinson. See also Marjorie S. Turner, *Joan Robinson and the Americans* (Armonk, NY: M. E. Sharpe, 1989), 87.

96. Deng Xiaoping, "The Working Class Should Make Outstanding Contributions to the Four Modernizations" (October 11, 1978), in SWDXP, 145–150.

97. "China Exchange" Folder, Box 8, Kenneth J. Arrow Papers, David M. Rubenstein Rare Book & Manuscript Library, Duke University.

98. "谷牧副总理会见美国经济代表团" [Deputy Premier Gu Mu Meets with American Economics Delegation], Xinhua News Agency (October 14, 1979); Lawrence R. Klein, "Autobiography" Nobelprize.org, at http://www.nobelprize .org/nobel_prizes/economic-sciences/laureates/1980/klein-bio.html.

99. Liu, *The Eighties*, 268.

100. Committee on Scholarly Communication with the People's Republic of China (CSCPRC), *Report of the CSCPRC Economics Delegation to the People's Republic of China (October 1979)* (Washington, DC: National Academy of Sciences, 1980), 3–7, 35–36, 44–45.

101. Kenneth Arrow, "China Trip Diary 1979," Box 2, Kenneth J. Arrow Papers, David M. Rubenstein Rare Book & Manuscript Library, Duke University.

102. Lawrence R. Klein, "The Sustainability of China's Economic Performance at the Turn of the Century," *International Journal of Business* 11, no. 3 (Summer 2006): 283–293, 318.

103. Margaret Thatcher Archives, October 31, 1979, "Record of a Discussion between the Prime Minister and the Federal Chancellor in the Federal Chancellery, Bonn" (Margaret Thatcher Archive sources are available at www .margaretthatcher.org).

104. "China: Visit by Premier Hua Guofeng," Margaret Thatcher Archives, August 14, 1979.

105. "Premier Hua Guofeng's Visit: Objectives and Briefing," Margaret Thatcher Archives, September 18, 1979.

106. Zhao, *Prisoner of the State*, 134.

107. Bo Yibo 薄一波, 薄一波书信集 [*Letters of Bo Yibo*] (Beijing: Zhonggong dangshi chubanshe, 2009), 2:624.

108. The group also included He Jianzhang, Jiang Yiwei, and Zhou Shulian, as well as also Sun Hongzhi (Party secretary at the Angang Steel Company). Xiao Donglian writes that from November 5 to December 6 another delegation led by Yuan Baohua and Deng Liqun visited the United States to study enterprise management, visiting Ford Motor Company, General Electric, Lockheed Aircraft Corporation, Coca-Cola, and other large companies, as well as some small- and medium-sized enterprises and some government departments (Xiao, "Observations," 26). On December 31, 1979, the study tour of the United States that Yuan Baohua had led submitted its report to the State Council, in which "scientific management," making

regular adjustments to plans, and use of more advanced technical fore-casting mechanisms were emphasized. "While this does not radically change the anarchy of capitalist production, it does reduce the blindness (of competition) in production" (ibid., 28–29). The report was praised by Bo Yibo (Bo, *Letters*, 2: 629).

109. Xue Muqiao 薛暮桥, "出访美国期间的两封家信" [Two Letters on Touring the United States] (1979), in 薛暮桥文集 [*Collected Works of Xue Muqiao*] (Bei-jing: Zhongguo jinrong chubanshe, 2011), 7:260.

110. 薛暮桥访美笔记 [*Xue Muqiao's Notes on Touring the United States*] (1979), in XMQNP; Ma Hong 马洪, "美国经济与管理教育" [The American Economy and Management Education], 经济研究参考资料 [*Reference Materials for Economic Studies*], no. 84 (1980), cited in Xiao, "Observations," 26; Xue Muqiao 薛暮桥, "访美观感" [Reflections on Visiting the United States], in 薛暮桥文集 [*Collected Works of Xue Muqiao*], 7:285–293.

111. Xiao, "Observations," 26; Ma, "The American Economy and Manage-ment Education"; National Delegation to the USA 国家经委访美代表团, "美国经济管理考察报告" [Report on American Economic Management], 经济研究参考资料 [*Reference Materials for Economic Studies*], no. 52 (1980), cited in Xiao, "Ob-servations," 26; Ma Hong 马洪, "在北京市委党校作的访美报告" [Report on My Visit to the United States at the Beijing Party School], 经济研究参考资料 [*Ref-erence Materials for Economic Studies*], no. 84 (1980): 31; 薛暮桥回忆录 [*Memoirs of Xue Muqiao*] (Tianjin: Tianjin renmin chubanshe, 1996), 332.

112. *Notes on Touring the USA*; see also Xue Muqiao 薛暮桥, "从宏观经济来看怎样提高经济效率" [How to Raise Economic Efficiency from a Macro Economic Perspective] (1981), in 薛暮桥文集 [*Collected Works of Xue Muqiao*], 9:60.

113. "于光远同志在全国经济学团体联合会筹备会上的讲话" [Comrade Yu Guangyuan's Speech at the Meeting of the Preparatory Committee of the All-China Federation of Economics Societies], in Keyser, *Professionalizing Research in Post-Mao China*, 45–46.

114. "Academy of Sciences Seeks Social Science Researchers," Xinhua News Agency, December 6, 1979, trans. in Foreign Broadcast Information Service, FBIS, December 16, 1979, L13, quoted in Keyser, *Professionalizing Research in Post-Mao China*, 41.

115. DXPNP, 580–581; Deng Xiaoping, "We Can Develop a Market Economy under Socialism," November 26, 1979, at http://www.china.org.cn /english/features/dengxiaoping/103388.htm.

116. Deng, "We Can Develop a Market Economy under Socialism."

117. Xiaoyuan Liu and Vojtech Mastny, eds., *Proceedings of the International Symposium: Reviewing the History of Chinese–East European Relations from the 1960s to the 1980s* (Zürich: ETH Zürich, 2004), 115.

118. Xiao "Observations," 31. The delegation also included Huang Hai and Chen Guoyan. Yu circulated his report, titled 匈牙利经济体制考察报告 [Report on an Investigation into Hungary's Economic System], to leading cadres.

119. GSJTL, 5:448.

120. Liu and Mastny, eds., *Proceedings of the International Symposium*, 162. The comment was made by Liu Qibao 刘琪宝.

CHAPTER THREE *A Swifter Vessel*

1. Zhao Renwei, author interview, Beijing, China, June 22, 2012. See also Edwin Lim 林重庚, "中国改革开放过程中的对外思想开放" [The Opening of Thinking to the Outside World in the Process of China's Reform and Opening], in 中国经济: 50; 人看三十年: 回顾与分析 [*China's Economy: Fifty People on Thirty Years: Reflections and Analysis*], ed. Wu Jinglian 吴敬琏 (Beijing: Zhongguo jingji chubanshe, 2008), 29–30; Liu Hong 柳红, 八〇年代: 中国经济学人的光荣与梦想 [*The 1980s: Chinese Economists' Glory and Dreams*] (Guilin: Guangxi shifan daxue chubanshe, 2010), 280–285.

2. Włodzimierz Brus had written, "The theory of a regulated market mechanism—strongly attacked on doctrinal grounds—in itself contains nothing that would make it alien to socialism or basically inconsistent with the premises of a socialist economy" (*The Market in a Socialist Economy* [London: Routledge, 1972], 138). Other advocates of forms of "market socialism"—some of whom did not welcome the term—also visited China, including Alexander Nove in 1979. "When visiting China in 1979, I was struck by the fact that the proposals being discussed by the Chinese for reforming their centralised economy were very much like the proposals which had been debated in the Soviet Union in the previous twenty years. (I said just this in Peking in the presence of a Soviet 'China' specialist, who nodded his head vigorously in agreement!)" (Alec Nove, *The Economics of Feasible Socialism Revisited*, 2nd ed. [London: HarperCollins, 1991], 143, 168).

3. Brus, *The Market in a Socialist Economy*, 138–141.

4. Ibid., 143–147.

5. Brus remained adamant that the market he described in his work should be viewed as a "real" market. "Undoubtedly, this is a peculiar market in which productive capacity and the output structure as well as aggregate demand and the basic elements of its structure are determined by central planning decisions," he wrote. "Despite such limitations, it is a real enough market to disclose actual, detailed substitution rates within the framework of the central planning decisions. There are sellers and purchasers of the means of production who make independent decisions on the basis of their reckoning of profitability. Prices, when compared with the expected results from a specific means of production, figure in the equilibrium of supply and demand for producer goods. . . . Price influences choice" (ibid., 181).

6. Jan Toporowski, "Obituary: Włodzimierz Brus," *The Guardian*, November 12, 2007; idem, "Obituary: Włodzimierz Brus," *Royal Economic Society Newsletter*, no. 139 (October 2007), at www.res.org.uk/SpringboardWebApp /userfiles/res/file/obituaries/brus.pdf.

7. Helena Wolinska had made a living by serving as a military prosecutor, a role in which she was alleged to have staged show trials and signed the death warrants of many so-called "enemies of the state." She had gone from being a victim of Nazi persecution to, according to the Polish government (which issued an order for her arrest years later), a persecutor of victims of Stalinism. See Anne Applebaum, "The Three Lives of Helena Brus," *Sunday Telegraph*, December 6, 1998, at http://www.anneapplebaum.com/1998/12/06/the-three -lives-of-helena-brus/.

8. Toporowski, "Obituary: Włodzimierz Brus."

9. Ibid.

10. Liu, *The Eighties*, 280.

11. Xue Yongying 薛永应, 董辅礽评传 [*Critical Biography of Dong Fureng*] (Wuhan: Wuhan daxue chubanshe, 2000), iv.

12. "Obituary: Włodzimierz Brus," *Royal Economic Society Newsletter*, no. 139 (October 2007); Xue, *Critical Biography of Dong Fureng*, 50–54.

13. Liu, *The Eighties*, 280–281.

14. The authors of 薛暮桥年谱 [*A Chronology of Xue Muqiao*], unpublished document, no pagination (cited hereafter as XMQNP), analyze several letters and printed materials to determine that the book, published by Renmin Publishing House, must have been released after December 22. See Ji Lu 季路, "人民出版社等七家出版社明年出书设想" [Publication Plans of the People's Press and Seven Such Presses], 出版工作 [*Publication Work*], no. 12 (1979): 19–22; "Letter from Xue Muqiao to Martha Avery," December 22, 1979, Box 188, Folder 7, Milton Friedman Papers, Hoover Institution Archives, Stanford, California.

15. See Joseph Fewsmith, *Dilemmas of Reform in China: Political Conflict and Economic Debate* (Armonk, NY: M. E. Sharpe, 1994), 68–70.

16. Frederick Teiwes and Warren Sun, "China's Economic Reorientation after the Third Plenum: Conflict Surrounding 'Chen Yun's' Readjustment Program, 1979–80," *China Journal*, no. 70 (July 2013): 176.

17. Xue Muqiao 薛暮桥, 中国社会主义经济问题研究 [*Research on Questions about China's Socialist Economy*] (Beijing: Renmin chubanshe, 1979). See also idem, 薛暮桥文集 [*Works of Xue Muqiao*] (Beijing: Zhongguo jinrong chubanshe, 2011), 19:204–205.

18. Tao Ying 陶膺 and Zhang Huan 张环, "一本印数近一千万册的经济著作" [An Economic Work Printed Ten Million Times], 出版史料 [*Information on Publication History*], no. 2 (2006): 57. With the success of the book, Xue became perhaps China's most famous economist. Zhao and other senior leaders paid attention to his writings—and on his eightieth birthday in 1984, Xue received a congratulatory note from Zhao himself, praising Xue's "half-century" of contributions to economic policy. See 赵紫阳文集 *1980–1989* [*Collected Works of Zhao Ziyang, 1980–1989*] (Hong Kong: Chinese University Press, 2016) (cited hereafter as ZZYWJ), 2:196 and 2:542.

19. Zhao Renwei, "Lecture 44," in 外国经济学讲座 [*Lectures on Foreign Economics*], ed. 外国经济学说研究会 [Foreign Economics Research Group] (Beijing: Zhongguo shehui kexue chubanshe, 1980–1981), 3:316.

20. Zhao Renwei 赵人韦, "就经济改革问题向布鲁斯教授提出几个问题" (December 30, 1979) [Some Questions for Professor Brus on Economic Reform Problems] in Liu, *The Eighties*, 281–282.

21. Rong Jingben 荣敬本 and Wu Jinglian 吴敬琏, "布鲁斯和锡克的经济模式述评" [Commentary on Brus's and Šik's Economic Models], in 吴敬连选集 [*Selected Works of Wu Jinglian*] (Taiyuan: Shanxi jingji chubanshe, 1989), 562–563.

22. Ibid., 563.

23. Lim, "The Opening of Thinking to the Outside World," 30.

24. Zhao, "Lecture 44," 325–328; Rong and Wu, "Commentary on Brus's and Šik's Economic Models," 565.

25. Liu, *The Eighties*, 284.

26. Rong Jingben, author interview, Beijing, China, September 3, 2013; Zhao Renwei, author interview, Beijing, China, June 22, 2012; Wu Jinglian, author interviews, Beijing, China, August 18, 2012, and September 7, 2013.

27. See, e.g., Sun Yefang 孙冶方, "论价值" [On Value], 经济研究 [*Economic Research*] (hereafter cited as JJYJ), no. 9 (September 1959): 42–46.

28. Meng Kui and Xiao Lin, "On Sun Yefang's Reactionary Political Position and Economic Program," 红旗 [*Red Flag*], no. 10 (1966), in *The People's Republic of China: A Documentary Survey, 1949–1979*, ed. Harold C. Hinton (Wilmington, DE: Scholarly Resources, 1980), 3:1372.

29. "Obituary: Sun Yefang Dies at 75; Top Chinese Economist," *New York Times*, February 24, 1983, A24, at http://www.nytimes.com/1983/02/24 /obituaries/sun-yefang-dies-at-75-top-chinese-economist.html.

30. Wu Jinglian, "The Evolution of Socialist Economic Theories and the Strategic Options of Reform in China." in *The Evolution of the Economic System: Essays in Honour of Ota Sik*, ed. Kurt Dopfer and Karl-Friedrich Raible (London: Macmillan, 1990), 269.

31. Sun Yefang 孙冶方, Diary of Sun Yefang, January 2, 1980, in Zhang Jianqing 张建清 Collection, quoted in XMQNP.

32. Cyril Lin, author interview, Oxford, England, June 24, 2014; Wu Jinglian, author interviews, Beijing, China, August 18, 2012, and September 7, 2013.

33. From a historiographic perspective, the harmony between Sun's ideas from the early 1960s and the ideas of European market socialists in the 1950s and 1960s (which Brus presented on his visit) emphasizes the necessity of advancing a truly global history of socialist economic thought in the twentieth century. As Barry Naughton has argued in *Growing out of the Plan: Chinese Economic Reform, 1978–1983* (New York: Cambridge University Press, 1995), Sun felt himself in dialogue with these thinkers, and the eventual convergence of these ideas in influencing Chinese reforms in the early 1980s indicates the importance of giving proper attention to the earlier connections as well.

34. Xiao Donglian 肖冬连, "中国改革初期对国外经验的系统考察和借鉴" [Observations of and References to Foreign Economic Systems during the Early Reform Period in China], 中共党史研究 [*Chinese Communist Party History Research*], no. 4 (2006): 32. The speech, delivered at the Central Party School work conference, was titled "关于经济工作的几个问题" [Some Questions Regarding Economic Work]. For details about Bo's background, see John Gittings, "Obituary: Bo Yibo," *The Guardian*, January 23, 2007, at http://www.theguardian .com/news/2007/jan/24/guardianobituaries.obituaries1.

35. Ezra Vogel, *Deng Xiaoping and the Transformation of China* (Cambridge: Belknap Press of Harvard University Press, 2011), 359.

36. Leng Rong 冷溶, ed., 邓小平年谱 *1975–1997* [*A Chronology of Deng Xiaoping 1975–1997*], 2 vols. (Beijing: Zhongyang wenxian chubanshe, 2004) (cited hereafter as DXPNP), 592–594; Deng Xiaoping, "The Present Situation and the Tasks Before Us" (January 16, 1980), in *Selected Works of Deng Xiaoping, 1975–1982* (Beijing: Foreign Languages Press, 1984) (cited hereafter as SWDXP), 231.

37. SWDXP, 230.

38. SWDXP, 235–236.

39. Mao Zedong, "关于红专问题的提示" [On the Question of "Red and Expert"] (January 31, 1958), in 毛泽东思想万岁 [*Long Live Mao Zedong Thought*]

(Red Guard Publication, April 1967), 17. Available in Fairbank Collection, Fung Library, Harvard University. See also John K. Fairbank, "'Red' or 'Expert'?" *New York Review of Books*, December 2, 1982, at http://www.nybooks.com /articles/1982/12/02/red-or-expert/.

40. SWDXP, 247.

41. Zhu Jiamu 朱佳木, ed., 陈云年谱: 一九〇五– 一九九五 [*Chronology of Chen Yun: 1905–1995*], 3 vols. (Beijing: Zhongyang wenxian chubanshe, 2000) (cited hereafter as CYNP), 3:255; Vogel, *Deng Xiaoping*, 363; ZZYWJ, 1:89. On March 17, 1980, Zhao Ziyang took over the Central Finance and Economics Small Group from Chen Yun (CYNP, 3:257).

42. Hu Yaobang, "Speech at the Second National Congress of the Chinese Scientific and Technical Association (Excerpts)," *Beijing Review*, no. 15 (April 14, 1980): 13–16.

43. Xiao, "Observations," 26.

44. Unsigned, "Betr.: China," *Der Spiegel*, December 1, 1980; Armin Gutowski, Wolfgang Klenner, and Kurt Wiesegart, *Situation und Perspektiven der chinesischen Wirtschaft. Verschuldungsnotwendigkeit und Finanzierungsspielraum* [*Situation and Perspectives of the Chinese Economy: Borrowing Necessities and Finance Capabilities*] (Hamburg: Institut für Wirtschaftsforschung, 1979); Yan Shou 严守, "西德古托夫斯基教授对我国财政金融问题提出的建议" [West German Professor Gutowski's Suggestions Regarding Our National Financial Problems], 金融研究 [*Finance Research*], no. 2 (1982): 64–65; Li Lanqing, *Breaking Through: The Birth of China's Opening-Up Policy* (Oxford: Oxford University Press, 2009), 387–388.

45. Ma Hong 马洪, "在北京市委党校作的访美报告" [Report to the Beijing Party School on My Visit to the United States] (December 27, 1979), 经济研究参考资料 [*Reference Materials for Economic Studies*], no. 84 (1980): 31.

46. Fewsmith, *Dilemmas of Reform*, 116.

47. Liu Guoguang 刘国光, "略论计划调节与市场调节的几个问题" [A Brief Comment on Several Problems with Planned Adjustments and Market Adjustments], JJYJ, no. 10 (1980): 3–11; Dong Fureng 董辅礽, "关于我国社会主义所有制形式问题" [On the Question of the Forms of China's Socialist Ownership], JJYJ, no. 1 (1979): 21–28; Jiang Yiwei 蒋一苇, "'企业本位论' 争议: 试论社会主义制度下企业的性质及国家与企业的关系" [Disputes on "Enterprise Standards": Characteristics and Relations between Enterprises and the State under a Socialist System], 经济管理 [*Economic Management*], no. 6 (July 14, 1980): 20–27.

48. National Economic System Reform Commission 国家经济体制改革委员会, ed., 中国经济体制改革规划集: 1979 年–1987 年 [*Collected Works on China's Economic Structural Reform Plan, 1979–1987*] ([Beijing]: Zhongguo zhongyang dangxiao chubanshe, 1988), 1–36.

49. Deng Xiaoping, August 1980, cited in Barry Naughton, "Deng Xiaoping: The Economist," *China Quarterly*, no. 135 (September 1993): 503.

50. On March 17, 1980, the State Council named this group the Central Finance and Economic Leading Small Group (中央财经领导小组) and increased its formal authority. Regarding these and other leading economists in China during this period, Andrew Watson has argued persuasively: "It is impossible to distinguish between their roles as academics, as Party theoreticians and as

members of governmental policy-making bodies. . . . It is scholars like these who establish the framework for much of the discussion that is taking place and who stimulate work at the lower levels." See Andrew Watson, "Social Science Research and Economic Policy Formulation: The Academic Side of Economic Reform," in *New Directions in the Social Sciences and Humanities in China*, ed. Michael B. Yahuda (London: Macmillan, 1987), 68.

51. Xue Muqiao 薛暮桥, 薛暮桥回忆录 [*Memoirs of Xue Muqiao*] (Tianjin: Tianjin renmin chubanshe, 2006), 272, 278.

52. Meng and Xiao, "On Sun Yefang's Reactionary Political Position and Economic Program," 3:1372.

53. Edwin Lim, interview with William Becker and Marie Zenni (World Bank Group, Oral History Program, Washington, DC, October 30–31, 2002), 19–20. For further discussion, see Harold K. Jacobson and Michel Oksenberg, *China's Participation in the IMF, the World Bank, and GATT* (Ann Arbor: University of Michigan Press, 1990), 59–60.

54. Chen Yixin 陈以新, "'世界银行' 在美国侵略亚洲中的作用" [The Role of the "World Bank" in American Aggression in Asia], 人民日报 [*People's Daily*] (cited hereafter as RMRB), September 27, 1962.

55. Lim, interview with Becker and Zenni, 2.

56. Ibid., 18–19.

57. "世界银行行长麦克纳马拉抵京" [World Bank President McNamara Arrives in Beijing], RMRB, April 12, 1980; "谷牧会见世界银行行长麦克纳马拉" [Gu Mu Meets World Bank President McNamara], RMRB, April 15, 1980; DXPNP, 620–621; Liqun Jin and Chi-kuo Wu, eds., 回顾与展望: 纪念中国与世界银行合作十五周年 [*Past and Future: Fifteen Years of Cooperation between China and the World Bank*] (Beijing: Ministry of Finance and Xinhua News Agency, 1995), 4–5.

58. Jin and Wu, *Past and Future*, 25.

59. "世界银行决定恢复我代表权" [World Bank Decides to Restore China's Representation], RMRB, May 17, 1980.

60. Jacobson and Oksenberg, *China's Participation in the IMF, the World Bank, and GATT*, 109–110; ZZYWJ, 1:48–49.

61. Lim, interview with Becker and Zenni, 20.

62. Author interview with Edwin Lim, Barnstable, Massachusetts, September 14, 2012.

63. Edwin Lim, "Learning and Working with the Giants," in *At the Frontlines of Development: Reflections from the World Bank*, ed. Indermit S. Gill and Todd Pugatch (Washington, DC: World Bank, 2005), 106; see World Bank, *China: Socialist Economic Development*, 3 vols. (Washington, DC: World Bank, 1983).

64. Teiwes and Sun, "China's Economic Reorientation after the Third Plenum," 165–166. The first five-year plan was not, in its initial form, a good illustration of "balance": it stressed rapid industrialization and allowed agriculture to fall behind. But Chen and Zhou revised the plan repeatedly and the eventual result was viewed very positively. Zhao Ziyang would later complain that Chen Yun continued to "uphold" the view that the first five-year plan should guide China's economic policy (Zhao Ziyang, *Prisoner of the State: The Secret Journal of Zhao Ziyang* [New York: Simon & Schuster, 2009], ch. 1).

65. I am grateful to an anonymous reviewer for this helpful elaboration of the "commodity economy" concept.

66. Susan Sontag, Noam Chomsky, Gabriel Kolko, Richard Poirier, and Arno J. Mayer, et al., "The Mandel Case," *New York Review of Books*, November 20, 1969, at http://www.nybooks.com/articles/1969/11/20/the-mandel -case/; *Ernest Mandel: A Life for the Revolution*, documentary by Chris Den Hond, 90 minutes, 2005, at https://www.youtube.com/watch?v=LXFFcJQSLrk. The Supreme Court upheld the Justice Department's decision to bar Mandel's entry into the United States. Justice Thurgood Marshall wrote that he was "stunned" in a memorable dissenting opinion: "I am convinced that Americans cannot be denied the opportunity to hear Dr. Mandel's views in person because their Government disapproves of his ideas. . . . For those who are not sure that they have attained the final and absolute truth, all ideas, even those forcefully urged, are a contribution to the ongoing political dialogue. . . . The progress of knowledge is an international venture." See *Kleindienst v. Mandel* 408 U.S. 753 (1972).

67. Ernest Mandel 曼德尔, 论马克思主义经济学 [*On Marxist Economics*] (Beijing: Shangwu yinshuguan, 1979).

68. Yang Jisheng 杨继绳, 中国改革年代的政治斗争 [*Political Battles during the Chinese Reform Period*] (Hong Kong: Tiandi tushu youxian gongsi, 2004), 148–150.

69. Zhao Renwei 赵人韦, "对改革初期'曼德尔旋风'的回忆与思考" [Memoirs and Reflections on the "Mandel Storm" during the Early Period of Reform], 经济学家茶座 [*Teahouse for Economists*], no. 2 (2004): 135.

70. Ibid., 136. Their critique was also published as a book review of the three chapters of Mandel's book that Hu Qiaomu had circulated. See "简评曼德尔〈论马克思主义经济学〉第十五至十七章" [Brief Commentary on Chapters 15 to 17 of Mandel's *On Marxist Economics*], in 经济学动态 [*Currents in Economics*], no. 11 (1980), cited in Yang Jisheng, *Political Battles during the Chinese Reform Period*, 156.

71. Yang, *Political Battles during the Chinese Reform Period*, 150.

72. Ibid.

73. Lawrence Lau, "A Giant, Mentor, Master," *China Daily*, November 4, 2013, at http://www.chinadailyasia.com/opinion/2013-11/04/content_15096156 .html.

74. "China Exchange," Box 8, Kenneth J. Arrow Papers, David M. Rubenstein Rare Book & Manuscript Library, Duke University.

75. Office Files of David Bell, Box 2, Folder 21, International Division, Ford Foundation Archives, Rockefeller Archive Center, Sleepy Hollow, New York.

76. Lawrence Klein, "Econometrics Lecture," Box 31, Lawrence Klein Papers, David M. Rubenstein Rare Book & Manuscript Library, Duke University.

77. Heng Ling, interview with Liu Guoguang, 2007, at http://casseng.cssn .cn/experts/experts_1st_group_cass_members/201402/t20140221_969619 .html.

78. Lau, "A Giant, Mentor, Master"; Lawrence R. Klein, "The Sustainability of China's Economic Performance at the Turn of the Century," *International Journal of Business* 11, no. 3, (Summer 2006): 283–318.

79. Office Files of F. X. Sutton, Box 58, Folder 12, International Division, Ford Foundation Archives; "China Exchange," Box 8, Kenneth J. Arrow Papers, David M. Rubenstein Rare Book & Manuscript Library, Duke University; Gregory Chow, *Understanding China's Economy* (Singapore: World Scientific, 1994), 61–71.

80. "Editors' Introduction," in *Lectures on Foreign Economics*, ed. Foreign Economics Research Group, 1:1.

81. Liu, *The Eighties*, 268.

82. "Editors' Introduction," in *Lectures on Foreign Economics*, ed. Foreign Economics Research Group 1:1.

83. Ibid., 1:2. These useful "elements" would be topics addressed in subsequent lectures.

84. Li Yining 厉以宁, ed., 宏观经济学和微观经济学: 现代国外经济学论文选 [*Macroeconomics and Microeconomics: Selected Papers of Contemporary Foreign Economics*] (Beijing: Shangwu yinshuguan, 1981).

85. Gao Hongye 高鸿业, interview with Han Tianyu 韩天雨 and Mao Zengyu 毛增余, in 与中国著名经济学家对话 [*Dialogues with China's Famous Economists*], ed. Han Tianyu 韩天雨 and Mao Zengyu 毛增雨 (Beijing: Zhongguo jingji chubanshe, 1999), 2:123.

86. Nicholas Kristof, " 'Mr. Stock Market': Selling China on a 'Public' Privatization," *New York Times*, January 8, 1989, F8, at http://www.nytimes.com /1989/01/08/business/mr-stock-market-li-yining-selling-china-on-a-public -privatization.html?pagewanted=all.

87. Teiwes and Sun, "China's Economic Reorientation after the Third Plenum," 182.

88. Fang Weizhong 房维中, ed., 风浪中前进: 中国发展与改革编年记事 [*Forward in the Storm: Chronology of China's Reform and Development, 1977–1989*], unpublished 2004 document. Available in the Fairbank Collection, Fung Library, Harvard University (cited hereafter as ZFLZQJ), 1980, 195.

89. Ibid., 1980, 196–199.

90. Teiwes and Sun, "China's Economic Reorientation after the Third Plenum," 182.

91. Ruan Ming 阮銘, 邓小平帝国 [*Deng Xiaoping Empire*] (Taipei: Yushanshe chuban shiye gufen youxian gongsi, 2009), 103, 106–108; CYNP, 3:262.

CHAPTER FOUR   *Navigating the Crosscurrents*

1. Yu Guangyuan, *A Talk with Yu Guangyuan*, ed. Aant Elzinga (Lund, Sweden: Research Policy Institute, 1981), 14.

2. This visit was organized by the Committee on Scholarly Communication with the People's Republic of China, founded in 1966 to promote academic exchanges. See Committee on Scholarly Communication with the People's Republic of China, "Index to Boxes held in WRLC Storage," accessed January 4, 2013, at https://library.gwu.edu/sites/default/files/grc/CSCPRC.pdf; Milton and Rose D. Friedman, *Two Lucky People: Memoirs* (Chicago: University of Chicago Press, 1998), 518.

3. "Will There Be a Recession? Economist Milton Friedman," *Time*, December 19, 1969 (cover article).

4. Milton Friedman, *Capitalism and Freedom* (Chicago: University of Chicago Press, 1962), viii, 15.

5. Erik Lundberg, "The Prize in Economics 1976: Presentation Speech," Nobelprize.org, at www.nobelprize.org/nobel_prizes/economics/laureates/1976/presentation-speech.html.

6. "Appearance on 'The Phil Donahue Show,'" Box 102, Milton Friedman Papers, Hoover Institution Archives, Stanford University, Palo Alto, CA (cited hereafter as "Friedman Papers").

7. "Letter from Lewis Branscomb to Milton Friedman," Friedman Papers, Box 114, Folder 14.

8. Friedman Papers, Box 189, Folders 1 and 7.

9. Li Yining 厉以宁, "现代资产阶级经济学消费行为理论述评" [The Theory of Consumer Behavior in Modern Bourgeois Economics], 北京大学学报（哲学社会科学版）[*Journal of Peking University (Philosophy and Social Sciences Edition)*], no. 2 (1979): 54–70, especially 56.

10. Yang Peixin 杨培新, "关于当前经济金融研究的几个问题" [Some Issues Concerning Contemporary Economic and Financial Research], 广东金融研究 [*Guangdong Finance Research*], no. 26 (June 1980): 2.

11. For a clear statement of how capitalist economies are "haunted" by inflation, see Peng Kuang-hsi, *Why China Has No Inflation* (Beijing: Foreign Languages Press, 1976), i.

12. Friedman Papers, Box 190, Folder 1.

13. Friedman Papers, Box 189, Folder 8.

14. Friedman and Friedman, *Two Lucky People*, 520–523.

15. Milton Friedman, *Friedman in China* (Hong Kong: Center for Economic Research, Chinese University Press, 1990), 4, 39. The book is a collection of his lectures in China.

16. Ibid., 75.

17. Ibid., 3.

18. Friedman and Friedman, *Two Lucky People*, 522.

19. Ibid., 531.

20. Yang, "Questions Concerning Contemporary Economic and Financial Research," 2–3.

21. Zhao Renwei, author interview, Beijing, China, June 22, 2012.

22. Frederick Teiwes and Warren Sun, "China's Economic Reorientation after the Third Plenum: Conflict Surrounding 'Chen Yun's' Readjustment Program, 1979–80," *China Journal*, no. 70 (July 2013): 183–185; 赵紫阳文集 *1980–1989* [*Collected Works of Zhao Ziyang, 1980–1989*] (Hong Kong: Chinese University Press, 2016) (cited hereafter as ZZYWJ), 1:126. See also 李先念年谱 [*Chronology of Li Xiannian*], 6 vols. (Beijing: Zhongyang wenxian chubanshe, 2011) (cited hereafter as LXNNP), 6:129–132 and ZZYWJ, 1:129–142.

23. Chen Yun, 陈云文选, *1956–1985* [*Selected Works of Chen Yun, 1956–1985*] (Beijing: Renmin chubanshe, 1986), 251; Zhu Jiamu 朱佳木, ed., 陈云年谱：一九〇五–一九九五 [*Chronology of Chen Yun: 1905–1995*], 3 vols. (Beijing: Zhongyang wenxian chubanshe, 2000) (cited hereafter as CYNP), 3:263–266.

24. CYNP, 3:264.

25. Xiao Donglian 肖冬连, "中国改革初期对国外经验的系统考察和借鉴" [Observations of and References to Foreign Economic Systems during the Early Reform Period in China], 中共党史研究 [*Chinese Communist Party History Research*], no. 4 (2006): 29–30.

26. Ota Šik, "Lebenslauf und Verzeichnis der wichtigsten wissenschaftlichen Arbeiten" [Curriculum Vitae and List of Primary Scientific Works] (1974), Papers of Ota Šik, Professor Universität St. Gallen und Zürich, 1984–1999 (Dossier) ZDA 2/2.19.0088, and "Wichtigste Daten des Lebenslaufes von Herrn Professor Dr. Ota Šik" [Primary Facts of the Curriculum Vitae of Professor Dr. Ota Šik] (2000), Papers of Ota Šik, Professor Universität St. Gallen und Zürich, 1984–1999 (Dossier) ZDA 2/2.19.0088.

27. Kurt Dopfer, "Emeritierung von Professor Dr. Ota Šik Wirtschaftssysteme," *Hochschule St. Gallen Information* (June 1989): 2, Papers of Ota Šik, Professor Universität St. Gallen und Zürich, 1984–1999 (Dossier) ZDA 2/2.19.0088.

28. Friedrich A. Hayek, "The Use of Knowledge in Society," *American Economic Review* 35, no. 4 (1945): 519–530; Murray N. Rothbard, "The End of Socialism and the Calculation Debate Revisited," *Review of Austrian Economics* 5, no. 2 (1991): 51–76.

29. Oskar Lange, "The Computer and the Market," in *Socialist Economics*, ed. Alec Nove and D. M. Nuti (Harmondsworth. UK: Penguin Books, 1972), 401–402.

30. Jeremi Suri, "The Promise and Failure of 'Developed Socialism': The Soviet 'Thaw' and the Crucible of the Prague Spring, 1964–1972," *Contemporary European History* 15, no. 2 (2006): 133–158.

31. Rong Jingben 荣敬本, "Lecture 45," in 外国经济学讲座 [*Lectures on Foreign Economics*], ed. Foreign Economics Research Group 外国经济学说研究会 (Beijing: Zhongguo shehui kexue chubanshe, 1980–1981), 3:336.

32. Rong Jingben, author interview, Beijing, China, September 3, 2013.

33. Ota Šik, *Plan and Market under Socialism*, trans. Eleanor Wheeler (White Plains, NY: International Arts and Sciences Press, 1967), 219.

34. Ibid., 170.

35. Ibid., 272.

36. Ibid., 167.

37. Ibid., 279, 295–296.

38. Ota Šik, *The Third Way: Marxist-Leninist Theory and Modern Industrial Society*, trans. Marian Sling (White Plains, NY: International Arts and Sciences Press, 1976), 405.

39. Dwight H. Perkins, "Reforming China's Economic System," *Journal of Economic Literature* 26, no. 2 (June 1988): 623.

40. Barry Naughton, *Growing out of the Plan: Chinese Economic Reform, 1978–1993* (New York: Cambridge University Press, 1995), 81, 82, 86.

41. Ao'ta Xike [Ota Šik], "论社会主义经济模式" [On the Socialist Economic Model], in 论社会主义经济体制改革 [*On Reform of the Socialist Economic System*], comp. Wu Jinglian 吴敬琏, Rong Jingben 荣敬本, et al. (Beijing: Falü chubanshe, 1982), 45–115.

42. Ibid. 46–47.

43. Ibid., 54, 58–59.

44. Ibid., 59, 81, 95–104.

45. Wu Jinglian, "Economics and China's Economic Rise" (paper presented at the Sixteenth World Congress of the International Economic Association, Beijing, China, July 4, 2011), 4; Zhao Renwei, author interview, Beijing, China, June 22, 2012. For examples, see Šik, "On the Socialist Economic Model," 63–65, 85–86, 96.

46. Šik, "On the Socialist Economic Model," 108. The "primary" role of price reform recalled the same assertion in *Plan and Market under Socialism*.

47. Šik, "On the Socialist Economic Model," 115.

48. Ibid., 114.

49. Rong Jingben 荣敬本, "忆改革开放三十年中的一段往事" [Remembering One Episode in Thirty Years of Reform and Opening], 经济学家茶座 [*Teahouse for Economists*], no. 37 (2008): 46–47.

50. Šik, "On the Socialist Economic Model," 112–113.

51. Wu Jinglian, "The Evolution of Socialist Economic Theories and the Strategic Options of Reform in China," in *The Evolution of the Economic System: Essays in Honour of Ota Sik*, ed. Kurt Dopfer and Karl-Friedrich Raible (London: Macmillan, 1990), 271; Wu Jinglian, author interviews, Beijing, China, August 18, 2012, and September 7, 2013.

52. Liu Hong 柳红, 八〇年代: 中国经济学人的光荣与梦想 [*The Eighties: Chinese Economists' Glory and Dreams*] (Guilin: Guangxi shifan daxue chubanshe, 2010), 292; Wu Jinglian, author interviews, Beijing, China, August 18, 2012, and September 7, 2013.

53. 薛暮橋年谱 [*A Chronology of Xue Muqiao*], unpublished document, no pagination (cited hereafter as XMQNP); Liu, *The Eighties*, 292; Wu Jinglian, author interviews, Beijing, China, August 18, 2012, and September 7, 2013.

54. Xue Muqiao 薛暮桥回忆录 [*Memoirs of Xue Muqiao*] (Tianjin: Tianjin renmin chubanshe, 2006), 301.

55. Xue Muqiao, 我国国民经济的调整和改革 [*China's National Economic Adjustment and Reform*] (Beijing: Renmin chubanshe, 1982), 387; Fang Weizhong 房维中, ed., 在风浪中前进: 中国发展与改革编年记 [*Forward in the Storm: Chronology of China's Reform and Development, 1977–1989*], unpublished 2004 document. Available in the Fairbank Collection, Fung Library, Harvard University (cited hereafter as ZFLZQJ), 1981, 238; "薛暮桥工作笔记" [Work Notes of Xue Muqiao], cited in XMQNP. See also ZZYWJ, 1:375.

56. Ota Šik, letter, November 13, 1983, "Korrespondenz Ausland 1980–1983," Schweizerisches Sozialarchiv, Zürich. See also Jiri Skolka, "Use of Input-Output Models in the Preparation of Price Reform in China," *Industry and Development*, no. 10 (1984): 61–73.

57. Lu Nan and Li Mingzhe, "Use of Input-Output Techniques for Planning the Price Reform," in *Chinese Economic Planning and Input-Output Analysis*, ed. Karen R. Polenske and Chen Xikang (New York: Oxford University Press, 1991), 83.

58. The equation consisted of several variables: $M = \delta_1 \omega L + \delta_2 K$, where M is price, δ_1 is average profit rate of labor in the two-channel price system, ω is

the sum of the diagonal matrices of the wage rate of workers and of farmers, L is the sum of the column vectors of labor input per unit of output, δ_2 is the average profit rate of capital in the two-channel price system, and $\bar{K}$ is the column vector of capital. Based on a statistical estimation, the coefficients δ_1 and δ_2 are calculated using the Cobb-Douglas production function. In the Chinese context, the key features of this equation were not only its incorporation of both labor and capital, but also its use of profit rates to calculate prices.

59. Lu and Li, "Use of Input-Output Techniques, 84–85. In addition to using lower levels of mathematics, sometimes entirely avoiding linear algebra, conventional socialist price formulae were based on labor inputs and generally disregarded capital, to say nothing of profit, leading to immense distortions.

60. Dong Fureng, "China's Price Reform," *Cambridge Journal of Economics* 10, no. 3 (1986): 297.

61. Lu and Li, "Use of Input-Output Techniques," 83.

62. Wu Jinglian, author interviews, Beijing, China, August 18, 2012, and September 7, 2013.

63. Deng Xiaoping, "Answers to the Italian Journalist Oriana Fallaci" (August 21 and 23, 1980), in *Selected Works of Deng Xiaoping, 1975–1982* (Beijing: Foreign Languages Press, 1984) (cited hereafter as SWDXP), 326–329.

64. Ezra Vogel, *Deng Xiaoping and the Transformation of China* (Cambridge: Belknap Press of Harvard University Press, 2011), 366.

65. Committee on Historical Manuscripts of the People's Republic of China 中国人民共和国史稿委会, ed., 邓力群国史讲谈录 [*A Record of Deng Liqun's Talks on the History of the Country*], internal manuscript (7 volumes, 2000–2002) (cited hereafter as GSJTL), 1:303, 308, (lectures on February 3, 1994, in Beijing, China).

66. Zhang Zhanbin 张湛彬, 改革初期的复杂局势与中央高层决策 [*The Complex Situation in the Early Reform Period and Policy Making in the Top Ranks of the Central Government*] (Beijing: Zhongguo guanli kexue yanjiuyuan bianji chuban yanjiusuo, 2008), 2:376; see also Geremie Barmé, "History for the Masses," in *Using the Past to Serve the Present: Historiography and Politics in Contemporary China*, ed. Jonathan Unger (Armonk, NY: M.E. Sharpe, 1993), 263.

67. Xiao Donglian 肖冬连, 中华人民共和国史, 第 10 卷: 歷史的轉軌 從撥亂反正到改革開放, 1979–1981 [*History of the People's Republic of China, vol. 10: The Turning Point of History: From Bringing Order out of Chaos to Reform and Opening, 1979–1981*] (Hong Kong: Dangdai Zhongguo wenhua yanjiu zhongxin, Zhongwen daxue, 2008), 249–258; Deng Liqun, 十二个春秋: 邓力群自述 [*Twelve Springs and Autumns: An Autobiography of Deng Liqun*] (Hong Kong: Bozhi chubanshe, 2006), 103–104, 160–162; CYNP, 3:270–272.

68. Vogel, *Deng Xiaoping*, 367–368.

69. It is no coincidence that allies of Chen Yun released a wave of articles seeking to bolster Chen's stature as an economic thinker whose works should be studied in the same way as Mao Zedong's writings. See Deng Liqun, "Seriously Study Chen Yun's Economic Theories" 世界经济导报 [*World Economic Herald*], June 15, 1981, trans. in Foreign Broadcast Information Service, FBIS-CHI-81-143, July 27, 1981. K15–K21.

70. CYNP, 3:277; CCP Central Committee, *Resolution on Certain Questions in the History of Our Party since the Founding of the People's Republic of China Adopted by the Sixth Plenary Session of the Eleventh Central Committee of the Communist Party of China on June 27, 1981* (Beijing: Foreign Languages Press, 1981).

71. Vogel, *Deng Xiaoping*, 368–369.

72. Teiwes and Sun, "China's Economic Reorientation after the Third Plenum," 186.

73. CCP Central Committee, *Resolution*.

74. Ma Hong, interview with Han Tianyu 韩天雨 and Mao Zengyu 毛增余, in 与中国著名经济学家对话 [*Dialogues with China's Famous Economists*], ed. Han Tianyu 韩天雨 and Mao Zengyu 毛增余 (Beijing: Zhongguo jingji chubanshe, 2005), 8:11. See also Yu, *A Talk with Yu Guangyuan*, 13.

75. Liu Hong 柳红, 吴敬琏 [*Wu Jinglian*] (Xi'an: Shaanxi shifan daxue chubanshe, 2002), 173. This is an authorized biography of Wu. Wu Jinglian, author interviews, Beijing, China, August 18, 2012, and September 7, 2013.

76. After a year at Princeton's Institute for Advanced Study, Kornai would be named F. W. Taussig Research Professor at Harvard in 1984, a visiting position, and then promoted to full professor in 1986. He retired in 2002. (See János Kornai, "Curriculum Vitae," at http://www.kornai-janos.hu/full%20CV.html.)

77. János Kornai, *By Force of Thought: Irregular Memoirs of an Intellectual Journey* (Cambridge, MA: MIT Press, 2006), 13–14 on Kornai's father; 25–37 on becoming a communist; 78–82 on his break with Marxism.

78. János Kornai, *Economics of Shortage* (New York: North-Holland, 1980), 4, 60–61. "Shortage," in Kornai's analysis, caused both households and firms to make forced substitutions between imperfect substitutes and forced savings because their demand for a good in shortage by definition exceeded its supply.

79. Ibid., 191, 193.

80. Robert Skidelsky, "Winning a Gamble with Communism," *New York Review of Books* 54, no. 9 (May 31, 2007), with the cartoon by David Levine. "The Hungarian János Kornai is the most famous, and certainly the most influential, economist to have emerged from postwar Communist Europe," wrote Skidelsky.

81. Kornai, *Economics of Shortage*, 194.

82. János Kornai, "Adjustment to Price and Quantity Signals in a Socialist Economy," in *The Economics of Relative Prices: Proceedings of a Conference Held by the International Economic Association in Athens, Greece*, ed. Béla Cšikós-Nagy, Douglas Hague, and Graham Hall (London: Macmillan, 1984), 61, 67–69, 76.

83. Kornai, *By Force of Thought*, 250.

84. "Discussion of the Paper by Professor Kornai," in *The Economics of Relative Prices*, ed. Cšikós-Nagy, Hague, and Hall, 81.

85. Ibid., 81.

86. János Kornai, "Birthday Greetings" (January 5, 2010), at http://www.kornai-janos.hu/news.html.

87. "Discussion of the Paper by Professor Kornai," in *The Economics of Relative Prices*, ed. Cšikós-Nagy, Hague, and Hall, 82.

88. Ibid., 82–83.

89. Ibid., 85.

90. The rapporteur, in his remarks, said, "The conference had witnessed an unusual event, an intervention at an IEA conference by a Chinese economist" ("Final Session," in *The Economics of Relative Prices*, ed. Cšikós-Nagy, Hague, and Hall, 530). See also Kornai, "Birthday Greetings," at www.kornai -janos.hu.

91. János Kornai, author interview, Budapest, Hungary, May 30, 2012.

92. Ibid.

93. "Final Session," in *The Economics of Relative Prices*, ed. Cšikós-Nagy, Hague, and Hall, 539.

94. Wu Jinglian, author interviews, Beijing, China, August 18, 2012, and September 7, 2013.

95. Naughton, *Growing out of the Plan*, 112–116.

96. Ota Šik, Letters of July 1981, October 26, 1981, November 6, 1981, "Korrespondenz Ausland 1980–1983," Schweizerisches Sozialarchiv, Zürich.

97. Yu Guangyuan 于光远, "发展经济科学 更好地为社会主义现代化建设服务" [Develop Economic Science to Better Serve the Construction of Socialist Modernization], 经济研究 [*Economic Research*], no. 10 (1981):10–13.

98. Ota Šik, letter, December 14, 1981, "Korrespondenz Ausland 1980–1983," Schweizerisches Sozialarchiv, Zürich.

CHAPTER FIVE   *Through Treacherous Waters*

1. Robert Lawrence Kuhn, *How China's Leaders Think: The Inside Story of China's Reform and What This Means for the Future* (Singapore: John Wiley & Sons [Asia], 2010), 419.

2. Zhu Jiamu 朱佳木, ed., 陈云年谱: 一九 〇 五–一九九五 [*Chronology of Chen Yun: 1905–1995*], 3 vols. (Beijing: Zhongyang wenxian chubanshe, 2000) (cited hereafter as CYNP), 3:289–290.

3. Fang Weizhong 房维中, ed., 风浪中前进: 中国发展与改革编年记事[Forward in the Storm: Chronology of China's Reform and Development, 1977–1989], unpublished 2004 document. Available in the Fairbank Collection, Fung Library, Harvard University (cited hereafter as ZFLZQJ), 1982, 28–31. The published version of this conversation, which includes only Chen's comments, is in Chen Yun 陈云, "加强和改进经济计划工作" [Strengthen and Improve Economic Planning Work] (January 25, 1982), in 陈云文选 1956–1985 [*Chen Yun's Selected Works, 1956–1985*] (Beijing: Renmin chubanshe, 1986), 278–280.

4. Deng Liqun 邓力群, "正确处理计划经济和市场调节之间的的关系" [Correctly Handle the Relation between the Planned Economy and Market Adjustments], in 计划经济与市场调节文集 [*Collected Essays on the Planned Economy and Market Adjustments*], ed. Hongqi chubanshe bianjibu (Beijing: Hongqi chubanshe, 1982), 1:79–83.

5. Yang Peixin 杨培新, "怎样观测当前的货币流通状况" [How to Regard the Current Situation of the Circulation of Money], 金融研究 [*Finance Research*], no. 11 (1981): 5.

6. Yu Guangyuan 于光远, "二十三个年头改革的功过是非" [Achievements and Failures in Twenty-Three Years of Reform], in 现代化、全球化与中国道路 [*Modernization, Globalization, and China's Path*], ed. Cao Tianyu 曹天予 (Beijing: Shehui kexue wenxian chubanshe, 2003), 21–55.

7. Chen Yizi 陈一谘, 陈一谘回忆录 [*Memoirs of Chen Yizi*] (Hong Kong: Xin shiji chuban ji chuanmei youxian gongsi, 2013), 314.

8. CYNP, 3:287; 李先念年谱 [*Chronology of Li Xiannian*], 6 vols. (Beijing: Zhongyang wenxian chubanshe, 2011) (cited hereafter as LXNNP), 6:159.

9. China Art Museum 中国美术馆, ed., 中国美术年鉴 1949–1989 [*Yearbook of Chinese Art 1949–1989*] (Nanning: Guangxi meishu chubanshe, 1993).

10. Zhao Ziyang, *Prisoner of the State* (New York: Simon & Schuster, 2009), 103–105; 赵紫阳文集 1980–1989 [*Collected Works of Zhao Ziyang, 1980–1989*] (Hong Kong: Chinese University Press, 2016) (cited hereafter as ZZYWJ), 2:273.

11. Rong Jingben 荣敬本, "忆改革开放三十年中的一段往事" [Remembering One Episode in Thirty Years of Reform and Opening], 经济学家茶座 [*Teahouse for Economists*], no. 37 (2008): 45–46.

12. Yu's speech was not published until that summer. See Yu Guangyuan 于光远, "开展经济体制改革理论问题的讨论" [Carry out Discussions of Theoretical Questions Regarding Reform of the Economic System], 人民日报 (*People's Daily*) (hereafter cited as RMRB), June 11, 1982, 5.

13. Ota Šik, letters of March 3, October, and November 1982 and April 4, 1983, "Korrespondenz Ausland 1980–1983," Schweizerisches Sozialarchiv, Zürich.

14. ZZYWJ, 1:453–454.

15. Zhou Chenghua 卓成华, "安志文: 中国改革的思考者" [An Zhiwen: The Mind of China's Reform], 中国老年 [*China's Elderly*], no. 3 (2010), at http://www .reformdata.org/index.do?m=wap&a=show&catid=100&typeid=&id=15066.

16. Yu, "Achievements and Failures in Twenty-three Years of Reform," 35–37.

17. Nina Halpern, "Learning from Abroad: Chinese Views of the East European Economic Experience, January 1977–June 1981," *Modern China* 11, no. 1 (January 1985): 97.

18. Liu, *The Eighties*, 204–206.

19. ZFLZQJ, 1982, 64–66.

20. Edwin Lim 林重庚, "中国改革开放过程中的对外思想开放" [The Opening of Thinking to the Outside World in the Process of China's Reform and Opening], in 中国经济: 50 人看三十: 回顾与分析 [*China's Economy: Fifty People on Thirty Years: Reflections and Analysis*], ed. Wu Jinglian 吴敬琏, et al. (Beijing: Zhongguo jingji chubanshe, 2008), 30–31. The formal name of the conference is 苏联东欧经济体制改革座谈会 [Symposium on Soviet and Eastern European Economic System Reform], and it is not to be confused with the much more famous 1984 Moganshan Conference.

21. 薛暮桥年谱 [*A Chronology of Xue Muqiao*], unpublished document, no pagination (cited hereafter as XMQNP).

22. 苏联、东欧经济体制改革座谈会简报, 第 1 期 [*Briefing on the Symposium on Soviet and Eastern European Economic System Reform*, vol. 1], the background briefing to the conference, submitted on July 11, 1982, obtained from a source who wishes to remain anonymous; ZZYWJ, 1:480–485.

23. XMQNP; Lim, "The Opening of Thinking to the Outside World," 31.

24. *Briefing on the Symposium*.

25. Liao Jili 廖季立, "廖季立在东欧经济体制改革座谈会上的发言" [Liao Jili's Speech at the Symposium on Soviet and Eastern European Economic System Reform] (July 1982). Document provided to the author by a source who wishes to remain anonymous.

26. Brus encouraged the Chinese economists to read János Kornai's *Economics of Shortage*; in their briefing, the Chinese economists cited the book's publication date but not Kornai's name, reflecting that in July 1983 they were not familiar with his work (*Briefing on the Symposium*, vol. 10) (July 18, 1982).

27. Xue Muqiao 薛暮桥, Liu Zhoufu 刘卓甫, and Liao Jili 廖季立, "关于布鲁斯为首的经济体制考察团来访情况的报告" [Report on the Visit of the Economic System Study Group Led by Brus] (August 10, 1982), in 国家体改委重要文件资料汇编 [*Compilation of Important Documents of the State Commission on System Reform*], ed. Important Documentary Materials of the State Commission on System Reform 国家体改委重要文件资料 (Beijing: Gaige chubanshe, 1999), 1–5. Document provided to the author by a source who wishes to remain anonymous.

28. This approach—which between July 1985 (in Bolivia) and December 1993 (in Russia) would become more systematically developed, especially by Jeffrey Sachs, as "shock therapy"—was particularly associated with Poland, which implemented a "big bang" reform on January 1, 1990. See, for example, Jeffrey Sachs, *Poland's Jump to the Market Economy* (Cambridge: MIT Press, 1993).

29. "林重庚谈中国经济体制改革" [Edwin Lim (Lin Chonggeng) Discusses China's Economic System Reform], in *Briefing on the Symposium*, vol. 5 (July 15, 1982).

30. Edwin Lim, author interview, Barnstable, Massachusetts, September 14, 2012.

31. XMQNP.

32. Ibid. I am grateful to Professor Xiaofei Tian and George Yin for their input on previous drafts of this translation.

33. Xue, Liu, and Liao, "Report on the Visit of the Economic System Study Group," 5.

34. Ibid.

35. CYNP, 3:299–305; Fewsmith, *Dilemmas of Reform*, 114; Lowell Dittmer, "The 12th Congress of the Communist Party of China," *China Quarterly*, no. 93 (March 1983): 108–124.

36. Hu Yaobang, "Report to the Twelfth Party Congress," Xinhua News Agency, September 1, 1982, trans. in Foreign Broadcast Information Service, FBIS-CHI-82-170, September 1, 1982, K4–K6.

37. "Chen Yun Supports Constitution, Zhao Report," Xinhua News Agency, December 2, 1982, trans. in Foreign Broadcast Information Service, FBIS-CHI-82-233, December 3, 1982, K4–K5: CYNP, 3:312–313.

38. Li Yining 厉以宁, "评美国凯恩斯学派与货币学派之间的论战" [On the Conflicts between the U.S. Keynesian School and the Monetarist School], 经济问题探索 [*Exploring Economic Problems*], no. 2 (1980): 40–49.

39. Li Yining 厉以宁 and Luo Zhiru 罗志如, 二十世纪的英国经济: "英国病" 研究 [*The Twentieth-Century English Economy: Research on "The English Disease"*] (Beijing: Renmin chubanshe, 1982), 2–3. Although the phenomenon itself was more commonly known as "the British Disease," Li and Luo's title has been consistently translated as "the English Disease."

40. Ibid., 9.

41. Ibid., 14, 238–239.

42. Nicholas Kristof, "'Mr Stock Market': Li Yining; Selling China on a 'Public' Privatization," *New York Times*, January 8, 1989, at http://www.nytimes.com/1989/01/08/business/mr-stock-market-li-yining-selling-china-on-a-public-privatization.html?pagewanted=all.

43. Li and Luo, *The Twentieth-Century English Economy*, 211, 349.

44. Ibid., 529–532.

45. Ford Foundation Papers, International Division, Office Files of F. X. Sutton, Box 58, Folder 12.

46. Liu Hong 柳红, 吴敬琏 [*Wu Jinglian*] (Xi'an: Shaanxi shifan daxue chubanshe, 2002), 175.

47. Wu Jinglian, author interviews, Beijing, China, August 18, 2012, and September 7, 2013.

48. Wu Jinglian, *Understanding and Interpreting Chinese Economic Reform* (Mason, OH: Thomson/South-Western, 2005), 362. Other statistics are drawn from Barry Naughton, *Growing out of the Plan: Chinese Economic Reform, 1978–1993* (New York: Cambridge University Press, 1995).

49. Hu Yaobang, January 17–18, 1983, in ZFLZQJ, 1983, 9, 38. See also ZZYWJ, 2:19–21.

50. Fewsmith, *Dilemmas of Reform*, 126.

51. Margaret M. Pearson, *Joint Ventures in the People's Republic of China: The Control of Foreign Direct Investment under Socialism* (Princeton: Princeton University Press, 1991), 54.

52. XMQNP; CYNP, 3:321.

53. ZZYWJ, 2:86–111. For an English translation, see Zhao Ziyang, "Report on the Work of the Government," June 6, 1983, trans. in Foreign Broadcast Information Service, FBIS-CHI-83-109, June 6, 1983, K8–K16.

54. CYNP, 2:337–338.

55. Xu Jilin, "The Fate of an Enlightenment: Twenty Years in the Intellectual Sphere (1978–98)," trans. Geremie R. Barmé and Gloria Davies, in *Chinese Intellectuals between State and Market*, ed. Edward Gu and Merle Goldman (London: RoutledgeCurzon, 2004), 186. The earliest use of "eradicate spiritual pollution" by Deng Liqun came during a speech to the Central Party School on June 4, 1983. Committee on Historical Manuscripts of the People's Republic of China 中国人民共和国史稿委员会, ed., 邓力群国史讲谈录 [*A Record of Deng Liqun's Talks on the History of the Country*], internal manuscript (7 volumes, 2000–2002) (cited hereafter as GSJTL), 4:446. See also Richard Baum, *Burying Mao: Chinese Politics in the Age of Deng Xiaoping* (Princeton: Princeton University Press, 1994), 427.

56. Shi Youxin, "No Spiritual Pollution Is Allowed on the Ideological Front," 红旗 [*Red Flag*], no. 20 (October 1983), 35–38, trans. in FBIS-CHI-83-224, November 18, 1983, K5–K9.

57. Naughton, *Growing out of the Plan*, 121.

58. "Strike Less Hard: The Death Penalty," *Economist* 308, no. 8847 (August 3, 2013).

59. Geremie R. Barmé, "China Blames the West for 'Spiritual Pollution,'" *National Times*, January 1984, 12.

60. ZZYWJ, 2:249; Fewsmith, *Dilemmas of Reform*, 127–129. These gains were mainly due to the payoffs from the rural reforms, discussed briefly in Chapter 2. The *Collected Works of Zhao Ziyang* shows that Zhao consistently advocated for "policy limits" (ZZYWJ, 2:275) on the Campaign to Combat Spiritual Pollution. In May 1984, Zhao acknowledged that this strategy had not entirely succeeded: "Because we were not clear enough about some of the policy limits [set by the central authorities], inappropriate practices appeared in some locations and work units. But when they were discovered, they were promptly corrected" (ZZYWJ, 2:382).

61. Chen Daisun 陈岱孙, "现代西方经济学的研究和我国社会主义经济现代化" [Research on Modern Western Economics and China's Socialist Economic Modernization], RMRB, November 16, 1983. This essay was originally published in 北京大学学报: 哲学社会科学版 [*Peking University Journal: Philosophy and Social Sciences*], no. 3 (1983): 2–5.

62. Leng Rong 冷溶, ed., 邓小平年谱 *1975–1997* [*A Chronology of Deng Xiaoping 1975–1997*], 2 vols. (Beijing: Zhongyang wenxian chubanshe, 2004). (cited hereafter as DXPNP), 954–959; ZFLZQJ, 1984, 11–13. See also Deng Xiaoping, "Make a Success of Special Economic Zones and Open More Cities to the Outside World" (February 24, 1984), in *Selected Works of Deng Xiaoping, Vol. III* (Beijing: Foreign Languages Press, 1994) (cited hereafter as SWDXP-3), 61–62.

63. For more on the importance of these "trading centers" (a Chinese term that today usually simply means "shopping mall"), see Bian Changtai 边长泰, "论贸易中心" [On Trading Centers], 财贸经济 [*Finance and Trade Economics*], no. 4 (1984): 22–25.

64. ZFLZQJ, 1984, 37–52; ZZYWJ, 2:333–345, especially 2:341–343. See also Fewsmith, *Dilemmas of Reform*, 131.

65. "福建省五十五名厂长、经理给省委领导写信: 请给我们' 松绑'" [Fifty-Five Fujian Factory Directors and Managers Write to Members of the Provincial Party Committee: Please "Untie" Us], RMRB, March 30, 1984.

66. "Provisional Regulations of the State Council on Further Expanding the Decision-Making Powers of State-Owned Enterprises," Xinhua News Agency, May 11, 1984, trans. in Foreign Broadcast Information Service, FBIS-CHI-84-096, May 16, 1984, K15–K17.

67. Hua Sheng, Xuejun Zhang, and Xiaopeng Luo, *China: From Revolution to Reform* (Basingstoke, UK: Macmillan, 1993), 103.

68. ZFLZQJ, 1984, 73.

69. "State Planning Commission to Conduct Major Reform of Planning System," 经济日报 [*Economic Daily*], October 6, 1984, trans. in Foreign Broadcast Information Service, FBIS-CHI-84-198, October 11, 1984, K1–K2. Zhao

Ziyang's arguments to the SPC officials for these changes are in ZFLZQJ, 1984, 108–112.

70. Fewsmith, *Dilemmas of Reform*, 132.

71. Hua, Zhang, and Luo, *China: From Revolution to Reform*, 103.

72. Theodore Schultz to Gregory Chow (copied to Kenneth Arrow), January 11, 1982, Kenneth Arrow Papers, "China Exchange" Box.

73. "赵紫阳会见庄至教授" [Zhao Ziyang Meets Professor Gregory Chow], RMRB, July 6, 1984.

74. 教授情况补充介绍 [Additional Information on the Professor], Gregory Chow's file from the Ministry of Education, dated July 12, 1984. I obtained this document from a source who wishes to remain anonymous.

75. Kenneth Arrow Papers, "China Exchange."

76. Additional Information on the Professor.

77. Kenneth Arrow Papers, "China Exchange"; Gregory Chow, "中国的经济改革: 一些建议" [Some Suggestions on China's Economic Reform] (handwritten letter to Zhao Ziyang), provided to the author by Gregory Chow.

78. Gao Shangquan 高尚全, 改革历程, 改革开放三十年 [*The Course of Reform: Thirty Years of Reform and Opening*] (Beijing: Jingji kexue chubanshe, 2008), 9.

79. Chen, *Memoirs of Chen Yizi*, 313; David Barboza, "Interviews with Wu Jinglian, Shelley Wu, and Wu's Biographer," *New York Times*, September 26, 2009, at www.nytimes.com/2009/09/27/business/global/27spy-text.html. Wu Jinglian, author interviews, Beijing, China, August 18, 2012, and September 7, 2013.

80. XMQNP.

81. Ma Hong 马洪, "关于社会主义制度下我国商品经济的再探索" [Further Exploration of China's Commodity Economy under a Socialist System], in ZFLZQJ, 1984, 136–137. The material they drew on included research conducted by Zhou Shulian 周叔莲 and Zhang Zhouyuan 张卓元.

82. Barboza, "Interviews with Wu Jinglian, Shelley Wu, and Wu's Biographer."

83. World Bank Country Study, *China: The Achievement and Challenge of Price Reform* (Washington, DC: World Bank, 1993), 6, 9.

84. Naughton, *Growing out of the Plan*, 250–251.

85. "李鹏在宴请匈牙利部长会议副主席马尔亚伊时说　中匈两国建设社会主义总目标是一致的" [Li Peng Says during Banquet with the Hungarian Deputy Prime Minister József Marjai: China and Hungary Share the Same Overall Goal of Building Socialism], RMRB, August 21, 1984. See also "赵紫阳会见马尔亚伊时希望特别注意发展中匈经济技术合作" [Zhao Ziyang Meets Marjai and Particularly Hopes to Develop China and Hungary's Economic and Technological Cooperation], RMRB, August 25, 1984; and "姚依林会见马尔亚伊" [Yao Yilin Meets Marjai], RMRB, August 26, 1984.

86. ZZYWJ, 2:131–141; FCO letter to No. 10 ("Visit by Mr Jozsef Marjai, Hungarian Deputy PM"), PREM19/1271 f154, at http://www.margaretthatcher.org/document/133802.

87. Hua, Zhang, and Luo, *China: From Revolution to Reform*, 108. That same month, Li Xiannian led a delegation to Yugoslavia and Romania that received much less attention than Marjai's visit to China, indicating the rising importance of Hungary relative to other reforming socialist countries at this juncture (LXNNP, 6:265–260).

88. Chen Yizi 陈一谘, 中国: 十年改革与八九民运 [*China: Ten Years of Reform and the 1989 Pro-Democracy Movement*] (Taipei: Lianjing chuban shiye gongsi, 1990), 75–77; idem, *Memoirs of Chen Yizi*, 309; Liu, *The Eighties*, 204–205.

89. Zhang Jun 张军, "莫干山上论战的价格改革" [The Price Reform War at Moganshan], in 不为公众所知的改革 [*The Reform Little Known to the Public*] (Beijing: Zhongxin chubanshe, 2010); for the number of participants, see Liu, *The Eighties*, 433. (Liu is the wife of Zhu Jiaming, one of the conference's organizers, and her account is largely drawn from his diary.)

90. Hua Sheng 华生, "双轨制始末" [The Whole Story behind the Dual-Track System], 中国改革 [*China Reform*], no. 1 (2005): 22–25.

91. Chen, *Memoirs of Chen Yizi*, 310–311. The question of whether Zhang Weiying, Hua Sheng, or others deserve credit for "inventing" the dual-track price system remains a controversial subject among Chinese economists, with competing claims of sources and witnesses. I have sought to tell a neutral account.

92. Hua, Zhang, and Luo, *China: From Revolution to Reform*, 124.

93. Hua, "The Whole Story behind the Dual-Track System."

94. Commission for Chinese Economic System Reform 中国经济体制改革委员会, ed., 中国经济体制改革十年 [*Ten Years of China's Economic System Reform*] (Beijing: Jingji guanli chubanshe, 1988), 454. The goal here was clearly to avoid a situation in which planners would play "catch up" with the gains in production enterprises made under the increased incentives of the dual-track system.

95. ZFLZQJ, 1984, 171–174. That September, Gao Shangquan had organized a series of seminars on the "commodity economy" at the Xiyuan Hotel (see Liu, *The Eighties*, 194–198).

96. Central Party Literature Research Center 中共中央文献研究室, ed., 十二大以来重要文献选编 [*Important Documents since the Twelfth National Party Congress*] (Beijing: Renmin chubanshe, 1986), 1:533–538; ZZYWJ, 484–488.

97. ZFLZQJ, 1984, 179; DXPNP, 994; ZZYWJ, 2:488.

98. ZFLZQJ, 1984, 179–184; CYNP, 3:360–361; ZZYWJ, 2:488–489.

99. ZFLZQJ, 1984, 181–184.

100. ZZYWJ, 2:490–508. For an English translation, see "Decision of the Central Committee of the CPC on Reform of the Economic Structure," Xinhua News Agency, October 20, 1984, trans. in Foreign Broadcast Information Service, FBIS-CHI-84-205, October 22, 1984, K1–K19.

101. Zhao, *Prisoner of the State*, 119.

102. DXPNP, 1006–1009; Deng Xiaoping, "Speech at the Third Plenary Session of the Central Advisory Commission of the Communist Party of China," October 22, 1984, in SWDXP-3, 90–99.

103. Ma Hong, "A Commodity Economy as it Can Exist under a Socialist System" (November 1984), in Ma Hong, *Chinese Economists on Economic Reform: Collected Works of Ma Hong*, ed. China Development Research Foundation (London: Routledge, 2014), 113; Wu Jinglian, author interviews, Beijing, China, August 18, 2012, and September 7, 2013; Zhao Renwei, author interview, Beijing, China, June 22, 2012.

104. Naughton rightly notes that Zhao and other reform-oriented leaders were likely "purposely using the vagueness of [these] concepts as a stratagem

to overcome resistance to reform" (*Growing out of the Plan*, 179). However, he does not explain how the economists who were charged with proposing and developing policies under the banner of these slogans dealt with the challenges such purposeful "vagueness" created.

105. Zhao Ziyang, "Report on the Work of the Government" (June 6, 1983), 1; ZZYWJ, 3:97–100.

106. Ibid., 262–263, 245–246. See also Edward S. Steinfeld, *Forging Reform in China: The Fate of State-Owned Industry* (Cambridge: Cambridge University Press, 1998), 189.

107. Deng Xiaoping, 建设有中国特色的社会主义: 增订本 [*Building Socialism with Chinese Characteristics: Revised Edition*] (Beijing: Renmin chubanshe, 1987), 86.

108. Naughton, *Growing out of the Plan*, 205, 220.

109. Hua, Zhang, and Luo, *China: From Revolution to Reform*, 112, 125.

110. Zhao Ziyang, "Report on the Work of the Government," March 27, 1985, trans. in Foreign Broadcast Information Service, FBIS-CHI-85-061, March 29, 1985, K1–K17. See ZZYWJ, 3:105–121 and 3:145–153.

111. Zhao, *Prisoner of the State*, 127–128.

112. Sergey Radchenko, *Unwanted Visionaries: The Soviet Failure in Asia at the End of the Cold War* (Oxford: Oxford University Press, 2014), 45.

113. CYNP, 2:370; Zhu Jiamu 朱佳木, "追忆陈云同志与阿尔希波夫交往的一段往事" [My Recollection of an Event in Comrade Chen Yun's Association with I. V. Arkhipov], 当代中国史研究 [*Contemporary China History Studies*], no. 3 (2007): 97–98; see also Radchenko, *Unwanted Visionaries*, 46.

114. Zhao, *Prisoner of the State*, 120–121.

115. Gilbert Rozman, *The Chinese Debate about Soviet Socialism, 1978–1985* (Princeton: Princeton University Press, 1987), 125.

116. Radchenko, *Unwanted Visionaries*, 47.

117. Numerous other senior Chinese government officials traveled abroad, even in the summer of 1985. To name just a few: Song Ping went to Mauritius and Madagascar; Gu Mu went to Japan; and Li Xiannian and Li Peng (no relation) visited the United States and Canada. See Library of Congress Research Division, *Current Chinese Leadership Update: A Report Prepared under an Interagency Agreement by the Federal Research Division* (May–August 1985), at www.dtic.mil/dtic/tr/fulltext/u2/a286876.pdf.

118. Ibid. (report by Beth Green), 1–4.

119. Ibid. (report by Andrea M. Savada), 1–7.

120. Margaret Thatcher, speech delivered at dinner for Chinese Premier (Zhao Ziyang), June 3, 1985, Thatcher Archive.

121. Barboza, "Interviews with Wu Jinglian, Shelley Wu, and Wu's Biographer."

122. See, for example, Wu Jinglian 吴敬琏, "经济改革初战阶段的发展方针和宏观控制问题" [Development Policy in the Beginning Stages of Economic Reform and Problems in Macro-control], RMRB, February 11, 1985.

123. Ibid., 5.

124. Wu Jinglian 吴敬琏, Li Jiange 李剑阁, and Ding Ningning 丁宁宁, "把国民经济的增长速度控制在适度的范围内" [Keep the Growth Rate of the National Economy within a Moderate Range], RMRB, May 17, 1985.

125. ZFLZQJ,1985, 164–166.

126. Guo Shuqing, *Chinese Economists on Economic Reform: Collected Works of Guo Shuqing*, ed. China Development Research Foundation (London: Routledge, 2012), xix.

127. Guo Shuqing, Liu Jirui, and Qiu Shufang, "Comprehensive Reform Is in Urgent Need of Overall Planning" (April 1985), in ibid., 28–36.

128. Zhu Jiaming 朱嘉明 and Liu Suli 刘苏里, "走世界, 看中国: 朱嘉明与刘苏里谈话录" [Travel the World and See China: Dialogue between Zhu Jiaming and Liu Suli], 领导者 [*Leaders*], no. 43 (2011): 120–130.

129. Zhu Jiaming 朱嘉明, "论我国正经历的经济发展阶段" [On China's Current Stage of Economic Development], 中青年经济论坛 [*Young Economists' Forum*], no. 2 (April 1985): 20; Susan Shirk, *The Political Logic of Economic Reform in China* (Berkeley: University of California Press, 1993), 284.

130. Zhu, "On China's Current Stage of Economic Development," 22.

131. Zhu Jiaming 朱嘉明, "中国改革的道路" [The Path of China's Reform], at http://www.21ccom.net/articles/zgyj/ggcx/article_2012110370279_2.html.

132. See Victor C. Shih, *Factions and Finance in China: Elite Conflict and Inflation* (Cambridge: Cambridge University Press, 2008); Naughton, *Growing out of the Plan*. I am grateful to an anonymous reviewer for suggesting the addition of this section.

133. Peng Kuang-hsi, *Why China Has No Inflation* (Beijing: Foreign Languages Press, 1976).

134. Guo Shuqing 郭树清, Liu Jirui 刘吉瑞, and Qiu Shufang 丘淑芳, "国民经济不能强行起飞" [The National Economy Cannot Break into Flight], 中青年经济论坛 [*Young Economists' Forum*], no. 3 (1985): 74–76. See also Wu Jian 吴健 and Weng Zhixing 翁志兴, "关于我国经济发展战略与世界经济发展趋势的几点认识" [Some Points of Understanding Regarding China's Economic Development Strategy and Trends in Global Economic Development], 世界经济 [*World Economy*], no. 6 (1985): 45–52.

135. Edwin Lim, Adrian Wood, et al., *China: Long-Term Development Issues and Options* (Baltimore: Johns Hopkins University Press, 1985).

136. Wu Jinglian, "Economics and China's Economic Rise" (paper presented at the Sixteenth World Congress of the International Economic Association, Beijing, China, July 4, 2011), in *The Chinese Economy: A New Transition*, ed. Masahiko Aoki and Jinglian Wu (New York: Palgrave Macmillan, 2012), 13–31.

137. Wu Jinglian, author interviews, Beijing, China, August 18, 2012, and September 7, 2013.

138. Lim, "The Opening of Thinking to the Outside World," 36.

139. Fewsmith, *Dilemmas of Reform*, 150; Hua, Zhang, and Luo, *China: From Revolution to Reform*, 112.

140. Xu Yi 许毅, "论建立综合财政的宏观协调平衡体系" [On the Establishment of a Comprehensive Financial Macro-coordinated Equilibrium System], 财政研究 [*Finance Research*], no. 5 (1985): 1–17.

CHAPTER SIX *Days on the River*

1. Liu Hong 柳红, 八〇年代: 中国经济学人的光荣与梦想 [*The 1980s: Chinese Economists' Glory and Dreams*] (Guilin: Guangxi shifan daxue chubanshe, 2010), 302.

2. Zhao Renwei, author interview, Beijing, China, June 22, 2012.

3. János Kornai, *Economics of Shortage* (New York: North-Holland, 1980), 1:60–61. The soft budget constraint was first introduced in János Kornai, "Resource v. Demand-Constrained Systems," *Econometrica* 47, no. 4 (July 1979): 801–819.

4. Mary Cairncross, diary entry for August 29, 1985; given to the author by Frances Cairncross.

5. Wu Jinglian, author interviews, Beijing, China, August 18, 2012, and September 7, 2013. See also Liu Hong 柳红, 吴敬琏 [*Wu Jinglian*] (Xi'an: Shaanxi shifan daxue chubanshe, 2002), 175.

6. Wu Jinglian, author interviews, Beijing, China, August 18, 2012, and September 7, 2013.

7. Béla Csikós-Nagy, Douglas Hague, and Graham Hall, eds., *The Economics of Relative Prices: Proceedings of a Conference Held by the International Economic Association in Athens, Greece* (London: Macmillan, 1984), 82.

8. Zhao Ziyang, *China's Economy and Development Principles: A Report* (Beijing: Foreign Languages Press, 1982), 47.

9. James Tobin to Don Brown, June 6, 1985, in "Correspondence, Miscellaneous, 1983–1988," Box 2, James Tobin Papers, Yale University Library Manuscripts and Archives, New Haven, CT.

10. Mary Cairncross, diary entry for August 29, 1985.

11. Yang Jigang 杨继刚 and Shi Xiaofan 史晓帆, "赵紫阳对参加'宏观经济管理国际讨论会'的中外代表说中国经济改革的目标坚定不移" [When Meeting with Chinese and Foreign Representatives to the "International Conference on Macroeconomic Management" Zhao Ziyang Says that China's Economic Reform Goals are Unwavering], 人民日报 [*People's Daily*] (cited hereafter as RMRB), September 1, 1985.

12. Alexander Cairncross, "Beijing. 1985," DC106 2/14, Papers of Sir Alexander Cairncross, University of Glasgow Archives, Glasgow, Scotland, UK.

13. Edwin Lim 林重庚, "中国改革开放过程中的对外思想开放" [The Opening of Thinking to the Outside World in the Process of China's Reform and Opening], in 中国经济: 50 人看三十: 回顾与分析 [*China's Economy: Fifty People on Thirty Years: Reflections and Analysis*], ed. Wu Jinglian 吴敬琏, et al. (Beijing: Zhongguo jingji chubanshe, 2008), 36.

14. "Decision of the Central Committee of the CPC on Reform of the Economic Structure," Xinhua News Agency, October 20, 1984, trans. in Foreign Broadcast Information Service, FBIS-CHI-84-205, October 22, 1984, K1–K19.

15. Chen Yun 陈云, "经济形势与经验教训" [The Economic Situation and Our Experiences and Lessons], December 16, 1980, in 陈云文选: 第三卷 [*Selected Works of Chen Yun: Volume 3*] (Beijing: Renmin chubanshe, 1995), 279.

16. Susan L. Shirk, *The Political Logic of Economic Reform in China* (Berkeley: University of California Press, 1993), 282–285. See also, for example, Wu Jinglian 吴敬琏, "经济改革初战阶段的发展方针和宏观控制问题" [Development Policy at the Beginning Stages of Economic Reform and Problems of Macro-control], RMRB, February 11, 1985; Guo Shuqing 郭树清, Liu Jirui 刘吉瑞, and Qiu Shufang 丘淑芳, "国民经济不能强行起飞" [The National Economy Cannot Break into Flight], 中青年经济论坛 [*Young Economists' Forum*], no. 3 (1985): 74–76; Xu Yi 许毅, "论建立综合财政的宏观协调平衡体系" [On the Establishment

of a Comprehensive Financial Macro-coordinated Equilibrium System], 财政研究 [*Finance Research*], no. 5 (May 1985): 1–17.

17. Wu Jinglian, *Understanding and Interpreting Chinese Economic Reform* (Mason, OH: Thomson/South-Western, 2005), 66.

18. Joseph Fewsmith, *Dilemmas of Reform in China: Political Conflict and Economic Debate* (Armonk, NY: M. E. Sharpe, 1994), 150.

19. Edwin Lim, "Learning and Working with the Giants," in *At the Frontlines of Development: Reflections from the World Bank*, ed. Indermit S. Gill and Todd Pugatch (Washington, DC: World Bank, 2005), 107. In the months ahead of the conference, Zhao referred to Lim's writings and opinions in internal deliberations over the Seventh Five-Year Plan and reform policy, further emphasizing the important role of the World Bank and of Lim himself at this moment. See, for example, 赵紫阳文集 *1980–1989* [*Collected Works of Zhao Ziyang, 1980–1989*] (Hong Kong: Chinese University Press, 2016) (cited hereafter as ZZYWJ), 3:151.

20. As shown in Chapter 3, Brus's earlier visit had been much discussed in China. See Zhao Renwei 赵人伟, "Lecture 44," in 外国经济学讲座 [*Lectures on Foreign Economics*], ed. Foreign Economics Research Group 外国经济学说研究会 (Beijing: Zhongguo shehui kexue chubanshe, 1980–1981), 3:316; and Rong Jingben 荣敬本 and Wu Jinglian 吴敬琏, "布鲁斯和锡克的经济模式述评" [Commentary on Brus's and Šik's Economic Models], in 吴敬连选集 [*Selected Works of Wu Jinglian*] (Taiyuan: Shanxi renmin chubanshe, 1989), 562–563.

21. Lim, "The Opening of Thinking to the Outside World," 37–38.

22. "Preliminary Proposal for an Economic Development Institute," February 24, 1953, WB-IBRD/IDA-045, Records of the World Bank Institute, World Bank Group Archives, Washington, DC; Alec Cairncross, interview with Charles Ziegler, January 10, 1985, 2, in World Bank Oral History Project, World Bank/IFC Archives, World Bank Group Archives, Washington, DC.

23. Alec Cairncross, *Living with the Century* (London: Lynx Press, 1998), 282–284. See also Unsigned, "英国学术院代表团来访" [English Academic Delegation Visits], 社会科学 [*Social Science*], no. 4 (1979): 118.

24. "Obituary: Sir Alec Cairncross," *Economist*, October 29, 1998, 121. This was a type that Cairncross would identify and praise in his biography of his friend Austin Robinson. See Alec Cairncross, *Austin Robinson: Life of an Economic Adviser* (London: Palgrave Macmillan, 1993).

25. Cairncross, *Living with the Century*, 47, 294.

26. Cairncross interview with Charles Ziegler, January 10, 1985, 2, 11.

27. Cairncross, *Living with the Century*, 500–501.

28. Cairncross, "Beijing. 29.8.85," DC106 2/14, Papers of Sir Alexander Cairncross, University of Glasgow Archives, Glasgow, Scotland, UK.

29. Lim, "The Opening of Thinking to the Outside World," 37–38. For details on Barre, see author interview, Edwin Lim, Barnstable, Massachusetts, September 14, 2012.

30. Lim, "The Opening of Thinking to the Outside World," 37.

31. Zhao Renwei 赵人伟, "1985 年'巴山轮会议'的回顾与思考" [Remembering and Reflecting on the 1985 Bashan Conference], 经济研究 [*Economic Research*] (cited hereafter as JJYJ), no. 12 (2008): 19; "Name and Room Num-

bers in the Ship," in 参加经济计划与宏观整理国际讨论会外宾名单及简介 [Names and Backgrounds of the Foreign Participants at the International Conference on Macroeconomic Management]. I obtained this document from a source who wishes to remain anonymous.

32. For an example of collaboration within the group, see Liu Guoguang 刘国光 and Zhao Renwei 赵人伟, "论社会主义经济中计划与市场的关系" [On the Relationship between Plan and Market in a Socialist Economy], JJYJ, no. 5 (1979): 46–55. In 1982, several of the same economists, including Xue Muqiao, Wu Jinglian, and Zhao Renwei, had participated in the much smaller World Bank conference with Eastern European economists in the resort town of Moganshan.

33. Wu Jinglian, "Economics and China's Economic Rise" (paper presented at the Sixteenth World Congress of the International Economic Association, Beijing, China, July 4, 2011), 9.

34. Wu Jinglian 吴敬琏, "从匈牙利的经验看我国当前的改革" [Viewing China's Present Reform from the Perspective of the Hungarian Experience], 经济社会体制比较 [*Comparative Economic and Social Systems*], no. 3 (1985): 1.

35. János Kornai, "The Dual Dependence of the State-Owned Firm in Hungary," in *China's Industrial Reform*, ed. Gene Tidrick and Chen Jiyuan (New York: Oxford University Press, 1987), 317–338.

36. Wu, "Viewing China's Present Reform from the Perspective of the Hungarian Experience," 1.

37. Josephine Woo (World Bank) to James Tobin, July 17, 1985, "China 1985," Box 13, Tobin Papers Collection, Yale University Library Manuscripts and Archives, New Haven, CT. See also Edwin Lim, interview with William Becker and Marie Zenni (World Bank Group, Oral History Program, Washington, DC, October 30–31, 2002), 28.

38. Edwin Lim, "Supplementary List of Topics That Could Be Added to the Presentations Given by Scholars from Abroad," in "China 1985," Box 13, Tobin Papers Collection, Yale University Library Manuscripts and Archives, New Haven, CT.

39. János Kornai, author interview, Budapest, Hungary, May 30, 2012.

40. John F. Burns, "In China, 'Capitalist Roaders' Can Now Cruise in Cadillacs," *New York Times*, June 29, 1985, A1.

41. János Kornai, *By Force of Thought: Irregular Memoirs of an Intellectual Journey* (Cambridge: MIT Press, 2006), 323.

42. Ibid., 323; János Kornai, author interview, Budapest, Hungary, May 30, 2012; James Tobin, "Suggestions for Chinese," September 2, 1985, China 1985," Box 13, James Tobin Papers, Yale University Library Manuscripts and Archives, New Haven, CT; Alexander Cairncross, "Beijing. 29.8.85," DC106 2/14, Papers of Sir Alexander Cairncross, University of Glasgow Archives, Glasgow, Scotland, UK.

43. Anthony Lewis, "Where Does It Stop?" *New York Times*, August 29, 1985, A25.

44. "Yangtse River Cruising" (advertisement), *Cruise Travel* (November/December 1985): 32.

45. Author interview, Edwin Lim, Barnstable, Massachusetts, September 14, 2012.

46. Xue Muqiao 薛暮桥, "开幕词" [Opening Address], in 宏观经济的管理和改革: 宏观经济管理国际讨论会言论选编 [*Macroeconomic Management and Reform: Selected Remarks from the International Conference on Macroeconomic Management*], ed. 中国经济体制改革研究会 [China Research Society on Economic System Reform] (Beijing: Jingji ribao chubanshe, 1986), 58–60.

47. Edwin Lim, "International Seminar on Economic Planning and Macromanagement: Tentative Program," in "China 1985," Box 13, James Tobin Papers, Yale University Library Manuscripts and Archives, New Haven, CT.

48. Wu, "Economics and China's Economic Rise," 9.

49. In Herman Wouk, *The Caine Mutiny* (Garden City, NY: Doubleday, 1951), a character based closely on Tobin is described as "measured, quiet speech, and a mind like a sponge . . . ahead of the field by a spacious percentage." Wouk and Tobin were Naval Reserve colleagues; the Pulitzer Prize–winning novel's character, named "Tobit," was explicitly modeled after Tobin (Ed Crooks, "Obituary: James Tobin Left a Legacy of Advances," *Financial Times*, March 19, 2002).

50. James Tobin, "The Economy of China: A Tourist's View," *Challenge* 16, no. 1 (March–April 1973): 20.

51. Ibid., 30.

52. James Tobin, "Suggestions for Chinese," September 2, 1985, "China 1985," Box 13, Tobin Papers Collection, Yale University Library Manuscripts and Archives, New Haven, CT. For the Chinese summary of this portion of his presentation, see Liu Guoguang 刘国光, et al., "经济体制改革与宏观经济管理: '宏观经济管理国际讨论会'评述" [Economic System Reform and Macroeconomic Management: A Commentary on the "International Conference on Macroeconomic Management"], JJYJ, no. 12 (1985): 11.

53. Tobin, "Suggestions." See also Liu, et al., "Economic System Reform and Macroeconomic Management," 12–13.

54. Tobin, "Suggestions." See also Liu, et al., "Economic System Reform and Macroeconomic Management," 11.

55. Tobin, "Suggestions." See also Liu, et al., "Economic System Reform and Macroeconomic Management," 12–13.

56. Zhao, "Remembering and Reflecting on the 1985 Bashan Conference," 2.

57. Zhang Zhouyuan 张卓元, "我们当代缺少国际经验" [Our Lack of International Experience Today], 时代人物周报 [*People of the Era*], August 16, 2005, at http://finance.sina.com.cn/economist/pingyixueren/20050816/11021890746.shtml.

58. Zhu Jiaming 朱嘉明, "论我国正经历的经济发展阶段" [On China's Current Stage of Economic Development], 中青年经济论坛 [*Young Economists' Forum*], no. 2 (1985): 13–23. For the opposing view, see Guo, Liu, and Qi, "The National Economy Cannot Break into Flight," 74–76.

59. Wu Jinglian, author interviews, Beijing, China, August 18, 2012, and September 7, 2013.

60. Author interview, Edwin Lim, Barnstable, Massachusetts, September 14, 2012; Wu Jinglian, author interviews, Beijing, China, August 18, 2012, and September 7, 2013.

61. Wu Jinglian 吴敬琏, "再论保持经济改革的良好经济环境" [Again Discussing Maintaining a Favorable Economic Environment for Economic Reform], JJYJ, no. 5 (1985): 4. For another example, see Wu Jinglian 吴敬琏, "科学社会主义同非科学的社会主义的斗争" [The Struggle between Scientific Socialism and Nonscientific Socialism], JJYJ, no. 4 (1981): 23.

62. Lim, "The Opening of Thinking to the Outside World," 39.

63. Lim, "International Seminar on Economic Planning and Macromanagement."

64. Kornai, *By Force of Thought*, 323.

65. János Kornai, author interview, Budapest, Hungary, May 30, 2012.

66. János Kornai, "Macropolicy and Reform: Hungarian Reform," "China 1985," Box 13, Tobin Papers Collection, Yale University Library Manuscripts and Archives, New Haven, CT. For the Chinese summary, see Liu, et al., "Economic System Reform and Macroeconomic Management," 3. For the detail on the handwritten notes, see János Kornai, author interview, Budapest, Hungary, May 30, 2012.

67. Wu Jinglian, author interviews, Beijing, China, August 18, 2012, and September 7, 2013.

68. Kornai, "Macropolicy and Reform: Hungarian Reform"; Liu, et al., "Economic System Reform and Macroeconomic Management," 4.

69. Kornai, "Macropolicy and Reform: Hungarian Reform."

70. Lim, "The Opening of Thinking to the Outside World," 38–39.

71. Kornai, "Macropolicy and Reform: Hungarian Reform." For the Chinese summary, see Liu, et al., "Economic System Reform and Macroeconomic Management," 3.

72. Ibid. This point is stressed even more clearly in Liu, et al., "Economic System Reform and Macroeconomic Management," 4, 5.

73. Guo Shuqing 郭树清, "国际知名学者和专家谈中国经济改革" [Famous International Scholars and Experts Discuss China's Economic Reform], 经济社会体制比较 [*Comparative Economic and Social Systems*], no. 3 (1985): 7; Liu, et al., "Economic System Reform and Macroeconomic Management," 10–11.

74. Kornai, *By Force of Thought*, 323.

75. James Tobin, "Discussion after Kornai" (handwritten notes), "China 1985," Box 13, James Tobin Papers, Yale University Library Manuscripts and Archives, New Haven, CT.

76. Zhao, "Remembering and Reflecting on the 1985 Bashan Conference," 12.

77. Yang Qi 杨启, quoted in Liu, *The Eighties*, 350.

78. Wu, "Economics and China's Economic Rise," 9.

79. Kornai, *By Force of Thought*, 324.

80. János Kornai, author interview, Budapest, Hungary, May 30, 2012.

81. Peter Nolan, *China's Rise, Russia's Fall: Politics, Economics and Planning in the Transition from Stalinism* (New York: St. Martin's Press, 1995), 75–76.

82. János Kornai, author interview, Budapest, Hungary, May 30, 2012.

83. James Tobin, "China, Sept. 3, p.m.," in "China 1985," Box 13, James Tobin Papers, Yale University Library Manuscripts and Archives, New Haven, CT.

84. Zhao "Remembering and Reflecting on the 1985 Bashan Conference," 5; Guo, "Famous International Scholars and Experts Discuss China's Economic Reform," 9.

85. James Tobin, "China Sept. 4 P.M.," in "China 1985," Box 13, James Tobin Papers, Yale University Library Manuscripts and Archives, New Haven, CT.

86. Michel Albert, "Conference lecture," in "China 1985," Box 13, James Tobin Papers, Yale University Library Manuscripts and Archives, New Haven, CT; Liu, et al., "Economic System Reform and Macroeconomic Management," 5.

87. Wu Jinglian, author interviews, Beijing, China, August 18, 2012, and September 7, 2013.

88. Lou Jiwei 楼继伟, "吸取南斯拉夫经验，避免强化地方分权" [Draw on Yugoslavia's Experience and Avoid Reinforcing a Dividing up of Power among Localities], 经济社会体制比较 [*Comparative Economic and Social Systems*], no. 1 (1986): 3.

89. János Kornai, author interview, Budapest, Hungary, May 30, 2012. See Liu, et al., "Economic System Reform and Macroeconomic Management," 7.

90. Alexander Cairncross, "Friday 6 Sept. 2 P.M.," DC106 2/14, Papers of Sir Alexander Cairncross, University of Glasgow Archives, Glasgow, Scotland, UK.

91. Mary Cairncross, diary entry for August 29, 1985.

92. Alexander Cairncross, "Wednesday, 4.9.85" and "Hangchow 6:30 A.M.," DC106 2/14, Papers of Sir Alexander Cairncross, University of Glasgow Archives, Glasgow, Scotland, UK; Lim, "The Opening of Thinking to the Outside World," 36.

93. Liu Jiexiu 刘洁修, ed., 汉语成语考释词典 [*Explanatory Dictionary of Chinese Idioms*] (Shanghai: Shangwu yinshuguan, 1989), 848.

94. Group photograph at the Bashan Conference, Yangtze River, September 1985. Provided to the author by Edwin Lim.

95. James Tobin, "Final Remarks," Box 13, James Tobin Papers, Yale University Library Manuscripts and Archives, New Haven, CT.

96. Ma Hong 马洪, "稳定经济，推进改革" [Stabilize the Economy, Advance Reform], 经济社会体制比较 [*Comparative Economic and Social Systems*], no. 1 (1986): 1–2.

97. Kornai, *By Force of Thought*, 324.

98. Meryl Gordon, "A Keynesian Who Refuses to Quit," *New York Times*, October 13, 1985, F28, at http://www.nytimes.com/1985/10/13/business/a-keynesian-who-refuses-to-quit.html?pagewanted=all.

99. An Zhiwen 安志文, "宏观经济管理国际讨论会对我国改革有参考价值的几点意见" [Several Suggestions with Relevance to China's Reform from the International Conference on Macroeconomic Management]. I obtained this document from a source who wishes to remain anonymous.

100. Wu Jinglian, author interviews, Beijing, China, August 18, 2012, and September 7, 2013.

101. This unusual designation had only been used a few times before in Chinese Communist Party (CCP) history, most notably in March 1955 to discuss

the removal of Gao Gang, the leader of the State Planning Commission in the early 1950s who was purged and committed suicide after allegedly plotting a coup. See David S. G. Goodman, "The National CCP Conference of September 1985 and China's Leadership Changes," *China Quarterly*, no. 105 (March 1986): 123–130.

102. Chen Yun, "We Must Correct the Tendency to Neglect Furthering Culture and Ideology" (September 24, 1985), in *Selected Works of Chen Yun: Volume III (1956–1994)]* (Beijing: Foreign Languages Press, 1999), 349–353; Zhu Jiamu 朱佳木, ed., 陈云年谱: 一九 o 五–一九九五 [*Chronology of Chen Yun: 1905–1995*], 3 vols. (Beijing: Zhongyang wenxian chubanshe, 2000), 3:383–385.

103. Chen Yun, "Combating Corrosive Ideology," *Beijing Review* 28, no. 41 (October 14, 1985): 15–16.

104. "Proposal of the Central Committee of the Chinese Communist Party for the Seventh Five-Year Plan for National, Economic and Social Development," Xinhua News Agency, September 25, 1985, trans. in Foreign Broadcast Information Service, FBIS-CHI-85-187, September 26, 1985, K2–K3; see also Wu, "Economics and China's Economic Rise," 10.

105. "Proposal of the Central Committee of the Chinese Communist Party for the Seventh Five-Year Plan for National, Economic and Social Development."

106. "13.9.85," DC106 2/14. Papers of Sir Alexander Cairncross, University of Glasgow Archives, Glasgow, Scotland, UK.

CHAPTER SEVEN   *In the Wake*

1. 赵紫阳文集 *1980–1989* [*Collected Works of Zhao Ziyang, 1980–1989*] (Hong Kong: Chinese University Press, 2016) (cited hereafter as ZZYWJ), 3:189; Fang Weizhong 房维中, ed., 在风浪中前进: 中国发展与改革编年记事 [Forward in the Storm: Chronology of China's Reform and Development, 1977–1989], unpublished 2004 document. Available in the Fairbank Collection, Fung Library, Harvard University (cited hereafter as ZFLZQJ), 1985, 227, 235–236. Fang Weizhong, the editor of this internal Party compendium, notes that Zhao left his prepared remarks and added these thoughts on p. 234.

2. ZFLZQJ, 1985, 235–236.

3. Ibid.

4. ZZYWJ, 3:189; ZFLZQJ, 1985, 227, 235–236.

5. Liu Guoguang 刘国光, et al., "经济体制改革与宏观经济管理: '宏观经济管理国际讨论会' 评述 [Economic System Reform and Macroeconomic Management: A Commentary on the "International Conference on Macroeconomic Management"], 经济研究 [*Economic Research*] (cited hereafter as JJYJ), no. 12 (1985): 3–19; "经济体制模式的选择与转换:'宏观经济管理国际讨论会'评述之一" [The Selection and Transformation of an Economic System Model: A Commentary on the "International Conference on Macroeconomic Management," Part I], 人民日报 [*People's Daily*] (cited hereafter as RMRB), December 27, 1985; "经济体制改革与宏观经济管理:'宏观经济管理国际讨论会'评述之二" [Economic System Reform and Macroeconomic Management: A Commentary on the "International Conference on Macroeconomic Management,: Part II],

RMRB, December 30, 1985. The same document had been published in slightly different forms; I cite from the *Economic Research* version.

6. Liu, et al., "Economic System Reform and Macroeconomic Management," 3.

7. Ibid., 17–18.

8. Ibid., 6, 8; ZZYWJ, 3:265.

9. ZFLZQJ, 1985, 242, 245.

10. Chen Yizi, et al., "Reform: Results and Lessons from the 1985 CESRRI Survey," *Journal of Comparative Economics* 11, no. 3 (1987): 462–478.

11. ZFLZQJ, 1985, 272.

12. This term is used in Zhao Renwei 赵人伟, "1985 年巴山轮会议的回顾与思考" [Remembering and Reflecting on the 1985 Bashan Conference]," JJYJ, no. 12 (2008): 17–28; uses of the term were numerous, e.g., Ai Zhigang 袁志刚, "也谈科尔奈' 非瓦尔拉均衡论': 与朱嘉明同志商榷" [Discussing Kornai's "Non-Walrasian Equilibrium Theory": A Discussion with Comrade Zhu Jiaming], JJYJ, no. 1 (1988): 61. During the same period, several other intellectual "fevers"—less consequential but conceptually analogous—swept through Chinese academic circles, including an existentialist "Sartre fever" in philosophy departments and a futurist "Toffler fever" in social science departments. These "fevers" in the 1980s are the subject of a forthcoming article by this author, tentatively titled "Fever Pitch: Sartre, Toffler, and Kornai in Beijing."

13. János Kornai 雅诺什· 科尔奈, 短缺经济学 [*Economics of Shortage*] (Beijing: Jingji kexue chubanshe, 1986).

14. Lu Zhongyuan 卢中原, "改革呼唤出来的经济理论家: 科尔奈及其经济学著作述评" [The Economic Theorist that the Reform Cried Out for: A Discussion on János Kornai and his Economic Writings], 读书 [*Dushu*], no. 6 (1985): 33. The transliteration of his name in Chinese is Yanuoshe Ke'ernai 雅诺什· 科尔奈. His last name is also sometimes rendered as Ke'ernei (科尔内). For other articles in this vein, see Li Zhenning 李振宁, "科尔奈经济思想的精华" [The Essence of Kornai's Economic Thought], JJYJ, no. 9 (1986): 25–29; and Lu Jianren 陆建人, "短缺经济学评介" [Review of *Economics of Shortage*], 世界经济与政治 [*World Economics and Politics*], no. 7 (1987): 55–57.

15. János Kornai, *By Force of Thought: Irregular Memoirs of an Intellectual Journey* (Cambridge: MIT Press, 2006), 325; János Kornai, author interview, Budapest, Hungary, May 30, 2012.

16. This information comes from the Chinese National Knowledge Infrastructure database, based on searches for the keywords "科尔奈" [Kornai], and "短缺经济学" [*Economics of Shortage*], on December 18, 2012.

17. Liu Xiaodong 刘晓东, "短缺经济学讨论会简述" [Summary of the Discussion Forum on the Economics of Shortage], 北京大学学报(哲学社会科学版) [*Journal of Peking University: Philosophy and Social Sciences*], no. 1 (1987): 71.

18. For two examples, see Jiang Shan 江山, "科尔内的' 短缺经济学' 和社会主义经济体制改革" [Kornai's *Economics of Shortage* and the Socialist Economy's Structural Reform], 经济社会体制比较 [*Comparative Economic and Social Systems*], no. 1 (1985): 30–37; and Jiang Yiguo 蒋一国 and Li Junze 李钧泽, "企业预算约束软化及其治理: 短缺经济学的启" [Lessons from *Economics of Shortage*: The Softening and Regulation of Enterprise Budget Constraints], 中央财政金

融学院学报 [*Journal of the Central College of Finance and Economics*], no. 5 (1987): 74–76.

19. Lu, "The Economic Theorist That the Reform Cried Out for," 31–33.

20. Li, "The Essence of Kornai's Economic Thought," 25–29.

21. Lu, "Review of *Economics of Shortage*," 55–56. As a reminder, the "soft budget constraint" refers to enterprise expectations that they will not suffer if they incur losses because the state will bail them out; "paternalism" refers to this attitude of the state toward enterprises.

22. Zhao Renwei 赵仁伟, "我国经济改革过程中的双重体制问题" [Problems of the Dual-Track System in China's Reform Process], JJYJ, no. 9 (1986): 18.

23. Xue Muqiao 薛暮桥, "薛暮桥同志在全国宏观经济管理问题讨论会开幕式上的讲话" [Comrade Xue Muqiao's Speech at the Opening Session of the National Conference on Issues in Macroeconomic Management], 计划经济研究 [*Planned Economy Research*], no. 9 (1986): 3.

24. Ibid.

25. Ibid., 5.

26. Another Bashan participant, Guo Shuqing, elaborated on this idea in a January 1987 article. Frequently using the term *hongguan tiaokong*, Guo wrote, "Since 1985, strengthening macro control has become the central task of reform," and he defined this "central task" in terms of the related needs to expand to "full" enterprise autonomy and to broaden the scope of the market. Guo Shuqing 郭树清, "我国经济体制现状与继续改革的方向" [The Current Situation of China's Economic System and the Direction of Continued Reform], 管理世界 [*Management World*], no. 1 (1987): 39, 46–48.

27. Liu Guoguang 刘国光, "中国经济大变动中的双重模式转换" [The Dual-Model Transition in China's Economic Transformation], 中国经济问题 [*China's Economic Problems*], no. 1 (1987): 2. Despite extremely similar titles, this essay is substantially different from the early 1986 paper presented at the CASS conference on the goal model of the reform—newly incorporating, for example, the direct references to Kornai.

28. Liu, "The Selection and Transformation of an Economic System Model," 2–4.

29. Ibid., 5.

30. Ibid., 6. Elsewhere, Liu uses Kornai to illustrate the dual dependence of enterprises under the dual-track system, echoing Zhao Renwei's analysis. See Liu Guoguang 刘国光, "中国经济体制改革的若干问题" [Some Problems in China's Economic System Reform], 财贸经济 [*Finance and Trade Economics*], no. 9 (1987): 1–8.

31. Liu Guoguang 刘国光, "关于发展社会主义商品经济问题" [Concerning Problems in Developing the Socialist Commodity Economy], 经济工作者学习资料 [*Study Materials for Economic Workers*], no. 28 (1986): 8.

32. Ibid., 6. According to Liu, "We want to learn all the knowledge that is conducive to the development of the socialist commodity economy, and that includes the experience and knowledge of the developed Western countries in managing the economy."

33. Liu Guoguang 刘国光, "在改革的实践中发展马克思主义经济理论" [Developing Marxist Economic Theory in Putting Reform into Practice], 中国社会科学 [*Social Sciences in China*], no. 5 (1987): 52–58. For an interesting contempo-

raneous discussion of Liu's views, see Du Hui 杜辉, "经济体制改革理论的冷静思考: 刘国光经济改革思想述评" [Cool-Headed Thinking about Economic System Reform Theory: An Evaluation of Liu Guogang's Ideas on Economic Reform], JJYJ, no. 7 (1988): 52–58, 33.

34. Lin Daojun 林道君, "四单位在南京联合举办 '经济体制改革理论和实践' 研讨会" [Four Work Units Jointly Host in Nanjing a "Discussion Forum on the Theory and Practice of Economic Structural Reform"], 经济管理 [*Economic Management*], no. 12 (1986): 73.

35. Liu Guoguang 刘国光, "中国经济大变动中的双重模式转换问题" [Problems of the Dual-Model Transition in China's Economic Transformation], in 经济体制改革的理论与实践' 研讨会 [*Collected Papers of the Discussion Forum on "Economic System Reform Theory and Practice"*], ed. Wang Haibo 汪海波, Lu Cheng 吕政, and Zhou Shaopeng 周绍鹏 (Beijing: Zhongguo jingji chubanshe, 1987), 9.

36. Zhou Shulian 周叔莲, "论我国经济体制改革的目标模式" [On the Goal Model of China's Economic System Reform], in ibid., 11. Zhou Shulian was one of the authors of the Bashan Report.

37. Ibid., 15–16, 32.

38. Xue Jiaji 薛家骥, "计划与市场相结合若干问题的思考" [Thoughts on Some Problems in Integrating Plan and Market], in ibid., 58, 60.

39. Susan Shirk argues that the willingness of Chinese enterprise managers to enact reforms to increase their power and funds was crucial to the success of the market reforms. She also observes that this situation in China differed from what experts on socialist transition generally expected (*The Political Logic of Economic Reform in China* [Berkeley: University of California Press, 1993], 286–289).

40. Economist Zhou Qiren characterized the Bashan Conference in these terms and described the excited reaction of his colleague Luo Xiaopeng after the conference (Zhou Qiren, author interview, Beijing, China, September 4, 2013).

41. Zhao Renwei 赵人伟, "一个经济学家的学术探索之旅: 读科尔奈的自传 '思想的力量'有感" [An Economist's Academic Adventure: Feelings about Kornai's Autobiography *By Force of Thought*], 经济社会体制比较 [*Comparative Economic and Social Systems*], no. 6 (2009): 185–186.

42. Zhang Jun 张军, "于光远与科尔奈的不同际遇" [The Different Fates of Yu Guangyuan and János Kornai], 东方早报 [*Eastern Daily*], November 12, 2013.

43. János Kornai and Zsuzsa Dániel, "The Chinese Economic Reform—As Seen by Hungarian Economists (Marginal Notes to Our Travel Diary)," *Acta Oeconomica* 36, nos. 3/4 (1986): 302.

44. When I interviewed Kornai in the summer of 2012, he answered even more simply: "It's very strange that in my own little country [I was ignored] most of the time, and in this giant country I was able to speak at a certain historical moment where one billion people wanted to hear exactly what I wanted to say. That was a very rare moment, and good luck" (János Kornai, author interview, Budapest, Hungary, May 30, 2012).

45. John F. Burns, "In China, a New 'Hundred Flowers' Drive," *New York Times*, June 16, 1986, at http://www.nytimes.com/1986/06/16/world/in-china-a-new-100-flowers-drive.html; Alexander Pantsov and Steven Levine,

Deng Xiaoping: A Revolutionary Life (Oxford: Oxford University Press, 2015), 329.

46. ZFLZQJ, 1986, 31–33; this report is also included in 吴敬琏选集 [*Selected Works of Wu Jinglian*] (Taiyuan: Shanxi renmin chubanshe, 1989), 446–449.

47. See Wu Ji 吴季, et al., "论经济增长的有效约束" [On Effective Constraints on Economic Growth]," JJYJ, no. 6 (1986): 19–24 (Wu Ji is a pen name for Wu Jinglian); Wu Jinglian 吴敬琏, "关于改革战略选择的若干思考" [Some Thoughts on the Choice of Reform Strategy], JJYJ, no. 2 (1987): 3–14. I am indebted to Joseph Fewsmith, *Dilemmas of Reform in China: Political Conflict and Economic Debate* (Armonk, NY: M. E. Sharpe, 1994), for his exceptionally lucid overview of the schism between the "coordinated reform" group and the "enterprise reform" group.

48. Hua Sheng 华生, et al., "微观经济基础的重新构造" [Restructuring the Microeconomic Base], JJYJ, no. 3 (1986): 21, 28.

49. Ibid., 21.

50. Ibid., 23–24. This group acknowledged that this idea also was international in origin. They wrote, "International experience that is worth emulation also shows that in a modern commodity economy the method of collecting returns from property is the most common form in which the interests of the proprietors (or legal owners) can be guaranteed, while leaving plenty of room for the managers (or business owners) to operate after the separation of management from ownership" (22–23).

51. Ma Ding 马丁 [Song Longxiang 宋龙祥], "当代我国经济学研究的十大转变" [Ten Major Changes in Contemporary China's Study of Economics], 工人日报 [*Workers' Daily*], November 2, 1985; the article was republished in 世界经济导报 [*World Economic Herald*], April 7, 1986. For an excellent analysis of this episode, see Merle Goldman, *Sowing the Seeds of Democracy in China: Political Reform in the Deng Xiaoping Era* (Cambridge: Harvard University Press, 1994), 160–163.

52. ZZYWJ, 3:229; Committee on Historical Manuscripts of the People's Republic of China 中国人民共和国史稿委员会, ed., 邓力群国史讲谈录 [*A Record of Deng Liqun's Talks on the History of the Country*], internal manuscript (7 volumes, 2000–2002), 4:200.

53. Ma. "Ten Major Changes."

54. ZFLZQJ, 1986, 36–37; ZZYWJ, 3:304–305.

55. Li Yining 厉以宁, "改革的基本思路" [The Fundamental Idea of the Reform], 北京日报 [*Beijing Daily*], May 19, 1986, 3; Fewsmith, *Dilemmas of Reform*, 186. As noted in Chapters 3 and 5, Li Yining's familiarity with Western economics was profound; in addition to writing book-length works about Thatcherite economics and other subjects, beginning in 1979 he had led the weekly lectures series of the Foreign Economics Research Group. See Foreign Economics Research Group 外国经济学说研究会, ed., 外国经济学讲座 [*Lectures on Foreign Economics*] (Beijing: Zhongguo shehui kexue chubanshe, 1980–1981).

56. Li Yining, author interview, Beijing, China, August 31, 2013.

57. Xiao Meng, author interview, Beijing, China, June 26, 2012; ZZYWJ, 3:460.

58. Wang Zhihua 王志华, "论具有中国特色的'模块集成式'体制" [On a System of "Integrated Units" with Chinese Characteristics], 复旦学报 [*Fudan University Journal*], no. 2 (1986): 41–43.

59. Hu Ruyin 胡汝银, "供给、所有制关系与短缺原因分析" [Analyzing Supply, Ownership Relations, and the Cause of Shortage], 世界经济文汇 [*Writings on the World Economy*], no. 2 (1987): 16, 18, 20, 22. For another critique of Kornai's ideas and their relevance to China by the same author, see Hu Ruyin 胡汝银, "短缺归因论" [On Shortage], 外国经济理论评述 [*Commentaries on Foreign Economic Theory*], no. 5 (1987): 28–33.

60. A young Institute for Chinese Economic Structural Reform economist named Zhang Weiying—one of the first to propose the dual-track system—also disparaged Kornai's influence on China. He complained, "Chinese economists have attached great importance to Kornai's *Economics of Shortage*. This has brought some progress to China's economic research but has also brought some trouble" (Zhang Weiying 张维迎, "总量分析、结构分析和预算软硬" [Aggregate Analysis, Structural Analysis, and Hard and Soft Budgets], JJYJ, no. 8 [1987]: 11). Zhang had also been part of a team of coauthors who voiced concerns about Kornai's influence; see Song Guoqing 宋国青, Zhang Weiying 张维迎, and Cheng Xiaonong 程晓农, "宏观经济讨论中的若干理论分歧" [Some Theoretical Differences in Macroeconomic Discussions], JJYJ, 4 (1987): 3–14. Song, et al., present a distinction between the intrinsic value of Kornai's ideas and the value of those ideas as "some authors have used them to analyze China's economy" (10), dismissing much of Kornai's work as "not of much practical value" (12).

61. Wu Jinglian 吴敬琏, "关于国家调节市场、市场引导企业的提法" [On the Idea of the State Managing the Market and the Market Guiding Enterprises], prepared for Jiang Zemin and submitted on June 10, 1991. Provided to the author by Wu Jinglian. "Manage" would win out by the following year.

62. Yang Jianming 杨建民, Liu He 刘鹤, and Cai Quan 蔡泉, "我国产业政策研究的回顾和深化" [Reviewing and Deepening China's Industrial Policy Research], 宏观经济研究 [*Macroeconomic Research*], no. 2 (1988): 15.

63. Hua Sheng 华生, Zhang Xuejun 张雪君, and Luo Xiaopeng 罗小朋, "中国改革十年: 回顾、反思和前景" [Ten Years of Chinese Reform: Review, Reflections, and Prospects], JJYJ, no. 9 (1988): 31.

CHAPTER EIGHT   *A Tempestuous Season*

1. Chen Yizi 陈一谘, 陈一谘回忆录 [*Memoirs of Chen Yizi*] (Hong Kong: Xin shiji chuban ji chuanmei youxian gongsi, 2013), 347–348; Gao Shangquan 高尚全, Chen Yizi 陈一谘, and Wang Xiaoqiang 王晓强, "匈牙利、南斯拉夫改革报告" [Report on the Reform in Hungary and Yugoslavia], in 艰难的探索: 匈牙利、南斯拉夫改革考察 [*A Difficult Exploration: An Investigation into the Reform in Hungary and Yugoslavia*] (Beijing: Zhongguo jingji guanli chubanshe, 1987), 15.

2. Chen, *Memoirs of Chen Yizi*, 347–350.

3. Gao, Chen, and Wang, "Report on the Reform in Hungary and Yugoslavia," 15–30. Other members of the delegation continued to discuss what they had learned. In October 1986, Ma Kai published a report on "price reform under the economic condition of shortage," analyzing the dual-track price

system and issues related to price reform based on Kornai's concept of "investment hunger" and both the Hungarian and Yugoslav experiences. See Ma Kai 马凯, 马凯集 [*Collected Works of Ma Kai*] (Harbin: Heilongjiang jiaoyu chubanshe, 1991), 195–212.

4. Fang Weizhong 房维中, ed., 在风浪中前进：中国发展与改革编年记事 [Forward in the Storm: Chronology of China's Reform and Development, 1977–1989], unpublished 2004 document. Available in the Fairbank Collection, Fung Library, Harvard University (cited hereafter as ZFLZQJ), 1986, 72–82; 赵紫阳文集 *1980–1989* [*Collected Works of Zhao Ziyang, 1980–1989*] (Hong Kong: Chinese University Press, 2016) (cited hereafter as ZZYWJ), 3:401–406. In July 1986, Zhao would praise the inspiration that Yugoslavia's reforms had offered to China (ZZYWJ, 3:424). See also "体改所兄弟姐妹唁文" [Message of Condolence from Chen's Friends at the Institute for Chinese Economic Structural Reform], April 19, 2014, 陈一谘先生纪念网站 [Memorial Website for Chen Yizi], at http://chenyizi.com/2014/04/19/tgs/.

5. *Journal of Comparative Economics* 11, no. 3 (September 1987): 291, and 515–516, which includes a full list of the participants and their affiliations.

6. Bruce Reynolds and Susan K. Sell, "China's Participation in Global Governance: Exchange Rates and Intellectual Property" (2012, unpublished draft, deleted in the final version). For the final version, see Bruce Reynolds and Susan K. Sell, "China's Role in Global Governance—Foreign Exchange and Intellectual Property: A Comparison," Indiana University, Research Center for Chinese Politics and Business, Working Paper No. #31 (November 2012), at https://www.indiana.edu/~rccpb/wordpress/wp-content/uploads/2015/11/Reynolds_Sell_RCCPB_31_Nov_2012.pdf.

7. Zhou Xiaochuan and Zhu Li, "China's Banking System: Current Status, Perspective on Reform," *Journal of Comparative Economics* 11, no. 3 (September 1987): 406–407.

8. Reynolds and Sell, "China's Participation in Global Governance" (unpublished draft), 22.

9. See Henry C. Wallich, *Mainsprings of the German Revival* (New Haven: Yale University Press, 1955).

10. ZFLZQJ, 1986, 138.

11. Ibid., 1986, 137; ZZYWJ, 3:460–462.

12. ZFLZQJ, 1986, 140–141; regarding his June views, see ZZYWJ, 3:401. In mid-August, returning to the issue of commodity prices in a discussion with the Central Finance and Economics Leading Group, Zhao would explicitly contrast China's situation to that in Hungary and Yugoslavia: "China does not have a situation like that in Hungary or Yugoslavia. We can control prices more easily than they can" (ZFLZQJ, 1986, 197).

13. Nicholas Lardy, *China's Unfinished Economic Revolution* (Washington, DC: Brookings Institution Press, 1998), 63–64.

14. Henry Harding, *China's Second Revolution: Reform after Mao* (Washington, DC: Brookings Institution Press, 1987), 73; Lardy, *China's Unfinished Economic Revolution*, 131–132. On the bankruptcy law, Lardy notes that, despite its intentions, the law was "rarely applied" and the more painful and effective reforms to state-owned enterprises did not truly begin until after 1993 (ibid., 23).

15. Wu Jinglian, *Understanding and Interpreting Chinese Economic Reform* (Mason, OH: Thomson South-Western, 2005), 294.

16. ZZYWJ, 3:254; Harold K. Jacobson and Michel Oksenberg, *China's Participation in the IMF, the World Bank, and GATT* (Ann Arbor: University of Michigan Press, 1990), 83, 87–88, 91–92.

17. For an insightful example that connects the World Bank reports to Kornai's ideas, see Zou Gang 邹刚 and Wang Zhigang 王志钢, "经营者利益与企业行为" [Managers' Interests and Enterprise Behavior], 经济体制改革 [*Economic System Reform*], no. 1 (1987): 24–27.

18. Xinhua News Agency, "赵紫阳会见林重庚首席代表" [Zhao Ziyang Meets with Chief Representative Edwin Lim], 人民日报 (*People's Daily*) (cited hereafter as RMRB), June 22, 1986; ZZYWJ, 3:415–420.

19. Huo En 霍恩 (photographer), "赵紫阳会见林重庚首席代表" [Zhao Ziyang Meets with Chief Representative Edwin Lim], RMRB, June 22, 1986; Edwin Lim, author interview, Barnstable, Massachusetts, September 14, 2012.

20. Lim's stature remained high for the rest of his tenure. His speeches were reported in the *People's Daily* and other outlets. For example, see Xinhua News Agency, "林重庚谈: 企业效率主要取决于竞争" [Edwin Lim Says Business Efficiency Depends Mainly on Competition], RMRB, May 29, 1989.

21. "World Bank Aids Modernization," *Beijing Review* 29, no. 12 (March 24, 1986): 36. The World Bank disburses two kinds of loans: International Bank for Reconstruction and Development (IBRD) loans, which charge interest, and International Development Association (IDA) loans, which are interest-free soft loans. China was eligible for both.

22. International Bank for Reconstruction and Development (IBRD), *Annual Report, 1981* (Washington, DC: IBRD, 1981), 120–121, 188; IBRD, *Annual Report, 1982* (Washington, DC: IBRD, 1982), 118–119, 184; IBRD, *Annual Report, 1983* (Washington, DC: IBRD, 1983), 126–127, 218; IBRD, *Annual Report, 1984* (Washington, DC: IBRD, 1984), 139, 142, 210; IBRD, *Annual Report, 1985* (Washington, DC: IBRD, 1985), 145–146, 166; IBRD, *Annual Report, 1986* (Washington, DC: IBRD, 1986), 137–138, 158; IBRD, *Annual Report, 1987* (Washington, DC: IBRD, 1987), 139–140, 160; IBRD, *Annual Report, 1988* (Washington, DC: IBRD, 1988), 131–132, 152; IBRD, *Annual Report, 1989* (Washington, DC: IBRD, 1989), 158–159, 178.

23. Liqun Jin and Chi-kuo Wu, eds., 回顾与展望: 纪念中国与世界银行合作十五周年 [*Past and Future: Fifteen Years of Cooperation between China and the World Bank*] (Beijing: Ministry of Finance and Xinhua News Agency, 1995), 27.

24. John Williamson, "What Washington Means by Policy Reform," in *Latin American Readjustment: How Much Has Happened*, ed. John Williamson (Washington, DC: Institute for International Economics, 1989); see also Joseph Stiglitz, *Globalization and Its Discontents* (New York: W. W. Norton, 2002).

25. Edwin Lim, author interview, Barnstable, Massachusetts, September 14, 2012.

26. Orville Schell, "Fang Lizhi: China's Andrei Sakharov," *Atlantic Monthly* (May 1988): 35–52.

27. Fang Lizhi 方励之, "民主、改革、现代化" [Democracy, Reform, and Modernization], (November 18, 1986), in Fang Lizhi, 危机感下的责任 [*Responsibility under Crisis*] (Singapore: Shijie keji chubanshe, 1989), 231.

28. Julie Kwong, "The 1986 Student Demonstrations in China: A Democratic Movement?" *Asian Survey* 28, no. 9 (September 1988): 970–971.

29. Jeffrey Wasserstrom, *Student Protests in Twentieth-Century China: The View from Shanghai* (Stanford: Stanford University Press, 1991), 299 (his first-hand account of living in Shanghai during this period).

30. "Obituary: Fang Lizhi," *Economist*, April 14, 2012.

31. Wasserstrom, *Student Protests in Twentieth-Century China*, 299.

32. Zhu Jiamu 朱佳木, ed., 陈云年谱: 一九〇五–一九九五 [*Chronology of Chen Yun: 1905–1995*], 3 vols. (Beijing: Zhongyang wenxian chubanshe, 2000) (cited hereafter as CYNP), 3:390, 392, 395.

33. "Hu Qiaomu, Deng Liqun on Nihilism, Liberalism," Xinhua News Agency, December 28, 1986, trans. in Foreign Broadcast Information Service, FBIS-CHI-86-250, December 30, 1986, K7.

34. Joseph Fewsmith, *Dilemmas of Reform in China: Political Conflict and Economic Debate* (Armonk, NY: M. E. Sharpe, 1994), 196.

35. Kwong, "The 1986 Student Demonstrations in China," 987.

36. Deng Liqun 邓力群, 十二个春秋: 邓力群自述 [*Twelve Springs and Autumns: An Autobiography of Deng Liqun*] (Hong Kong: Bozhi chubanshe, 2006), 401–407. Deng Liqun recalled that, as early as 1983, he and Chen Yun had criticized Hu Yaobang, but Deng Xiaoping had protected his then-protégé. See Committee on Historical Manuscripts of the People's Republic of China 中国人民共和国史稿委员会, ed., 邓力群国史讲谈录 [*A Record of Deng Liqun's Talks on the History of the Country*], internal manuscript (7 volumes, 2000–2002) (cited hereafter as GSJTL), 7:190.

37. Leng Rong 冷溶, ed., 邓小平年谱 *1975–1997* [*A Chronology of Deng Xiaoping, 1975–1997*], 2 vols. (Beijing: Zhongyang wenxian chubanshe, 2004) (cited hereafter as DXPNP), 1160–1162; CYNP, 3:400; Zhao Ziyang, *Prisoner of the State* (New York: Simon & Schuster, 2009), 172.

38. ZFLZQJ, 1987, 56; Richard Baum, *Burying Mao: Chinese Politics in the Age of Deng Xiaoping* (Princeton: Princeton University Press, 1994), 206–207; CYNP, 3:401–402; Edward A. Gargan, "Deng's Crushing of Protest Is Described," *New York Times*, January 14, 1987, at http://www.nytimes.com/1987/01/14/world/deng-s-crushing-of-protest-is-described.html; James H. Williams, "Fang Lizhi's Expanding Universe," *China Quarterly*, no. 123 (September 1990): 479.

39. I am grateful to an anonymous reviewer for drawing my attention to this point. See also Joseph Fewsmith, "What Zhao Ziyang Tells Us about Elite Politics in the 1980s," *China Leadership Monitor*, no. 30 (Fall 2009): 1–20.

40. Zhao, *Prisoner of the State*, 176–179.

41. Ibid., 169–170.

42. Ibid., 173; ZZYWJ, 4:17 and 4:21–23. On January 5, 1987, Yang Shangkun traveled to Shanghai to brief Li Xiannian on the meeting and the decisions regarding Hu and Zhao; see 李先念年谱 [*Chronology of Li Xiannian*], 6 vols. (Beijing: Zhongyang wenxian chubanshe, 2011) (cited hereafter as LXNNP), 6:372. According to Zhao, this is where Li issued this warning.

43. *Selected Works of Deng Xiaoping, Vol. III* (Beijing: Foreign Languages Press, 1994) (cited hereafter as SWDXP-3), 203. See also ZFLZQJ, 1987, 76–77.

44. Ibid.

45. ZFLZQJ, 1987, 82–86.

46. DXPNP, 1173–1174; ZFLZQJ, 1987, 112–114; ZZYWJ, 4:47–48.

47. ZFLZQJ, 1987, 115–122.

48. Ibid., 1987, 123; ZZYWJ, 4:75.

49. Zhao, *Prisoner of the State*, 188. Their first draft of a list of liberals to be punished included economist and CASS leader Yu Guangyuan, who was added by Deng Liqun. Zhao, who had long looked to Yu to support international intellectual exchanges, overrode Deng Liqun and decided that Yu could perform a self-criticism without further punishment (ibid., 191). Zhao's continuing difficulties in managing the attacks on "bourgeois liberalization" in the spring and summer of 1987 were underscored in a May 1987 speech on propaganda and theory (ZZYWJ, 4:96–98).

50. Ibid., 187.

51. Ibid., 199. Deng Xiaoping's chronology records a meeting with Zhao, Yang Shangkun, Wan Li, Bo Yibo, and Hu Qili at Deng's house that day, but only states that the meeting was to discuss personnel issues related to the Thirteenth Party Congress (DXPNP, 1200).

52. Li Xiannian also wrote a letter supporting Deng Liqun and praising his work, but to no avail (LXNNP, 6:404). For the description of Deng Liqun, see Zhao, *Prisoner of the State*, 9.

53. Stanley Rosen, "China in 1987," *Asian Survey* 28, no. 1 (1988): 36–40; ZZYWJ, 4:123. For a different perspective, see Susan L. Shirk, *The Political Logic of Economic Reform in China* (Berkeley: University of California Press, 1993), 308–312.

54. Zhao, *Prisoner of the State*, 205.

55. Ibid. See also ZZYWJ, 4:48.

56. SWDXP-3, 247–248.

57. Barry Naughton, *Growing out of the Plan: Chinese Economic Reform, 1978–1993* (New York: Cambridge University Press, 1995), 223.

58. Zhao Minshan 赵岷山, "二十个城市推行承包责任制的调查" [An Investigation into the Implementation of Long-Term Contracting in Twenty Cities], in 优秀统计分析报告选编 [*Selected Exemplary Statistical Analysis Reports*], ed. State Statistical Bureau 国家统计局办公室 (Beijing: Zhongguo tongji chubanshe, 1989), 442–448.

59. Peter Geithner, letter of May 15, 1986, and "Memorandum: Opening the Beijing Office," June 18, 1987, Developing Countries Program, Office Files of William Carmichael, Box 1, Folder 22, Ford Foundation Papers.

60. Edwin Lim 林重庚, "中国改革开放过程中的对外思想开放" [The Opening of Thinking to the Outside World in the Process of China's Reform and Opening], in 中国经济: 50 人看三十年: 回顾与分析 [*China's Economy: Fifty People on Thirty Years: Reflections and Analysis*], ed. Wu Jinglian 吴敬琏, et al. (Beijing: Zhongguo jingji chubanshe, 2008), 40.

61. Wu Jinglian 吴敬琏, "经济学家、经济学与中国改革" [Economists, Economics, and China's Reform], 财经杂志 [*Caijing Magazine*], March 3, 2008, at http://www.caijing.com.cn/2008-03-03/100050778.html.

62. Peter F. Drucker, "No Jobs for the Millions Is China's Nemesis," *Wall Street Journal*, November 19, 1987. Drucker was attacked by his colleague at the Claremont Graduate Institute, sinologist Steven W. Mosher, in a subsequent letter to the editor, for letting off the "totalitarian" Chinese Communist Party too easily (Steven W. Mosher, "Letters to the Editor: China's Economic Puzzle," *Wall Street Journal*, January 8, 1988).

63. "Zhao Ziyang's Visit to Hungary, Evaluation by Delegation Members," July 1987, History and Public Policy Program Digital Archive, Historical Archives of the Hungarian State Security (ABTL), trans. by Katalin Varga, at http://digitalarchive.wilsoncenter.org/document/119354; ZZYWJ, 2:134. The detail about An Zhiwen's attendance is noted in Wolfgang Bartke, *Who Was Who in the People's Republic of China* (Munich: K.G. Saur, 1997), 1:7.

64. Xiaoyuan Liu and Vojtech Mastny, eds., *China and Eastern Europe, 1960s–1980s: Proceedings of the International Symposium: Reviewing the History of Chinese–East European Relations from the 1960s to the 1980s, Beijing, 24–26 March 2004* (Zürich: ETH Zürich, 2004), 168. These comments were made by Zhu Ankang.

65. Ibid., 165. See also ZZYWJ, 4:126–129.

66. Fewsmith, *Dilemmas of Reform*, 210–214; Qimiao Fan, "State-Owned Enterprise Reform in China: Incentives and Environment," in *China's Economic Reforms: The Costs and Benefits of Incrementalism*, ed. Qimiao Fan and Peter Nolan (Basingstoke, UK: Macmillan, 1994), 149–150. For comments from Zhao Ziyang on the contract responsibility system and related policies, see ZZYWJ, 4:61–62, 4:87–89, 4:95, 4:283–288, 4:382, and 4:391–394.

67. Zhang Xuejun 张学军, "对我国宏观经济研究中若干基本观点的评价" [An Evaluation of Some Basic Viewpoints in China's Macroeconomic Research], 经济研究 [*Economic Research*] (cited hereafter as JJYJ), no. 8 (1987): 5–7. In the same article, Zhang gives lukewarm reviews to an article by another economist, Deng Yingtao, which he characterizes as derivative of Kornai. He writes, "Deng's article cannot match Kornai in the force of its analysis and the maturity of its theoretical system" (5).

68. Ibid., 6–7.

69. Wu Jinglian 吴敬琏, "关于宏观经济问题的分歧" [Concerning Differences on Macroeconomic Issues], JJYJ, no. 11 (1987): 52. Never one to miss an opportunity to allude to international support for his ideas, Wu also described his support for price reform in the following terms: "Like many other Chinese and foreign economists, I believe that, at present, the price reform . . . lags far behind the entire reform, especially the reform aimed at expanding the decision-making power of enterprises, and that determined steps should be taken so that it can catch up" (47).

70. Deliberations leading up to the Thirteenth Party Congress took place, in part, during debates about the proper agenda for 1988. In July 1987, Zhao outlined his priorities for 1988, headlined by "deepening the reform of the enterprise management system" (ranging from increasing "competitiveness" to "perfecting self-restraint") and including a wide range of other reforms at both the microeconomic and macroeconomic levels (ZFLZQJ, 1987, 226). However, the large ideological ambitions (as opposed to the narrower policy ambitions) of the 1987 congress were its primary significance.

71. See Reuters photographs in Michel Oksenberg, "China's 13th Party Congress," *Problems of Communism* 36, no. 6 (November–December 1987), 2 and 7.

72. LXNNP, 6:416; Baum, *Burying Mao*, 215–216. Tony Saich, "The Thirteenth Congress of the Chinese Communist Party: An Agenda for Reform?" *Journal of Communist Studies* 4, no. 2: 203–204; Oksenberg, "China's 13th Party Congress," 5–7.

73. Other analyses, primarily by political scientists, have highlighted the admittedly "skeletal and suggestive" proposals for political reform in the "neo-authoritarian" model then in vogue in China (Baum, *Burying Mao*, 220–222).

74. Zhao Ziyang 赵紫阳, 沿着有中国特色的社会主义道路前进 [*Advance along the Road of Socialism with Chinese Characteristics*] (Beijing: Renmin chubanshe, 1987), 26–27; see also ZZYWJ, 4:217–254.

75. Zhao, *Prisoner of the State*, 123. Of course, it is also possible Chen was simply not feeling well. But this portrayal draws on Zhao's interpretation of Chen's early exit.

CHAPTER NINE   *The Narrows of the River*

1. Adi Ignatius, "Introduction" to Zhao Ziyang, *Prisoner of the State* (New York: Simon & Schuster, 2009), ix–x. For Zhao Ziyang's exchange with the press, see 赵紫阳文集 *1980–1989* [*Collected Works of Zhao Ziyang, 1980–1989*] (Hong Kong: Chinese University Press, 2016) (cited hereafter as ZZYWJ), 4:257–264.

2. Robert Weatherley, *Politics in China since 1949: Legitimizing Authoritarian Rule* (London: Routledge, 2006), 136. Zhao Ziyang maintained his position on the Leading Small Group for Financial and Economic Affairs after he was promoted to general secretary. At present, President Xi Jinping leads it. (See Wu Peng, "Closer Look: Xi's Leadership of Top Economic Group Follows Pattern," *Caixin*, June 20, 2014, at http://english.caixin.com/2014-06-20/100693367.html.)

3. Fang Weizhong 房维中, ed., 在风浪中前进: 中国发展与改革编年记事 [Forward in the Storm: Chronology of China's Reform and Development, 1977–1989], unpublished 2004 document. Available in the Fairbank Collection, Fung Library, Harvard University (cited hereafter as ZFLZQJ), 1987, 335–342; ZZYWJ, 4:283–288.

4. Wu Jinglian, "Economics and China's Economic Rise" (paper presented at the Sixteenth World Congress of the International Economic Association, Beijing, China, July 4, 2011), in *The Chinese Economy: A New Transition*, ed. Masahiko Aoki and Jinglian Wu (New York: Palgrave Macmillan, 2012), 14.

5. Joseph Fewsmith, *Dilemmas of Reform in China: Political Conflict and Economic Debate* (Armonk, NY: M. E. Sharpe, 1994), 214–217.

6. ZZYWJ, 2:577–587; Fuh-Wen Tzeng, "The Political Economy of China's Coastal Development Strategy: A Preliminary Analysis," *Asian Survey* 31, no. 3 (March 1991): 273.

7. ZFLZQJ, 1987, 334; ZZYWJ, 4:271; Zhao, *Prisoner of the State*, 145–146.

8. Zhao, *Prisoner of the State*, 145–146.

9. Zhao Ziyang acknowledged this influence. See ibid., 145–146. For a fuller analysis of the growth model in these countries, see Ezra F. Vogel, *The Four Little Dragons: The Spread of Industrialization in East Asia* (Cambridge: Harvard University Press, 1991).

10. Wei-Wei Zhang, *Ideology and Economic Reform under Deng Xiaoping, 1978–1993* (London: Kegan Paul International, 1996), 194.

11. Deng Xiaoping, "We Should Draw on the Experiences of Other Countries" (June 3, 1988), in *Selected Works of Deng Xiaoping, Vol. III* (Beijing: Foreign Languages Press, 1994) (cited hereafter as SWDXP-3), 261–262; ZZYWJ, 4:372. In 1992, Chinese officials would begin to characterize the four Asian tigers as models for the future in a new way. On his Southern Tour in 1992, for example, Deng praised Singapore in broad terms: "Thanks to a strict administration, Singapore has good public order. We should learn from its experience and surpass it in this respect." As China was negotiating to establish diplomatic relations with South Korea in August 1992, Deng added, "The experience of other countries shows that some of them—Japan, South Korea and parts of Southeast Asia, for example—have gone through one or more periods of rapid development. . . . We must have this ambition" (SWDXP-3, 365). The *New York Times* reported that Wu Bangguo, Shanghai Party secretary, "reportedly told a visitor that China aimed to learn from the policies of South Korea and Singapore in developing their economies" (Nicholas D. Kristof, "China Sees Singapore as a Model for Progress," *New York Times*, August 9, 1992, at http://www.nytimes.com/1992/08/09 /weekinreview/the-world-china-sees-singapore-as-a-model-for-progress.html).

12. Zhu Jiamu 朱佳木, ed., 陈云年谱: 一九〇五—一九九五 [*Chronology of Chen Yun: 1905–1995*], 3 vols. (Beijing: Zhongyang wenxian chubanshe, 2000) (cited hereafter as CYNP), 407–408, 420.

13. Committee on Historical Manuscripts of the People's Republic of China 中国人民共和国史稿委员会, ed., 邓力群国史讲谈录 [*A Record of Deng Liqun's Talks on the History of the Country*], internal manuscript (7 volumes, 2000–2002) (cited hereafter as GSJTL), 1:410.

14. Zhao, *Prisoner of the State*, 146.

15. Tzeng, "The Political Economy of China's Coastal Development Strategy," 273.

16. ZFLZQJ, 1988, 7. Zhao met with Chen Yun on January 29, 1988, but CYNP does not record the contents of their meeting. On February 15, 1988, speaking with Li Peng and Hu Qili, Chen said he supported the "two ends extending abroad" but warned his colleagues not to underestimate the difficulty of what they were undertaking (CYNP, 3:409–410).

17. ZZYWJ, 4:366–367; "Chao on Coastal Area's Development Strategy," *Beijing Review* 31, no. 6 (February 8–14, 1988): 15–19.

18. Tzeng, "The Political Economy of China's Coastal Development Strategy," 271.

19. 薛暮桥年谱 [*A Chronology of Xue Muqiao*], unpublished document, no pagination.

20. Ibid.

21. ZFLZQJ, 1988, 23–27, 28–32.

22. Ibid., 1988, 3, 47.

23. Ibid., 1988, 48. See Tian Yuan 田源, "价格改革与产权制度转换" [Price Reform and the Changeover in the Property Rights System], 经济研究 [*Economic Research*] (cited hereafter as JJYJ), no. 2 (1988): 11–18.

24. ZFLZQJ, 1988, 60.

25. Ibid., 1988, 90; Zhao, *Prisoner of the State*, 146; ZZYWJ, 4:375.

26. ZFLZQJ, 1988, 102–107.

27. Ibid., 1988, 107–115.

28. It did seem that foreign experts largely believed China was suffering from demand-pull inflation during this period, with the Japanese economist Ryutaro Komiya—who visited Beijing in April 1988—stating that the phenomenon "had not come to an end by mid-1987" (Wu Jinglian, *Understanding and Interpreting the Chinese Economy* [Mason, OH: Thomson/South-Western, 2005], 367).

29. ZZYWJ, 3:157; ZFLZQJ, 1988, 119; ZZYWJ, 4:420–423.

30. Leng Rong 冷溶, ed., 邓小平年谱 *1975–1997* [*A Chronology of Deng Xiaoping, 1975–1997*], 2 vols. (Beijing: Zhongyang wenxian chubanshe, 2004) (cited hereafter as DXPNP), 978–979; "We Must Safeguard World Peace and Ensure Economic Development" (May 29, 1984), in SWDXP-3, 66–67.

31. See Herbert S. Yee, "The Three World Theory and Post-Mao China's Global Strategy," *International Affairs* 59, no. 2 (Spring 1983): 239–249.

32. Chen Yizi 陈一咨, 陈一咨回忆录 [*Memoirs of Chen Yizi*] (Hong Kong: Xin shiji chuban ji chuanmei youxian gongsi, 2013), 505–509.

33. Zhu Jiaming 朱嘉明, Chen Yizhong 陈宜中, Qian Yongxiang 钱永祥, and Wang Chaohua 王超华, "中国改革的道路" [The Path of China's Reform], November 3, 2012, at http://www.21ccom.net/articles/zgyj/ggcx/article_20121 10370279_2.html.

34. Chen, *Memoirs of Chen Yizi*, 505–509.

35. Ibid., 509–512.

36. Zhu Jiaming 朱嘉明, "智慧: 在于避免偏见" [Wisdom Lies in Refraining from Bias], 读书 [*Dushu*], no. 6 (1988): 120. Zhu also used the Brazilian experience in developing its interior regions to argue for development policies for western China. See Zhu Jiaming 朱嘉明, "关于中国西部地区开发的若干问题" [Several Issues Regarding the Development of China's Western Regions], 改革 [*Reform*], no. 1 [1989]: 98–101.

37. Guo Shuqing 郭树清, "经济改革中的政策配合问题" [What Policies Suit Reforms Best], 管理世界 [*Management World*], no. 1 (1989): 75–76. Guo cites a translation of Ludwig Wilhelm Erhard's *Prosperity through Competition* (London: Thames and Hudson, 1958), 来自竞争的繁荣 (Beijing: Shangwu yinshuguan, 1983), as well as Alexander Cairncross's *Years of Recovery: British Economic Policy, 1945–1951* (New York: Methuen, 1985) and, most interestingly, János Kornai's remarks at the 1985 Bashan Conference (Guo, "The Question of Coordinating Policy," 75). He also cites his own article on the Bashan Conference: Guo Shuqing 郭树清, "国际知名学者和专家谈中国经济改革" [World-Renowned Scholars and Experts Discuss China's Economic Reform], 经济社会体制比较 [*Comparative Economic and Social Systems*], no. 3 (1985): 6–11.

38. Peng Shuzi, "The Causes of the Victory of the Chinese Communist Party over Chiang Kai-Shek, and the CCP's Perspectives: Report on the Chinese Situation to the Third Congress of the Fourth International," *International*

Information Bulletin (Socialist Workers Party) (February 1952), at https://www
.marxists.org/archive/peng/1951/nov/causes.htm.

39. Dong Jianmin 董建民 and Liu Ren 刘仁, "近年来我国通货膨胀问题讨论
综述" [Summary of the Discussion on the Recent Problem of Inflation in Our
Country], 财经科学 [*Finance and Economics*], no. 2 (1989): 63. See also Chang
Qing 常清, "论模式转换时期的通货膨胀" [Discussions on Inflation during the
Change of Model], 财经科学 [*Finance and Economics*], no. 10 (1988): 1–9.

40. Dong and Liu, "Summary of the Discussion on the Recent Problem of
Inflation," 66.

41. Twentieth-century China had witnessed serious inflation, including a
spectacular episode of hyperinflation near the end of the Guomindang (Nationalist Party, KMT) rule of the Chinese mainland. Fighting against the Japanese,
the KMT government struggled to make up for the war deficit and resorted to
printing currency. By May 1949, several months before the establishment of
the PRC, the price index was over 350,000 times the price index in June 1937.
Suisheng Zhao writes, "Inflation became the dominant feature of urban economic life during the last years of KMT rule" (Suisheng Zhao, *A Nation-State
by Construction: Dynamics of Modern Chinese Nationalism* [Stanford: Stanford
University Press, 2004], 114; see also Lloyd E. Eastman, "Nationalist China
during the Sino-Japanese War, 1937–1945," in *The Nationalist Era in China,
1927–1949*, ed. Lloyd E. Eastman, et al. [Cambridge: Cambridge University
Press, 1991], 152–160). Rana Mitter discusses the related phenomenon of high
inflation in the CCP's Yan'an base camp, showing that it was a source of Mao's
emphasis on self-sufficiency (*Forgotten Ally: China's World War II, 1937–1945*
[Boston: Houghton Mifflin Harcourt, 2013], 272–273).

42. Wu Guoguang 吴国光, 趙紫陽與政治改革 [*Political Reform under Zhao Zi-
yang*] (Taipei: Yuanjing chuban shiye gongsi, 1997), quoted in Ezra F. Vogel,
Deng Xiaoping and the Transformation of China (Cambridge: Belknap Press of
Harvard University Press, 2011), 469.

43. Cheng Xiaonong, "Decision and Miscarriage: Radical Price Reform in
the Summer of 1988," in *Decision-Making in Deng's China: Perspectives from
Insiders*, ed. Carol Lee Hamrin and Suisheng Zhao (Armonk, NY: M. E.
Sharpe, 1995), 190. Li Peng was still consulting with Chen Yun with some
regularity; they met on May 28, 1988 (CYNP, 3:413).

44. Vogel, *Deng Xiaoping*, 600.

45. ZFLZQJ, 1988, 138–140.

46. Ibid., 1988, 140–141.

47. Ibid., 1988, 143.

48. Ibid., 1988, 146.

49. Ibid., 1988, 154–155; ZZYWJ, 4:445–446. Throughout 1988, Zhao continued to refer to Brazil's experiences with inflation (see, for example, ZZYWJ,
4:549).

50. ZZYWJ, 4:445–446; Xue Muqiao, "Afternoon Session, May 30, 1988,"
in XMQNP.

51. Cheng, "Decision and Miscarriage," 193.

52. Xue, "Afternoon session, May 30, 1988."

53. See, for example, ZZYWJ, 4:476–483. An even broader range of cutting-
edge economic ideas began to appear in Chinese economic circles at this time.

Ronald Coase, the Nobel Prize–winning scholar of institutional economics who would become popular in China in the 1990s, wrote to his Chinese graduate student Sheng Hong in 1988 that he had a "firm belief that an understanding of what is happening, and has happened, in China will greatly help us to improve and enrich our analysis of the influence of the institutional structure on the working of the economic system" (see http://iep.gmu.edu/wp-content /uploads/2012/04/WangNingCoaseInterviewDec2010.pdf, p. 3). See also Sheng Hong 盛洪, "中国的过渡经济学" [China's Transitional Economics], in 中国的过渡 经济学 [*China's Transitional Economics*], ed. Sheng Hong (Shanghai: Shanghai renmin chubanshe, 2009), 6–7.

54. Mi Ling Tsui, ed., *China: Presenting River Elegy*, Deep Dish TV, at https://archive.org/details/ddtv_40_china_presenting_river_elegy/.

55. Rana Mitter, *A Bitter Revolution: China's Struggle with the Modern World* (Oxford: Oxford University Press, 2004), 264. Mitter offers an excellent, succinct analysis of *River Elegy* (ibid., 264–272).

56. Cheng, "Decision and Miscarriage," 193.

57. Many of these reports were collected and translated into English. See Joseph Fewsmith, ed. and trans., "China's Midterm Economic Structural Reform, 1988–1995," *Chinese Law and Government* 22, no. 4 (Winter 1989–1990); Wu Jinglian and Bruce Lloyd Reynolds, "Choosing a Strategy for China's Economic Reform," *American Economic Review* 78, no. 2 (1988): 461–466. Fewsmith hypothesizes that Liu "cast his lot with the conservatives" because his "influence had waned," as Wu, Li, and others had become prominent in the preceding years (*Dilemmas of Reform*, 224).

58. Wu, "Economics and China's Economic Rise," 14.

59. Li Yining 厉以宁, "价格改革为主还是所有制改革为主" [Should Price Reform or Ownership Reform Have Priority?], 金融科学 [*Financial Science*], no. 2 (1988): 86–88.

60. Vogel, *Deng Xiaoping*, 469; Wu Guoguang 吴国光, 赵紫阳与政治改革 [*Zhao Ziyang and Political Reform*] (Hong Kong: Taipingyang shiji chubanshe, 1997) (cited hereafter as ZZYYZZGG), 526–531.

61. Cheng, "Decision and Miscarriage," 194.

62. Zhao, *Prisoner of the State*, 231, 236. I am grateful to an anonymous reviewer for suggesting that I include this point.

63. Cheng, "Decision and Miscarriage," 195.

64. Ibid., 194.

65. Fewsmith, *Dilemmas of Reform*, 226.

66. ZFLZQJ, 1988, 191–193.

67. Ibid., 1988, 198–221; CYNP, 3:414.

68. ZZYYZZGG, 526, 530; DXPNP, 1243.

69. ZZYYZZGG, 529; ZFLZQJ, 1988, 224.

70. Xiao Huanhuan 肖欢欢 and Ni Ming 倪明, "1988 年 9 月初武汉市民抢购金 饰" [Wuhan Residents Rush to Purchase Gold Jewelry in Early September 1988], 广州日报 [*Guangzhou Daily*], June 7, 2008, at http://news.hexun.com/2008-09-09 /108681287.html and http://news.hexun.com/2008-09-09/108682010.html.

71. "激荡三十年: 1978–2008" [*The Vibrant Thirty Years: 1978–2008*], episode 11: Yicai, directed by Zeng Jie 曾捷, 2008, at https://www.youtube.com/watch ?v=XaFuWneg30k&feature=youtu.be&t=5m35s/.

72. Liu Binyan, *China's Crisis, China's Hope* (Cambridge: Harvard University Press, 1990), 5; Reuters, "China Presses Curbs on Spending," June 15, 1988, at http://www.nytimes.com/1988/06/15/world/china-presses-curbs-on-spending.html.

73. Times Wire Services, "Panic Buying Clears Shelves in Chinese City," *Los Angeles Times*, August 16, 1988, at http://articles.latimes.com/1988-08-16/news/mn-711_1_bank-run.

74. The original survey was authored by An Zhiwen 安志文 and released on October 15, 1988; reprinted in "贯彻三种全会精神增强改革信心" [Acting in the Spirit of the Third Plenary Session of the Thirteenth Central Committee and Strengthening Confidence in the Reform], 中国经济体制改革 [*China's Economic System Reform*] 36, no. 12 (December 23, 1988): 6–9.

75. ZFLZQJ, 1988, 227–230; CYNP, 3:414–415.

76. ZFLZQJ, 1988, 231–234. See also ZZYWJ, 4:484–496.

77. Zhao, *Prisoner of the State*, 227.

78. Vogel, *Deng Xiaoping*, 470.

79. Yao Yilin had met with Chen Yun on September 7 (CYNP, 3:415).

80. ZFLZQJ, 1988, 236–242; DXPNP, 1247–1248.

81. Zhao, *Prisoner of the State*, 233–236.

82. Friedman Papers, Box 189, Folder 10, and Box 189, Folder 7.

83. Milton and Rose D. Friedman, *Two Lucky People: Memoirs* (Chicago: University of Chicago Press, 1998), 537; Edward H. Crane, "Foreword: Crisis and Opportunity," in *Economic Reform in China: Problems and Prospects*, ed. James A. Dorn and Wang Xi (Chicago: University of Chicago Press, 1990), ix. Jiang's attendance at the meetings is recorded in ZFLZQJ, 1988, 234–235.

84. Milton Friedman, "Using the Market for Social Development," *Cato Journal* 8, no. 3 (Winter 1989): 567–579.

85. Friedman Papers, Box 114, Folder 14.

86. Pu Shan, "Planning and the Market," *Cato Journal*, 8, no. 3 (Winter 1989): 581–583.

87. Friedman and Friedman, *Two Lucky People*, 540.

88. Milton Friedman, *Friedman in China* (Hong Kong: Centre for Economic Research, Chinese University Press, 1990), 107–111.

89. Wu Jinglian, "Economics and China's Economic Rise," 24.

90. Friedman and Friedman, *Two Lucky People*, 42.

91. Ibid., 607–609.

92. Zhang Liang 张亮, "赵紫阳会见弗里德曼时说中国已大体具备推行股份制条件" [When Meeting with Friedman, Zhao Ziyang States that China has Largely Implemented the Conditions for a Joint-Stock System], 人民日报 [*People's Daily*] (cited hereafter as RMRB), September 20, 1988. See also ZZYWJ, 4:510–518. This Chinese-language transcript matches Friedman's transcript cited below.

93. Friedman and Friedman, *Two Lucky People*, 611–612.

94. Ibid., 610–611.

95. Ibid., 543.

96. Ibid., 614–615.

97. Steven N. Cheung, "Deng Xiaoping's Great Transformation," *Contemporary Economic Policy* 16, no. 2 (April 1998): 125–135. Cheung, a former student, accompanied Friedman on the 1988 trip as his translator.

98. GSJTL, 4:206–207, 221.

99. Friedman Papers, Box 114, Folder 14.

100. Friedman and Friedman, *Two Lucky People*, 543.

101. Zhang Liang 张亮, "未来世界经济发展总趋势令人乐观: 访西方货币学领袖米尔顿·弗里德曼" [Future Optimism about Trends in Global Economic Development: Interview with Leading Western Monetarist Milton Friedman], RMRB, September 24, 1988; for a different phrasing, see ZZYWJ, 4:513.

102. Friedman Papers, Box 190, Folder 2.

103. Gregory Chow, 1988. Notes on Economic Exchanges, Kenneth Arrow Papers.

104. Reuters, "Friedman Says Inflation May Cripple China," *Los Angeles Times*, September 14, 1988, at http://articles.latimes.com/1988-09-14/business /fi-1701_1_milton-friedman; Milton Friedman, "Letter to the Editor," *Stanford Daily*, October 27, 1988.

105. Anthony Lewis, "For Which We Stand," *New York Times*, October 2, 1975.

106. Friedman, "Letter to the Editor."

107. Peter Brimelow, "Why Liberalism Is Now Obsolete: An Interview with Nobel Laureate Milton Friedman," *Forbes* 142, no. 13 (December 12, 1988): 161.

108. Richard Baum, *Burying Mao: Chinese Politics in the Age of Deng Xiaoping* (Princeton: Princeton University Press, 1994), 234–236; CYNP, 3:416.

109. Vogel, *Deng Xiaoping*, 472.

110. ZFLZQJ, 1988, 243, 246; see also ibid., 1988, 250–252; ZZYWJ, 4:528–538.

111. ZFLZQJ, 1988, 272–275.

112. Fewsmith, *Dilemmas of Reform*, 231.

113. CYNP, 3:416–417; ZFLZQJ, 1988, 278–280; for the October 24, 1988 price report, see ZFLZQJ, 1988, 281–284.

114. ZZYWJ, 4:553–560.

115. Zhao, *Prisoner of the State*, 222; ZFLZQJ, 1988, 286–296.

116. Baum, *Burying Mao*, 241.

117. See articles by Yan Jiaqi 严家其 and Su Shaozhi 苏绍智, in 世界经济导报 [*World Economic Herald*], January 9, 1989, 15; and Wen Yuankai 温元凯, "得知识分子得天下, 失知识分子失天下" [To Gain Intellectuals Is to Gain Everything, and to Lose Intellectuals Is to Lose Everything], 世界经济导报 [*World Economic Herald*], February 20, 1989, 1. These examples, and most others from the *World Economic Herald*, are drawn from Li and White's excellent article on the history of the publication. See Li Cheng and Lynn T. White, III, "China's Technocratic Movement and the *World Economic Herald*," *Modern China* 17, no. 3 (July 1991): 342–388.

118. CYNP, 419; DXPNP, 1266–1267.

119. Oleg T. Bogomolov, ed., *Market Forces in Planned Economies: Proceedings of a Conference Held by the International Economic Association in Moscow, USSR*

(Basingstoke, UK: Macmillan, in association with the International Economic Association, 1990), xii–xvi, 245.

120. Wu Jinglian and Zhao Renwei, "The Dual Pricing System in China's Industry," *Journal of Comparative Economics* 11, no. 3 (1987): 309–318.

121. Dong Fureng 董辅礽, "经济运行机制的改革和所有制的改革" [Reform of the Economic Mechanism and Reform of Ownership], JJYJ, no. 7 (1988): 27–33.

122. ZZYWJ, 4:647. The beginning of 1989 was a busy time for international exchanges, and even the septuagenarian theoretician Hu Qiaomu traveled to the United States for the first time for several weeks of study and touring. See Ye Yonglie 叶永烈, 胡乔木 [*Hu Qiaomu*] (Beijing: Zhonggong zhongyang dangxiao chubanshe, 1994), 214–215; Zhang Zhanbin 张湛彬, 改革初期的复杂局势与中央高层决策 [*The Complex Situation in the Early Reform Period and Policy Making in the Top Ranks of the Central Government*] (Beijing: Zhongguo guanli kexue yanjiuyuan bianji chuban yanjiusuo, 2008), 3.

123. Gregory C. Chow, *Interpreting China's Economy* (Singapore: World Scientific, 2010), 427. Chow played an active role in Hong Kong affairs, including in its dealings with the mainland. See ZZYWJ, 4:630–633.

124. An Zhiwen 安志文 and Liu Hongru 刘鸿儒, "关于和台湾经济学家座谈的报告" [Report on the Symposium with Taiwanese Economists] (March 25, 1989), in 国家体改委重要文件资料汇编 [*Compilation of Important Documents of the State Commission on System Reform*], ed. Important Documentary Materials of the State Commission on System Reform 国家体改委重要文件资料 (Beijing: Gaige chubanshe, 1999); "国家体改委关于国营企业利改税问题座谈会情况的报告" [Report by the State Commission for Structural Reform on the Issue of Tax-for-Profit in State-Owned Enterprises], in ibid., 2:799–804. Documents provided to the author by a source who wishes to remain anonymous.

125. Friedman Papers, Box 189, Folder 10, and Box 189, Folder 7.

126. Zhao, *Prisoner of the State*, 132–133.

127. Guo Shuqing 郭树清, "经济体制改革近期与长远的统一问题" [The Issue of Integration in Short-Term and Long-Term Economic Structural Reform], JJYJ, no. 3 (1988): 44.

128. Chen Yizi, "The Decision Process Behind the 1986–1989 Political Reforms," in *Decision-Making in Deng's China*, 149–150, ed. Hamrin and Zhao; Merle Goldman, *Sowing the Seeds of Democracy in China: Political Reform in the Deng Xiaoping Era* (Cambridge: Harvard University Press, 1994), 232–237.

129. Chen, "The Decision Process Behind the 1986–1989 Political Reforms," 142–143.

130. ZZYYZZGG, 73. The publication of the *Collected Works of Zhao Ziyang, 1980–1989* provides important new material for scholars studying China's political reform efforts during the 1980s, particularly in the period from 1986 to 1989, when Deng Xiaoping encouraged Zhao to explore political reform. See, for example, ZZYWJ, 3:468–477, 3:490–493, and 4:202–216.

131. See, for example, Wu Jinglian 吴敬琏, "'寻租'理论与我国经济中的某些消极现象" [Rent-Seeking Theory and Some Negative Phenomena in China's Economy], 经济社会体制比较 [*Comparative Economic and Social Systems*], no. 5 (September 1988): 1–2. Because of the opportunities created by the market re-

forms and the continuing existence of the dual system, Wu wrote, "The concept in Western economics of 'rent-seeking' has developed, albeit in our very different social context." Wu appeared to draw substantially on the work of American economist Nicholas Lardy.

132. Andrew J. Nathan, "China's Political Trajectory: What Are the Chinese Saying?" in *China's Changing Political Landscape: Prospects for Democracy*, ed. Cheng Li (Washington, DC: Brookings Institution Press, 2008), 37–38.

133. See, for example, He Jiacheng 何家成, "东欧经济改革中的政治问题" [Political Issues in Eastern Europe's Economic Reform], 政治学研究 [*Political Studies Research*], no. 2 (1989): 66–72. He Jiacheng had been one of the two junior economists assigned to prepare a first draft of the Bashan Report in 1985.

134. Zhao Renwei 赵人韦, Chen Dongqi 陈东琪, and Wang Zhongmin 王忠民, "市场化改革进程中的实物化倾向" [The Tendency of Paying in Kind in the Course of Market-Oriented Reforms], JJYJ, no. 4 (1989): 9.

135. Ibid., 16.

136. In addition to the economic reforms that are the subject of this book, analysts including David Shambaugh have noted that studies of postcommunist and noncommunist states have also influenced some of the political and institutional reforms undertaken by the CCP. See David Shambaugh, *China's Communist Party: Atrophy and Adaptation* (Washington, DC: Woodrow Wilson Center Press; Berkeley: University of California Press, 2008).

137. Vogel, *Deng Xiaoping*, 595–639; Baum, *Burying Mao*, 248. See also Philip J. Cunningham, *Tiananmen Moon: Inside the Chinese Student Uprising of 1989* (New York: Rowman & Littlefield, 2009); Andrew J. Nathan, *China's Crisis: Dilemmas of Reform and Prospects for Democracy* (New York: Columbia University Press, 1990).

138. See Chapter 10. New sources—including interviews with participants, memoirs, and leaked military documents—are revealing previously poorly understood dynamics, for instance, the extent of discord within the military leadership during martial law. Furthermore, a series of books and articles published around the twenty-fifth anniversary of June 4, 1989, inaugurated a new wave of scholarly interest, which promises to deepen substantially our understanding of this crucial, tragic episode. See, for example, Louisa Lim, *The People's Republic of Amnesia: Tiananmen Revisited* (Oxford: Oxford University Press, 2014); Rowena Xiaoqing He, *Tiananmen Exiles: Voices of the Struggle for Democracy in China* (New York: Palgrave Macmillan, 2014); Andrew Jacobs and Chris Buckley, "Tales of Army Discord Show Tiananmen Square in a New Light," *New York Times*, June 2, 2014, at http://www.nytimes.com/2014/06/03 /world/asia/tiananmen-square-25-years-later-details-emerge-of-armys-chaos .html?_r=0.

139. Fewsmith, *Dilemmas of Reform*, 230–231; ZFLZQJ, 1989, 31–40.

140. DXPNP, 1269–1270; ZFLZQJ, 1989, 50–52.

141. Ian Johnson, "The Ghosts of Tiananmen Square," *New York Review of Books* 61, no. 10 (June 5, 2014): 31–33; see also Zhang Liang, *The Tiananmen Papers*, ed. Andrew J. Nathan and Perry Link (New York: Public Affairs, 2001).

142. Stephen Kotkin, with a contribution by Jan T. Gross, *Uncivil Society: 1989 and the Implosion of the Communist Establishment* (New York: Modern

Library, 2009), 117–131; Timothy Snyder, "1989: Poland Was First!" *New York Review of Books*, December 9, 2009, at http://www.nybooks.com/blogs/nyrblog/2009/dec/09/1989-poland-was-first/. There is evidence that leaders of the student movement were directly inspired by what they saw in Eastern Europe. Wang Dan, for example, commented on March 4, 1989: "The star of hope rises in Eastern Europe. . . . This forcefully testifies to the fact that democracy is not a given but must be fought for by the people from below" (Wang Dan, "The Star of Hope Rises in Eastern Europe," in *China's Search for Democracy: The Student and Mass Movement of 1989*, ed. Suzanne Ogden, et al. [Armonk, NY: M. E. Sharpe, 1992], 46–47). The *World Economic Herald* also provided insight into this international orientation. On April 3, 1989, the *Herald* ran an article by Zhang Weiguo, reporting on a symposium on state-owned enterprises and declaring, "[M]any Chinese economists believe the state economic system is at a dead end *world-wide*" (emphasis added). See Zhang Weiguo, "The Crisis of the State-Ownership System," *World Economic Herald*, April 3, 1989, 10, quoted in Li and White, "China's Technocratic Movement."

143. ZZYWJ, 4:645; Baum, *Burying Mao*, 250. Deng was watching these events closely and discussed the "Color Revolutions" on April 8, 1989 (DXPNP, 1271).

144. Mary Sarotte, "China's Fear of Contagion: Tiananmen Square and the Power of the European Example," *International Security* 37, no. 2 (Fall 2012): 161, 171.

145. Unsigned, "必须旗帜鲜明地反对动乱" [It Is Necessary to Take a Clear-Cut Stand Against the Disturbances], RMRB, April 26, 1989.

146. "Student Response to the Editorial" and "April 27 Demonstrations" (April 24–30), in Zhang, *Tiananmen Papers*, 76–82.

147. Ibid., 57.

148. Li and White, "China's Technocratic Movement," 352, 379; on Zhao reading the *World Economic Herald*, see ZZYWJ, 2:199. The article criticizing Li Peng was written by Hu Jiwei, who had been chief editor and director of the *People's Daily*.

149. Editorial Board, "Statement of Our Views on the Shanghai Party Committee's 'Decision' to Reorganize the *World Economic Herald*," in *China's Search for Democracy*, ed. Ogden, et al. 157–158.

150. Li and White, "China's Technocratic Movement," 343.

151. Fang Lizhi, "Prologue: On Patriotism and Global Citizenship," in *The Broken Mirror: China After Tiananmen*, ed. George Hicks (London: Longman, 1990); James H. Williams, "Fang Lizhi's Expanding Universe," *China Quarterly*, no. 123 (September 1990): 482.

152. "Politburo Standing Committee Meets" (May 8), in Zhang, *Tiananmen Papers*, 126–129. See also CYNP, 3:423; Vogel, *Deng Xiaoping*, 608–609; ZZYWJ, 4:657–662.

153. "The Standing Committee Meets at Deng Xiaoping's Home" (May 17), in Zhang, *Tiananmen Papers*, 184–190; Baum, *Burying Mao*, 257.

154. Zhao, *Prisoner of the State*, 48.

155. Zhang, *Tiananmen Papers*, 194.

156. Baum, *Burying Mao*, 260–261.

157. Zhao, *Prisoner of the State*, 25–34.

158. Baum, *Burying Mao*, 271.

159. Quoted in ibid., 272, citing Andrew G. Walder and Xiaoxia Gong, "Workers in the Tiananmen Protests: The Politics of the Beijing Workers Autonomous Federation," *Australian Journal of Chinese Affairs*, no. 29 (January 1993): 19.

160. "Who Ordered the Arrest of Bao Tong?" (May 26–28), in Zhang, *Tiananmen Papers*, 308.

161. Vogel, *Deng Xiaoping*, 624–631.

162. "Western Infiltration, Intervention, and Subversion" (June 1), in Zhang, *Tiananmen Papers*, 338–348.

163. "The CCP Elders Decide to Clear the Square" (June 2), in Zhang, *Tiananmen Papers*, 354–362. The sense of an international plot was underlined in a May speech by President George H. W. Bush on changes occurring in the Soviet bloc. Bush, who had visited Beijing in February, declared, "The superiority of free societies and free markets over stagnant socialism is undeniable" (George H. W. Bush, commencement address delivered at Texas A&M University, May 12, 1989, at http://www.presidency.ucsb.edu/ws/?pid=17022). See CYNP, 3:424.

164. Vogel, *Deng Xiaoping*, 624–631.

165. Zhao, *Prisoner of the State*, 33.

CHAPTER TEN   *At the Delta*

1. Ezra Vogel, *Deng Xiaoping and the Transformation of China* (Cambridge: Belknap Press of Harvard University Press, 2011), 619, 629–631; Jonathan Mirsky, "Tiananmen: How Wrong We Were," *New York Review of Books*, Blog, May 20, 2014, at www.nybooks.com/blogs/nyrblog/2014/may/20/tiananmen -how-wrong-we-were/.

2. These security briefings hypothesized about the implications of both student protests and conservative responses; for example, "Deng almost certainly regards himself and his reform policies as the real target of attacks on Zhao" (*National Intelligence Daily*, May 11, 1989, Top Secret, National Security Archive).

3. June 4, 1989, Telegram 01070 (Confidential), 1–3, National Security Archive.

4. Chen Yizi 陈一咨, 陈一咨回忆录 [*Memoirs of Chen Yizi*] (Hong Kong: Xin shiji chuban ji chuanmei youxian gongsi, 2013), 635–638.

5. Fang Lizhi, "The Past and the Future" (written November 1989), trans. by Perry Link, *New York Review of Books* 58, no. 11 (June 23, 2011); George H. W. Bush, "Diary, June 10," in George Bush and Brent Scowcroft, *A World Transformed* (New York: Knopf, 1998), 99.

6. Leng Rong 冷溶, ed., 邓小平年谱 *1975–1997* [*A Chronology of Deng Xiaoping, 1975–1997*], 2 vols. (Beijing: Zhongyang wenxian chubanshe, 2004) (cited hereafter as DXPNP), 1279–1280; Fang Weizhong 房维中, ed., 在风浪中前进: 中国发展与改革编年记事 [*Forward in the Storm: Chronology of China's Reform and Development, 1977–1989*], unpublished 2004 document. Available in the Fairbank Collection, Fung Library, Harvard University (cited hereafter as

ZFLZQJ), 1989, 73. See also Richard Baum, *Burying Mao: Chinese Politics in the Age of Deng Xiaoping* (Princeton: Princeton University Press, 1994), 294–295.

7. DXPNP, 1281–1282; Deng Xiaoping, "Urgent Tasks of China's Third Generation of Collective Leadership" (June 16, 1989), in *Selected Works of Deng Xiaoping, Vol. III* (Beijing: Foreign Languages Press, 1994) (cited hereafter as SWDXP-3), 302–303. See ZFLZQJ, 1989, 76–82.

8. ZFLZQJ, 1989, 76; Barry Naughton, *Growing out of the Plan: Chinese Economic Reform, 1978–1993* (New York: Cambridge University Press, 1995), 274–276.

9. Zhu Jiamu 朱佳木, ed., 陈云年谱: 一九〇五–一九九五 [*Chronology of Chen Yun: 1905–1995*], 3 vols. (Beijing: Zhongyang wenxian chubanshe, 2000) (cited hereafter as CYNP), 3:426–427; DXPNP, 1282–1283.

10. Li Peng 李鹏, "关于赵紫阳同志在反党反社会主义的动乱中所犯错误的报告" [Report on Comrade Zhao Ziyang's Mistakes in the Anti-Party, Anti-Socialist Turmoil] (June 24, 1989), at http://news.xinhuanet.com/ziliao/2005-01/17/content_2469759.htm; Editorial, "Only Socialism Can Develop China," 人民日报 (*People's Daily*) (cited hereafter as RMRB), July 22, 1989, trans. in Foreign Broadcast Information Service, FBIS-CHI-89-140, July 24, 1989, 34; "中国共产党第十三届中央委员会第四次全体会议公报" [Communiqué of the Fourth Plenary Session of the Thirteenth Central Committee of the CCP], June 23, 1989, at http://cpc.people.com.cn/GB/64162/64168/64566/65386/4441846.html; "Li Peng's Report on Zhao's Mistakes Published," 东方日报 (*Eastern Daily*) (Hong Kong), July 16, 1989, trans. in Foreign Broadcast Information Service, FBIS-CHI-89-136, July 18, 1989, 21–23.

11. Quoted in Joseph Fewsmith, *China since Tiananmen: The Politics of Transition* (New York: Cambridge University Press, 2001), 31.

12. "Remarks" by various speakers, Secretariat of the Fourth Plenum of the CCP Thirteenth Central Committee, June 23–24, 1989, in Zhang Liang, *Tiananmen Papers*, ed. Andrew J. Nathan and Perry Link (New York: Public Affairs, 2001). This comment was allegedly made by Song Renqiong.

13. Zhao Ziyang, *Prisoner of the State* (New York: Simon & Schuster, 2009), 123.

14. Deng, "Urgent Tasks."

15. Chen Xitong 陈希同, 关于制止动乱和平息反革命暴乱的情况报告: 1989年6月30日在第七届全国人民代表大会常务委员会第八次会议上 [*Report on the Suppression of Unrest and Quelling the Counterrevolutionary Rebellion: Speech at the Eighth Meeting of the Standing Committee of the Seventh National People's Congress on June 30, 1989*] (Beijing: Renmin chubanshe, 1989), 2–3.

16. Ibid.

17. Friedman Papers, Box 189, Folder 8; for Fan's letter, see Friedman Papers, Box 189, Folder 10.

18. Unsigned, "The Birth of the Institute," *Newsletter: The 1990 Institute*, December 1990, 1.

19. Friedman Papers, Box 190, Folder 1.

20. DXPNP, 1284.

21. Bush and Scowcroft, *A World Transformed*, 104–111.

22. John W. Garver, "The Chinese Communist Party and the Collapse of Soviet Communism," *China Quarterly*, no. 133 (March 1993): 1–26.

23. DXPNP, 1286; Vogel, *Deng Xiaoping*, 645. The party elders whom Deng told at Beidaihe were Yang Shangkun and Wang Zhen. Chen Yun also gave his support to Jiang, meeting with him on August 16, 1989. See CYNP, 3:427.

24. Deng Liqun 邓力群, 十二个春秋: 邓力群自述 [*Twelve Springs and Autumns: An Autobiography of Deng Liqun*] (Hong Kong: Bozhi chubanshe, 2006), 405–407.

25. CYNP, 3:427–429; Fewsmith, *China since Tiananmen*, 36.

26. Barry Naughton, ed., *Wu Jinglian: Voice of Reform in China* (Cambridge: MIT Press, 2013), 171.

27. Todd M. Johnson, letter to Victor Rabinowitch, June 21, 1989, and memorandum, July 12, 1989, in "Consulting–National Academy of Sciences–Committee on Economics Education and Research in China–1984–1991, 1993," Herbert A. Simon Papers, Carnegie Mellon.

28. Gregory Chow, "Report" (May 1990), quoted in Gregory Chow, letter of January 2, 1991, Kenneth Arrow Papers, "China Exchange" Box.

29. DXPNP, 1296–1297, 1304–1305; Maureen Dowd, "2 U.S. Officials Went to Beijing Secretly in July," *New York Times*, December 19, 1989, at http://www.nytimes.com/1989/12/19/world/2-us-officials-went-to-beijing-secretly-in-july.html; and Fang, "The Past and the Future."

30. Dowd, "2 U.S. Officials Went to Beijing"; Brent Scowcroft, "Toast by the Honorable Brent Scowcroft, Assistant to the President for National Security Affairs, Beijing, December 9, 1989," *New York Review of Books*, June 23, 2011, at http://www.nybooks.com/articles/2011/06/23/toast-brent-scowcroft-beijing/.

31. Shahid Javed Burki, "World Bank Operations: Some Impressions and Lessons," in *At the Frontlines of Development: Reflections from the World Bank*, ed. Indermit S. Gill and Todd Pugatch (Washington, DC: World Bank, 2005), 127–128.

32. Xiaoyuan Liu and Vojtech Mastny, eds., *China and Eastern Europe, 1960s–1980s: Proceedings of the International Symposium: Reviewing the History of Chinese–East European Relations from the 1960s to the 1980s, Beijing, 24–26 March 2004* (Zürich: ETH Zürich, 2004). 14. This fact was shared by Vojtech Mastny.

33. "齐奥塞斯库访华获积极成果" [Ceaușescu's Visit to China Achieves Positive Results], RMRB, November 19, 1988; "我党代表团团长乔石转交: 中共中央致罗共十四大的贺词" [Head of the CCP Delegation Qiao Shi Sends Message of Congratulations on Behalf of the Central Committee of the CCP to the Romanian Communist Party's Fourteenth Congress], RMRB, November 23, 1989.

34. Bush and Scowcroft, *A World Transformed*, 175–179.

35. Nicholas Kristof, "Upheaval in the East: China; In Reaction to Rumania, A Hardening in Beijing," *New York Times*, January 7, 1990, at http://www.nytimes.com/1990/01/07/world/upheaval-in-the-east-china-in-reaction-to-rumania-a-hardening-in-beijing.html.

36. Uli Schmetzer, "China Loses Its Favorite Socialist Archetype," *Chicago Tribune*, December 25, 1989, at http://archives.chicagotribune.com/1989/12/25/page/6/article/china-loses-its-favorite-socialist-archetype.

37. Geremie R. Barmé, "To Screw Foreigners Is Patriotic: China's Avant-Garde Nationalists," *China Journal*, no. 34 (July 1995): 209–234.

38. Yuan Hongbing 袁红冰, 荒原风 [*Wind on the Plains*] (Beijing: Xiandai chubanshe, 1990); Xu Guangqiu, "Anti-Western Nationalism in China, 1989–99," *World Affairs* 163, no. 4 (Spring 2001): 153.

39. János Kornai, *The Socialist System: The Political Economy of Socialism* (Oxford: Oxford University Press, 1992), 570–574. Presumably because of these controversial claims about China, the book would not be published in the PRC until 2007; see 社会主义体制: 共产主义政治经济学, trans. by Zhang An 张安 (Beijing: Zhongyang bianyi chubanshe, 2007). In the translation, several sentences were removed, including the prospect of "rejecting Marxism" (p. 572 in the English, omitted on p. 533 in the Chinese). Even so, a number of prominent students of Kornai have published essays on his enduring relevance to Chinese debates. See Eric Maskin and Chenggang Xu, "Soft Budget Constraint Theories: From Centralization to the Market," in *The Economics of Transition: The Fifth Nobel Symposium in Economics*, ed. Erik Berglöf and Gérard Roland (London: Palgrave Macmillan, 2007), 12–36; and Yingyi Qian and Chenggang Xu, "Innovation and Bureaucracy under Soft and Hard Budget Constraints," *Review of Economic Studies* 65, no. 1 (January 1998): 151–164.

40. Alec Cairncross and Cyril Z. Lin, "The Private Sector that is Driving China," *Financial Times*, January 8, 1993, 13. By 2010, Kornai told the Chinese newsmagazine *Caijing*: "I would prefer to refrain from drawing universally valid conclusions from the transformation in Eastern Europe. . . . The whole region has a population no bigger than a single Chinese province, yet how varied the experiences of these small and medium-sized countries have been!" See Ma Guochuan 马国川, "科尔奈: 中国改革再建言" [Kornai: Further Comments on China's Reform], 财经 [*Caijing*], no. 7 (March 29, 2010), at http://magazine.caijing.com.cn/2010-03-28/110404798.html.

41. Rong Jingben 荣敬本, "Foreword" to Rong Jingben 荣敬本 and Liu Jirui 刘吉瑞, 比较经济学 [*Comparative Economics*] (Shenyang: Liaoning renmin chubanshe, 1990), trans. in *Chinese Economic Studies* 25, no. 2 (Winter 1991–1992): 3–7.

42. Xue Muqiao 薛暮桥, "牢记历史经验 坚决执行治理整顿的方针" [Remember the Lessons from History and Persist in Implementing the Principles of Management and Rectification], RMRB, December 18, 1989.

43. Fewsmith, *China since Tiananmen*, 247.

44. Central Party Literature Research Center, 中共中央文献研究室, ed., 江泽民思想年编: 一九八九一二〇〇八 [*Chronology of Jiang Zemin's Thought: 1989–2008*] (Beijing: Zhongyang wenxian chubanshe, 2010), 30–32; Jiang Zemin 江泽民, "爱国主义和我国知识分子的使命" [Patriotism and the Mission of Our Country's Intellectuals], May 3, 1990, at http://news.xinhuanet.com/ziliao/2005-02/18/content_2591767.htm.

45. Xu, "Anti-Western Nationalism in China," 156.

46. George H. W. Bush: "Statement by Press Secretary Fitzwater on the Renewal of Most-Favored-Nation Trade Status for China," May 24, 1990, in

Gerhard Peters and John T. Woolley, American Presidency Project, at http://www.presidency.ucsb.edu/ws/?pid=18518/.

47. Xue's phrase (管住货币, 放开价格) had a long history. He had been using it for many years; some of his colleagues traced it to Milton Friedman's reflections on the "Erhard miracle." (Wu Jinglian, author interviews, Beijing, China, August 18, 2012, and September 7, 2013.) Xue's 1990 letter to the State Planning Commission is Xue Muqiao 薛暮桥, "再论建立在商品经济基础上的计划管理体制" [More on a Planned Management System Built on a Market Economy], in 薛暮桥文集 [*Collected Works of Xue Muqiao*] (Beijing: Zhongguo jinrong chubanshe, 2011), 14:20.

48. Lawrence Lau to Lawrence Klein, March 15, 1990, Lawrence Klein Papers, Box 27, Correspondence 1990 A–M.

49. Kenneth Arrow to Gregory Chow, December 20, 1990, Kenneth Arrow Papers, "China Exchange."

50. 薛暮桥年谱 [*A Chronology of Xue Muqiao*], unpublished document, no pagination; Naughton, ed., *Wu Jinglian*, 172–173. The other conservative was Xu Yi, a planning official.

51. Naughton, ed., *Wu Jinglian*, 224–229.

52. See Fewsmith, *China since Tiananmen*, 27.

53. Zhang Yingfang 张映芳 and Shi Zhiqin 史志钦, "'陈云同志论著研讨会' 讨论综述" [Summary of the "Forum on the Works of Comrade Chen Yun"], 中共党史研究 [*Research on the History of the Chinese Communist Party*], no. 5 (1990): 93–95; Liu Guoguang 刘国光, "关于治理整顿和深化改革的几个问题" [Several Issues Regarding Rectifying and Deepening Reform], in 中国社会科学院研究生院学报 [*Chinese Social Science Academy Graduate School Research Report*], no. 6 (1990): 1–13.

54. Baum, *Burying Mao*, 320–321.

55. Gao Xin 高新 and He Pin 何频, 朱容基传: 从反党右派到邓小平继承人 [*A Biography of Zhu Rongji: From an Anti-Party Rightist to Deng Xiaoping's Successor*] (Taipei: Xinxinwen wenhua shiye gufen youxian gongsi, 1993), 212.

56. XMQNP, citing "著名经济学家薛暮桥说: 我们与资本主义国家既竞争又合作 不采取世界公认的办法不行" [Renowned Economist Xue Muqiao: Competing and Cooperating with Capitalist Countries, We Have to Follow Procedures Accepted Worldwide], 经济日报 [*Economic Daily*], November 17, 1990. A summary of Xue's speech was also published in the *Guangming Daily* on December 1.

57. Quoted in Baum, *Burying Mao*, 321.

58. Pieter Bottelier, "China and the World Bank: How a Partnership Was Built," Stanford Center for International Development Working Paper No. 277, April 2006, 7.

59. Naughton, *Growing out of the Plan*, 298–299; Fewsmith, *China since Tiananmen*, 47.

60. DXPNP, 1322–1324; *SWDXP-3*, 350–352.

61. DXPNP, 1326–1328; *SWDXP-3*, 353–355.

62. Victor C. Shih, *Factions and Finance in China: Elite Conflict and Inflation* (Cambridge: Cambridge University Press, 2008), 144–146.

63. Laurence Brahm, "Zhu Rongji: A Rare Talent," *South China Morning Post*, March 10, 2003.

64. DXPNP, 1330–1331; Hu Shuli 胡舒立, Huo Kan 霍侃, and Yang Zheyu 杨哲宇, "改革是怎样重启的: 社会主义市场经济体制的由来" [How Reform Was Restarted: Origins of the Socialist Market Economic System], 中国改革 [*China Reform*], no. 12 (2012), at http://magazine.caixin.com/2012-11-29/100466603 .html. My account here draws on this superb investigative report published by *Caixin* reporters in *China Reform* magazine on the twentieth anniversary of the 1993 codification of the "socialist market economy" concept into the Chinese constitution.

65. Naughton, *Growing out of the Plan*, 285–287.

66. Gao and He, *A Biography of Zhu Rongji*, 218. See also Vogel, *Deng Xiaoping*, 668.

67. He Xiaoming 何晓明, "市场经济下的货币政策与信贷调节" [Monetary Policy and Credit Adjustment in a Market Economy], 经济体制改革内部参考 [*Internal Reference Material on Economic System Reforms*], no. 9 (1993): 7–10.

68. Gao Di 高狄, "社会主义必定代替资本主义 (摘要)" [Socialism is Bound to Replace Capitalism (Abstract)], RMRB, December 17, 1990.

69. See Shih, *Factions and Finance in China*, 142. Shih points to a speech by Jiang in September 1991, at a central work conference, as another example of Jiang's balancing act during this period. Jiang met with Chen Yun on July 6, 1990, August 16, 1991, and January 15, 1992 (CYNP, 3:433–434, 438, 440).

70. Central Party Literature Research Center, ed., *Chronology of Jiang Zemin's Thought*, 63–66; front page editorial, "要进一步改革开放" [China Should Further Its Reform and Opening Up], RMRB, September 2, 1991.

71. David M. Lampton, "How China Is Ruled," *Foreign Affairs* 93, no. 1 (January/February 2014): 74–84.

72. Xinhua News Agency, "China-Hungary Bilateral Relations," May 16, 2007, at http://news.xinhuanet.com/english/2007-05/16/content_6106973.htm.

73. Ann Scott Tyson, "China Party Protégés Float Plan for Reform," *Christian Science Monitor*, February 11, 1992, at http://www.csmonitor.com/1992 /0211/11011.html.

74. Chen Yuan 陈元, "我国经济的深层问题和选择" [The Deep Problems and Choices of Our Country's Economy], 经济研究 (Economic Research) (cited hereafter as JJYJ), no. 4 (1991): 18–26. See Fewsmith, *China since Tiananmen*, 49, 85–86.

75. Shih, *Factions and Finance in China*, 144–146.

76. *Zhu Rongji on the Record: The Road to Reform, 1991–1997*, trans. by June Y. Mei (Washington, DC: Brookings Institution Press, 2013), 6.

77. Shih, *Factions and Finance in China*, 146.

78. *Zhu Rongji on the Record*, 13.

79. Another illustration of his careful study of these concepts came on October 29, 1991, when Zhu called for "controlling redundant construction" by controlling bank lending (*Zhu Rongji on the Record*, 44).

80. Baum, *Burying Mao*, 334.

81. Ibid., 457.

82. Deng Liqun 邓力群, "正确认识社会主义社会的矛盾, 掌握处理矛盾的主动权" [Correctly Understand the Conflicts in a Socialist Society and Seize the Initiative to Handle Them], RMRB, October 23, 1991.

83. Chen Jun 陈君 and Hong Nan 洪南, eds., 江泽民与社会主义市场经济体质的提出: 社会主义市场经济 20 年 [*Jiang Zemin and the Proposal of a Socialist Market Economic System: Reflections on 20 Years of a Socialist Market Economy*] (Beijing: Zhongyang wenxian chubanshe, 2012), 1–8.

84. Hu, Huo, and Yang, "How Reform Was Restarted."

85. Zhou Xiaochuan 周小川, "十四大确立社会主义市场经济为体制改革目标的历史意义" [The Historical Significance of the Establishment of the Socialist Market Economy as the Objective of Structural Reform during the Fourteenth Party Congress], and Guo Shuqing 郭树清, "回忆 1991 年讨论经济体制改革目标的系列座谈会" [Remembering the 1991 Series of Discussion Forums on the Objectives of Economic System Reforms], in *Jiang Zemin and the Proposal of a Socialist Market Economic System*, ed. Chen and Hong, 53–70, 71–90.

86. Zhou, "The Historical Significance of the Establishment of the Socialist Market Economy," 55.

87. Naughton, ed., *Wu Jinglian*, 240.

88. Ibid., 233–235.

89. Guo, "Remembering the 1991 Series of Discussion Forums," 76–79; detail about the "socialist market economy" is from Zhou, "The Historical Significance of the Establishment of the Socialist Market Economy."

90. Hu, Huo, and Yang, "How Reform Was Restarted."

91. DXPNP, 1334–1341; Suisheng Zhao, "Deng Xiaoping's Southern Tour: Elite Politics in Post-Tiananmen China," *Asian Survey* 33, no. 8 (August 1993): 739–756.

92. Deng Xiaoping, "Excerpts from Talks Given in Wuchang, Shenzhen, Zhuhai, and Shanghai" (January 18–February 21, 1992), in *SXDXP-3*, 361–363.

93. As noted in Chapter 1, this was certainly not the first time Deng had used this metaphor, though his "Cat Theory" would become synonymous with the Southern Tour. During a July 1962 famine Deng had argued to the Central Committee that farmers should use the "household responsibility system" to raise agricultural production, saying, "It doesn't matter whether a cat is yellow or black, so long as it catches the mouse," garnering Chen Yun's agreement. Several days later, Deng again used the phrase in a public setting, although the "yellow" was widely misquoted to "white," which Deng evidently decided, by the Southern Tour, that he preferred. The metaphor was directly criticized during the Cultural Revolution, with Mao allegedly saying of Deng, "This is a man who doesn't grasp class struggle. . . . This is his 'white cat, black cat,' he doesn't care whether it's imperialism or Marxism." See Li Yanzeng 李彦增, "邓小平同志'黑猫白猫论'背后的故事" [The Story Behind Comrade Deng Xiaoping's Black Cat, White Cat Theory], at http://cpc.people.com.cn/GB/85037/8530953.html.

94. Vogel, *Deng Xiaoping*, 670–672.

95. Zhao, *Prisoner of the State*, 751.

96. Alexander Pantsov and Steven I. Levine, *Deng Xiaoping: A Revolutionary Life* (New York: Oxford University Press, 2015), 425. I am grateful to an anonymous reviewer for bringing this point to my attention.

97. DXPNP, 1345–1346; Shih, *Factions and Finance in China*, 148.

98. Ann Scott Tyson, "China Economists Break Silence, Condemn Marxist Retrenchment," *Christian Science Monitor*, March 23, 1992, at http://www.csmonitor.com/1992/0323/23013.html.

99. Fang Sheng 方生, "对外开放和利用资本主义" [Opening to the Outside World and Using Capitalism], RMRB, February 23, 1992.

100. Tyson, "China Economists Break Silence."

101. *Zhu Rongji on the Record*, 54–59.

102. Ibid., 73.

103. Chen incorrectly dates the conference to 1984.

104. Fewsmith, *China since Tiananmen*, 84.

105. Chen Yuan 陈元, "我国经济运行研究的几个方法和理论问题" [Several Methodological and Theoretical Issues Regarding Research on the Chinese Economy], JJYJ, no. 2 (1992): 29.

106. Ibid., 36–37.

107. Naughton, ed., *Wu Jinglian*, 247.

108. Zhu Rongji, "Some Comments on the Current Economic Situation and Macroeconomic Controls" (October 20, 1992), in *Zhu Rongji on the Record*, 110–111; Wu Jinglian, *Understanding and Interpreting the Chinese Economy* (Mason, OH: Thomson/South-Western, 2005), 148.

109. Nicholas Lardy, *Integrating China into the Global Economy* (Washington, DC: Brookings Institution Press, 2002), 25.

110. Hu, Huo, and Yang, "How Reform Was Restarted."

111. DXPNP, 1347–1348.

112. CYNP, 3:442–443; Shih, *Factions and Finance in China*, 151; Vogel, *Deng Xiaoping*, 682–683. Hu Qiaomu died on September 28, likely solidifying Chen's sense that an era had ended.

113. DXPNP, 1352–1355; Central Party Literature Research Center, ed., *Chronology of Jiang Zemin's Thought*, 86–89.

114. Jiang Zemin 江泽民, "加快改革开放和现代化建设步伐, 夺取有中国特色社会主义事业的更大胜利" [Accelerating the Reform, the Opening to the Outside World, and the Drive for Modernization so as to Achieve Greater Successes in Building Socialism with Chinese Characteristics], October 12, 1992, at http://cpc.people.com.cn/GB/64162/64168/64567/65446/4526308.html. Some translations are adapted from the *Beijing Review*, at http://www.bjreview.com.cn/document/txt/2011-03/29/content_363504_3.htm.

115. Vogel, *Deng Xiaoping*, 684.

116. See Tony Saich, "The Fourteenth Party Congress: A Programme for Authoritarian Rule," *China Quarterly*, no. 132 (December 1992): 1136–1160.

117. Zhu, "Some Comments on the Current Economic Situation and Macroeconomic Controls," 109–122.

118. Li Jingwen to Lawrence Klein, Letter of March 8, 1991, Box 28, and Diane L. Galloway-May (Ford Foundation) to Li Jingwen, Letter of January 25, 1991, Box 29, both in Lawrence Klein Papers, Duke University.

119. Franco Modigliani to Chen Yuan, Letter of June 10, 1991, Box E10, Modigliani Papers, Duke University.

120. "Att: Pro. Lawrence Klein," Telegram of October 9, 1992, Box 28, Lawrence Klein Papers, Duke University.

121. "Diary: Beijing," DC106 2/14. Papers of Sir Alexander Cairncross, University of Glasgow Archives, Glasgow, Scotland, UK.

122. Naughton, *Growing out of the Plan*, 289–290. The firm was Anshan Iron and Steel Company, where Naughton conducted interviews.

123. Baum, *Burying Mao*, 377.

124. *Zhu Rongji on the Record*, 131–132. Zhu's article was published in 经济日报 [*Economic Daily*] on February 11, 1993.

125. Shih, *Factions and Finance in China*, 152.

126. Constitution of the People's Republic of China (adopted December 4, 1982 and amended on March 29, 1993), Article 7, at http://www.npc.gov.cn/englishnpc/Law/2007-12/05/content_1381974.htm.

127. Zhu Rongji, "Thirteen Measures for Strengthening Macroeconomic Controls" (June 9, 1993), in *Zhu Rongji on the Record*, 133–143.

128. Wu Jinglian and Zhou Xiaochuan, "A Comprehensive Design for the Near and Medium-Term Reform of the Economic System" (June 1993), in *Wu Jinglian*, ed. Naughton, 251–260.

129. Some reports on the conference state that Franco Modigliani attended. Based on my review of his personal papers, Modigliani did travel to China during this period for several exchanges, including a meeting in 1991 with senior officials at the PBOC that included Chen Yuan (noted above) and a 1994 conference in Beidaihe on inflation, but it seems he did not attend the Dalian Conference. See Box E12, Modigliani Papers, Duke University.

130. Peter Harrold, E. C. Hwa, and Jiwei Lou, eds., *Macroeconomic Management in China: Proceedings of a Conference in Dalian, June 1993* (Washington, DC: World Bank, 1993); Hu, Huo, and Yang, "How Reform Was Restarted"; Wu Jinglian, "Economics and China's Economic Rise" (paper presented at the Sixteenth World Congress of the International Economic Association, Beijing, China, July 4, 2011), 12; Ye Sen 叶森, Lou Jiwei 楼继伟, and Zhang Xiaochong 张小冲, 中国宏观经济管理国际研讨会论文集 [*Collected Works from the International Symposium on Chinese Macroeconomic Management*] (Beijing: Gaige chubanshe, 1993). Other participants included Wu Xiaoling and Liu Kegu.

131. Shahid Javed Burki, "Foreword," to *Macroeconomic Management in China: Proceedings of a Conference in Dalian*, ed. Harrold, Hwa, and Lou, vii.

132. Baum, *Burying Mao*, 382; Shih, *Factions and Finance in China*, 152–153.

133. Wu, *Understanding and Interpreting*, 372.

134. Zhu Rongji, "'Three Ground Rules' for Financial Work" (July 7, 1993), in *Zhu Rongji on the Record*, 144.

135. Naughton, *Growing out of the Plan*, 292, 304.

136. Milton and Rose D. Friedman, *Two Lucky People: Memoirs* (Chicago: University of Chicago Press, 1998), 553.

137. Friedman Papers, Box 190, Folder 1. Several economists (including Justin Yifu Lin, who later became chief economist of the World Bank) wrote seeking to take him up on this challenge.

138. Friedman and Friedman, *Two Lucky People*, 556.

139. "江泽民会见弗里德曼教授" [Jiang Zemin Meets Professor Friedman], RMRB, October 27, 1993.

140. Zhao, *Prisoner of the State*, 149.

141. Hu, Huo, and Yang, "How Reform Was Restarted."

142. "中共中央关于建立社会主义市场经济体制若干问题的决定" [Decision of the Central Committee of the Communist Party of China on Some Issues Concerning the Establishment of a Socialist Market Economic System], November 14, 1993, at http://cpc.people.com.cn/GB/64162/134902/8092314 .html. An English translation is available at *Beijing Review* 36, no. 47 (November 22–28, 1993): 12–31.

143. Ibid. See also Wu, *Understanding and Interpreting*, 224–225, 269–270.

CONCLUSION

1. Daniel H. Rosen and Beibei Bao, "China's Fiscal and Tax Reforms: A Critical Move on the Chessboard," July 11, 2014, at http://rhg.com/notes/chinas -fiscal-and-tax-reforms-a-critical-move-on-the-chessboard/. Under these reforms, the ratio of China's fiscal revenue to gross domestic product (GDP) had fallen from 28.2 percent in 1979 to 12.3 percent in 1993, and the ratio of central to total government revenue had declined from 40.5 percent in 1984 to 22 percent in 1993.

2. Wu Jinglian, *Understanding and Interpreting Chinese Economic Reform* (Mason, OH: Thomson/South-Western, 2005), 269–270; Barry Naughton, *The Chinese Economy: Transitions and Growth* (Cambridge: MIT Press, 2007), 431.

3. Richard Baum, *Burying Mao: Chinese Politics in the Age of Deng Xiaoping* (Princeton: Princeton University Press, 1994), 382; Wu, *Understanding and Interpreting*, 228.

4. Naughton, *The Chinese Economy*, 431.

5. Rosen and Bao, "China's Fiscal and Tax Reforms." They continue: "Zhu's reforms solved the problems of the 1990s, but sowed the seeds for today's, including local government reliance on land financing, and the dangerous practice of using local government financing vehicles (LGFV) which was buoyed by Beijing's stimulus program in 2008. . . . [T]he National Audit Office has identified massive and unsustainable debt creation by local governments and LGFVs, along with dangerous entanglement with shadow banks. These systemic risks have pushed the Xi leadership to accept the need for a new round of fundamental reform."

6. Zhang Yugui 章玉贵, "比较经济学对中国经济理论发展的影响" [The Influence of Comparative Economics on the Development of China's Economic Theories (1978–2005)], 财经研究 [*Journal of Finance and Economics*] 33, no. 2 (2007): 70–79; Wu Jinglian 吴敬琏, Zhou Xiaochuan 周小川, et al., 公司治理结构、债务重组和破产程序: 重温 1994 年京伦会议 [*Company Management Structure, Debt Restructuring, and Bankruptcy Procedures: Revisiting the 1994 Beijing-Jinglun Conference*] (Beijing: Zhongyang bianyi chubanshe, 1999). Other Chinese participants included officials like Chen Qingtai, and leading economists including Qian Yingyi, Rong Jingben, Li Jiange, and Wu Xiaoling.

7. Wu, *Understanding and Interpreting*, 155, 174.

8. Ibid., 226.

9. Information from ChinaVitae, at www.chinavitae.com.

10. Patrick E. Tyler, "Yao Yilin, A Hard-Liner, Is Dead at 77," *New York Times*, December 13, 1994, at http://www.nytimes.com/1994/12/13/obituaries /yao-yilin-a-hard-liner-is-dead-at-77.html; idem, "Chen Yun, Who Slowed China's Shift to Market, Dies at 89," *New York Times*, April 12, 1995, at http://www.nytimes.com/1995/04/12/obituaries/chen-yun-who-slowed-china -s-shift-to-market-dies-at-89.html?pagewanted=all.

11. Baum, *Burying Mao*, 383; Orville Schell and David Shambaugh, eds., *The China Reader: The Reform Era* (New York: Vintage Books, 1999); Seth Faison, "Deng Xiaoping Is Dead at 92: Architect of Modern China," *New York Times*, February 20, 1997, at http://www.nytimes.com/1997/02/20/world/deng -xiaoping-is-dead-at-92-architect-of-modern-china.html?pagewanted=all; Patrick E. Tyler, "As Deng Joins the Immortals, Jiang Vows to Keep the Faith," *New York Times*, February 26, 1997, at http://www.nytimes.com/1997/02/26 /world/as-deng-joins-the-immortals-jiang-vows-to-keep-the-faith.html ?pagewanted=all; BBC News, "On This Day 1997: China's Reformist Deng Xiaoping Dies," at http://news.bbc.co.uk/onthisday/hi/dates/stories/february /19/newsid_2565000/2565613.stm.

12. CNBC Asia, "Death of Deng Xiaoping," at www.youtube.com/watch ?v=rpE8eRsPOZQ/.

13. Wu, *Understanding and Interpreting*, 86–88.

14. Nicholas R. Lardy, *Integrating China into the Global Economy* (Washington, DC: Brookings Institution Press, 2002), 16; Naughton, *The Chinese Economy*, 288–289, 307; Wu, *Understanding and Interpreting*, 375.

15. WTO Press Release, "WTO Successfully Concludes Negotiations on China's Entry," September 17, 2001, at http://www.wto.org/english/news_e /pres01_e/pr243_e.htm; Wu, *Understanding and Interpreting*, 295, 229.

16. Lardy, *Integrating China into the World Economy*, 3.

17. Yang Jiang, *China's Policymaking for Regional Economic Cooperation* (Basingstoke, UK: Palgrave Macmillan, 2013), 88. For a somewhat different viewpoint, see Joseph Fewsmith, "The Political and Social Implications of China's Accession to the WTO," *China Quarterly*, no. 167 (September 2001): 587–588.

18. Wu, *Understanding and Interpreting*, 300.

19. Pete Engardio, "Online Extra: 'China is a Private Sector Economy,'" *Bloomberg BusinessWeek*, August 22, 2005, at http://www.bloomberg.com/news /articles/2005-08-21/online-extra-china-is-a-private-sector-economy.

20. Xinhua News Agency, "China FDI Inflow Rises 6.4 Percent in 2015," January 14, 2016, at http://news.xinhuanet.com/english/2016-01/14/c _135009494.htm; Xinhua News Agency, "China's Total Export, Import Values Down 7 Percent in 2015," January 13, 2016, at http://news.xinhuanet.com /english/photo/2016-01/13/c_135005612.htm.

21. Joseph Kahn, "China Gives Zhao's Death Scant Notice," *New York Times*, January 18, 2005, at http://www.nytimes.com/2005/01/18/world/asia /china-gives-zhaos-death-scant-notice.html.

22. Philip P. Pan, "China Plans to Honor a Reformer," *Washington Post*, September 9, 2005, at http://www.washingtonpost.com/wp-dyn/content/article /2005/09/08/AR2005090802120.html.

23. Julian Gewirtz, "Bury Zhao Ziyang, and Praise Him," *Foreign Policy*, April 8, 2014, at http://foreignpolicy.com/2015/04/08/zhao-ziyang-china-ccp -deng-xiaoping-tiananmen/.

24. Bob Davis, "Who Is Chinese Central Banker Zhou Xiaochuan?" *Wall Street Journal*, September 24, 2014, at http://blogs.wsj.com/economics/2014/09 /24/who-is-chinese-central-banker-zhou-xiaochuan/; Carl Walter, "The Nine Lives of China's Central Bank Chief Zhou Xiaochuan," *Forbes Asia*, September 26, 2014, at www.forbes.com/sites/carlwalter/2014/09/26/the-nine -lives-of-zhou-xiaochuan/.

25. Liyan Qi, "China Finance Minister: Government to Keep Policy Steady: Policy Makers to Focus on Combination of Growth Objectives, Lou Jiwei Says," *Wall Street Journal*, September 22, 2014.

26. Fu Jianli, "Guo Shuqing Gives Shandong 'New Deal,'" August 30, 2013, Caixin Online, at http://english.caixin.com/2013-08-30/100575793.html.

27. They also coauthored a book in 1991, see Li Yining 厉以宁, Li Keqiang 李克强, Li Yuanchao 李源潮, and Meng Xiaosu 孟晓苏, 走向繁荣的战略选择 [*The Strategic Decision Toward Prosperity*] (Beijing: Jingji ribao chubanshe, 1991). For further graduate school writings by Li Keqiang, see Li Keqiang 李克强, "论我国经济的三元结构" [On the Three-Part Structure of China's Economy], 中国社会科学 [*Social Sciences in China*], no. 3 (1991): 65–82.

28. Bob Davis and Lingling Wei, "Meet Liu He, Xi Jinping's Choice to Fix a Faltering Chinese Economy," *Wall Street Journal*, October 6, 2013, at http://www .wsj.com/articles/SB10001424052702304906704579111442566524958.

29. "China and the World Bank: 2030 Vision," February 28, 2012, *Economist*, at www.economist.com/blogs/analects/2012/02/china-and-world -bank; Liyan Qi and Tom Orlik, "Economist: World Bank Suggestions for China Reform Garbage," *Wall Street Journal*, March 27, 2012, at http://blogs .wsj.com/chinarealtime/2012/03/27/economist-world-bank-suggestions-for -china-reform-garbage/.

30. See "Edwin Lim," Institute for New Economic Thinking, at http:// ineteconomics.org/conference/hongkong/edwin-lim/.

31. "Justin Yifu Lin," World Bank, at http://econ.worldbank.org/WBSITE /EXTERNAL/ EXTDEC/0,contentMDK:23211510~pagePK:64165401~piPK :64165026~theSitePK:469372,00.html; Yingyi Qian, curriculum vitae, Tsinghua University School of Economics and Management, at http://crm.sem .tsinghua.edu.cn/UploadFiles/File/201210/ 20121009165911564.pdf. Even as Chinese graduate programs improve, recent data point to this trend continuing: In 2014, the *China Daily* reported that fully 33 percent of the total enrollment of international graduate students in the United States came from China (Paul Welitzkin, "Better Grad Programs Keep Students at Home," *China Daily*, November 14, 2014, at http://usa.chinadaily.com.cn/china/2014-11/14/content _18912187.htm).

32. "Communiqué of the Third Plenary Session of the 18th Central Committee of the Communist Party of China," at http://www.china.org.cn/china

/third_plenary_session/2014-01/15/content_31203056.htm; Xi Jinping 习近平, "关于中共中央关于全面深化改革若干重大问题的决定的说明" [Explanation Concerning the CCP Central Committee Resolution Concerning Some Major Issues in Comprehensively Deepening Reform], trans. by China Copyright and Media, at https://chinacopyrightandmedia.wordpress.com/2013/11/19 /explanation-concerning-the-ccp-central-committee-resolution-concerning -some-major-issues-in-comprehensively-deepening-reform/.

33. Xi, "Explanation."

34. Ibid.

35. "Top Chinese Economists Debate Role of Government in Economy," Caixin Online, July 11, 2014, at http://m.english.caixin.com/pad/2014-07-11 /100702690.html. As this debate shows, a more extreme pro-market faction than ever existed in the 1980s has also emerged, with outspoken economists like Zhang Weiying and his mentor Mao Yushi, who attended Lawrence Klein's summer econometrics workshop in 1980, asserting their intellectual lineage from Hayek and Milton Friedman and calling for the radical removal of the state's role in the economy. However, we must also recall that the recent evolution in China began with a socialist system, in which every movement toward the market had to be justified—whereas, in the West, markets are often the starting point, and advocates for greater government intervention during Keynes' time as well as our own rise to fame precisely because they write against the backdrop of a strong market system and advocate for new and heightened roles for government.

36. Ma Guochuan 马国川, "科尔奈: 中国改革再建言" [Kornai: Further Comments on China's Reform], 财经 [Caijing], no. 7 (2010), at http://magazine .caijing.com.cn/2010-03-28/110404798.html.

37. See Evan Osnos, "Born Red: How Xi Jinping, an Unremarkable Provincial Administrator, Became China's Most Authoritarian Leader Since Mao," New Yorker, April 6, 2015, at http://www.newyorker.com/magazine/2015/04/06 /born-red; Andrew Jacobs and Chris Buckley, "Move Over Mao: Beloved 'Papa Xi' Awes China," New York Times, March 7, 2015, at http://www.nytimes.com /2015/03/08/world/move-over-mao-beloved-papa-xi-awes-china.html.

38. International Monetary Fund, World Economic Outlook, October 2014, at http://www.imf.org/external/pubs/ft/weo/2014/02/weodata/index.aspx.

39. "China," World Trade Organization Trade Profiles, at http://stat.wto .org/CountryProfile/WSDBCountryPFView.aspx?Country=CN&/; "China Eclipses U.S. as Biggest Trading Nation," Bloomberg News, February 10, 2013, at http://www.bloomberg.com/news/articles/2013-02-09/china-passes-u-s-to -become-the-world-s-biggest-trading-nation.

40. "China's Foreign-Exchange Reserves Decline to $3.23 Trillion," Bloomberg News, February 6, 2016, at www.bloomberg.com/news/articles/2016-02 -07/china-s-foreign-exchange-reserves-decline-to-3-23-trillion.

41. Xinhua News Agency, "Xi Eyes More Enabling International Environment for China's Peaceful Development," November 30, 2014, at http://news .xinhuanet.com/english/china/2014-11/30/c_133822694.htm. Foreign Minister Wang Yi delivered a speech in October 2014 that raised many of these same themes, explicitly referencing international law and rules of the road the PRC

would "uphold"—but making it clear that "as China grows stronger," it will seek "to build a fairer and more reasonable international political and economic order." See Wang Yi, "China, a Staunch Defender and Builder of International Rule of Law," Xinhua News Agency, at http://en.people.cn/n/2014/1024/c90883 -8799769.html.

42. See Chris Buckley, "China Takes Aim at Western Ideas," *New York Times*, August 19, 2013, at http://www.nytimes.com/2013/08/20/world/asia /chinas-new-leadership-takes-hard-line-in-secret-memo.html.

43. Chris Buckley, "China Warns Against 'Western Values' in Imported Textbooks," *New York Times*, Sinosphere Blog, January 30, 2015, at http:// sinosphere.blogs.nytimes.com/2015/01/30/china-warns-against-western -values-in-imported-textbooks/.

44. See David Shambaugh, *China Goes Global: The Partial Power* (Oxford: Oxford University Press, 2013).

45. "Quotation of the Day," *New York Times*, December 20, 2014; Al Kamen, "Hungary's Viktor Orban Has No Appetite for Democracy," *Washington Post*, October 13, 2011, at https://www.washingtonpost.com/politics/hungarys -viktor-orban-has-no-appetite-for-democracy/2011/10/11/gIQAfIJaiL_story .html; Geoffrey York, "South African President Heaps Lavish Praise on Authoritarian China," *Globe and Mail*, August 25, 2010, at http://www .theglobeandmail.com/news/world/south-african-president-heaps-lavish -praise-on-authoritarian-china/article4389110/. See also Ian Bremmer, *The End of the Free Market: Who Wins the War Between States and Corporations?* (New York: Portfolio, 2010) and the special issue of the *Economist* on "The Rise of State Capitalism," January 21, 2012, at http://www.economist.com/node /21543160.

46. Xi Jinping 习近平, "在纪念邓小平同志诞辰110周年座谈会上的讲话" [Speech at the Forum Commemorating the 110th Anniversary of Deng Xiaoping's Birth], Xinhua News Agency, August 20, 2014, at http://news.xinhuanet.com /politics/2014-08/20/c_1112160001.htm.

47. Zhang Pinghui, "Party Mouthpiece Compares Xi with Deng as the 'New Architect of Reform,'" *South China Morning Post*, November 14, 2014.

48. Kenneth Lieberthal and Wang Jisi, *Addressing U.S.-China Strategic Distrust* (Washington, DC: John L. Thornton Center at the Brookings Institution, 2012).

49. Andrew Browne, "Can China Be Contained?" *Wall Street Journal*, June 12, 2015, at http://www.wsj.com/articles/can-china-be-contained-1434118534.

50. Statement by Representative Christopher Smith, "Is Academic Freedom Threatened by China's Influence on U.S. Universities?" (Congressional Hearing on Academic Freedom and China's Influence on U.S. Universities, Subcommittee on Africa, Global Health, Global Human Rights, and International Organizations, Washington, DC, December 4, 2014), at http://foreignaffairs .house.gov/hearing/subcommittee-hearing-academic-freedom-threatened -chinas-influence-us-universities.

51. Wu Jinglian, "Economics and China's Economic Rise," in *The Chinese Economy: A New Transition*, ed. Masahiko Aoki and Jinglian Wu (New York: Palgrave Macmillan, 2012), 33.

52. Numerous other categorizations are possible, of course, and fuller development of these frameworks is part of the important theoretical work that lies ahead for historians. The framework suggested here is simply an illustrative taxonomy that has yielded insights for this project.

53. See Rebecca Blumstein, Helen Gao, Julian Gewirtz, and Evan Osnos, "Can the Next Generation in China and America Share the Future?" (panel discussion at the Aspen Ideas Festival, July 3, 2015, video recording at www .aspenideas.org/session/can-next-generation-china-and-america-share -future/).

54. János Kornai, "Birthday Greetings" (January 5, 2010), at http://www .kornai-janos.hu/news.html. See also János Kornai, *By Force of Thought: Irregular Memoirs of an Intellectual Journey* (Cambridge: MIT Press, 2006), 179.

Key Chinese Figures

Chen Yun

陈云

1905–1995. One of the "Eight Immortals" of the Chinese Communist Party (CCP) who participated in the founding of the People's Republic of China (PRC); consistent advocate of the plan as "primary" and the market as "secondary" (the so-called "bird-cage" economy). Despite periodic pushbacks, he ultimately lost influence over economic policy to Zhao Ziyang, the reformist general secretary.

Deng Liqun

邓力群

1915–2015. Leading Marxist theoretician and CCP propaganda official. Conservative ally of Chen Yun; he was criticized by Deng Xiaoping as "stubborn like a Hunan mule." Head of the Policy Research Office of the CCP Secretariat. Led the Campaign to Combat Spiritual Pollution in 1983.

Dong Fureng

董辅礽

1927–2004. Received a PhD from the Moscow Institute of the National Economy. Deputy director, then director, of the Institute of Economics of the Chinese Academy of Social Sciences (CASS). Invited Włodzimierz Brus to visit China. Early advocate of enterprise ownership reform. Attended the 1989 International Economic Association conference in Moscow.

Gao Shangquan

高尚全

1929–. Official at the System Reform Commission and leader of the Institute for Chinese Economic Structural Reform. Attended the Bashan Conference. Traveled to Hungary and Yugoslavia to participate in a study tour in 1986.

Guo Shuqing

郭树清

1956–. Conducted graduate work at CASS. Worked in the System Reform Commission. Associated with Wu Jinglian and the "coordinated reform" group. Attended the Bashan Conference and the 1987 International Seminar on State-Owned Enterprise Reform. Currently governor of Shandong Province.

Hu Qiaomu

胡乔木

1912–1992. Leading Marxist theoretician and preeminent CCP wordsmith. Author of many important documents and speeches. Delivered 1978 address on "objective economic laws." Praised Ernest Mandel. Became increasingly conservative in the 1980s. Associated with Chen Yun and Deng Liqun.

Hua Guofeng

华国锋

1921–2008. Mao's designated successor in 1976. Restored the Party's emphasis on economic modernization and promoted the "foreign leap forward." Attacked for upholding the Maoist "two whatevers." Outmaneuvered by Deng Xiaoping before the 1978 third plenum.

Li Yining

历以宁

1930–. Organized the lecture series of the Foreign Economics Research Group, 1979–1980. Led translation efforts in the early 1980s. Critiqued Wu Jinglian's "coordinated reform" group and championed the "enterprise reform" group.

Liu Guoguang

刘国光

1923–. Prominent CASS economist, later vice president of CASS. Helped to organize the visits to China of Włodzimierz Brus and Ota Šik, and the 1982 Moganshan Conference. Mentor to Zhao Renwei. Attended the 1985 Bashan Conference and was the lead author of the Bashan Report.

Ma Hong

马洪

1920–2007. Vice president, and later president, of CASS. Led Zhao Ziyang's State Council research group on structural reform. Met Ota Šik in 1981. With Xue Muqiao, led the Price Research Center. Mentor to Wu Jinglian. Attended the 1985 Bashan Conference and delivered the closing remarks.

Rong Jingben

荣敬本

1933–. Deputy director of the Central Compilation and Translation Bureau under the Central Committee. Involved in the lecture series of the Foreign Economics Research Group, 1979–1980. With Wu Jinglian, he prepared the report on Ota Šik's visit, which was later deemed "invalid."

Sun Yefang

孙冶方

1908–1983. Leading economist under Mao Zedong. Imprisoned for proposing market socialism during the Cultural Revolution. After rehabilitation in 1977, served as senior adviser to the Institute of Economics of CASS. Met with Włodzimierz Brus in 1980.

Wu Jinglian

吴敬琏

1930–. Researcher at the Institute of Economics of CASS. Student of Sun Yefang. In 1981, accompanied Ota Šik in China, and met János Kornai at a conference in Athens. Attended the 1983 Moganshan Conference. Studied at Yale, 1983–1984. Appointed executive secretary of the State Council Development Research Center in 1984. Led the "coordinated reform" group. Attended the 1985 Bashan Conference and the 1987 International Seminar on State-Owned Enterprise Reform. Adviser to Jiang Zemin and Zhu Rongji.

Xue Muqiao

薛暮桥

1904–2005. Senior economic policy maker under both Mao Zedong and Deng Xiaoping. Led Zhao Ziyang's State Council research group on institutional reform. Met with Ota Šik in 1981. With Ma Hong, led the Price Research Center. Attended the 1982 Moganshan Conference and the 1985 Bashan Conference, at which he delivered the opening remarks.

Yu Guangyuan

于光远

1915–2013. Vice president of CASS. Participated in a study tour of Yugoslavia in 1978. Led Zhao Ziyang's State Council research group on theory and method. In the face of conservative pushback, he advocated research on international economics.

Zhao Renwei

赵人伟

1933–. Researcher, and later director, of the CASS Institute of Economics. Involved in the lecture series of the Foreign Economics Research Group, 1979–1980. Accompanied Włodzimierz Brus in 1979–1980. Studied at Oxford, 1982–1984. Attended the 1985 Bashan Conference.

Zhao Ziyang

赵紫阳

1919–2005. Premier, 1980–1987. CCP general secretary, 1987–1989. For much of this period, he directed economic reform and international engagement. Head of the System Reform Commission. Placed under house arrest during the Tiananmen crisis of 1989.

Zhou Xiaochuan

周小川

1948–. Conducted graduate work at Tsinghua University. Attended the Bashan Conference and the 1987 International Seminar on State-Owned Enterprise Reform. Worked under Wu Jinglian on the proposal for a "Midterm Economic Structural Reform." Currently chief of China's central bank.

Acknowledgments

I OWE A GREAT debt of gratitude to my professors at Harvard and Oxford: Erez Manela, who guided me at every turn and inspired me with his dedication and vision; Rana Mitter, for his support and wisdom, now and to come; Emma Rothschild, who encouraged me to pursue the history of economic thought—and this project in particular—with her characteristic generosity of ideas and time; and David Armitage, Niall Ferguson, Henrietta Harrison, William Kirby, Micah Muscolino, and Serhii Plokhii.

In the research for this book, I was fortunate to interview a wide variety of participants in these events and their relatives. In China, these include He Jiacheng, Hu Deping, Fred Hu, Hu Shuli, Li Yining, Yifu Justin Lin, Lu Mai, Qian Yingyi, Rong Jingben, Susan Su, Wang Haijun, Wu Jinglian, Xiao Meng, Zhang Weiying, Zhao Renwei, and Zhou Qiren; in Hong Kong, Lawrence Lau; in Europe and the United States, Frances Cairncross, Gregory Chow, János Kornai, Edwin Lim, and Cyril Lin. I am extraordinarily grateful to them for sharing their memories and perspectives.

Many experts offered their time and advice. I extend my thanks to James Fallows, Joseph Fewsmith, Karl Gerth, Adi Ignatius, Susan Jakes, Elisabeth Köll, Nicholas Kristof, Li Danhui, Roderick Mac-Farquhar, Evan Osnos, Dwight Perkins, Jeffrey Prescott, Michael Puett, Kevin Rudd, Shen Zhihua, Susan Shirk, Terry Sicular, Edward Steinfeld, Michael Szonyi, John Thornton, Ezra Vogel, Wang Jisi, Ngaire Woods, Wen Yu, Philip Zelikow, and Zuo Jun. I am grateful to the two anonymous reviewers for Harvard University

377

Press, whose meticulous review and helpful input improved this book.

I feel tremendous gratitude to the teachers who helped me develop the skills and passions that allowed me to write this book: Eugenia Pan, Liu Mengjun, Victoria Zhu, and Wang Miaomiao, who taught me the Chinese language; and Gerard Casanova at the Hopkins School, who took me seriously as a historian before I did so myself.

Over the past twenty-six years, I have been lucky to know many bold Chinese thinkers, writers, and reformers whose work has motivated my commitment to China and whose friendships I treasure. Hu Shuli challenged me as a writer and scholar of China, welcomed me into her home, and stands as an inspiration for those who support reform in China. Li Xin, Wang Xixin, Xiao Meng, Xu Zhiyong, and Yang Zheyu inspire me with their dedication and warmth. I owe a special debt of gratitude to Fan Shitao, whose enthusiasm for this project helped me see it through—and whose scholarly career promises to be a brilliant one.

My goals and beliefs have been shaped by the remarkable people who have supported and mentored me. In addition to those already mentioned, I also thank Naomi Baird, Stacy Baird, Bill Budinger, Sewell Chan, Emily Chertoff, Molly Dektar, Noah Feldman, Yiqin Fu, Adam Goodheart, Jorie Graham, Sofia Groopman, Woo Lee, Marne Levine, Charlotte Lieberman, James McAuley, Melissa Obegi, Matt Perault, Peter Sacks, Mubeen Shakir, Elizabeth Sherwood-Randall, Timothy Steinert, Strobe Talbott, Jacob Taylor, Zoe Weinberg, Ben Wilcox, and Mark Wu.

For financial support, I am grateful for awards from the Rhodes Trust, the Weatherhead Center for International Affairs at Harvard, and the Thomas H. Hoopes Prize Committee. At Harvard University Press, I benefited from the wise counsel and steady hand of Kathleen McDermott and the team, including Margaux Leonard, Mary Ribesky, and Timothy Jones.

Historians depend on sources, but we also depend on the kindness and enthusiasm of the rare people like Nancy Hearst, librarian in the Fairbank Collection of the H. C. Fung Library at Harvard. Nancy was a continual source of new documents and leads as I researched and wrote the book, and then she meticulously proofread every word. Many generations of China scholars have benefited from her remarkable knowledge and dedication. I feel lucky now to count myself among their number.

Finally, I dedicate this book to my brother, Alec Gewirtz; my mother, Zoë Baird; and my father, Paul Gewirtz, who showed me the meaning of partnership. Thank you for a lifetime of support and love.

Index